URBAN DESIGN IN THE ARAB WORLD

Urban Design in the Arab World
Reconceptualizing Boundaries

Edited by

ROBERT SALIBA
American University of Beirut, Lebanon

LONDON AND NEW YORK

First published 2015 by Ashgate Publishing

Published 2016 by Routledge
2 Park Square, Milton Park, Abingdon, Oxon OX14 4RN
605 Third Avenue, New York, NY 10017

First issued in paperback 2021

Routledge is an imprint of the Taylor & Francis Group, an informa business

Copyright © Robert Saliba 2015

Robert Saliba has asserted his right under the Copyright, Designs and Patents Act, 1988, to be identified as the editor of this work.

All rights reserved. No part of this book may be reprinted or reproduced or utilised in any form or by any electronic, mechanical, or other means, now known or hereafter invented, including photocopying and recording, or in any information storage or retrieval system, without permission in writing from the publishers.

Notice:
Product or corporate names may be trademarks or registered trademarks, and are used only for identification and explanation without intent to infringe.

Publisher's Note
The publisher has gone to great lengths to ensure the quality of this reprint but points out that some imperfections in the original copies may be apparent.

British Library Cataloguing in Publication Data
A catalogue record for this book is available from the British Library.

Library of Congress Cataloging-in-Publication Data
Saliba, Robert.
  Urban design in the Arab world : reconceptualizing boundaries / by Robert Saliba.
    pages cm. -- (Design and the built environment)
  Includes bibliographical references and index.
  ISBN 978-1-4724-0976-8 (hardback) -- ISBN 978-1-4724-0977-5 (ebook) -- ISBN 978-1-4724-0978-2 (epub) 1. City planning--Arab countries. 2. Urbanization--Arab countries. I. Title.
  HT169.A7S25 2015
  307.1'21609174927--dc23
                                                                        2014046516

ISBN 13: 978-1-03-209851-7 (pbk)
ISBN 13: 978-1-4724-0976-8 (hbk)

Contents

List of Figures   *vii*
List of Tables and Boxes   *xi*
Notes on Contributors   *xiii*
List of Abbreviations   *xvii*

1   Framing Urban Design on the Margins: Global Paradigms and Regional Implications   1
      Robert Saliba

2   Medina; the "Islamic," "Arab," "Middle Eastern" City: Reflections on an Urban Concept   17
      Nezar AlSayyad

PART I   **THE DISCURSIVE: RECONCEPTUALIZING BOUNDARIES BETWEEN THE DIVERSE AND THE CONFLICTIVE**

3   The Cultural Discourse: On Regionalism in Urban Design and the Role of the Aga Khan Award for Architecture   29
      Omar Abdulaziz Hallaj

4   The Participative Discourse: Community Activism in Post-War Reconstruction   39
      Howayda Al-Harithy

5   The Corporate Discourse: Learning from Beirut's Central Area Renewal   51
      Angus Gavin

6   The Greening Discourse: Ecological Landscape Design and City Regions in the Mashreq   65
      Jala Makhzoumi

PART II   **THE HYBRID: BLURRING BOUNDARIES BETWEEN DESIGN DISCIPLINES**

7   Cultural Infrastructure for the Margins: A Machinic Approach to Nahr Beirut   85
      Lee Frederix

8   Architectural Urbanism: Proposals for the Arab World   97
      Sam Jacoby

PART III   **THE OPERATIONAL: BRIDGING BOUNDARIES BETWEEN RESEARCH AND PRACTICE**

9   Aleppo 2025 City Development Strategy: A Critical Reflection   115
      Ali Saad and Thomas Stellmach

| 10 | Community-Based Design as Mediator between Academia and Practice: The Case of Souq Sabra, Beirut
Rabih Shibli | 131 |
| 11 | [Trans]Forming Nahr Beirut: From Obsolete Infrastructure to Infrastructural Landscape
Sandra Frem | 147 |

PART IV   THE VISIONARY: CROSSING BOUNDARIES BETWEEN THE UTOPIAN AND THE REAL

12	Sites of Globalization: New Cities; Reflecting on the Dialectics between Designer and Client *Anne Marie Galmstrup*	167
13	Sites of Worship: From Makkah to Karbala; Reconciling Pilgrimage, Speculation and Infrastructure *Robert Saliba*	177
14	Sites of Conflict: Baghdad's Suspended Modernities versus a Fragmented Reality *Caecilia Pieri*	199
15	Sites of Contestation: Tahrir Square; From Appropriation to Design *Robert Saliba, Hussam Hussein Salama and Nathan Cherry*	213

PART V   PROSPECTS: FUTURE URBAN DESIGN AGENDAS

| 16 | Estidama as a Model for Sustainable Urbanism in the Arab World: The Case Study of Abu Dhabi
John Madden | 227 |
| 17 | Re-Engineering the Twenty-First-Century City: Future Directions for Urban Design in the Arab World
Anne Vernez Moudon | 243 |

Index   *263*

List of Figures

1.1	Sites of globalization, the King Abdullah Financial District (KAFD), Saudi Arabia	10
1.2	Sites of worship, oblique view of Karbala, Iraq	11
1.3	Sites of conflict, concrete T-wall encircling the Hotel Palestine, Baghdad, Iraq	12
1.4	Sites of contestation, Tahrir Square demonstrations, Cairo, Egypt	13
3.1	Detail of *Plan Cadastral, Ville D'Alep, Cironscription VII, Section 5, Feuille 1, 1930*	30
3.2	Traditional and modern mosques in Al-Hajarayn, Wadi Hadhramout, Yemen	31
3.3	A selection of projects nominated for the 11th cycle of the Aga Khan Award for Architecture	35
4.1	Destruction in residential neighborhoods in the southern suburb of Beirut – al-Dahiya	42
4.2	Haret Hreik charette	43
4.3	The al-Qleileh post-war landscape	45
4.4	Four Ecological Landscape Associations (ELAs) identified	45
4.5	UNIFIL post refurbished through funding secured by SPNL from Birdlife International	46
4.6	Beit bil-Jnoub	49
5.1	A new kind of Master Plan	53
5.2	Upgrading and landscaping Beirut's city center Ring	54
5.3	A family of Streetwall Controls to ensure the form and continuity of the street	56
5.4	Bank Audi Plaza: An exemplary streetwall building (Kevin Dash)	57
5.5	Saifi Village	57
5.6	The Garden of Forgiveness: Still waiting to be realized (Gustafson Porter)	59
5.7	Massing model: The New Waterfront District (SOM)	62
5.8	The Etoile: Beirut's meeting point in the downtown's historic core	64
6.1	The rapid expansion of three cities in the Mashreq	66
6.2	The Western image of parkland landscapes dominates the conception of green areas in cities of the Mashreq (view of Al Jalaa Park, Damascus, Syria)	68
6.3	View of the homogenized urban landscape of Amman, Jordan, the hilly terrain barely perceptible	69
6.4	The diverse landscape of the urban hinterland in the Mashreq	69
6.5	Productive community garden in downtown Frankfurt	71
6.6	From city park to infrastructural landscapes, representation of the shifting paradigm in urban greening	71
6.7	The spatially dynamic and temporally expansive ecological landscape planning framework provides a layered reading of the diverse rural, regional heritage in the Mashreq (Makhzoumi 2014)	73
6.8	Agricultural land comprises 33 percent of the municipal area of Saida	74
6.9	View of the Abu Nuwas River Corniche green corridor	76
6.10	Saida USDS conceptual model of the green–blue network	78
6.11	Baghdad CCDP landscape master plan	78
7.1	The study area: Beirut's geographical margins	91
7.2	Articulations of network and territory	93
7.3	Synthetic ecologies	95

8.1	Marcin Ganczarski, changing relations between the church and piazza in Rome	98
8.2	Marcin Ganczarski, urban transformation of Rome	99
8.3	Deena Fakhro, typological analysis	101
8.4	Deena Fakhro, typological transformation of the airport to an Islamic walled city and university	102
8.5	Deena Fakhro, airport–university in Makkah	103
8.6	Fadi Mansour, *A Monument of Radical Neutrality*	105
8.7	Yasmina El Chami, *From City of Capital to Capital City*	107
8.8	Yasmina El Chami, *From City of Capital to Capital City*	109
9.1	The visual landscape of Aleppo	116
9.2	Collaboration integration across planning levels and stakeholder sectors	117
9.3	East–West disparity of residential areas and allocation of industry in the East	119
9.4	The Aleppo masterplan superimposed on the existing city showing the large scope of the planned project	121
9.5	Illustrative map of the Aleppo Vision 2025 outlining the spatial strategy	122
9.6	Aleppo 2025 response to multiple LA21 targets	124
9.7	Map that summarizes Uberbau's proposed amendments to the masterplan	125
10.1	Map demarcating the main landmarks surrounding the area of intervention	132
10.2	A 3D model of the Urban Agriculture Training Center in Ain Al Helwa	133
10.3	Schematic representation of the operational framework enabling the implementation of Community Based Projects	134
10.4	An aerial image locating landmarks and clusters in Sabra neighborhood	136
10.5	Photograph of Souq Sabra showing the Ghobeiri and Beirut municipal boundary lines coinciding along the market street	136
10.6	Photographic documentation	137
10.7	Market dynamics	137
10.8	Map as prepared by AUB students on Souq Sabra	139
10.9	Analytical maps of Souq Sabra as prepared by the students	140
10.10	Drawings tailored to fit site specificities	141
10.11	AUB students in action	143
10.12	Pictures taken of Sabra market before and after the implementation of works	144
11.1	Coastal rivers in Lebanon	151
11.2	Morphologies of Nahr Beirut, which show the river district as the last open space in Beirut	152
11.3	Intermittent flow cycles of Nahr Beirut, its different pollutants, and the appropriation of its infrastructure as public space	153
11.4	The infrastructural landscape: The river as a civic and performative landscape	155
11.5	Nahr Beirut will treat the city's water using micro-organisms; treated water will be given back to city and will cover 70 percent of its non-potable needs	155
11.6	Living systems type 1—living machines	156
11.7	Case study of the Nabaa platform	156
11.8	Living systems type 2	157
11.9	Sectional and plan diagram of the river as a connector	158
11.10	Transversal bridging typologies	158
11.11	New pedestrian friendly mobility networks around Nahr Beirut	159
11.12	The decanalization of the river has rendered some of the ramps and bridges going over the former canal walls obsolete	159
11.13	The network of different public spaces overlaying the infrastructural landscapes	160

11.14	The river opens up to the city with linear promenades and terminal wetland parks that treat urban runoff	161
11.15	Major phases for implementation: Space reservation, network establishment and introduction of public spaces, decanalization of Nahr Beirut	161
12.1	KAFD: Bird's eye view from the conceptual design stage and construction view in 2013	169
12.2	Dirab: Bird's-eye view of the concept design	170
12.3	Inspirational images for the KAFD project	171
12.4	KAFD: (a) conceptual view from the main street; (b) construction view in 2012	172
12.5	Dirab: Views from the residential area	173
13.1	Bird's-eye view of the clock tower in Makkah	179
13.2	Hierarchy of streets and open spaces in the vicinity of the Haram in Makkah, showing the historical encroachment of residential areas on the Haram edge	181
13.3	Map showing the clearance of the periphery of the Haram area in Madinah	181
13.4	Iraq's holiest Shia cities	182
13.5	High-rise ring zone in central Makkah	183
13.6	Subdivision of the Haram's periphery in Makkah into megadevelopment projects	184
13.7	Istanbul: The use of a street on Friday as prayer space	187
13.8	Islamic cultural centers in the Eighteenth Arrondissement of Paris	187
13.9	Jabal Omar competition	191
13.10	Urban requalification of the Abu Hanifa Mosque in the Adhamiyah neighborhood of Baghdad	193
14.1	Physical growth of Baghdad from 1920 to present	199
14.2	Baghdad's built up area in the late Ottoman era, 1908	200
14.3	Rashid Street (called "New Street" until the late 1920s)	201
14.4	Map of Adhamiyah and Waziriya neighborhoods in the 1930s showing the juxtaposition of the traditional fabric sector (next to the river) and the new quarters with orthogonal grids and detached and semi-detached housing	202
14.5	King Ghazi Street (today Kifah Street)	203
14.6	Doxiadis's master plan of 1958	204
14.7	Peripheral growth during this period can be noted by comparing a bus route map from 1961 and a tourism map from 1971	205
14.8	Postcard of Bab-Sharqi showing typical buildings of the late 1950s as articulation between the old and the new city	206
14.9	Schematics of dwelling types from the PolService of 1979	206
14.10	The enlarged Haifa Street	208
14.11	Sectarian map of Baghdad in April 2007	209
14.12	Several levels of walling have become distinctive markers of Baghdad today, transforming neighborhoods into privatized areas as seen in Abu Nuwas, April 2013 and Jadriya, February 2011	210
15.1	The transformation of the *Saha* of Sultan Hassan Mosque to a modern square during the late nineteenth-century modernization project	215
15.2	Freedom of expression in Tahrir Square	217
15.3	Comparison between Tahrir and other squares in Western cultures	220
16.1	The four pillars of Estidama (sustainability)	228
16.2	Impact of Estidama	229
16.3	The Estidama Pearl Rating System (PRS)	230
16.4	Numbers of building and villas that have been rated	231

16.5	Plan 2030 concept sketch titled: *The Human City*	232
16.6	The Capital District	234
16.7	Oblique view of Masdar development proposal	235
16.8	Traditional passive design techniques in Islamic architecture	237
16.9	Solar shading analysis	237
16.10	Transportation strategy, Masdar	238
16.11	Pedestrian routes with passive and active solar shading	238
16.12	Grid orientation and built form, Masdar	239
16.13	Zero waste and material reuse strategy	239
17.1	Gross Domestic Product (GDP) per capita and motorization	244
17.2	Expanses of roads and parking in Istanbul, Dubai, Aleppo and Beirut	246
17.3	Evidence from environmental research	248
17.4	Seoul: Sejongno Avenue before and after Gwanghwamun Plaza	252
17.5	Seoul Plaza in front of City Hall before and after	253
17.6	Seoul, Cheonggyecheon	254
17.7	New York City: Broadway and First Avenue	255
17.8	Shanghai public bicycles	257

List of Tables and Boxes

Tables

1.1	Urban design matrix	5
6.1	Greening components of the Saida USDS exemplify transdisciplinarity by breaching the disciplinary boundaries of environmental resources, ecological systems, livelihoods, and amenity and landscape heritage	79
12.1	Agenda: New city versus maturing city	171
12.2	Vision: From a global and local viewpoint	173
12.3	Process: From negotiation toward collaboration	175
13.1	Analytical urban design framework, with the generic attributes of holy cities expressed as columns, and key urban design issues as rows	178

Boxes

3.1	Modernist codification of public space	30
3.2	Normalizing modern Islamic identity	31

Notes on Contributors

Howayda Al-Harithy is Professor of Architecture and a former Chair of the Department of Architecture and Design at the American University of Beirut. She was a visiting professor at the Department of Fine Arts at Harvard University in 1994, at the Department of Architecture at MIT in 1993 and in 2000 and at the Center for Contemporary Arab Studies at Georgetown University in 2005–6. Her research in Islamic art and architecture focuses on the Mamluk period. More recent research focuses on urban heritage and post-war reconstruction projects as applied to the contemporary practice in the Arab world. She is the editor of and contributor to a recently published book entitled *Lessons in Post-War Reconstruction: Case Studies from Lebanon in the Aftermath of the 2006 War* (Routledge 2010).

Nezar AlSayyad is Professor of Architecture, Planning and Urban History at the University of California at Berkeley where he currently serves as Chair of the University's Center for Middle Eastern Studies (CMES). In 1988, AlSayyad co-founded the International Association for the Study of Traditional Environments (IASTE). Today, he serves as the Association's president and editor of its highly acclaimed peer-reviewed journal, *Traditional Dwellings and Settlements Review*. AlSayyad is the author, co-author, editor or co-editor of many books, most recently *Cinematic Urbanism* (2006); *The Fundamentalist City? Religiosity and the Remaking of Urban Space* (2010); *Cairo: Histories of a City* (2011); and *Traditions: The Real, the Hyper, and the Virtual in the Built Environment* (2014).

Nathan Cherry is the director of RTKL's Los Angeles-based Planning and Urban Design group. With 25 years of experience as an architect and planner, he specializes in large downtown redevelopments, urban transit districts, sports and entertainment districts, and airport city plans. He is recognized as an innovator in urban design and resilience, and has co-authored several books and numerous articles on the subject, including *Grid / Street / Place* (APA Planners Press 2009) and *Reconsidering Jane Jacobs* (APA Planners Press 2011). He also lectures at the University of Southern California.

Lee Frederix is a Beirut-based artist and designer who earned his BA in Architecture from Georgia Tech and his MArch in Landscape Urbanism from Notre Dame University. He currently serves as Visiting Assistant Professor at the Lebanese American University (LAU) in the School of Architecture and Design. His recent work investigates urban transgressions, practices within the public realm that defy both conventions of social behavior and municipal regulation.

Sandra Frem is an architect and urbanist researching the potential of infrastructure to revitalize cities. She is a founding member of platau—platform for architecture and urbanism. She studied at the Lebanese University and the Massachusetts Institute of Technology where she graduated with a SMArchS in Urbanism. Her thesis *Nahr Beirut: Projections on an Infrastructural Landscape* (2009) won the SMArchS Award. She participated in several international conferences (Rio de Janeiro, Cambridge, Delft, Frankfurt, Beirut). She was a faculty member at the Lebanese American University's School of Architecture between 2009 and 2013. Frem currently works in Beirut and her present research focuses on Mediterranean geography.

Anne Marie Galmstrup joined Henning Larsen Architects (HLA) in 2004, and became an associate partner in 2007 (and partner in 2013). She graduated from the Bartlett School of Architecture in London and has a BA in Architecture from the Royal Danish Academy of Fine Arts in Copenhagen. She founded the Imagination student summer schools and currently serves as visiting lecturer at Istanbul Technical University. She has led the HLA design studio in Istanbul since 2012 and is in charge of HLA's projects in Turkey and Levant.

Galmstrup has worked on projects in the Middle East and Turkey for more than 10 years and lived in the region since 2009.

Angus Gavin is a consultant in urban planning and was with Solidere, Beirut, from its formation in 1994 until June 2013, as Planning Advisor to the Chairman, Head of the Urban Development Division and Solidere International's Director of Urban Development. Before joining Solidere he was consultant to Dar Al-Handasah, leading the Master Plan team for reconstruction of Central Beirut. Previously he was with London Docklands Development Corporation as Development Manager and Head of Urban Design for the Royal Docks Area. Gavin received his MA in Architecture from Cambridge and Master's in Urban Design from Harvard. He has taught at the University of Virginia and University College London, and was principal author of *Beirut Reborn* (John Wiley 1996).

Omar Abdulaziz Hallaj is an independent architect and development consultant. His professional work concentrates on linking institutional, legal and socio-economic concerns to the production of the built environment. He served in the past as CEO of the Syria Trust for Development, Team Leader for the German Technical Cooperation Project for the Development of Historic Cities in Yemen (GIZ), and partner in SURADEC, an urban planning and heritage management consortium in Aleppo, Syria. He has researched, published and lectured on the history, economics and development policies in the MENA region. He was a recipient of the Aga Khan Award for Architecture; he also served as chairperson of the Master Jury and is currently serving on the Award's Steering Committee.

Sam Jacoby is a chartered architect with a diploma from the Architectural Association School of Architecture and a doctorate from the Technical University of Berlin. He has worked for architectural and planning offices in the United Kingdom, the United States and Malaysia, and trained as a cabinet-maker in Germany. Currently he is director of the post-graduate Projective Cities programme at the AA (projectivecities.aaschool.ac.uk) and a teaching fellow at The Bartlett, University College London. Jacoby co-edited *Typological Formations: Renewable Building Types and the City* (2007) and an Architectural Design issue on urbanism, *Typological Urbanism: Projective Cities* (2011).

John Madden is Senior Planning Manager of the Department of Sustainable Development and Urban Design at the Abu Dhabi Urban Planning (UPC) with emphasis on the development and implementation of the Estidama (sustainability) Program. Before joining the UPC, Madden had worked within the Central Area Planning Division at the City of Vancouver, Canada, on a variety of projects including mega waterfront and downtown historic preservation plans, the Trade and Convention Centre expansion program, an industrial lands strategy, as well as the award winning Downtown Transportation Plan. Madden was also one of the lead project planners for privately-held lands within Southeast False Creek, Vancouver's most recent mega development on the edge of Vancouver's central downtown.

Jala Makhzoumi is a landscape architect, with expertise in ecological design and planning. Her approach to landscape is holistic and developmental, mediating community needs with ecosystem health, biodiversity protection and landscape heritage conservation. Her professional and academic expertise includes post-war recovery, energy efficient site planning and sustainable urban greening. Makhzoumi is an affiliate faculty at the American University of Beirut. Her publications include *Ecological Landscape Design and Planning: The Mediterranean context* (co-author Pungetti; Spon 1999) and *The Right to Landscape, Contesting Landscape and Human Rights* (co-editors Egoz and Pungetti; Ashgate 2012) and *Horizon 101* (Dar Qonboz 2010), a reflective collection of paintings and prose on landscape and identity.

Anne Vernez Moudon is Professor of Architecture, Landscape Architecture, and Urban Design and Planning; she is Adjunct Professor of Epidemiology and Civil and Environmental Engineering at the University of Washington, Seattle, where she directs the Urban Form Lab (UFL). She holds a BArch (University of California, Berkeley) and a Doctor ès Science (École Polytechnique Fédérale, Lausanne, Switzerland). Moudon consulted with organizations in Europe, Latin America and Asia. She published articles in urban design, transportation and public health journals. Her books include *Built for Change: Neighborhood Architecture in San Francisco* (MIT Press 1986), *Public Streets for Public Use* (Columbia University Press 1991) and *Monitoring Land Supply with Geographic Information Systems* (with M. Hubner, John Wiley & Sons 2000).

Caecilia Pieri is the Head of the Urban Observatory at the French Institute of the Near-East, Beirut. She focuses on modern heritage as a social marker and tool for politics. She received her PhD at the EHESS, Paris, on the modernization of Baghdad, where she has been conducting fieldwork for 11 years. An expert within the UNESCO World Heritage for the safeguard of the built modern heritage in the Arab world, she is the author of *Baghdad Arts Deco, 1920–1950* (American University of Cairo Press 2011) and *Baghdad. La construction d'une capitale moderne, 1920–1960* (Presses de l'Ifpo 2014).

Ali Saad is partner at Uberbau, Berlin. He was responsible for the office's key projects in strategic urban design and architecture, such as Berlin Central State Library, Moscow ZIL Factory, Astana Expo 2017 and Paris Territory North-East. In 2009 he was consulting the GIZ in the framework of the Aleppo CDS. Saad was a project leader of the Grand Paris Project at LIN in Berlin, and an assistant professor, lecturer and researcher at TU Berlin investigating the transformation of post-World War II city models in Europe, the Middle East and South Asia. His works and texts have been published in books, magazines and exhibitions nationally and internationally.

Hussam Hussein Salama is Assistant Professor of Architecture and Urban Planning at Qatar University and was a Dubai Initiative Research Fellow at Harvard University, The Kennedy School of Government. Salama earned a Master of Architecture and a PhD in Planning from the University of Southern California, Los Angeles. His research focuses on urban development and public spaces in the Middle East during the era of globalization with emphasis on the Gulf Region. Salama held several teaching and research positions at the University of Southern California, Harvard University and the British University of Egypt.

Robert Saliba is a professor at the Department of Architecture and Design, the American University of Beirut, and served as the coordinator of the graduate program in Urban Planning and Policy and Urban Design between 2008 and 2011. He has conducted extensive research on Beirut's historic formation and post-war reconstruction, and published three reference monographs: *Beyrouth Architectures: Aux Sources de la Modernité* (Parenthèses 2009), *Beirut City Center Recovery: the Foch-Allenby and Etoile Conservation Area* (Steidl 2004) and *Beirut 1920–1940: Domestic Architecture between Tradition and Modernity* (The Order of Engineers and Architects 1998). He has served as a land use consultant with the World Bank and UN-Habitat on the state of the environment in Lebanon and worked as an urban design consultant and a city planning associate at the Community Redevelopment Agency in Los Angeles, California.

Rabih Shibli is a lecturer at the Department of Landscape Design and Ecological Management at the American University of Beirut (AUB), which he joined after receiving his master's degree in Urban Design from the same university. In September 2006 he founded and directed Beit Bil Jnoub, a non-profit civil organization that was heavily involved in the reconstruction process in the aftermath of the July War. Since October 2009, he has served as the team leader of the Community Projects and Development Unit (CPDU) at the Center for Civic Engagement and Community Service (CCECS), which has been engaged in the development and implementation of a number of sustainable projects along the Lebanese territory.

Thomas Stellmach is partner at Uberbau, Berlin and consultant for UN-Habitat. His focus of interest is strategic urban planning in a transforming world. Recent work includes the strategic plan for Germany's Ruhr region, and city transformation and extension projects in Baghdad and Moscow. He has taught at the Berlage in Rotterdam and the University for Science & Arts in Aleppo, Syria, and lectured at Tsinghua University in Beijing, Strelka in Moscow, UPC in Barcelona, and AUB in Beirut among others. He supports the programme for achieving sustainable urban development for UN-Habitat and coordinates pilot projects in the Philippines, Rwanda and Mozambique.

List of Abbreviations

4WD	Four-wheel drive
AA	Architectural Association
AFP	Agence France Presse
AUB	American University of Beirut
BCD	Beirut's Central District
BCE	Before Common Era
BMI	Body Mass Index
BREEAM	Building Research Establishment Environmental Assessment Methodology
BRT	Bus Rapid Transit
BUA	Built-up Area
CBL	Community Based Learning
CCDP	Comprehensive City Development Plan
CCECS	Center for Civic Engagement and Community Service
CDR	Council for Development and Reconstruction
CDS	City Development Strategy
CEE	Civil and Environmental Engineering
CEO	Chief Executive Officer
CNU	Congress of New Urbanism
CO	Carbon Monoxide
COO	Chief Operations Officer
CPA	Coalition Provisional Authority
CPDU	Community Projects and Development Unit
CSP	Concentrated solar power
CVD	Cardio-vascular diseases
DALYs	Disability-adjusted life year loss
DHL	Adrian Dalsey, Larry Hillblom, Robert Lynn
DNA	Deoxyribonucleic Acid
DOE	Department of Energy
EC	European Commission
ELAs	Ecological Landscape Associations
ELC	The European Landscape Convention
ENP	European Neighborhood Partnership
ENPI-CBC	The European Neighborhood Policy Instrument and Cross Border Cooperation
EU	European Union
GCC	Gulf Cooperation Council
GDP	Gross Domestic Product
GHG	Greenhouse Gas
GIS	Geographic Information System
GIZ	Gesellschaft für Internationale Zusammenarbeit
GNP	Gross National Product
GTZ	German Technical Cooperation/Deutsche Gesellschaft für Technische Zusammenarbeit
HFSHD	Hariri Foundation for Sustainable Human Development
HIV/AIDS	Human Immunodeficiency Virus/Acquired Immune Deficiency Syndrome
HPCH	Health Promotion and Community Health

IBA	Important Bird Area
IBRD	International Bank for Reconstruction and Development
IDB	Iraqi Development Board
IRENA	International Renewable Energy Agency
IUCN	The International Union for the Convention of Nature
JODC	Jabal Omar Development Company
KAFD	King Abdullah Financial District
LA21	Local Agenda 21
LDEM	Department of Landscape Design and Ecological Management/ Landscape Design and Eco-System Management
LED	Light Emitting Diode
LEDO	Lebanese Environment and Development Observatory
LEED	Leadership in Energy and Environmental Design
MArch	Master of Architecture
MENA	Middle East and North Africa
MIST	Masdar Institute of Science and Technology
MS	Master of Science
NDP	National Democratic Party
NGO	Non-Governmental Organization
NIDDK	National Institute of Diabetes and Digestive and Kidney Diseases
NOx	Nitrous Oxides
NYC	New York City
NYDOT	New York Department of Transportation
OEA	The Lebanese Order of Engineers and Architects
OIRA	Office of Institutional Research and Assessment
OMA	Office for Metropolitan Architecture
ORNL	Oak Ridge National Laboratory
PADCO	Planning and Development Collaborative International
PPP	Public Private Partnership
PQP	Pearl Qualified Professional
PROAP	Projectos de Arquitectura Paisagista
PRS	Pearl Rating System
PRT	Personal rapid transit system
PWD	Public Works Department
R&D	Research and Development
RMJM	Robert Matthew Johnson-Marshall
RU	Reconstruction Unit
SMS	Short Message Service
SOM	Skidmore Owings & Merrill
SOV	Single Occupant Vehicle
SPNL	Society for the Protection of Nature in Lebanon
SUV	Sports Utility Vehicle
TSE	Treated sewage effluent
UHI	Urban heat island effect
UIA	Union of International Architects
UN	United Nations
UNDP	United Nations Development Programme
UNESCO	United Nations Educational, Scientific and Cultural Organization
UNHSP	United Nations Human Settlements Program
UNIFIL	United Nations Interim Force in Lebanon

List of Abbreviations

UPC	Abu Dhabi Urban Planning Council
USD	United States Dollar
USDS	Urban Sustainable Development Strategy
VOC	Volatile Organic Compound
WHO	World Health Organization

Chapter 1
Framing Urban Design on the Margins: Global Paradigms and Regional Implications

Robert Saliba

Introduction

The title of this book incorporates two problematic yet promising concepts: *Urban Design* and the *Arab World*. The first designates, "a [young] discipline that has been unable to develop any substantial theory on its own" (Cuthbert 2003: viii) and the second remains an elusive term, geographically, politically and ethnically. Despite these qualifications, urban design is a lively and strong emerging discipline profoundly anchored in professional practice, real world projects, and future visions. Moreover, the *Arab world*, despite its geographical ambiguity, is an emblematic term profoundly ingrained in common parlance, academic discourse and media diffusion, that generally brings images of a region rampant with constructed and ambiguous national identities, overwhelming wealth and poverty, religious mix, and most recently the Arab uprisings, a bottom-up revolution shaking the foundations of pre-established long-standing hierarchies. Accordingly, the Arab world is a prime territory for questioning urban design as a discipline in flux, due to its abundance of *sites of globalization*, *sites of worship*, *sites of conflict* and *sites of contestation*. Such diversity invites a multiplicity of opportunities for shaping, upgrading and rebuilding urban form and civic space while subjecting global paradigms to regional and local realities.

This book is also about urban designers *on the margins*, and how they narrate their cities, how they engage with their discipline, and how they negotiate their distance *away from* and *with respect to* global disciplinary trends. As such, the term *margins* implies three complementary connotations: on the global level, it invites speculation on how contemporary urban design is being impacted by the new conceptualizations of center–periphery originating from the *post-colonial discourse*; on the regional level, it is a speculation on the *specificity of urban design thinking and practice* within a particular geographical and cultural context (here, the Arab world); and finally, on the local level it is an attestation to a *major shift in urban design focus* from city centers to their margins with unchecked suburban growth, informal development and disregard for leftover spaces.

Contextualizing Arab Urbanism

In Chapter 2, entitled "Medina; the 'Islamic,' 'Arab,' 'Middle Eastern' City: Reflections on an Urban Concept," Nezar AlSayyad deconstructs chronologically the web of assumptions tied with the terms *Arab*, *city* and *urban*. He clearly demonstrates the elusive and dynamic nature of such notions as the Islamic city, the Arab city and the Middle Eastern city (used often interchangeably) as evolving intellectual constructs spanning one century of colonialism, nationalism and globalism. On the one hand, *Middle East* is a geopolitical construct dating back to British colonialism, flexible enough to include Turkey and Iran, and expandable enough to encompass Afghanistan and Pakistan in a *Greater Middle East* under the post-9/11 Bush administration. On the other hand, *Arab* is mainly associated with the rising pan-Arabism of the late 1950s and early 1960s, instigated by the charismatic figure that was Egypt's Gamal Abdul Nasser. Merging the geopolitical and the ethnic, current urban literature is using the two terms conjointly: the "Arab Middle East" (Al-Asad 2008), and the "Arab/Middle Eastern City" denote cities inhabited by Arabs in the Middle Eastern regions (Elsheshtawy 2004, 2008).

What all of these designations have in common is to question and evade the term *Islamic* as a qualifier of the cities in the region despite the fact that *Islamic* is the most enduring characterization of Arab urbanism since the turn of the twentieth century, and that it is profoundly ingrained in the Orientalist tradition as well as in contemporary regional imaginary. As argued by AlSayyad in City Debates 2012 (the international conference on contemporary urban issues that I organized at the American University of Beirut), "the point here is not to isolate the Islamic element, the point was to recognize that even though Islam existed in the background, it is not the main shaper of a particular urban process or urban form all the time or even in given moments in time." He traces this progressive disjunction between the religious, the ethnic and the geopolitical to three successive waves of scholarship: the Orientalist tradition of the pre-1960s, the revisionist tradition of the late 1960s and 1970s, and the nationalist tradition of the 1980s. While the first, based on Orientalist scholarship, propagated a stereotypical model of the *Islamic city* generalized from a small number of locations, the second linked urban form to the political dynamics through which the city operated, taking an inductive approach and still partially relying on the Orientalist model. The third is mainly the outcome of nationalist scholars operating in the region, who were dissatisfied with the legacy of colonialism, and shared a common belief that national identity could be re-established by reflecting the Muslim way of life in the form and culture of cities. Founded in the 1980s and struggling with this notion of Islamic identity is the well-known Aga Khan Award for Architecture. In formulating its mission and philosophy, the organization was confronted with the dialectic between Islam, and the diversity of communal practices in the region; this is clearly conveyed by Hallaj in Chapter 3:

> The positing of a Muslim collective was always problematic as the award was not concerned with a specific ideological construct of Islam but could not be made independent of it ... The successive juries that served as the trend setters of the Award were carefully selected to avoid giving the Award any specific ideological bias. The focus was always on communities rather than on Islam. The world inhabited by Muslim communities was thought to be sufficiently diversified that no single ideological construct could be capable of dominating it. The main concern was to put forward alternative practices that would help these communities refocus the world around their local identities and needs. The Award thus evolved into one of the strongest advocates for regionalism in the professional spheres of architecture and urbanism.

Deconstructing Arab Urbanism

This shift from Islam to regionalism has been reinforced by the theoretical breaks introduced by postmodernism, poststructuralism and post-colonialism in the late twentieth and early twenty-first centuries. The Orientalist, revisionist and nationalist views are being challenged, leading to important paradigmatic changes in conceptualizing urban form.

One reactionary track is promoting a shift from the traditional/Orientalist reading with its religious interpretation of urban form and its static vision of the past as a source of authenticity. Elsheshtawy qualifies such a view as "outdated and counterproductive," leading to "a narrative of loss" (Elsheshtawy 2004: 4) and Hamadeh considers it as rooted in the dual city construct, "freezing the image of a society in time and space thus maintaining differentiation between the colonizers and the colonized" (Hamadeh 1992: 241–59). Through this post-colonial discourse, a more dynamic view of modernity and nationalism is strongly emerging, where the colonial urban legacy is positioned as an integral part of the national identity construct, and where the provincial city is seen as capable of shaping its unique responses to metropolitan modernity. Furthermore the provincial city is reframed within the contemporary globalization discourse where the concept of heritage conservation has shifted from the museumification of medieval cores to the *manufacturing of heritage* (AlSayyad 2001) for tourist consumption.

A second track positions the local actors and stakeholders as participants in the process of early modernization in lieu of being passive receivers. Colonialism is therefore interpreted as a simultaneous indicator of Western hegemony, and a conscious choice by the colonized to join Western modernity. In *Urbanism: Imported or Exported?* Nasr and Volait argue that "[p]lanning and architectural discourse can be shaped by domestic realities (such as economic and social structures and political intents) as much as by the experience of professional planners (whether indigenous or foreign)." Colonial heritage is therefore envisaged as a result of the hybridization between "Native Aspirations and Foreign Plans" mutually and dialectally impacting each other (Nasr and Volait 2003: xiii). This complexification of the historical discourse has permeated recent investigations of not only the urban, but also the architectural. In *Weaving Historical Narratives: Beirut's Last Mamluk Monument*, Al-Harithy (2008) identifies three different narratives of post-war conservation: the religious, the archeological and the architectural. All three are woven around the same monument to serve socio-political and/ or economic ends. Such an approach is anchored in the dynamic signification of buildings as opposed to their inherent meaning, introducing a poststructuralist perspective to heritage conservation.

Reframing the Margins

> Is there such a thing as Third World literature? Is it possible to establish—without falling prey to vulgarity and parochialism—the fundamental virtues of the literatures of the countries that make up what we call the Third World? In its most nuanced articulation—in Edward Said, for example—the notion of a Third World literature serves to highlight the richness and the range of the literatures on the margins and their relation to non-Western identity and nationalisms … It is clear, nonetheless, that there is a sort of narrative novel that particular to the countries of the Third World. Its originality has less to do with the writer's location than with the fact that he knows he is writing far from the world's literary centers and the he feels this distance inside himself … If there is anything that distinguishes Third World literature, it is not the poverty, violence, politics, or social turmoil of the country from which it issues but rather the writer's awareness that his work is somehow remote from the centers where the history of his art—the art of the novel—is described, and he reflects this distance in his work … At the same time, this sense of being an outsider frees him from anxieties about originality. (Pamuk 2008: 168–9)

The above quote by Pamuk inspired the subtitle of this book: *Reconceptualizing Boundaries*. Adapting Pamuk's quote to address urban design instead of literature, I started by asking: "Is there such a thing as Third World [urban design that] serves to highlight the richness and the range of [the new townscapes] on the margins and their relation to non-Western identity and nationalisms?" Within the post-colonial discourse, this question has been asked by many historians in recent decades in an attempt to re-appropriate colonial history into national histories and to reframe Western-imposed modernity as self-imposed and accepted local modernities (Lu 2010). This quest boils down to challenging, reconceptualizing, negating and/or reframing the classic binaries core/periphery and tradition/modernity as mediated by colonialism, postmodernity and globalism.

Interestingly, this debate is increasingly initiated by scholars coming from the periphery but operating in the core, reversing the Orientalist trend whereby the scholars from the core theorized the periphery. Some of the answers that transpired from this line of questioning include Lu's argument for an "open globality based, not on asymmetry and dominance between core and periphery, but on connectivity and dialogue on an equal basis," and the recognition of other modernities "as legitimate spaces of knowledge production" (2010: 24, 25); in other words Lu argues for erasing the notion of margins. Moreover, Ananya Roy (2003) maintains that economic globalization operates "through multiple and uneven geographies" both "multi-scaled and multi-sited" and "through a hardening of regionalism, parochialism and fundamentalism" (2004: 1). Therefore, "it requires stepping outside the grid of global cities," bringing forward the necessity that *"globalization must be understood at its margins* [my emphasis], rather than simply at the core" (2004: 6). Such margins are conceptualized by AlSayyad as a *third space*, a *hybrid space*, a space of non-synthesis between the global and the local, a space where discourses encounter and transform each other, and where generic and overused concepts of identity are being constantly redefined and relativized. Identity is no more about rootedness, but about constructiveness; there is no longer a single history of Cairo, but *histories of Cairo*, or of Beirut, Damascus and Baghdad. In AlSayyad's work, urbanism is no more a synthetic concept about the technical and design expertise for reshaping cities, but about scanning the townscapes of the margins to detect emergences, and question trends.

Articulating a Regional Geography of Urban Design

For the past two decades, the image of the Middle Eastern city has wavered in the public and professional imagination between two extremes: the global hub and the post-war city, the first exemplified by Dubai and the second by Beirut. Between the two, a vast array of intermediate landscapes exists, ranging from suburban informal settlements to metropolitan new towns and expanding holy cities. Over the past two decades, diverse attempts to classify these landscapes were made in built-environment literature. In 2004, Elsheshtawy differentiated between *traditional, fringe* and *oil rich* cities, with all three categories merging historical, geographical and economic designations. Four years later he simplified his classifications to *struggling* and *emerging* cities, referring to the *great divide* that exists between the burgeoning Gulf cities and traditional centers like Cairo or Damascus, with the influx of money and development models from the former to the latter termed as *gulfication* or *dubaization*.

A third categorization, advanced by Al-Asad (2008) and intersecting with the previous two, merges economic status and *types of urban narratives*. Al-Asad contends that, for the past decade and a half, there has been a shift from "the micro-scale of architecture to the macro urban scale" and from the search for localized architecture identities (in the 1970s and 1980s) to an attempt to fit within overall global development. This created two narratives "with one being prevalent in the area's *middle and lower-income countries* [my emphasis] and the other in the *affluent, oil-rich countries* of the Gulf Cooperation Council (GCC)." The first narrative revolves around heritage conservation at an urban scale from Sana'a, Aleppo, Cairo, Jerusalem and Hebron; it also extends to infrastructural upgrades, tourism and new master plans as main catalysts for development. The second narrative revolves around *branding*, with themed districts, high-end developments and massive man-made islands (the Dubai model). Applying both narratives, the reconstruction of Beirut's Central District (BCD) illustrates the reconfiguration of "complete urban districts through large investment companies working in coordination, and often partnership, with governmental authorities" (Al-Asad 2008: 26).

Although BCD has been qualified by Al-Asad as "primarily an urban development project" (2008: 26), it illustrates another major catalyst of urban design interventions in the region: post-war reconstruction. Besides generating major changes in urban form and social practices, post-war reconstruction has stimulated emergency urban involvement and accelerated the rate of urban planning and design thinking and testing. In countries like Lebanon, post-war reconstruction has led to a wide range of urban interventions from central district restoration and development (Khoury and Khalaf 1993; Rowe and Sarkis 1998; Saliba 2004) to suburban neighborhood rebuilding (Harb 2001; Ghandour and Fawaz 2010; also Chapter 4), from refugee camp reconstruction (Hanafi and Hassan 2010; Ramadan 2009) to rural landscape recovery (Al-Harithy 2010; Makhzoumi 2010; also Chapter 4).

In this regard, AlSayyad (2010) points to the emergence of a new subfield called *reconstruction studies*, and adds that "this new specialty, which may be loosely situated within the larger field of interdisciplinary urban studies[,] requires an engagement with other fields like migration studies, refugee studies, post-war studies, social movements, political mobilization, physical planning and urban design" (2010: vii).

Urban Design Matrix

To better frame this diversity of approaches within the disciplinary bounds of urban design, I have identified five generic issues underlying place-making: (1) identity; (2) infrastructure; (3) ecology; (4) public space; and (5) private development. As such, urban design is premised on the basis of preserving and enhancing the identity of place, integrating mobility, insuring sustainability, improving the quality of open space, and regulating private development. Such generic issues are usually addressed through *market-, community-, conceptual-* or *empirical-based* perspectives that encompass regional, city, district and block scales. The resulting matrix (Table 1.1), although diagrammatic, is intended to be a synthetic framework that helps to locate conceptually the different case studies and thematic discussions in this book in terms of emphasis, intellectual position and scale of intervention.

Table 1.1   Urban design matrix

Continuum	Areas of intervention/ typical landscapes	Generic issues					Ideological frameworks			
		Identity	Ecology	Infrastructure	Civic space	Private development	Market-based	Community-based	Formal/conceptual-based	Empirical-based
Urban/inner-city	Central districts/ historic cores									
	Infrastructural breaks									
	Transitional districts									
	Demarcation lines									
	Inner-city neighborhoods									
Urban/periphery	Peripheral districts									
	Infrastructural sites									
	Transitional industrial zones									
Sub-urban	Informal settlements									
	Refugee camps									
	Highway strips									
	Subdivisions									
Peri-urban	Coastal recreational and agricultural areas									
	River valleys									
Rural	Villages									
	Reserves									

Approach of this Book

An extensive body of knowledge has been produced over the last three decades on urbanism in the Arab world. What importance has been specifically given to urban design in the discourse on development, redevelopment and reconstruction? To what extent has the published professional and academic work emphasized the unique role of urban design as a key discipline in *reinstating urbanity* and in giving shape to the diverse types of settlements throughout the Arab world?

The literature on urbanism in general and on urban design in particular, which largely emerged in the 1980s, has revolved mainly around three axes: the geographical, the historical and the thematic. Conference proceedings as well as individual articles have usually been articulated around comparative city profiles (City Debates 2011; Elsheshtawy 2004, 2008; Bianca 2000). Historical studies have focused on post-colonial practices and the domestication of Western design models during colonial, independence and contemporary periods (Hamadeh 1992; Ghorayeb 1995; Davie 1996; Nasr and ; 2003; Saliba 2004, 1998; Eddé 2010). Most of the thematic studies have concentrated on two types of urban design practice: post-war reconstruction and urban conservation. With the ongoing cycle of destruction and reconstruction expanding throughout the region, cities are subjected to a variety of warfare from military raids to terrorist bombings. Such cycles are being documented and analyzed through national-scale reconstruction monographs (Al-Harithy 2010) that complement the extensive literature that has been written on capital cities like Beirut for the last two decades and mentioned above (Khoury and Khalaf 1993; Rowe and Sarkis 1998; Saliba 2004; Harb 2001; Ghandour and Fawaz 2010; Hanafi and Hassan 2010; Ramadan 2009; Makhzoumi 2010).

Although most of these studies were written by built-environment professionals coming from backgrounds in architecture, landscape and physical planning, I would argue that urban design itself has rarely been positioned as a key starting point for investigation. Instead, the studies tend to merge the physical, the legislative, the political and the socio-economic under the umbrella term of Urbanism in an effort to be comprehensive. Backing this attitude is the general belief that "it is unlikely that the field of urban design will ever become a discipline with its own teachings, separate from the established architecture, landscape, and planning professions" (Moudon 1992: 337). Furthermore, most of the research in this category follows an empirical approach, favoring case studies and a comparative perspective in order to deduce applicable lessons from past mistakes. This may be traced to the fact that urban design invites short- to medium-term physical intervention and rarely allows time and space for reflective thinking.

In parallel, another body of work focuses specifically on urban design and originates from three main sources: (1) studio publications by design schools; (2) books and brochures by professional firms; and (3) a restricted body of research on urban morphology. Programs in architecture and urbanism in Europe and the United States have made it a point during the last two decades to conduct design workshops for their students in the region. Beirut was the most sought after "hot spot" in the 1990s and may have become the most designed city worldwide by international students. Also, publications by planning and design firms have played an important role beyond their initial function as real estate promotional tools, acting as guides for *good practice* in urban design (Gavin and Maluf 1996; Saliba 2004). Finally, studies in urban morphology may be the only attempt at substantiating urban design studies within a conceptual foundation by decrypting the logic that underlies the deconstruction and reconstruction of urban form (Nasr 2003; Dominiczak 1998; Saliba 1990).

As explained above, the focus of this book will be on urban design as a distinctive discipline; it will be articulated around four tracks related to urban design thinking: the *discursive*, the *hybrid*, the *operational*, the *visionary*. Each track will be problematized in view of its global relevance and regional specificity and I will focus on how such constructs intersect with sites and practices and bring forward urban design issues of ideology and context. The book ends with a *prospective* section advancing future agendas for urban design in the region.

Part I: The Discursive: Reconceptualizing the Boundaries between the Diverse and the Conflictive

Today's cities no longer make sense. Maybe they should not make sense. (Schwarzer 2000: 127)

This track investigates how the diversity of design positions during the last two decades has created a dynamic and reactive regional dialogue through an increased fluidity in the transfer of ideas and concepts between the *emerging* and *struggling* cities on the margins. Here, urban design is conceived of as a catalyst for change, as a channel for importing and domesticating models, for creating regional paradigms, and for interrogating mutual perceptions between international and local practitioners. Is such a diversity of positions promoting replication, collage, hybridization or innovation? Is there an emerging *geography of design exchange* with its regional centers and peripheries, its own instruments of regionalization, and an autonomous discourse? Are we moving toward a "discursive urbanism," one that is more accepting of the complexities and multiplicities shaping urban form in the Arab world? This first section of the book investigates four types of discourse that have strongly emerged since the 1990s: the *cultural*, the *participative*, the *corporate* and the *greening* or ecological. Each brings its own logic to urban design, both as ideology and as praxis.

The *cultural discourse* is examined by Omar Abdulaziz Hallaj (Chapter 3) through a critical investigation of the Aga Khan Award for Architecture, in terms of the evolving dialectics underlying the nomination of the winning projects. A major feature of the Award is its geographic scope, encompassing the entire region and therefore providing a common reference to assess the diversity of practices. Hallaj states: "the positing of a Muslim collective was always problematic as the award was not concerned with a specific ideological construct of Islam but could not be made independent of it." Therefore the focus has shifted to community, attempting to identify and promote best practices, self-reliance and self-confidence for Muslim communities to solve their own problems. Hallaj continues: "Yet, in its very insistence on not being ideologically normative, the Award produced an unintended professional normative role that sees the built environment as a product of small scale collective action," mostly non-replicable due to contextual specificity.

More focused geographically on Lebanon and thematically on post-war reconstruction, the *participative discourse* is examined by Howayda Al-Harithy (Chapter 4) in terms of professional activism by a group of academicians and practitioners affiliated with the American University of Beirut who volunteered their expertise in the aftermath of the 2006 war between Lebanon and Israel. Strategies for community participation are discussed through three different cases, all initiated by the limited role of the Lebanese government as an active participant in post-war reconstruction: (1) *initiation of public debate* in the case of Haret Hreik, a large-scale urban reconstruction site in the southern suburbs; (2) *community advising and technical aid* for the agricultural recovery of a rural site, the village of al-Qleileh; and (3) *capacity building* for the reconstruction of an individual family home as pilot project. The importance of such initiatives is to test the engagement of the university in community work and to "initiate a change in current planning practices in Lebanon."

Angus Gavin (Chapter 5) illustrates the *corporate discourse* through a promotional and detailed account of Beirut's Central District reconstruction two decades after the war. As stated by Gavin in City Debates 2012, Solidere, the real estate company entrusted with reconstruction, has its strategy premised on the fact that "cities are everywhere in competition. We have sought the talents of internationally acclaimed architects and public space designers to help reposition Beirut as the Levant's multi-confessional, cosmopolitan city of history, culture, education and commerce: leisure destination of choice for the Arab world, the diaspora and a growing clientele from the US, Europe and Asia." As such, Solidere was able to establish a *brand* of successful place making that is now being exported to other countries in the region.

Finally, the *greening discourse* by Jala Makhzoumi (Chapter 6) focuses on the "environmental challenges" facing cities in the Mashreq in the wake of the twenty-first century due to the changing scale and pattern of physical urbanization, and the emergence of "regional agglomerations" and "urban growth corridors" undermining the relationship between urban cores and peripheries. The *greening discourse* is problematic since it still conceives of landscape interventions in terms municipal parks, and fails "to address the environmental and ecological impact of urban growth" and "to acknowledge the natural heritage of the city." Makhzoumi posits ecological landscape design and planning at the heart of the greening strategies at city and metropolitan scales by taking two projects as case studies: the Saida Urban Sustainable Development Strategy (USDS) and Baghdad Comprehensive City Development Plan (CCDP). She argues in both projects for the merging of two discourses, the "city-region" and "urban livability" broadening the concept of urban greening to embrace environmental as well as economic and social considerations.

Prevailing discourses are not only limited to the *cultural, social, corporate* and *ecological*. Schwarzer contends that "the city can be found not within one movement or another, but only amid the conflictive and shifting relations between movements" (Schwarzer 2000: 127). As such, this first part of the book is an invitation to examine, compare, juxtapose and contrast different discourses that are starting to replace unitary views of the city in the Arab world with an alternative construct: *a city of difference* where variety and complexity are being celebrated beyond the generalizations and the constricting views of the Orientalists and the Modernists.

Part II: The Hybrid: Blurring Boundaries between Design Disciplines

The interlocking disciplines of architecture, urban design and physical planning are being challenged in their ways of thinking and shaping city space by new patterns of physical urbanization and growing environmental concerns. Emerging disciplines such as *ecological landscape design* (covered in Chapter 6 by Jala Makhzoumi as underlying the greening discourse) and *landscape urbanism* (covered in Chapter 7 by Lee Frederix as a tool to investigate socio-cultural networks in marginal spaces) are providing alternative means for conceptualization that stress ecology over morphology; network surface over urban form; and the confluence of architecture, landscape, city and infrastructure. These dynamic and integrated visions are emphasizing the *holistic* and the *interdisciplinary*, while widening the scope of design investigation. Concurrently, attempts at grounding urban design theory in the social sciences are leading to a new understanding of urban space, locating it at the intersection of social theory, human geography and cultural studies. To what extent has urban design in the region kept pace with these changing paradigms, and how far does contemporary urban design theory account for regional specificities?

In broadening the definition of infrastructure to include socio-cultural networks, Lee Frederix (Chapter 7) conceptualizes the Nahr Beirut [*Beirut River*] as the site for intervention strategies that would initiate change *from within*, locating a socially marginalized subculture within the marginal spaces of the city. This approach plays on indeterminacy by applying the notion of *machinic process*, inspired by landscape urbanism, to systems and networks already present within the site. His proposed *cultural infrastructure* is the result of "a process-based intervention that acts as a systemic catalyst and reconfigures the site as a horizontal network open for future permutations and appropriation" by motivated individuals within the community.

Finally, Sam Jacoby (Chapter 8) posits the notion of *architectural urbanism*, an alternate approach to design thinking that is based on the premise that "typal and typological reasoning" provide the primary cross-disciplinary framework between architecture, urban design and master planning. Accordingly, the student proposals that he discusses for an *aerotropolis* in Jeddah and a *univerCity* in Beirut illustrate the benefits of continuously rethinking types themselves, along with their potential effects on the design and conceptualization of the city.

Part III: The Operational: Bridging Boundaries between Research and Practice

As a profession-oriented discipline, urban design defines itself through *operational research* and *reflective practice*. With the waning of Modernism, design research has retracted from the universal to focus on the regional and the local, and has expanded its scope from the morphological to the ecological, communal and speculative. Practice itself has acquired an evaluative edge with the increasing accountability of the designer to the community and to the market, as well as the mounting public expectations with regard to sustainability and participation. How is urban design "on the margins" responding to these global challenges? How is recent design-based research reflective of paradigmatic shifts in urban design thinking? And is there an active engagement between urban design research and professional practice?

One of the recent common observations of cities across the Arab world has been the lack of institutional or governmental intervention in the planning process. In light of this deficiency, the three chapters in Part III illustrate alternative paradigms for the planning procedure, where the decision-making process is appropriated by various groups, thereby opening possibilities of participatory approaches and re-asserting the public right to space. The three approaches are operational in the sense that they emphasize process over results and act as facilitators in bridging the gap between communities and their spaces in the absence of traditional top-down action.

Ali Saad and Thomas Stellmach (Chapter 9) carry out a critical reflection on the limitations of traditional planning methods in Aleppo; in contrast, they propose an alternate approach that "acknowledge[s] the existing dynamics shaping the city as the base for defining future spatial qualities for steering urban development." This approach was tested in a cooperative project between the Gesellschaft für Internationale Zusammenarbeit (GIZ) and municipal authorities, with the planners playing a didactic role. Throughout the process, local stakeholders were introduced to the spatial structure of the city and learned to understand their own communities from a strategic and sustainable perspective.

Operating in areas of the city where the presence of the state fades, encouraging the formation of self-governing bodies, Rabih Shibli (Chapter 10) depicts projects carried out by the Community Projects and Development Unit (CPDU) at the American University of Beirut (AUB). The projects involve students, faculty members and community representatives improvising various models that depend on local knowledge and consensus building in order to counteract the absence of state intervention or support. As such, "community-based design" is conceived "as a pedagogical tool that constitutes a mediating platform between design education and practice."

Finally, Sandra Frem (Chapter 11) re-envisions urban rivers, "allowing them to regain their civic, and environmental significance" within the Arab city. Her project for Nahr Beirut redefines the role of infrastructure in contemporary urbanism to integrate spaces of social, economic and ecological importance, as well as addressing the regional water shortages. Attempting to bridge the gap between research and practice, Frem posits design research as a starting point of any potential planning process while instigating "a participatory framework of dialogue between the different actors: producers of space (private sector), regulators (public sector) and users (communities). The goal is to create—through such project—a platform for negotiation, which exists at the intersection of the different interests and priorities."

Part IV: The Visionary: Crossing Boundaries between the Utopian and the Real

The urban design project has always been a mediator between idealized pasts and idealizing futures and a channel for importing and domesticating modernity. As mentioned above, for the past two decades, the ideals of the city in the Arab world shifted from a quest for the local, national and regional to a "preference for internationally-prevalent models" (Al-Asad 2008: 26). These models range from a fascination with Western imagery of commercial strips, towers and avant-garde high-tech deconstructivist architecture on one hand, to packaged historical landscapes for tourist consumption on the other. However, the physical, social and cultural geography of the Arab world is too diverse to be encapsulated in two extreme representations. The vast extent of intermediate landscapes encompasses a huge diversity of *sites of globalization* (Figure 1.1), *sites of worship* (Figure 1.2), *sites of conflict* (Figure 1.3), *sites of contestation* (Figure 1.4), and so on. What are the underlying dialectics that connect and differentiate these diversified landscapes? Are the margins still a colonial testing ground for the ideals of the center, or just a market for overused and discarded ideas and concepts? How are the dreams of globalization being subjected to a new emerging political consciousness and to the immediacy of the here and now?

These questions are addressed through case studies encompassing prototypical sites that are representative of the region's iconic locations and dynamics of urbanization. From new urban and metropolitan districts in Riyadh, to the urban renewal of *Holy Shrine* cities from Makkah to Karbala, to the pending globalization of Baghdad's post-war urbanism, to Tahrir Square's "design for revolution," generic urban design issues are being subjected to regional and local specificities; reinterpreted by international as well as local consultants; negotiated with a variety of agents both public and private; and subjected to a wide range of implementation frameworks.

Anne Marie Galmstrup from Henning Larsen Architects (Chapter 12) reflects on the process of mediating between the global vision of the client and the local/participative vision of the consultant in designing two projects for Riyadh and its metropolitan area: a master plan for the King Abdullah Financial District; and a 200-hectare site for the accommodation of biomedical facilities and associated office and residential spaces. Robert Saliba (Chapter 13) synthesizes the experience of three international design firms who worked on iconic sites of worship in Saudi Arabia and Iraq, and the difficulty in "reconciling pilgrimage, infrastructural demands and real estate speculation." Caecilia Pieri (Chapter 14) traces the successive attempts of Baghdad to modernize its urban form and space, and outlines the post-war metropolization and fragmentation that the capital is undergoing as a consequence of the continuing conflict and pending globalization. And finally, Tahrir Square, the embodiment of the Arab Spring in the collective imagery, is explored by a scholar and a professional, Hussam Hussein Salama and Nathan Cherry (Chapter 15), contributing their respective views on the historical "formation and transformation" of the square and the "urban design tools [that] could help to optimize the square's function as the cradle of a new democratic Egypt."

Figure 1.1 Sites of globalization, the King Abdullah Financial District (KAFD), Saudi Arabia
Source: Henning Larsen Architects.

Figure 1.2 Sites of worship, oblique view of Karbala, Iraq
Source: Dewan Architects & Engineers.

Figure 1.3 Sites of conflict, concrete T-wall encircling the Hotel Palestine, Baghdad, Iraq
Source: Caecilia Pieri 2013.

Figure 1.4 Sites of contestation, Tahrir Square demonstrations, Cairo, Egypt
Source: http://commons.wikimedia.org/wiki/File:Tahrir_Square_-_February_9,_2011.png (image by Jonathan Rashad via Wikimedia Commons) [accessed: October 11, 2014].

Part V: Prospects: Future Urban Design Agendas

The book concludes with two chapters outlining key directions for the future of research and practice of urban design in the Arab world.

John Madden (Chapter 16) introduces "Estidama as a Model for Sustainable Urbanism in the Arab World" based on the urban design and sustainability policy directions laid out in the *Abu Dhabi Urban Structure Framework Plan: 2030* (Plan 2030). Beyond being a "philosophy and a mindset," Estidama has its own regulatory and policy formulation, as well as its Pearl Rating System (PRS) similar to other third party international rating systems like LEED and BREEAM. Madden illustrates the application of Estidama in two pilot projects which are part of strategic initiatives of Plan 2030: the Capital District forming the gateway to Abu Dhabi, and Masdar, a 640-hectare site with mixed-use development planned to accommodate 40,000 residents and 50,000 employees. Madden argues for the replicability of the Plan 2030 strategic thinking: "The Estidama PRS was formulated and launched in Abu Dhabi not as a static policy or regulation that can simply be adopted in other cities. Rather, it is a system that has evolved from a need to respect and incorporate unique Arab cultural influences in the built environment and to encourage contemporary expressions of Arab urbanism at large."

Starting from recent worldwide research on the negative impacts of over-reliance on inner-city motorized transport, Anne Vernez Moudon (Chapter 17) proposes to "re-engineer the twenty-first-century city" as a future agenda for "urban design in the Arab world." Based on an extensive body of evidence on land consumption by vehicular infrastructure, and the resulting environmental toxicity linked to increasing rates of asthma and cancers, obesity, type 2 diabetes and cardio-vascular diseases, Moudon provides an eye-opening perspective on linking public health to infrastructure and urban design, backed by successful case studies ranging from Seoul to New York. She clearly states that:

> Urban designers have a chance to play an effective role because they have by tradition been the go-between urban planning and development. Together with urban planners, urban designers must proactively integrate transportation into their portfolios and cease to leave the transportation sector to transportation specialists ... Urban designers' versatility, relative lack of dogmatic principles (specifically relative to transportation and urban planning), and comprehensive approach to cities make them well-positioned to become facilitators of not only a rapprochement between transportation and urban planning, but also of a return to considering people (the person and the collective) as the center of urban life.

References

Al-Asad, M. 2008. *The Contemporary Built Environment in the Middle East: Architecture and Urbanism in the Middle East*. Washington, DC: The Middle East Institute.

Al-Harithy, H. 2008. Weaving Historical Narratives: Beirut's Last Mamluk Monument. *Muqarnas: An Annual on Islamic Art and Architecture* [online], 25, 215–30. Available at: http://www.jstor.org/stable/27811121 [accessed: May 13, 2014].

Al-Harithy, H. (ed.) 2010. *Lessons in Post-War Reconstruction: Case Studies from Lebanon in the Aftermath of the 2006 War*. London: Routledge.

AlSayyad, N. (ed.) 2001. *Consuming Tradition, Manufacturing Heritage: Global Norms and Urban Forms in the Age of Tourism*. London: Routledge.

AlSayyad, N. 2010. Foreword, in *Lessons in Post-War Reconstruction: Case Studies from Lebanon in the Aftermath of the 2006 War*, edited by H. Al-Harithy. London: Routledge, vii–ix.

Bianca, S. 2000. *Urban Form in the Arab World Past and Present*. London: Thames & Hudson.

City Debates. 2011. "Contemporary Urbanism in the Arab World" Conference, May 12–13, 2011, the Department of Architecture and Design, the American University of Beirut. Further information: http://www.aub.edu.lb/fea/citydebates/Pages/2011/index.html.

Cuthbert, A.R. 2003. *Designing Cities: Critical Readings in Urban Design*. Chichester: Wiley.

Davie, M. 1996. *Beyrouth et ses Faubourgs, 1840–1940: Une Integration Inachevée (Cahiers du CERMOC)*. Beirut: Centre D'etudes et de Recherches sur le Moyen–Orient Contemporain.

Dominiczak, J. 1998. Warsaw and Gdansk as Two Distinctive Approaches to Post-Second World War Reconstruction: Urban Design Potential and the Problem of Method, in *Urban Triumph or Urban Disaster: Dilemmas of Contemporary Post-War Reconstruction*, edited by S. Barakat, J. Caleme and E. Charlesworth. New York: Post-War Reconstruction & Development Unit, University of York, 15–22.

Eddé, C. 2010. *Beyrouth: Naissance d'une Capitale: 1918–1924*. Paris: Sindbad.

Elsheshtawy, Y. 2004. *Planning Middle East City: An Urban Kaleidscope in a Globalizing World*. London: Routledge.

Elsheshtawy, Y. 2008. *The Evolving Arab City: Tradition, Modernity and Urban Development*. London: Routledge.

Gavin, A. and Maluf, R.B. 1996. *Beirut Reborn: The Restoration and Development of the Central District*. London: Academy Editions.

Ghandour, M. and Fawaz, M. 2010. Spatial Erasure: Reconstruction Projects in Beirut. *ArteEast* [online]. Available at: http://www.arteeast.org/2012/02/05/spatial-erasure-reconstruction-projects-in-beirut/ [accessed: March 14, 2014].

Ghorayeb, M. 1995. Aux Sources de la Modernité de Beyrouth: 1860–1940. *Environmental Design: Journal of the Islamic Environmental Design Research Centre*, 1(2), 122–9.

Hamadeh, S. 1992. Creating the Traditional City: A French Project, in *Forms of Dominance: On the Architecture and Urbanism of the Colonial Enterprise*, edited by N. AlSayyad. Aldershot: Avebury, 241–59.

Hanafi, S. and Hassan, I.S. 2010. (In)-Security and the Post-War Scene in Nahr el Bared Refugee Camp. *Journal of Palestine Studies* [online], 40(1), 27–48. Available at: http://www.jstor.org/stable/10.1525/jps.2010.XL.1.027 [accessed: January 22, 2014].

Harb, M. 2001. Urban Governance in Post-War Beirut: Resources, Negotiations, and Contestations in the Elyssar Project, in *Capital Cities: Ethnographies of Urban Governance in the Middle East*, edited by S. Shami. Toronto: Centre for Urban & Community Studies, University of Toronto Press, 111–33.

Khoury, P.S. and Khalaf, S. (eds) 1993. *Recovering Beirut: Urban Design and Post-War Reconstruction*. Leiden: Brill Academic Publishers.

Lu, D. (ed.) 2010. *Third World Modernism: Architecture, Development and Identity*. New York: Routledge.

Makhzoumi, J. 2010. Marginal Landscapes, Marginal Rural Communities: Sustainable Post-War Recovery in Southern Lebanon, in *Lessons in Post-War Reconstruction: Case Studies from Lebanon in the Aftermath of the 2006 War*, edited by H. Al-Harithy. London: Routledge, 127–57.

Moudon, A.V. 1992. A Catholic Approach to Organizing What Urban Designers Should Know. *Journal of Planning Literature*, 6(4), 331–49. Available at: http://jpl.sagepub.com/content/6/4/331 [accessed: December 14, 2012].

Nasr, J. 2003. Morphology of Disaster: Challenges for Research. *Urban Morphology*, 7(2), 105–6.

Nasr, J. and Volait, M. 2003. *Urbanism Imported or Exported? Native Aspirations and Foreign Plans*. Chichester: John Wiley & Sons Ltd.

Pamuk, O. 2008. *Other Colors: Writings on Life, Art, Books and Cities*. New York: Alfred A. Knopf. Translated by M. Freely (2007).

Ramadan, A. 2009. Destroying Nahr el-Bared: Sovereignty and Urbicide in the Space of Exception. *Political Geography*, 28(3), 153–63. Available at: http://dx.doi.org/10.1016/j.polgeo.2009.02.004 [accessed: May 13, 2014].

Rowe, P.G. and Sarkis, H. (eds) 1998. *Projecting Beirut: Episodes in the Construction and Reconstruction of a Modern City*. Munich: Prestel.

Roy, A. 2003. Global Histories: A New Repertoire of Cities. Paper to the Conference: *New Global History and the City*, St. Petersburg, January 9–12, 2003. Available at: http:// www.journalinks.nl/Mijn%20webs/Global%20Histories.doc [accessed: July 9, 2008].

Saliba, R. 1990. *Morphological Investigation of Downtown Beirut: Towards an Urban Design Framework*. Beirut: American University of Beirut, Department of Architecture, Course A505.

Saliba, R. 1998. *Beirut 1920–1940: Domestic Architecture between Tradition and Modernity*. Beirut: Order of Engineers and Architects.

Saliba, R. 2004. *Beirut City Center Recovery: The Foch-Allenby and Etoile Conservation Area*. Göttingen: Steidl.
Schwarzer, M. 2000. The Contemporary City in Four Movements. *Journal of Urban Design*, 5(2), 127–44. Available at: http://dx.doi.org/10.1080/713683960 [accessed: May 13, 2014].

Chapter 2
Medina; the "Islamic," "Arab," "Middle Eastern" City: Reflections on an Urban Concept

Nezar AlSayyad

The idea of the "Islamic" city, the "Arab" city, the "Middle Eastern" city, often referred to in both Western and Arab literature as the "Medina," has been with us now for almost a century. Indeed, in the second half of the twentieth century, the term has received its fair share of attention from scholars in numerous disciplines from architectural history to urban geography. The evolution of the concept seems to have paralleled the development of scholarship on the urban form of the cities of Islam culminating in the conceptualization of the Medina as the "Islamic city" (AlSayyad 1998: 1).[1]

Initially the discourse on the influence of Islam in the urban realm brought about the "Arab," "Near Eastern" and "Middle Eastern" city debates. Each of these categories embodies particular cultural, identity and geo-political assumptions. For example, "Arab" is closely tied to Arab nationalism and identity. The term "Arab urbanism" did not exist in the scholarly literature until the late 1950s and early 1960s and specifically under the influence of the rising "pan-Arabism" of Gamal Abdul Nasser's Egypt. In line with this conception, most contemporary understandings of the "Arab" city entail cities within the geo-political construct of the "Arab" world. Reference to the "Middle Eastern" city usually includes Turkey and Iran, whereas reference to the "Greater Middle East"—a term coined after the events of September 11, 2001 to promote the Bush Administration's Greater Middle East Initiative—includes Turkey, Iran, and also Afghanistan and Pakistan. Nonetheless, one should ask Middle of what and East of where? The question that arises from the preponderance of categories used to describe cities in the Arab world is whether it is enough that these cities are tied together by something unique, be it Islam, the Arabic language, a common culture, or particular geo-political conditions.

The Evolution of the Concept of the Medina

The word *Medina* [from *Madaniyah*] represents one of the principal Arab expressions of the idea of civilization. In the Arabic language, the word *Madaniyah*, meaning urbanization/urbanism, is not totally synonymous with *Hadarah* or civilization, but the two words and their meanings are clearly linked. Rarely has there been an Islamic *Hadarah* without *Madaniyah*. This situation is not unique to Islam or to Arabic. European civilization, as well, was directly a product of a system of urban settlements, and the English word "civilization" itself is derived from the Latin *civitas* meaning "city" (AlSayyad 1998: 1–2).

Etymologically, the word Medina is derived from the Aramaic *Din*, a word that signified justice and submission. Medina developed as a place where a presiding government achieved security and administered justice. The word *Din* evolved later in the Arabic language to mean "submission" and "obedience" and later to signify religion (Al-Waly 1983: 109). In Arabic, the word Medina is used in the Quran 13 times, four of which are in reference to the city of Memphis in Egypt, two are to the city of Antioch in Syria, three are to unidentified cities in the Middle East, and four are to Yathrib, the city to which the Prophet Muhammad

---

1 This chapter is an expansion of an earlier version of the argument in my piece "The Study of Islamic Urbanism: An Historiographic Essay" published in *Built Environment*, 1996, 22(2), Special Issue *Islamic Architecture and Urbanism: Middle Eastern Perspectives*, where I served as a guest editor. It also builds on a short piece, "Arab Muslim Cities," in *Design Book Review*, 14, published in spring 1988, in which I review the literature of that time about the "Islamic city." Some of my positions on the subject have remained the same, but others have changed as evident in this chapter.

emigrated and where he established the first Islamic nation (Al-Waly 1983: 110), signifying the Arabs' knowledge of the importance of permanent settlements. It is not difficult to speculate about the benefits of invoking a somewhat generic term like Medina to describe a small city or town with a unique government like Muhammad's Yathrib, the first Medina (AlSayyad 1998: 2).

It is no surprise then that during the early years of the Islamic conquest, new cities that were established or conquered were not necessarily or automatically designated "Medinas." Garrison towns like Kufa, Basra and Fustat were designated as *Amsar* [sing: *Misr*] before they were referred to as Medinas (AlSayyad 1998: 2). Only when these towns acquired a predominantly Muslim population, were they then referred to as Medinas. The Medina was to be the subject of inquiry among many Arab historians, chroniclers and philosophers from Al-Farabi's *Al-Madinah Al-Faḍilah* (Al-Farabi and Wafi 1973) or ideal city, to Ibn Khaldun's *Muqqademah* (Ibn Khaldun and Al-Ibar 1959).

The Medina in Orientalist and Arab Scholarship

However, the concept of the Medina as we know it today owes its origin to Orientalist scholarship. The theorization of the Medina as the Islamic city began mainly in the service of the colonial project. After Napoleon's short-lived urban-based occupation of Egypt (1798–1801), the study of the Orient by the Europeans evolved into a systematic discipline. In the decades following the French invasion of Algeria in 1830, French scholars were commissioned to describe different aspects of the country in massive descriptive volumes. Hence, the first studies of the Islamic city were produced in the Maghrib by French scholars, and were later pursued by British, German and American scholars in different parts of the Middle East in the early twentieth century (AlSayyad and Tureli 2009: 599–600). Philologists were among the earliest scholars to pay attention to Islamic urbanism. This can be explained principally by the fact that many of these scholars were trained in religious studies, and ancient languages, and they adopted the same approaches commonly used in their time to study the bible and its history, and the urbanism of the people of Islam. In retrospect, as other scholars such as architectural and art historians and urban geographers participated in the debate, the nature of inquiry changed from a search for a basic Islamic essence for architecture and urban form to a discussion about the degree that can be attributed to the role of Islam in shaping the city (AlSayyad and Tureli 2009: 599–600).

In terms of method, there have been two approaches to the Islamic city both influenced by the ideas of Max Weber (1958). The art historical approach analyzed the Islamic city formally using morphological and typological analysis. The second approach, more sociological in content, examined the structural characteristics of the urban order. Both of these approaches converged to describe a model for the Islamic city that was somewhat static and unchanging. Weber had theorized the medieval European city in comparison to its non-Western Oriental counterpart. While attempting to explain the origins of modern capitalism, he credited the Christian religion for the uniqueness of the European city and singled it out as the locus of the European civilizational order. Weber claimed the superiority of the European city over its Oriental counterparts in India, China and the Near East, a matter for which he would be later severely criticized. In addition, he also overlooked the impact of European colonialism on the cities of the Orient as he dismissed the latter as cities altogether. Nevertheless, Weber's thinking continued to inform studies of the city in general and of Islamic urbanism in particular, throughout the twentieth century (AlSayyad and Tureli 2009: 600).

Weber identified five characteristics of the European medieval city: fortifications, market, guild associations, the landed nobility, and the independence of the church. Based on his analysis of Oriental cities, he argued that several of these characteristics may have existed in the Orient, but they came together in a functioning manner only in the European medieval city (Weber 1958). While he did not conduct a specific study of the cities of Islam, as such, he volunteered several comments on what he believed was the negative role of Islam in the development of urban culture. Weber and later his followers argued that Islamic cities lacked the corporate institutions and the civic life that existed in the European medieval city (AlSayyad and Tureli 2009: 600).

In the Orientalist tradition, Islam was credited with significantly increasing the degree of urbanization in the Middle East. It was assumed that Islam introduced a unique Islamic urban form. The development of this conceptual idea was paralleled by the development of graphic models by architect and planners of the city's physical form. The stereotypical model of the Islamic city consists of a mosque, a palace, a citadel, a market and residential quarters with inward-oriented housing (German 1983: 599–601).

In the West, the first interest in the nature of the Islamic city was spurred by the writings of the Marçais brothers. Their work is still cited in most books and articles on Muslim cities because it provides a general framework within which to pursue further examination of particulars. In a classic article, "L'Islamisme et la Vie Urbanine" (Marçais 1928), William Marçais introduced the idea that Islam was essentially an "urban" religion that had produced a civilization whose essence was its cities. In this article Marçais contended that Friday prayers in the congregational mosque were a reflection not only of the necessity of urban living but for the continued survival of Islam itself. He then described what he called "the quintessential Islamic city," which he claimed was centered on a Friday mosque, a nearby market, and a series of public baths (AlSayyad 1996: 91).

The ideas introduced by William Marçais in the 1920s and 1930s were followed up by his brother Georges and by Roger Le Tourneau. In two articles published in 1940 and 1945 (Marçais 1940; Marçais 1945: 517–33), Georges Marçais identified what he considered the unique morphology of a Muslim city, with ethnically segregated residential quarters and hierarchically ordered bazaars. He developed this conception by noting a distinct difference between ethnically organized residential areas and non-residential areas, as well as by spatial mapping out the hierarchical organization of markets. Le Tourneau's work on Fez, culminating in a 1957 book (Le Tourneau 1957), continued this line of research. It too, however, relied on a specifically North African model of the Islamic city. The intent of this research was to establish a unique character of the Islamic city that differentiates it from its medieval European counterpart (AlSayyad 1996: 92).

Operating in a different region and a few years later but on the Syrian cities of Damascus and Aleppo, Jean Sauvaget—another French Orientalist—drew a slightly different picture, showing how Muslim cities evolved from pre-Islamic origins (Sauvaget 1934, 1941). That line of inquiry was followed up in the 1950s by another French scholar, Xavier De Planhol, whose model of an Islamic city emphasized a linear bazaar, an elevated citadel, and irregular alleyways feeding the residential quarters. De Planhol was one of the first scholars to bluntly put a special derogatory spin on the meaning of urban form in Islam. He wrote:

> Irregularity and anarchy seem to be the most striking qualities of Islamic cities. The effect of Islam is essentially negative. It substitutes for a solid unified collectivity, a shifting and inorganic assemblage of districts; it walls off and divides up the face of the city. By a truly remarkable paradox this religion that inculcates an ideal of city life leads directly to a negation of urban order. (De Planhol 1959: 23)

The choice of words here is a clear indication of a specific norm, which equated regularity with order and development, and associated it with the West, while irregularity was considered an Islamic trait reflective of urban chaos (AlSayyad 1996: 92). By the late 1950s, then, two different models of Muslim urbanism had emerged within European scholarship. One was based on examples from North Africa represented mainly by the Marçais brothers, the other based on examples from the Levant represented mainly by Sauvaget. Neither of these models, however, incorporated much about the characteristic institutional structure, economic bodies, or social organization of Muslim society (AlSayyad 1996: 92).

It took the work of Gustave von Grunebaum to bring all these strands together to produce a fully developed Orientalist model of the prototypical Islamic city. After it appeared in 1955, von Grunebaum's classic article "The Structure of the Muslim Town" was widely used to teach and discuss the form of the Islamic city. In this work, von Grunebaum merged the work of the Marçais brothers on Morocco and Sauvaget on Syria into a compromise of elements, which he called "the typical physical form of a Muslim city" (von Grunebaum 1955: 141–58).[2] Then, using Kroeber's culturist theory (Kroeber 1952),[3] he married this formalist analysis to the institutional structure and socio-economic organization of urban Islam identified by earlier Orientalists like Massignon (1956) and Brunschvig (1947). Von Grunebaum's work showed all of the negative, reductionist

---

2 Gustave von Grunebaum had many articles and books on Islamic cities and civilization, the most important being "The Structure of the Muslim Town" (1955).

3 Kroeber's classic work, *The Nature of Culture* (1952), was used by many scholars of this generation.

tendencies of Orientalist scholarship. His method of accepting Islam as incapable of change and his definition of the Islamic city in terms of equivalent institutions found in medieval Europe were serious flaws in his model (AlSayyad 1996: 92).

Ironically, by the 1960s the von Grunebaumian stereotype had become accepted by many scholars from the Islamic world itself. This could be observed in the work of R. Jairazbhoy, Abdel Ismail and Ahmed Monier. Jairazbhoy (1965), an Indian scholar, used examples from Mughal India and the Arab Middle East to agree with von Grunebaum's notion that irregularities in the form of Muslim cities were not a result of the absence of controlling authorities. He suggested that Islam's desire to ensure the safety and independence of its urban inhabitants resulted in an appropriate form of residential segregation and commercial grouping. Jairazbhoy's book repeated the von Grunebaumian stereotype on the Indian subcontinent (AlSayyad 1996: 93). The work of other scholars like Adel Ismail (1969) and Ahmed Monier (1971) achieved the same effect in the Middle East. In the work of both these Egyptian researchers the von Grunebaumian stereotype was used in its entirety as an underlying basis for discussion. With hindsight, then, it appears that the concept of the Islamic city first evolved, developed and matured as a result of cumulative research done by "Orientalist" scholars from the West and "Oriental" scholars from the Muslim world. These writers largely drew on one another in a chain of authority that went all the way back to the Marçais brothers and Sauvaget. Ironically, a similar chain may also be found in the *Arab Chronicles*, which all writers used as primary research evidence (AlSayyad 1996: 93).

Ira Lapidus' (1967) research in the late 1960s marked the beginning of a different series of books on Muslim cities that formed a second identifiable wave of scholarship. This was justifiably critical of earlier literature, and established what I call the revisionist phase. Lapidus concentrated on exploring the urban structure of three major Muslim cities—Aleppo, Cairo and Damascus—during the Mamluk era. Instead of testing the Weberian proposition (Weber 1958)[4] that the urban entities of the Muslim Middle East were not really cities, he reformulated the issue by asking what forces established Muslim cities as functioning urban political units. He concluded by suggesting that Muslim urban society was not an entity defined by any single political or socio-economic body, but rather a society which divided essential powers and functions among its different component groups (AlSayyad 1996: 93). This system of relations constituted the government of Muslim cities, whose urban form was the outcome of interactions between these subsidiary groups. Lapidus' principal contribution lay in his attempt to map out the relationship between the military elites, the Ulama or religious leaders, and the local notables and merchants and their role in managing the city. This model, which contains Weberian traces, remains useful in understanding the cities of Islam within the temporal framework of the Middle Ages (AlSayyad 1996: 93). Entering the 1970s, Hourani and Stern followed Lapidus' line of reasoning in their book *The Islamic City* (Hourani and Stern 1970). Referring to Weber's critical components of the city, they suggested that although Islamic cities may have lacked some of Weber's components, they were still able to flourish and maintain a high level of urban activities (AlSayyad 1991b: 26).

The Medina under the Nationalist Scholars

The independence struggles of the 1950s and 1960s had been settled with the establishment of new nation states in the Middle East and the 1970s brought an increasing dissatisfaction with the inherited colonial structure and an awareness of the religious values implicit in Muslim cultural systems. Many of the newly independent nation states were now examining their own history and the subject of the Muslim city in order to devise operational guidelines for building and planning practices.

It is possible to classify the schools of scholarship among Middle East scholarship of the 1980s and 1990s into three distinct groups: the politically motivated, the philosophically inspired, and the legally based. While the three groups employ very different methods in the study of Islamic urbanism, they share the unwavering belief that the Islamic way of life was reflected in the form and culture of its cities (AlSayyad 1996: 94).

---

4 The work of Max Weber remains an important foundation for any work on the sociology of urbanism, particularly his book *The City* (1958).

The attempt to carve out an urban identity for themselves after independence explains the many conferences and symposiums on the Muslim city sponsored by research groups and political organizations throughout the Arab world. The literature from that time, often sponsored and published by national public institutions and government bodies, best reflect the views of the first group. For example, the respected Arabic journal from Kuwait, *Alam Al-Fikr* (1982), published a special issue in the early 1980s entitled *The Arab City*, containing contributions in a similar vein from well-known Arab scholars that maintained a somewhat nationalistic tone, which reflected the authors' pride in the history of Arab culture. Several conferences on Middle Eastern and Muslim urbanism inside and outside the Muslim world also took place at this time. A variety of organizations were active in sponsoring such meetings. One was the Aga Khan Award for Architecture, which also published several interesting books oriented to serve the award program, and whose philosophy can be clearly linked to educational objectives propagated through the institution's educational unit at Harvard and the Massachusetts Institute of Technology. Another was the Organization of Arab Towns, which sponsored several international conferences and which published one principal volume, *The Arab City* (Serageldin and El-Sadek 1981) edited by Ismail Serageldin that dealt with the identity and evolution of the Muslim city from past to present and offered strategies for future planning (AlSayyad 1996: 94). The Saudi government sponsored several conferences on the Islamic city, most notably the one held at King Faisal University, which attempted to identify the so-called "Islamic essence of architectures and urban existence" in the Muslim world and published as a book with the title *Islamic Architecture and Urbanism* (German 1983).

The publication of Edward Said's seminal book *Orientalism* (Said 1979) should have had some impact on studies of the city. Said argued that early Orientalist research was imbued with the idea of the Orient as mysterious, unchanging and ultimately inferior. This powerful paradigm was not always fully understood by many researchers of the Islamic city, particularly those that operated in Islamic countries. This becomes clear when looking at an important conference held in Sanaa in 1987 under the sponsorship of the Professors World Peace Academy, which clearly displayed these rising nationalistic tendencies. Its proceedings, edited as a book by Abdul Aziz Saggaf (1987), contained work from different interdisciplinary contributors covering historic and contemporary issues in Middle Eastern urbanism. In a brief introduction, Saggaf, a distinguished Yemeni scholar, explained that the book would not treat the Islamic city as a historical phenomenon, but as a contemporary entity capable of providing a harmonious environment for its inhabitants. Saggaf's position is a good example of the reactionary tendencies of this group of nationalist scholars. He began by quoting what he considered to be a controversial paragraph from Lapidus (Saggaf 1987: 3):

> We can no longer think of Muslim cities as unique ... None of the characteristic bodies of Muslim society were specifically urban forms of organization ... Cities were physical entities but not unified social bodies defined by characteristically Muslim qualities. (Lapidus 1969: 73)

He then responded to this passage by providing a view that stood for the position of many of his colleagues:

> Of course, most scholars take issue with Professor Lapidus since Muslim cities do have certain distinctive features. They have a unique layout and physical design, the central focus point of which is always a Maidan around a castle or palace on one hand and the central mosque on the other hand. (Saggaf 1987: 3)

It was ironic that in reaction to a perceived, but not real, dismissal by Lapidus of the concept of the Islamic city, Saggaf reverted to the same Orientalist model invented by von Grunebaum that had been the source of controversy in the scholarship on Muslim urbanism. It was as if in defense of the concept of the Islamic city, it was now legitimate for the national scholars to use the flawed work of the Orientalists whose work was already being contested and even discredited in the West for its biases (AlSayyad 1996: 95).

Not all research on Islamic urbanism in that time, however, followed the above lines of analysis. Although their work was not as widely disseminated, another group of researchers attempted to bring together the study of Muslim philosophy and Muslim architecture and urban form. This is the second group I have referred to above as basing their understanding of the city on philosophical ideas. The use of Sufism (as one branch of Islamic religious and spiritual practice) by this group informed their interpretations of urban form. The centrality of the mosque and the royal quarters, for example, received a new interpretation that drew upon a particular understanding of the cosmos in Islam. The early Orientalist notion was that the centrality of these elements was a representation of centralized authority. But in the work of the Iranian-born scholars Nader Ardlan and Laila Bakhtiar (1973) this original notion has been replaced by the idea that the centrality emerged from a latent spiritual belief related to the concept of oneness in Islam (AlSayyad 1996: 95).

Finally, a third group, which I label the legalists, is a group of scholars who sought legal or juridical explanations for the configurations of urban form within the Islamic city. Although members of this group are rather diverse in their orientations, they have all focused on the relationship between social structure and the legal mechanisms that governed the production of urban form in its service. Using individual case studies from different Arab regions, they later generalize their finding to a generic type that becomes for them the Islamic city. Among the noteworthy works produced in this category are those published in Arabic by Besim Hakim (1986), Jamel Akbar (1988) and Saleh Al-Hathloul (1992), all written originally in English but some were reissued years later in an Arabic edition. Using Islamic law rulings, rendered to resolve urban conflicts and building disputes, they have identified the process through which Muslim law, as they believe, ultimately shaped Muslim cities (AlSayyad 1996: 95). Perhaps the most egregious example of this approach is Besim Hakim's *Arabic-Islamic Cities*, which concludes by reaffirming the Orientalist position regarding Islamic cities, stating that "the earlier reliance on Islam as main basis for analysis was essentially sound" (Hakim 1986: 137). These books are a reminder of the different research cycles that we go through as academics. First we had the Orientalists, then the revisionists, then the nationalist scholars with their various nationalist, philosophical or legalist inclinations (AlSayyad 1996: 95).

The Medina in Post-Colonial Discourse

Edward Said's influence started to show in the work of some American scholars. Janet Abu-Lughod's seminal article "The Islamic City" (Abu-Lughod 1987) critiqued the Orientalist chain of authority that plagued studies of the Islamic city and warned against making generalizations based on singular cases. I argued that the Islamic city model was inadequate because as a stereotype it did not account for the great variation that existed in the vast Islamic world. For example in *Cities and Caliphs* (AlSayyad 1991a), I tried to show that the planned garrison towns of medieval Egypt, Syria and Iraq were shaped mainly by administrative motives and that their growth was neither unstructured nor solely determined by Islam. In the case of existing towns that were occupied by the Arabs in the early years of the conquest, the process of their Islamization often involved compromises to deal with predominantly non-Muslim populations. In that book, I not only critiqued the Islamic city concept but I went further by suggesting that individual caliphs' political visions had more influence on the genesis of Islamic cities, such as Damascus and Cairo, than did Islam.

In *Forms of Dominance*, I further attempted to unsettle the Islamic city trope by asking why is colonialism not invoked as an interpretative tool in discussing the Arab conquest of the Levant and Egypt in the seventh century? (AlSayyad 1992: 27). As I attempted to put forth a new paradigm to understand the "Islamic city as a colonial enterprise," urban geographers like Eckart Ehlers (1992) contributed to the debate by pointing to the need to include the contemporary city into studies of the Islamic city, and by emphasizing the influence of such institutions as the religious endowment *Waqf* and the phenomenon of rent capitalism. In the past two decades, the work on Ottoman cities is challenging the Arab ideal of the Islamic (AlSayyad and Tureli 2009: 601).

In this chapter, I pointed out how the idea of a stereotypical Muslim city was constructed by a series of Western authorities who drew upon a small sample of cities from a variety of locations. This stereotype was then elaborated in concert with the development of Orientalist scholarship. As the flawed basis of such Orientalist work became evident, the stereotype was challenged by a number of revisionist writers. However, aspects of the original stereotype are still being championed by some Arab and Muslim scholars for political reasons either at the national or the institutional academic scale (AlSayyad 1996: 96). The debate started to shift in the final years of the twentieth century. A new, more mature understanding of modernity, aided by the work of scholars like Tim Mitchell (1988), Gaytri Spivak (1988) and others, brought about a different perspective on urbanism. I had argued in many works then that the dualistic positioning of the traditional city against the modern city, as well as notions of "progress," imposed an insider/outsider dichotomy, that serves to naturalize and stabilize the "traditional" (AlSayyad 2004). The "traditional" in this case was assumed to be the persistent Islamic practices at the urban level in the modernizing and globalizing cities of the Arab world. Today, one can only hope that this traditional/modern dichotomy as a mechanism for understanding urbanism has finally been put to rest.

The Medina in the Post-9/11 Era

A decade into the twenty-first century, we are now concerned with understanding how Islamism is construed as a pertinent basis for social organization and rights claims that shape cities. We are interested in learning about how contemporary Islamic urban practices animate current debates about planning, development, governance and identity in cities in the Arab world. From Turkey in the north to Sudan in the south and from Tunisia in the west to Indonesia in the east, Islam is being revived as a major organizing force with the establishment of Islamic parties; this has major implications on the production on the built environments in the cities of the Arab world and beyond. Indeed the focus has become the principle lens through which cities in the Arab world are viewed, both externally by the West, particularly after the events of September 11, 2001, and internally by Arab governments, civil society organizations, planners and ordinary citizens. Additionally, the very active "Islamic heritage industry" and the projects that attempt to re-inscribe contemporary Arab cities with an "Islamic" character has brought the debates on the role of religion in public life to the fore. Have we arrived at "the fundamentalist city" (AlSayyad and Massoumi 2011) as recent scholarship implies?

The Arab Spring has given rise to new democratic spaces never experienced before in the Arab world but at the same time it has brought to power undemocratic and even fundamentalist regimes to government. With the increased visibility of Islamism after September 11, 2001, the twenty-first century witnessed an increase in scholarship that attempts to understand the relationship between Islamic religiosity, the *practice* of Islamic piety, and urban social and spatial processes. This body of work includes scholars like Mona Harb. Harb in fact takes this further by examining the link between Islamic "religiosity" and spatiality in Beirut. She analyzes Hezbollah's spatial strategies in Beirut's southern suburbs and how the group appropriates, controls and orders public space via processes of symbolization that mark territory and render it with specific meanings, and she argues that Hezbollah's strategies, including clientelistic social service networks, religious symbolism and territorial markings, embody the "Islamic milieu" and are a primary reason for the group's success (Harb 2011: 125–54). Harb's work is in dialogue with Asef Bayat's (2007) exploration into the politics of "Islamizing" the urban space in Tehran and Cairo, arguing that the "Islamist order" of the socially conservative movements has reinforced the notion of "Islamic exceptionalism," which is "expressed most visibly and immediately in urban public space" (2007: 50) by explicit, as well as implicit, interventions. From the proliferation of cultural centers celebrating Muslim achievements, to symbolic markings and the construction of mosques, the city is ordered into sanctioned versus unsanctioned spaces of piety as Saba Mahmood (2005) called them.

For me perhaps the transformation in the discourse regarding Islam and the city is best summed up by the conceptualization of the "fundamentalist city." I argue that the city is being transformed into a space in which "religious fundamentalisms … claim it as a new domain beyond the idea of the nation." I suggest that the cities of the Arab world are being transformed "into fragmented landscapes made up of spaces of exception" (AlSayyad 2011: 24). I do not accept Bayat's notion of "post-Islamism," which offers a more optimistic conceptualization of the role of Islam in the city, because I believe the events of the Arab Spring have proven him wrong.

In this chapter, I have attempted to raise a set of questions relevant to a discussion of the Islamic city. My intention has simply been to reveal linkages between a particular system of ideas and the nature of conclusions reached. It should be clear that what is needed today is a culturally informed, ethnically conscious and gender-sensitive interdisciplinary approach. Only an approach that can both analyze the intents of the propagators of Islamic cities, and account for the dynamic balance that developed between their inhabitants and their governments, can explain why these urban entities continue to be hotly debated as a main mechanism to understand the mysterious other.

References

Abu-Lughod, J. 1987. The Islamic City-Historic Myth, Islamic Essence and Contemporary Relevance. *International Journal of Middle East Studies* [online], 19(2), 155–76. Available at: http://dis.fatih.edu.tr/store/docs/852311CoC46E6x.pdf [accessed: August 22, 2013].

Akbar, J. 1988. *Crisis in the Built Environment: The Case of the Muslim City*. Singapore: Concept Media Pte Ltd.

Akbar, J. 1988. *Imarat Al-Ard fi Al-Islam*. Beirut: Mo'asset Ulam Al-Quran. Beirut: Al-Resalah Publishers.

Al-Farabi and Wafi, A.W. 1973. *Al-Madinah Al-Faḍilah*. Cairo: Dar Alam Al-Kutub lil-Ṭab Wa-Al-Nashr.

Al-Fikr Al-Araby. 1982. Special volumes on the Arab city, 4, 30–31. Title translated from the Arabic.

Al-Hathloul, S. 1992. *Al-Madinah Al-Arabiah AlIslamiah*. Riyadh, Saudi Arabia.

AlSayyad, N. 1991a. *Cities and Caliphs*. New York: Greenwood.

AlSayyad, N. 1991b. *The Typical Muslim City in Cities and Caliphs*. New York: Greenwood.

AlSayyad, N. (ed.) 1992. *Forms of Dominance: On the Architecture and Urbanism of the Colonial Enterprise*. Aldershot: Avebury.

AlSayyad, N. 1996. The Study of Islamic Urbanism: An Historiographic Essay. *Built Environment* [online], 22(2), 91–7. Available at: http://www.jstor.org/stable/23288983 [accessed: December 6, 2012].

AlSayyad, N. 1998. Contesting the Madînah: Dualities in the Study of Islamic Urbanism. *Islamic Culture*, LXXII(4), 1–20.

AlSayyad, N. (ed.) 2004. *The End of Tradition?* London: Routledge.

AlSayyad, N. 2011. The Fundamentalist City? in *The Fundamentalist City? Religiosity and the Remaking of Urban Space*, edited by N. AlSayyad and M. Massoumi. London: Routledge, 3–26.

AlSayyad, N. and Massoumi, M. (eds) 2011. *The Fundamentalist City? Religiosity and the Remaking of Urban Space*. London: Routledge.

AlSayyad, N. and Tureli, I. 2009. Urban Geography: Islamic Urbanism, in *International Encyclopedia of Human Geography*, edited by R. Kitchin and N. Thrift. Oxford: Elsevier, 599–601.

Al-Waly, T. 1983. The City in Islam. *Al-Fikr Al-Araby*, 4(29), 108–33. Title translated from the Arabic.

Ardlan, N. and Bakhtiar, L. 1973. *The Sense of Unit*. Chicago: University of Chicago Press.

Bayat, A. 2007. *Making Islam Democratic: Social Movements and the Post-Islamist Turn*. Stanford: Stanford University Press.

Brunschvig, R. 1947. Urbanisme medieval et droit musulmane. *Revue des Etudes Islamiques*, 47, 89–101.

De Planhol, X. 1959. *World of Islam*. Ithaca: Cornell University Press.

Ehlers, E. 1992. The City of the Islamic Middle East, in *Modeling the City: Cross-Cultural Perspectives*, edited by E. Ehlers, J. Bahr and C.D. Harris. Bonn: In Kommission bei Ferd. Dummlers, 231–9.

German, A. (ed.) 1983. *Islamic Architecture and Urbanism—Selected Papers: Proceedings of a Symposium Organized by the College of Architecture and Planning*. Dammam, Saudi Arabia: King Faisal University.

Hakim, B. 1986. *Arabic-Islamic Cities*. London: Kegan Paul.

Harb, M. 2011. On Religiosity and Spatiality: Lessons from Hezbollah in Beirut, in *The Fundamentalist City? Religiosity and the Remaking of Urban Space*, edited by N. AlSayyad and M. Massoumi. London: Routledge, 125–54.

Hourani, A. and Stern, S.M. (eds) 1970. *The Islamic City*. Oxford: Bruno Cassirer.

Ibn Khaldun, A.R. and Al-Ibar, T. 1959. *Al-Muqaddemah*. Beirut: Dar Al-Nahad.

Ismail, A. 1969. *Origin, Ideology and Physical Pattern of Arab Urbanization*. Karlsruhe: University Dissertations.

Ismail, A. (ed.) 1969. Origin, Ideology and Physical Pattern of Arab Urbanization. *Ekistics*, 195.

Jairazbhoy, R. 1965. *Art and Cities of Islam*. New York: Asia Publishing House.

Kroeber, A.L. 1952. *The Nature of Culture*. Chicago: University of Chicago Press.

Lapidus, I. 1967. *Muslim Cities in the Later Middle Ages*. Cambridge, MA: Harvard University Press.

Lapidus, I. (ed.) 1969. *Muslim Cities and Islamic Societies, in Middle Eastern Cities*. Berkeley: University of California Press.

Le Tourneau, R. 1957. *Les Villes Musulmanes de l'Afrique du Nord*. Algiers: La Maison des Livres.

Mahmood, S. 2005. *Politics of Piety: The Islamic Revival and the Feminist Subject*. Princeton: Princeton University Press.

Marçais, G. 1940. L'Urbanisme Musulmane, in *Congrès de la Federation des Socieses Savantes de L'Afrique du Nord*. Algiers, 31–48.
Marçais, G. 1945. La Conception des villes dans L'Islam. *Revue d'Alger*, 517–33.
Marçais, W. 1928. L'Islamisme et la Vie Urbaine, in *L'Academie des inscriptions et belles-lettres: Comptes Rendus*. Paris, 27–60.
Massignon, L. 1956. *Opera Minora*. Paris: Editions du Cenacle.
Mitchell, T. 1988. *Colonizing Egypt*. Cambridge: Cambridge University Press.
Monicr, A. 1971. *Cities of Islam*. Beirut: Beirut American University Press.
Saggaf, A. (ed.) 1987. *The Middle East City*. New York: Paragon House.
Said, E. 1979. *Orientalism*. New York: Vintage Books.
Sauvaget, J. 1934. Esquisse d'une histoire de la ville de Damas. *Revue Etude Islamiques*, special issue.
Sauvaget, J. 1941. *Alep*. Paris: Librairie Orientaliste.
Serageldin, I. and El-Sadek, S. (eds) 1981. *The Arab City*. Riyadh: Arab Urban Development Institute.
Spivak, G.C. 1988. *Can the Subaltern Speak?* Basingstoke: Macmillan.
Von Grunebaum, G. 1955. The Structure of the Muslim Town, in *Islam: Essays in the Nature and Growth of a Cultural Tradition*, edited by G. von Grunebaum. London: Routledge and Kegan Paul, 141–58.
Weber, M. 1958. *The City*. D. Martindale (ed.) and G. Neuwirth (trans.). Glencoe, IL: Free Press.

PART I
The Discursive: Reconceptualizing Boundaries between the Diverse and the Conflictive

Chapter 3
The Cultural Discourse: On Regionalism in Urban Design and the Role of the Aga Khan Award for Architecture

Omar Abdulaziz Hallaj

The Post-Colonial Public Space

Urban design is a field of human activity that involves collective imagination, enterprise and values. However, the obvious need to coordinate and negotiate human activity has only recently gained a discursive nature as the practice became self-reflective and the process of urban form-making became closely linked to the efforts of demarcating the *public* against the *private* and *center* against *margins*. In the post-colonial city, urban design was further subjected to paradigms that engendered the *public* as a newly constructed imagined identity. Succumbing to internationalist trends was both a proof of belonging to the modern world but also a sign of subjugation to the colonial. The urban form of the post-colonial city can be creative and locally adaptive, but never originary.[1] The paradigms that framed the question of urban form were often defined elsewhere. Complex issues of city making, such as the multi-layered demarcations of center versus margin, public versus private, and wealth versus abjection were often deferred in favor of symbolic representations of national or ethno-religious identities. The process of localizing the discourse on urban design involved many cultural stakeholders. In this chapter I will concentrate on the role of the Aga Khan Award for Architecture in contributing the emerging language and practice of urban design in the Muslim world.[2]

The paradigms that controlled the urban form of the post-colonial city differed little from those of the colonial period. They were mainly preoccupied with formulaic, formalistic and for the most part idealistic concerns. The modern parts of the city were celebrated as proof that the city provided an image of belonging to the world. The colonized assimilated the lessons of modernity left behind by the colonizers, especially that many of the theoretical and practical advances of the urban design discipline were developed in the colonies (Rabinow 1989; Wright 1991). But these advances were often reflections on debates taking place in Western design discourse and practice. What was missing for the most part is local agency. The practice of urban design in the post-colonial space inherited colonial visions and dilemmas. However, local practice failed to link the discipline's main tenets to local political processes of defining the public in the political, economic and social senses. Urban form-making was relegated to the domain of regulatory statutes based on inherited norms and standards rather than evolved from direct experience or needs. The process of creating an aesthetic *public* has therefore taken a different path than the process of defining a socio-political *public*.

---

    1 The ability to redefine a state of being from one's own experience was coined by Robert Mugerauer using the term *originary* as opposed to *original* to avoid the nostalgic connotations often misunderstood in reading Heidegger (Mugerauer 2012).
    2 Though the Award is concerned with a greater concept of Muslim communities worldwide, this chapter will draw its examples primarily from the Arab region to provide a framework for the formation of a cultural discourse on architectural and urban design in the Arab speaking region. The intention is to complement other research on the region presented in the conference. Many of the issues presented here are specific and generalizations should be avoided.

Box 3.1   **Modernist codification of public space**

Figure 3.1   Detail of *Plan Cadastral, Ville D'Alep, Cironscription VII, Section 5, Feuille 1, 1930*
Note: Modern wide streets, traditional throughways and small alleyways are all designated as public domain on the cadastral maps.
Source: Open records of the City of Aleppo.

In 1926, the French colonial mandate in Syria and Lebanon embarked on a mission to develop a comprehensive cadastral system (Figure 3.1). The mapping process was done with great technical precision but with utter irreverence to the social context of the cities and towns being mapped. Semi-public alleyways were perceived in the Western framework of *public domain*, thus ending centuries-old common law understanding of these spaces as self-policed, locally maintained spaces (Marcus 1989; Semerdjian 2008). The process of codifying the city came as part of a major package of urban legislations (the codes of: cadastral law, state public and private properties, eminent domain and the building regulations*). The normative practice of bringing all space under the watchful eye of the modern state continues until today, with dire consequences, particularly in the spontaneous settlements. Encroaching on residual semi-public space is legally criminalized despite social tolerance and support.

* Refer to Syria–Lebanon codes 144 dated 1925, 161 dated 1926, 186 and 188 dated 1926 and their subsequent amendments.

Box 3.2   Normalizing modern Islamic identity

Figure 3.2   Traditional and modern mosques in Al-Hajarayn, Wadi Hadhramout, Yemen
Source: Author's collection.

Throughout the Arab–Muslim territories, iconic urban forms are being demolished and replaced in favor of idealized forms of Arab and/or Muslim identities. National governments have invested substantially in funding public projects with the intention of consolidating the representation of the nation. However, another trend is at work. Through semi-formal networks of funding, patrons mostly with connections to the rich Gulf States are pushing for homogenized representations of Islam. The pictures are from the city of Al-Hajarayn in Yemen (Figure 3.2), where many of the city's traditional mosques were demolished to make way for mosques built according to *modern Islamic methods*.

Normalizing the Practice

The normative processes defining the post-colonial construction of the *public* revolved for the longest period around two types of ideological constructs: the national and the ethno-religious identities. Though other paradigms of collective social contracts were proposed none really managed to break the hold of the two populist ideologies. Both ideologies idealized the creation of iconic urban space in terms of imagined identities imbued with aesthetic and symbolic values. The practice of city-making, however, engenders complex and multi-layered designations of space. Urban form in Arab–Muslim cities (like in all other cities of the world) is often negotiated, fought over, and resolved through demarcating and challenging boundaries along economic, social and political divides.[3] The limited scope of post-colonial ideological constructions of collective identities deferred the complex questions that did not fit into dominant paradigms. The real issues of the city were tucked beyond the public discourse. Public officials often regurgitate unfeasible solutions based on standards they have learned from their previous colonizers. Increasingly, with the shifting of local economic structures to favor rapid and often spontaneous urbanization, major segments of the city became marginalized. Moreover, as the limited wealth was despairingly distributed among its inhabitants, the city could not sustain the economic expectations of its population. Its internal marginalization was thus synchronic with its marginalization on the regional and international scene. The combined economic and social marginalization of urban residents bunched them into all sorts of subaltern collectivities[4] with the obvious absence of the one collective identity that should have counted the most: citizenship.

Beyond Regionalism

The Aga Khan Award for Architecture was initiated 35 years ago against this background, where collective identity was fiercely debated but never in the realm of the built environment. It was born out of a concern over the increased marginalization of Muslim communities both in the international arena and within their local communities. The positing of a Muslim collective was always problematic as the award was not concerned with a specific ideological construct of Islam but could not be made independent of it.[5] The successive juries that served as the trendsetters of the Award were carefully selected to avoid giving the Award any specific ideological bias. The focus was always on communities rather than on Islam. The world inhabited by Muslim communities was thought to be sufficiently diversified that no single ideological construct could be capable of dominating it. The main concern was to put forward alternative practices that would help these communities refocus the world around their local identities and needs. The Award thus evolved into one of the strongest advocates for regionalism in the professional spheres of architecture and urbanism.[6]

However, the careful crafting of the Award procedures to avoid ideological hegemony produced a different type of center/periphery problematic. To avoid a normative practice based on religion, the Award became identified with local social practices of space making. Once again, the development of the built environment was celebrated mainly around limited ranges of *publics*. In searching for innovation, juries were eager to recognize ingenuity and not the methodical work that goes into system building and replication. The main understanding was that the Award's mission was to define best practices, highlight positive initiatives and encourage self-confidence in Muslim communities to solve their own problems mainly through the agency of

---

3 Darrow Zenlund (1991) traced the contestation of urban codes and urban narrative in the daily practices of multitudes of stakeholders in the city of Aleppo, Syria. The case study could serve as a clear example of how post-colonial narratives on the city assimilated the colonial ones and adapted them to allow the different stakeholders to lay claim on the city.

4 Most sociological research about marginalization in the Arab region has concentrated on the formation of class identity. Building on Marxian principles, sociologists like Hanna Batatu have inspired a slew of research for the last 20 years. The main trends of this scholarly work move in the direction of gradual shifts from traditional identities (like ethnicity, and sectarian identities) toward the consolidation of class (Batatu 1992, 1999). However, very little anthropological fieldwork was actually done on the ground in marginalized communities. Often, traditional forms of collective solidarity are coexistent side by side with modern forms of collective organization such as political parties and sub-sectarian alliances. In reality identity should be regarded as a fluid construct that evolves according to the narrow interests of people and communities. The unfolding of the Arab Spring social movements is perhaps the clearest indicator on how subaltern identities were dynamic and flexible.

5 One can read in the first monograph issued by the Award how the members of the first Steering Committee were extending themselves to keep the definition of Islam open. They wanted to map through the nominations and winning projects the field in which the Award was to work. The introductory statements were meant to open the door for a new exploration into contemporary Muslim cultures rather than an attempt to frame *Islam* (Holod 1983).

6 To promote its mission, the Award organized scores of seminars over the years. Titles such as *Regionalism in Architecture*, *Modern Approaches to Regionalism* and *Symbolism in Its Regional and Contemporary Context* were not uncommon (Katz 1980; Powell 1985, 1989).

civil society. The public involvement in such range of activities is often unique and non-replicable; replication being a normative imposition that the Award was clearly trying to avoid. Thus, processes dependent on *public* agents beyond the reach of individual communities were less likely to be recognized by the Award. Over the years the Award gained a solid professional image as one of the most solid socially orientated architectural awards. Yet, in its very insistence on not being ideologically normative, the Award produced an unintended professional normative role that sees the built environment as a product of small scale collective action.

From Normative Discourse to Advocacy

During the jury deliberations in the previous cycle[7] (in which I had the honor to participate), the jury debated the issue rather extensively. There was a common denominator running through many of the nominated projects. The jury identified certain *profiles* that characterized nominated projects. At the end, as we selected the winning projects, we tried to choose a wide range of collective agency roles in the built environment (public, private and non-profit). We were trying to demonstrate that the diversity of the Muslim world is not only a matter of ideology and geography (Hallaj 2011). There was a diversity of agency. We even tried to challenge the very understanding of the Muslim community by selecting winning projects from non-Muslim communities (something that has actually been done but only on a very limited basis in the past). And yet, what was once again recognized through our selection was limited. Innovations in replication, in systems' development, in code building and breaking, and in deconstructing marginalization and not only in remedying its symptoms were naturally absent. And while it is hard to speculate on the reason, one major rational was the fact that most nominations received by the Award for that year fit into what has become a *stereotype* or a *profile* for potential winning projects.

The 11th cycle of the Award witnessed a small innovation. The shortlist was published for the first time. In the past, the general public had access only to the final list of winning projects. This time, the Steering Committee of the Award wanted to expand its outreach and to open the debate about the nature of the Ummah constituting the Muslim realm that the Award is trying to serve. Along with this move it became possible for the first time to point to projects that can be used as case studies, and to engage them as material evidence for efforts being carried out in the field. The shortlist was published in advance of the announcement of the final winners. It includes a wide range of projects, some were clearly not deserving of the Award for one reason or another but they had the potential to serve the public discourse on the built environment. The publishing of the shortlist was mainly geared to drive more diversified future nomination. The Award was expanding its nominations every cycle but the expansion was often quantitative and poorly reflected the diversification of issues.

Of the 401 nominated projects for the last cycle, the jury encountered the usual score of *Islamic Style* projects. Now they run from small scale to urban projects. But these projects rarely afford any new understanding of issues. They bring to the table standard construction procedures, typical client–architect relationships, low community participation in the process, and very often the only thing Islamic about them is a myriad of cut and paste details that mix and match architectural references from Muslim histories. If the current nomination list is a good sample, then the Muslim world is building a substantial part of its environment based on normative symbolism that has become almost obligatory in the eyes of patrons who want to be perceived as leaders in the Muslim world. From attempts at inventing traditions to hyper nostalgia, the Award continues to attract a fair share of nominations where *Islam* is seen as a last layer to be added onto a building to localize it: regionalism in its most rudimentary form.

---

7 This text was written following the 11th Aga Khan Award for Architecture and deals mainly with the results of the nomination cycle from 2008 to 2010. At the time of the publication, the results of the new 12th cycle are already known, though the short list was published again prior to the presentation of the final announcement of the permeated projects. Five projects were awarded in the latest edition of the Award. Many of the arguments presented in this chapter were further reinforced with the new selection.

Agency in the Public Sphere

However, the jury was not particularly looking for Muslim identity in the symbolism of built form, as much as in the agency that creates the built environment. In a world where Muslim communities are part of a global reality and complex networks of interests, the manifestation of Islam was sought beyond the used up symbolic forms of the past. Rather, the jury was concerned with projects where multiple agents with different agendas could work together, negotiate the production of the built form and reconcile conflicting identities. Conviviality[8] on a global scale was one way modern Muslim identities could be merged within global cultural networks without losing their own voice. We were not looking at projects that reflected regional forms within a global context, but at regional agents that were able to use form to integrate their communities into the global system. Yet, integrating projects into the world comes with responsibilities on a global scale: the environment, respect for cultural diversity, and the search for cultural dialogue.

Another portion of the Award nominations came in the guise of super modern, constructivist, de-constructivist, high-tech, neo-classical and other non-site-specific styles (Figure 3.3a). These nominations have become more forthcoming as the Award was given in the past to some very modern projects to recognize engineering innovations, innovative construction processes and new forms of institutional expressions and building typologies. The fact that the Award's previous non-winning projects were never known to the public may have contributed to nominators thinking that the winning projects were recognized simply because of their *modernness*, as a sign that the Award is finally giving in to the reality that the Muslim world must now be integrated in the modern world. This is perhaps indicative that people, who look back to the previous Awards to discern trends, are often merely looking at visual clues. Architectural awards have a strong tendency to normalize the practice of design simply because the practice itself is still very visually oriented.

On an urban scale, the jury was faced with dozens of nominations of the sort described above. Attempts at developing instant urbanity by importing readymade concepts, styles and even institutional brands are becoming a common practice in some rapidly developing Muslim countries. Wholesale university campuses, new beach-line and in-the-sea developments, theme cities, and so on, are creating a real demand for professional services that can only be met by standardized design solutions. The painstaking effort of integration of new developments into existing fabrics and the participation of community in the process is rarely taken into consideration. In these cases, nominations to the Award reflect an understanding of the regionalist mission of the Award simply as a geographical category: this is an Award for good quality architecture in this region. Very often the design process in the nondescript developments is given the epithet of *design excellence* to cover the fact that it has no local relevance.

Another category of projects has by now become a standard yard stick for the Award: the small, environmentally sensitive, site-specific and innovative but respectful of community ethos, type of projects. These projects are true works of dedication to a cause. They are often non-replicable in as far as the conditions that led to their development are non-transferable. However, these projects are also recurring in the Award's nomination list at an increasing rate. The jury was particularly concerned that a certain *Aga Khan Award style* was developing. It is perhaps a positive outcome of the Award that people are becoming more aware of the need to engage the community, respect the environment, use local materials and integrate the building into the site. But the Award should be alarmed that certain normative poetics are emerging as a result. This is entirely different from recognizing innovative systems of replication. However, system replication should not fall back into form replication, or else international style is no different from *local style* in robbing people of the true expressions of local identity.

It remains to be seen if the publishing of the shortlist is going to influence a new drive for a critical review of the Award's criteria for recognizing a winning project. The shortlist is not about projects that were almost good enough; it is about expanding the public debate on what constitutes a break from the norm. To cover this particular line of the Award's mission I would like to highlight four projects from the last cycle (two projects from the shortlist and two winning projects).

---

8 The term was pinned through the discussion of the Madinat al-Zahra Museum, one of the winning projects. The term is a poor translation of *conviviencia*, a cultural period that dominated Andalusian Spain and merged the various cultures of the Iberian Peninsula for a good part of the medieval period.

The Cultural Discourse 35

Placed on the shortlist was the Souq Waqif in Qatar (Figure 3.3b), a broad gesture for preserving local culture facing the rapidly globalizing nature of the modern city. It is not a conservation project, because much of the original physical fabric was beyond preservation. But through a sensitive approach at recollecting and painstakingly documenting the remaining fabric, the urban morphology was recreated and a major investment ensued to assure that this very rare sample of an urban heritage is preserved for future generations.

Souq Waqif is a place that celebrates the diverse cultures contributing to the creation of a modern state. An alternative to the generic shopping mall was opened to the residents of the city. Yet, the project was a top-down investment, a form of open-air mall where property was bought by the local authorities and then rented (or given) to businesses or cultural initiatives who offer a local flavor to the ever expanding consumer culture of large size malls in the region. While, the project involved a deep respect for the local identity and represented a painstaking attempt at retrieving elements of a not-so-distant past, it will remain to be seen if it will evolve into a viable motor for local culture or simply a place of consumption.

The American University of Beirut Campus was also placed on the shortlist along with various new buildings on the site (the business school and the student center). The project was in stark contrast to most of the instant urbanity that other university campuses in the region were putting forward as a solution to the needs of expansion. Instead of abandoning the site or redeveloping it, the plan was to carefully densify it while

Figure 3.3 A selection of projects nominated for the 11th cycle of the Aga Khan Award for Architecture

Note: (a) the Petronas Towers in Kuala Lumpur received the Aga Khan Award in the 2004 cycle; (b) Souq Waqif, Doha, Qatar; (c) view of Avenue Habib Bourquibah.
Source: (a) author's collection; (b) photographer Ziad Chawkat, courtesy of the Aga Khan Trust for Culture; (c) photographer Saleh Jabeur, courtesy of the Aga Khan Trust for Culture.

paying utmost respect to its ecology. Attempts were made to engage the campus and surrounding community (albeit not fully developed) in the process. New constructions made great efforts to be environmentally friendly. Yet, despite all its sensitive design work, the campus remains disengaged from the city and the few square meters that were relegated back to the public realm outside the site were limited gestures and did not constitute a strategy for active engagement between community and university.

Wadi Hanifa in Saudi Arabia is a very special project. It is one of the largest sites ever considered for the Award; it runs some dozen of kilometers along the banks of an old wadi. Runoff water from the city was naturally treated, the site, once an environmental disaster zone of landfills, was rehabilitated and the risk of floods was clearly mitigated. Moreover, in the process the largest green zone in the city became once more accessible to its residents. The Greater Riyadh Authority developed the project over several phases in what seemed like a sensible strategy for using public funds systematically and not just a small one-off project. The Wadi Hanifa may have some technical design deficiencies but overall it was recognized because it was about systems development and not just space making.

Finally, the restoration and revitalization of recent urban heritage in Tunis was recognized wholeheartedly by the jury because it attempts to reconcile the various *pasts* of the city into one urban space. The once *cordon sanitaire* established by the French colonial authorities, to separate the modern city form the Medina, is lined by colonial era buildings. Dozens of monuments face up to the main avenue of Habib Bourquibah (Figure 3.3c) with facades ranging from neo-baroque to neo-Islamic in style. But behind the main street, little neighborhoods were slowly degenerating. Through a mixture of direct funding and small incentives, the Associations de la Sauveguard de la Ville de Tunis managed to reweave the urban fabric physically, economically and socially. Shortly after, it came as no surprise when we witnessed the great civil society activists launching their major demonstrations in the newly rediscovered public space. The zone has been re-opened to city residents of all backgrounds to re-engage in it.

The Aga Khan Award has gained an important role as a platform for regionalism in the discourse on architecture and the built environment. The role of the Award in countering the international style hegemony over local culture is perhaps a topic for serious research in the future. Yet, no one can deny the strong impact it has left on changing local practices and perceptions. Nonetheless, it is important to distinguish between its impact on stylistic and discursive practices and its impact on systems of production of the built environment, especially at the urban level. The Award process, with all its emphasis on identifying collective construction processes, still needs to engender serious debate on constructing the collective.

References

Batatu, H. 1992. *The Old Social Classes and the Revolutionary Movements of Iraq*. Princeton: Princeton University Press.
Batatu, H. 1999. *Syria's Peasantry, the Descendants of Its Lesser Rural Notables, and Their Politics*. Princeton: Princeton University Press.
Hallaj, O.A. 2011. The Short List, in *Implicate Explicate*, edited by M. Mostafavi. Baden: The Aga Khan Award for Architecture and Lars Muller Publishers, 264–268.
Holod, R. 1983. Introduction, in *Architecture and Community: Building in the Islamic World Today*, edited by R. Holod. New York: Aperture and the Aga Khan Award for Architecture, 14–20.
Katz, J.G. (ed.) 1980. *Architecture as Symbol and Self-Identity*. Geneva: The Aga Khan Award for Architecture.
Marcus, A. 1989. *The Middle East on the Eve of Modernity: Aleppo in the Eighteenth Century*. New York: Columbia University Press.
Mugerauer, R. 2012. *Heidegger and Homecoming: The Leitmotif in the Later Writings*. Toronto: University of Toronto Press.
Powell, R. (ed.) 1985. *Regionalism in Architecture*. Singapore: Concept Media and the Aga Khan Award for Architecture.
Powell, R. (ed.) 1989. *Criticism in Architecture*. Singapore: Concept Media and the Aga Khan Award for Architecture.
Rabinow, P. 1989. *French Modern Norms and Forms of the Social Environment*. Cambridge, MA: MIT Press.

Semerdjian, E. 2008. *Off the Straight Path: Illicit Sex, Law, and Community in Ottoman Aleppo.* Syracuse: Syracuse University Press.
Wright, G. 1991. *The Politics of Design in French Colonial Urbanism.* Chicago: University of Chicago Press.
Zenlund, D. 1991. *Post-Colonial Aleppo, Syria: Struggles in Representation and Identity.* Austin: University of Texas Press.

Syrian and Lebanese Codes

Code 144 dated 1925 defining the Public Domain.
Code N. 161 dated 1926 for public expropriations.
Codes N. 186, and 188 dated 1926 and subsequent amendments for establishing the cadastral records and the Real Estate Court.

Chapter 4

The Participative Discourse: Community Activism in Post-War Reconstruction

Howayda Al-Harithy

This chapter explores the role of professional activism in post-war reconstruction, based on the experiences of the Reconstruction Unit (RU), a group of academicians and practitioners affiliated with the American University of Beirut. Members of this group, with which I was associated, volunteered their expertise in the aftermath of the 2006 war between Lebanon and Israel. The RU's comprehensive vision integrated physical reconstruction with socioeconomic revitalization, operating at the levels of problem assessment, conceptual planning and technical aid. Considering the limited role of the Lebanese government at the time, we intended our efforts to be participatory and community based, and we engaged with a great variety of individuals and agencies on the ground, including municipalities, NGOs and the Shia social, political and religious group Hezbollah.

This chapter highlights three diverse examples of the RU's interventions. First, it examines the unit's work with regard to the Beirut neighborhood of Haret Hreik, a large-scale urban reconstruction project. The challenge here was political and the aim was to initiate public debate. Next, it looks at al-Qleileh, a rural area in southern Lebanon, where the challenge was environmental and the goal was agricultural recovery and long-term development. Finally, it relates the case of Beit Bil Jnoub, a nonprofit organization created to assist individual homeowners. Our challenge in the third case was technical, and the aim was capacity building.

Throughout the course of our work in the years following the 2006 war, the RU attempted to engage with communities outside the rigid confinement of exclusive sectarian territories. We wanted to respond to the polarized climate of the time by systematically reclaiming open space for everyone. By engaging as activists and volunteers in the post-war reconstruction, we also sought, as academics, to question the boundaries between the university and its surroundings, and to initiate a change in current planning practices in Lebanon.

In order to generate discourse beyond the group and its fieldwork and create a learning process yet to come, we reflected on our experiences in a book in 2010. The book, which I edited, was titled *Lessons in Post-War Reconstruction: Case Studies from Lebanon in the Aftermath of the 2006 War*. The examples presented here are recountings of selected sections of that book. These will serve both to introduce the context of the 2006 reconstruction and illustrate our range of experiences responding to it.

The 2006 Post-War Condition

The 2006 war began on July 12 after Hezbollah captured two Israeli soldiers in an attempt to negotiate an exchange of prisoners. Israel subsequently waged full-scale war for 33 days, targeting sites across Lebanon. The war ultimately claimed the lives of 1,183 civilians and left more than 4,000 people wounded. More than 250,000 people were permanently displaced, while close to a million people were temporarily displaced (Fattouh and Kolb 2006: 97).

The war has been described as the "costliest Arab-Israeli war in Lebanon's history" (Salem 2006: 18). Direct damage to civilian infrastructure and industries was estimated by the Council for Development and Reconstruction (CDR) to be $3.6 billion. Indirect economic loss related to the tourist industry and to an air and sea blockade raised this total to $7 billion (Dibeh 2008: 157). The United Nations (UN) put the cost of the war even higher, estimating it at $15 billion (Fattouh and Kolb 2006: 101). More importantly, the war forced Lebanon, which has a long history with wars, to grapple with a vast new challenge while still engaged in reconstruction following its own 1975–90 civil war. To respond to this new disaster, the country turned to the international community for aid, and in particular other Arab countries such as Kuwait, Saudi Arabia and Qatar.

The position of the government was made clear from the first day of the ceasefire. Its role in the reconstruction process was limited to fundraising and providing compensation to those who had lost their homes. This, claimed many analysts, opened the door for non-governmental actors to intervene and at times take the lead. It also meant that NGOs and international agencies needed to operate without clear coordination or an overall guiding strategy. At the forefront of these groups was Jihad al-Bina, the construction NGO of Hezbollah. In most cases it was the first agency to arrive on the scene, conduct surveys, coordinate with donors and municipalities, and offer services to those who lost homes or businesses. According to Hamieh and Mac Ginty (2009: S106):

> As soon as the fighting came to a halt in August 2006, Hezbollah leader Hassan Nasrallah appeared on television pledging that his organization would help to rebuild homes and compensate those whose homes had been destroyed. Well in excess of USD 100 million in cash was distributed within 72 hours of the cessation of hostilities. Hezbollah seemed the most effective on-the-ground actor as it directed bulldozers to raze damaged buildings and its volunteers staffed registration centers to assess the needs of returnees. The party justified its reconstruction activities as another part of its 'war of resistance'.

Even as foreign donations arrived, the Lebanese government played a minimal role. Many countries contributed financial assistance either as compensation for homeowners or to rebuild infrastructure. Saudi Arabia, Qatar, Kuwait and Iran were the major contributors. Of these, Qatar and Iran opted to pay for projects directly, without going through government institutions. Indeed, this absence of a major government role or all-encompassing strategy meant that the burden of reconstruction fell largely on individual Lebanese citizens who had lost their homes. The need here was acute, since nearly half the damage inflicted during the war was to the country's housing stock. "Housing compensation was estimated by the United Nations Development Programme (UNDP) as the largest direct cost of the war" (Hamieh and Mac Ginty 2009: 5).

It was clear that Israel's strategy had been twofold: on the one hand, to hit Hezbollah military targets, but on the other to seek to undercut support for the group by attacking the civilian infrastructure. The most telling evidence of this was Israel's selective destruction of total villages or neighborhoods, such as the massive destruction suffered by Beirut's southern suburbs.

The Founding of the Reconstruction Unit at the American University of Beirut

It was against this scenario of an absent government, a paralyzed nation and a displaced population that our group of professionals, which included architects, designers and planners, initiated its efforts to assist the recovery process. Being largely associated with the American University of Beirut (AUB), we organized under the umbrella of the university, and founded the Reconstruction Unit on August 18, 2006, within the Department of Architecture and Design. The RU was intended to provide a flexible forum that would allow for growth and effective cross-disciplinary cooperation. Our self-described mission included the following passage:

> The Unit aims to conduct its work within a larger framework and a comprehensive vision that *integrates physical reconstruction with social and economic revitalization.* The work is therefore intended to be *participatory and community based.* It will operate both at the level of conceptual planning and technical aid and the level of assessment and problem definition on the ground. The Unit also aims to work with individuals and agencies on the ground, especially municipalities, conduct surveys and assess needs—immediate, medium and long term. Accordingly, it will formulate problem definitions, objectives and intervention strategies. This comes with a complete awareness that each site has its particular set of problems and issues to respond to with the proper approach and tools. Thus, the Unit's role is to guide the process of reconstruction towards

an effective, site-specific and sustainable integrated product. (Reconstruction Unit 2006, http://staff.aub.edu.
lb/~webtfrcs/reconstruction2.htm)

Members of the RU worked individually and collectively, with each member playing a different role based on his or her contacts and expertise. That led to a number of different intervention sites and strategies, and resulted in products that ranged from design proposals, to studio assignments, to written papers, to debates. Site visits with students, engagements with municipalities, and meetings with individuals and community groups were all part of this strategy. The following sections recount three of these experiences largely in the words of the practitioners who led them, as taken from *Lessons in Post-War Reconstruction*.

Influencing the Politics of Reconstruction in Haret Hreik

Haret Hreik, in Beirut's southern suburbs, was a main administrative and residential center for Hezbollah. A principal target of Israeli air attacks, it was largely destroyed by the end of the war. Our work with regard to its reconstruction was coordinated by Mona Harb and Mona Fawaz. As faculty of the Graduate Programs of Urban Planning & Policy and Urban Design, both Fawaz and Harb were, at the time, part of the Haret Hreik task team of the RU. Fawaz also organized in January 2007 a three-day workshop that resulted in the widely disseminated local monograph titled *The Reconstruction of Haret Hreik: Design Options for Improving the Livability of the Neighborhood* (Fawaz and Ghandour 2007).

This intervention was the most complex we became involved in, not only because Haret Hreik was the site of what Harb and Fawaz (2010) described as "the most significant urbicide" of the July 2006 war, but because its reconstruction was solely led and implemented by Hezbollah as a translation of its Secretary General's promise to rebuild it "more beautiful than it was."

Against the rush of Hezbollah to intervene and the absence of a framework for action, architects and planners within the Reconstruction Unit mobilized to facilitate public debate over the area's future. We strongly believed that decisions pertaining to Haret Hreik needed to be generated through an open public process. In order to influence this process, we launched a number of strategies to instigate informed debate. Our efforts translated to three successive interventions: (1) organizing an international urban design ideas competition; (2) developing planning proposals and publicizing them; and (3) engaging the Hezbollah reconstruction company assigned to Haret Hreik, Wa'd, in a public debate. The following are excerpts from Harb and Fawaz's chapter that offer an overview of these activities:

> Al-Dahiya is the Party's capital city, where its key cadres and members reside; where the headquarters of its large network of service institutions are located; where most of its constituency lives; where the Party's ideology is physically materialized in the built environment; and where its political economy thrives the most. During Israel's 33-day war on Lebanon in summer 2006, the Israeli air force raided Al-Dahiya repeatedly … All neighborhoods in Al-Dahiya were hit, but the most significant urbicide took place in Haret Hreik, the strategic quarter of the Party. Municipal estimates indicate that over 250 apartment buildings were razed. (Harb and Fawaz 2010: 21; see Figure 4.1)

> In the then newly established Reconstruction unit (RU) at the American University of Beirut (AUB), a group of us who were already familiar with al-Dahiya and its politics decided to combine efforts and take part in the reconstruction of these neighborhoods. We believed Haret Hreik to be an integral part of the city's social and urban fabric, and we thought that its reconstruction should recognize and strengthen this neighborhood's place in the capital. Except for Hezbollah, whose apparatus was extensively mobilized even during the war, the reconstruction took place in a general ambience of indifference and *laissez-faire*: both public and civil society stakeholders believed that Hezbollah would inevitably control the reconstruction of al-Dahiya, which they recognized as the Party's turf, and therefore refrained from intervening. As researchers who had worked closely with Hezbollah's institutions over the past fifteen years, we wanted to challenge this attitude … Our aim was to introduce the (absent) dimension of the *public* in both the process and form of planning, despite the highly politicized post war context of reconstruction. (Harb and Fawaz 2010: 21–2)

Figure 4.1   Destruction in residential neighborhoods in the southern suburb of Beirut – al-Dahiya
Source: Robert Saliba.

Hezbollah's reconstruction policy in al-Dahiya confirmed the reading that had been initially made by most observers: the party exclusively controlled the process, involving only selected actors from its own apparatus … Hezbollah's policy choices in the reconstruction of al-Dahiya asserted its domination over this section of the city and its urgent need to renew its legitimacy amongst its urban constituency. (Harb and Fawaz 2010: 25–6)

The government ignored the opportunity provided by reconstruction for public agencies to interact with dwellers on new grounds that could depart from the conflicting interactions that characterized their relationship. Instead it relied exclusively in this post-war reconstruction on compensation as a strategy. (Harb and Fawaz 2010: 27)

Amid these two powerful protagonists, the dwellers were locked-in. The compensation policy of the state was poorly disseminated and dwellers were poorly informed … (Hilal 2008). (Harb and Fawaz 2010: 28)

The idea of an international competition was the first serious attempt we made to influence the planning process … The initiative had the merit of soliciting ideas for improving the neighborhood's livability in order to widen the horizons of possible intervention, within the constraints imposed by local actors, but without dictating a final option. We hoped to create a partnership between the local authority (Haret Hreik Municipality) which would act as the owner of the competition, thus strengthening the role of local actors, and the Lebanese Order of Engineers who would bring in a professional overview to the process. (Harb and Fawaz 2010: 31)

In parallel, and through many visits and discussions with public actors, municipal agents, members in the council of the Lebanese Order of Engineers and Architects (OEA), and Hezbollah local authorities, we worked to reverse an initial wariness *vis à vis* the idea of an international competition … We eventually gained the trust of many who expressed a clear endorsement. (Harb and Fawaz 2010: 31–2)

[T]he OEA board voted in favour of endorsing the competition and its brief, providing seed funds for its initiation; the Haret Hreik Municipal Council unanimously endorsed its role as the competition owner …

[S]hortly after this endorsement, a decision was taken among high-ranking Hezbollah members to call-off the competition. (Harb and Fawaz 2010: 32)

Figure 4.2   Haret Hreik charette
Note: RU members at the Department of Architecture and Design at AUB, January 17–20, 2007 (left); *The Reconstruction of Haret Hreik: Design Options for Improving the Livability of the Neighborhood* (2007) booklet cover (right).
Source: Mona Harb (left); Fawaz, Ghandour 2007 (right).

We overcame our disappointment and came up with a different approach for initiating a public debate …

In January 2007, building on the information gathered for the international design competition brief, a multi-disciplinary group of twenty architects, urban planners and designers, landscapers, and others came together for a three-day workshop. (Harb and Fawaz 2010: 33)

Aware that Hezbollah was proceeding with its own design project, we were eager to develop a number of avenues through which we would engage Wa'd's project designers. Concrete design options, we believed, had the merit also of channeling a public debate on the reconstruction away from political polarization towards issues of public concern, such as the quality and nature of open/public space in the reconstruction project. (Harb and Fawaz 2010: 33–4; see Figure 4.2)

The outcome of the workshop was then taken to local stakeholders. By then, it was clear that the most interested stakeholders were the Municipality of Haret Hreik and Hezbollah, the latter weighing considerably more in the balance of power. In February 2007, our team organized separate presentations, one at the Municipality and the other at Wa'd's temporary offices, in the presence of a number of influential members of the Party who we knew to be closely involved in the decisions regarding this reconstruction …

Our choice to engage the Municipality, which by then, was clearly sidelined by the Party, was engineered to strengthen the local public actor's position with a set of proposals built on the guidelines we had developed with several of its members while working on the competition brief. It was clear, however, that the Municipality had withdrawn from playing a role in the process while the Hezbollah reconstruction decision-makers present at the meeting largely dismissed our proposals … The idea of engaging stakeholders in the reconstruction process seemed more remote than ever.

In the following months, we worked to develop and distribute the ideas formulated during the workshop in the form of a booklet which was published in June 2007. (Harb and Fawaz 2010: 34)

On 19 November 2008, Wa'd's CEO Hassan Jeshi presented the project publically in the Department of Architecture and Design at AUB. The Wa'd project guidelines were described for the first time, accompanied by a one-week exhibition displaying a number of plans and building designs. By then, Wa'd had initiated the construction of about 190 buildings which were in various stages of completion. Hezbollah's design team was ready to engage the public and reveal the principles it had adopted in the process of reconstruction. (Harb and Fawaz 2010: 36–7)

[T]his initiative triggered interest in the project and led to other invitations; we had helped set up the exposure of the project and we organized debates within Beirut. The second presentation took the form of a public debate in which the Haret Hreik Task Team was invited to present its proposals alongside Wa'd's ... Eventually, Wa'd's CEO was forced to concede that the project had focused on private buildings, that Wa'd could not claim to replace a public planner, and that a potential public intervention to complement the project's accomplishment, which consisted essentially of rebuilding the homes of neighborhood dwellers, was required.

This was, to us, a very significant moment. (Harb and Fawaz 2010: 37)

Marginal Landscapes, Marginalized Rural Communities: Sustainable Post-War Recovery in Southern Lebanon

The second intervention I will describe was coordinated by Jala Makhzoumi—at the time, the coordinator of the Landscape Design and Ecological Management (LDEM) program at AUB, whose research and professional practice was focused on devising and implementing ecological design methodologies in the Mediterranean context (also see Chapter 6 by the same author). It was located at the al-Qleileh village and reflected the fact that the 2006 war had destroyed villages, fields and orchards in southern Lebanon as well as heavily populated areas in the vicinity of Beirut. It thus argued against the validity and suitability of an entirely urban-oriented discourse on reconstruction. In particular, the destruction in rural areas reached beyond homes and villages to target the whole countryside in an effort to destroy the local agricultural economy.

The central position and motivation of this intervention was the conviction that a sustainable post-war recovery in southern Lebanon had to be based on economic development with a long-term focus. It thus sought to create a multifaceted strategy to address economic, social and environmental issues endemic to rural peripheries. It adopted the "Ecological Landscape Associations" (ELAs) approach as a dynamic framework that "integrate[s] ecological and cultural knowledge into the design process" (Makhzoumi and Pungetti 1999: 214).

The following are excerpts from Makhzoumi's chapter that offer an overview of the work in the village of al-Qleileh:

As a member of the RU team, I was eager to volunteer my professional expertise as a landscape architect and to explore the landscape approach to post-war recovery in al-Qleileh. My initial objective was practical: how to provide public places for the community to congregate pending the clearing of cluster bombs from the village open landscapes. Meeting this objective, I was faced with two challenges. The first was the absence of a public land that could serve for the purpose ... The second challenge was integral to the meaning of the community landscape in a Lebanese village ...

I explored answers to these questions through weekly site visits to the village (September to the end of October 2006), where I applied the methodology of ecological landscape design to secure an in-depth assessment of the village's physical setting and equally to understand post-war socio-cultural dynamics in the village. Engaging with local community representatives, I gained insight into their aspirations and their expectations of post-war reconstruction. Slowly, I managed to construct a reading of the physical and socio-cultural landscape at al-Qleileh. The in-depth landscape reading subsequently served as a framework for writing post-war recovery narratives through a landscape design studio project. (Makhzoumi 2010: 136)

The challenge of proposing community landscapes in post-war al-Qleileh was put to senior landscape design students ... The project's aim was to propose multi-functional post-war community landscapes. In parallel was a pedagogic aim of fostering awareness among young designers about the human and material complexity of post-war discourse in rural Southern Lebanon. (Makhzoumi 2010: 142–3; see Figure 4.3)

The Participative Discourse 45

The students were divided into four groups, each assigned one of the four identified ELAs as a platform for exploring community perceptions and post-war aspirations and as a potential site for post-war recovery narratives. (Makhzoumi 2010: 143; see Figure 4.4)

Figure 4.3   The al-Qleileh post-war landscape
Note: Sustained damage to the village core reduced dwelling units to rubble (above); the gap remaining after cleaning the rubble (below).
Source: Rabih Shibli.

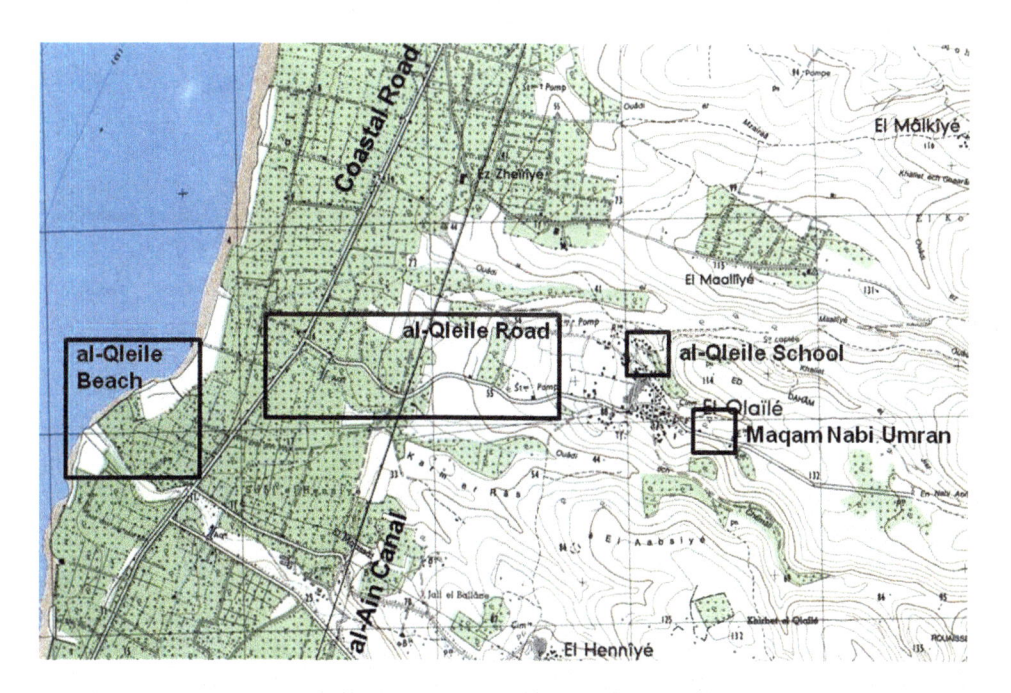

Figure 4.4   Four Ecological Landscape Associations (ELAs) identified
Note: The natural landscape of al-Qleileh beach; the agricultural landscape of the coastal plain; the marginal landscape of the school complex; and the cultural-religious landscape of the Maqam Nabi 'Umran in the upper foothills.
Source: Jala Makhzoumi.

The first narrative, *al-Qleileh Main Road*, acknowledges that livelihoods from citrus and banana plantations are a key to sustaining the village economy. The landscape narrative builds on current use of the road by farmers to access orchards and fields and the fact that the road is no longer in use[, as well as] the exceptional scenic quality of the agricultural landscape. The recovery narrative proposes to rehabilitate the road, framing it to serve as a venue for wholesale marketing of agricultural produce during weekdays and for leisurely strolling, cycling and picnicking during the weekends. (Makhzoumi 2010: 143–4)

The narrative for *Maqam Nabi 'Umran* looks to the cultural, historical heritage … [. T]he *maqam* is that of Virgin Mary's father, who is equally revered by Muslims and Christians … The community landscape proposed for the *maqam* reintegrates the segmented landscape of the *maqam* (a partially excavated Byzantine church) and the *maqam* itself, a citrus orchard acquired by the Waqf al-Shi'i (Endowed land). (Makhzoumi 2010: 144–5)

The landscape narrative for *al-Qleileh School* … addresses the spatial and visual separation of the school building from the Mediterranean view and the outlying communal landscape … The landscape narrative's aim was threefold: to open up the school to the surrounding landscape through a series of open spaces that serve for outdoor learning, active and passive activities and informal gathering places; to relocate the school parking downhill, rehabilitating the space into a large community gathering place for the local community; and to rehabilitate the network of pedestrian paths that linked the school to the village. (Makhzoumi 2010: 146–7)

The forth narrative, *al-Qleileh coast* … was inspired by two fluke discoveries: that the beach and adjoining seasonal estuary are an important stop-over for migratory birds and that the sandy beach is a nesting site for Mediterranean sea-turtles, *Caretta caretta* … Like the three previous narratives, a multifunctional landscape is envisioned that declares the beach a community protected site, generating livelihoods from nature-tourism while serving as a platform to promote awareness of environment and biodiversity …

[T]he four landscape narratives address human and material post-war discontinuities in al-Qleileh. (Makhzoumi 2010: 147)

The one narrative that was implemented—that of the al-Qleileh beach—proved successful because of an early partnership with the Society for the Protection of Nature in Lebanon (SPNL). [http://www.spnlb.org/] This national NGO served to provide continuity by carrying through the academic project, seeing through to

Figure 4.5 **UNIFIL post refurbished through funding secured by SPNL from Birdlife International**
Note: Building and tower serve as information center, base for local community training and bird watching (left); detail of the landscape narrative for the al-Qleileh beach (right).
Source: Jala Makhzoumi.

implementation and beyond. SPNL, in collaboration with Birdlife International, secured recognition of al-Qleileh beach as an Important Bird Area (IBA). With recognition secured, international funding for community capacity-building related to the IBA was also secured ... The abandoned UNIFIL post was refurbished to service the proposed nature tourism and the observation tower repaired to serve for bird watching ... Local residents were trained as guides for the bird watching and the village built its potential to service nature related tourism. Recognizing and protecting the al-Qleileh's natural heritage, entrusting stewardship to the village, and the benefits accrued to the local community empowers them to negotiate with global funding agencies to fulfill their future hopes and aspirations. (Makhzoumi 2010: 151–2; see Figure 4.5)

The recovery narratives of landscape designers aspire to rectify political, social and economic marginalization in rural peripheries, using natural, cultural and human resources in the region as leverage for sustainable development. (Makhzoumi 2010: 152)

Beit bil-Jnoub: A Grassroots Approach to Reconstruction

The third intervention I will describe was coordinated by Rabih Shibli—at the time, a lecturer at LDEM and later, team leader at the Community Projects and Development Unit (CPDU) in the Center for Civic Engagement and Community Service (CCECS) at AUB (see Chapter 10 by the same author). Working initially in al-Qleileh (the same site as the last example), he targeted individual homeowners in hopes of assisting them as they struggled to rebuild their homes and lives from damage inflicted during the war. His mechanism was an NGO, Beit bil-Jnoub [House in the South], which he founded in September 2006 with a group of other volunteer activist architects.

Beit bil-Jnoub had three principal objectives: (1) allowing for a speedy recovery for the victims while preventing the reoccurring trends of chaotic reconstruction; (2) building capacities through training programs, despite urgent demands for securing shelters fast; and (3) introducing a ground-up participatory process to engage homeowners directly apart from the highly politicized environment.

The following are excerpts from Shibli's chapter that offer an overview of his work:

> The affected population was left in a vulnerable state and faced a critical time. The manner in which their built environment would be restored was the least of their worries. In other words, they were in dire need of shelter by any means—and fast. As such, the nature of our "participatory approach" failed to present itself at first as a "constructive" and smooth process. It required much effort to encourage the owners of demolished houses to truly engage, in a full sense of the term. And it was not until we became familiar with each household at a personal level that we could ourselves begin to make any real progress ...
>
> On 15 August, Hezbollah's Secretary-General appeared on al-Manar Television declaring the Party's strategy. *Iwa'* was the means for providing decent and suitable furniture and a year's rent of a house to any Lebanese family that lost its home in the month-long war ...
>
> On 16 August, the Lebanese Council of Ministers issued a decree No. 146 ... The decree established a mechanism by which compensations were distributed to affected individuals by the Council of the South and the Central Fund for the Displaced under the supervision of the Higher Council of Relief, which reports directly to the presidency of the Council of Ministers. (Shibli 2010: 189)

The national policy made the compensation mechanism its priority and neglected to formulate a comprehensive strategy that tackled the critical issues which surfaced in the aftermath of the war. (Shibli 2010: 191)

Dissatisfied with the rebuilding mechanism set up by the Council of the South for the village and rebelling against what they perceived as an "insensitive" Municipal Council, the residents of al-Qleileh found themselves in a difficult situation. Here the top-bottom reconstruction approach was being practiced. The people's needs were not being met. Yes, there was a need for immediate and decent shelter. There was also a big chasm with regard to the order of the priorities. Out of the 820 houses of the village, 330 were destroyed ...

Ad hoc rebuilding mechanisms sprang up all over the site: in absence of planning guidelines and technical assistance, the reconstruction set up in al-Qleileh became three fold:

1. The Council of the South was the main stakeholder in charge of the surveying and compensation mechanism.
2. The Municipality played the role of a 'town planner'.
3. The construction foremen played the roles of designer and builder.

This was the problem. We felt there was no regard for the uniqueness of South Lebanon or of a Southern Lebanese village. (Shibli 2010: 193)

In this context, I began an operation in al-Qleileh using the only two tools that I could: my ties to the community and my laptop. 3D modeling had a significant effect on engaging affected household heads in the design process. Soon after, wire-frame blue prints were materialized in hollow bricks and concrete slabs. Word spread, overwhelmingly increasing demand for architectural drawings. Sustaining the promising results achieved in al-Qleileh entailed involving more activist architects in the rebuilding process. (Shibli 2010: 196)

The personal initiative that had initially focused on just one village grew to a collective form of teamwork in three locations, namely al-Qleileh, Zibqine and Siddiqine. The efforts exerted had therefore to be consolidated under an indicative umbrella: Beit bil-Jnoub (House in the South) was the name we decided on. (Shibli 2010: 198; see Figure 4.6a)

Our entry points into each village were coordinated with their respective mayors. (Shibli 2010: 199)

To ensure sustainable presence given to our limited field visits, a local partner was selected to mediate between Beit bil-Jnoub and the local community. (Shibli 2010: 200)

Beit bil-Jnoub defined the scope of the work under three main scenarios:

1. [D]esigning and monitoring the rebuilding of totally damaged houses;
2. [I]ntroducing corrective measures to structured buildings;
3. [E]nabling affected household heads to manage the reconstruction. (Shibli 2010: 203; see Figure 4.6b)

The first year of fieldwork was a vast experience for the team as we began to make sense of the dynamics (political, social and economic)[.] ... Beit bil-Jnoub began campaigning for more structured efforts to secure a higher impact in the field. In this respect, we made contact with the international agencies and NGOs which were setting up programmes of intervention in the aftermath of the 2006 war. (Shibli 2010: 209)

Under the project entitled "Good governance for Enhanced Post-War Reconstruction in South Lebanon," a cooperative strategy was then developed between Beit bil-Jnoub and UN-HABITAT, covering twenty-one affected villages in the union of Municipalities of Sour, Bint Jbeil and Jabal 'Amil in order to respond to reconstruction challenges ... In each one of the three unions, we established fully-equipped technical offices; each office was composed of a team leader (architect or a civil engineer), two architects, two civil engineers, one land surveyor and one field officer. Proposed interventions addressed two particular aspects of the reconstruction process that were lacking in the Lebanese government's response plan:

1. Technical assistance for local authorities and affected communities to assess, plan and monitor the reconstruction operation.
2. Capacity building to strengthen municipal recovery and management operation. (Shibli 2010: 209–10)

Figure 4.6   Beit bil-Jnoub
Note: (a) the cover of the guidance kit distributed to community members, showing a picture of one of the houses designed by Beit bil-Jnoub; (b) a Beit bil-Jnoub team member with affected family members filling in a reconstruction survey form (Zibqine, October 2007).
Source: Rabih Shibli.

Conclusion

The book *Lessons in Post-War Reconstruction* was intended as a record of the bottom-up approaches to the reconstruction process adopted by a group of designers and planners as they volunteered their expertise in a post-war reconstruction effort. In it, they reflected on the "intersection of different interest groups in the reconstruction process as well as the politics that motivated their agendas and approaches, particularly in the absence of a central government vision and strategy" (Al-Harithy 2010: 14).

The reconstruction process in the aftermath of the 2006 war in Lebanon was complex and rapid. The fact that the recovery process was not a conventional government-led effort meant that volunteer experts had to mobilize and innovate in order to be effective. They also had to reach out to local municipalities as their key targets and partners.

Collectively, the diverse interventions, despite their varying levels of success and failure, offered multiple lessons for non-governmental initiatives and models that may be applicable to other post-war-reconstruction contexts. Each of the cases I have highlighted here also yielded its own particular lessons.

Overall, the Reconstruction Unit learned three very important lessons, which we tried to keep in mind throughout our engagement: (1) to retain innovative flexibility in order to negotiate involvement and solutions; (2) to sustain the technical and professional edge; and (3) to maintain political independence in a tense, polarized political environment.

As Nezar AlSayyad (2010: ix) wrote in a foreword to *Lessons in Post-War Reconstruction*: "This we learn is a reconstruction effort from the ground up and it shows that informed and politically conscious socially active architects, contrary to popular belief, are able to get involved in positive ways with the public and to arouse public passion and discourse around issues of rebuilding."

References

Al-Harithy, H. (ed.) 2010. *Lessons in Post-War Reconstruction: Case Studies from Lebanon in the Aftermath of the 2006 War*. London: Routledge.
AlSayyad, N. 2010. Foreword, in *Lessons in Post-War Reconstruction: Case Studies from Lebanon in the Aftermath of the 2006 War*, edited by H. Al-Harithy. London: Routledge, vii–ix.

Dibeh, G. 2008. The Business Cycle in Postwar Lebanon. *Journal of International Development*, 20(2), 145–60. Available at: http://onlinelibrary.wiley.com/doi/10.1002/jid.1394/abstract [accessed: May 12, 2014].

Fattouh, B. and Kolb. J. 2006. The Outlook for Economic Reconstruction in Lebanon after the 2006 War. *The MIT Electronic Journal of Middle East Studies*, 6, 96–114.

Fawaz, M. and Ghandour, M. 2007. *The Reconstruction of Haret Hreik: Design Options for Improving the Livability of the Neighborhood*. Beirut: American University of Beirut, Reconstruction Unit at the Department of Architecture and Design.

Hamieh, C.S. and Mac Ginty, R. 2009. A Very Political Reconstruction: Governance and Reconstruction in Lebanon after the 2006 War. *Disaster*, 33(3), S103–S123. Available at: http://onlinelibrary.wiley.com/doi/10.1111/j.1467-7717.2009.01101.x/abstract [accessed: May 12, 2014].

Harb, M. and Fawaz, M. 2010. Influencing the Politics of Reconstruction in Haret Hreik, in *Lessons in Post-War Reconstruction: Case Studies from Lebanon in the Aftermath of the 2006 War*, edited by H. Al-Harithy. London: Routledge, 21–45.

Hilal, N. 2008. Governance and Public Participation in Post-War Reconstruction Projects: Haret Hreik, Beirut as a Case Study. MUPP Thesis. American University of Beirut. Department of Architecture and Design.

Makhzoumi, J. 2010. Marginal Landscapes, Marginalized Rural Communities: Sustainable Post-War Recovery in Southern Lebanon, in *Lessons in Post-War Reconstruction: Case Studies from Lebanon in the Aftermath of the 2006 War*, edited by H. Al-Harithy. London: Routledge, 127–57.

Makhzoumi, J. and Pungetti, G. 1999. *Ecological Landscape Design and Planning*. London: Taylor & Francis.

Salem, P. 2006. The Future of Lebanon. *Foreign Affairs*, 85(6), 13–22. Available at: http://www.jstor.org/stable/20032139 [accessed: May 12, 2014].

Shibli, R. 2010. Beit bil-Jnoub: A Grassroots Approach to Reconstruction, in *Lessons in Post-War Reconstruction: Case Studies from Lebanon in the Aftermath of the 2006 War*, edited by H. Al-Harithy. London: Routledge, 187–213.

Chapter 5
The Corporate Discourse: Learning from Beirut's Central Area Renewal

Angus Gavin

Introduction: The Exchange Model

Beirut's post-war Central Area renewal, now at its midway stage, is widely recognized as a successful model of inner-city regeneration, delivering restoration, new development and public space of the highest quality. Its Public Private Partnership (PPP) framework is unique in the way it leveraged hidden value from disaster. But, driven by the specifics of central Beirut at the close of the civil war—large-scale destruction, squatterization and uncontrolled landfill on the city center waterfront—it is unlikely to be transferable as an institutional framework for other urban projects.

However, aspects of its urban planning, implementation and development control regimes may offer valuable, transferable experience. The urban design behind them is not *market-based*, but *market-responsive*, as indeed all contemporary urban design should be—professionally sophisticated and keenly aware of the need to chart an informed course between the creation of value and protection of the public interest. These planning mechanisms, developed for Beirut, are certainly now emulated by other city-makers elsewhere in the region as well as by Solidere on other projects outside Lebanon. Many such projects have been introduced to Solidere by governments and private landowners. They do so, recognizing the company's acquired expertise in large urban projects, and in place-making skills that carry a strong regional *brand* and Mediterranean feel, much in demand.

I have dubbed central Beirut's PPP the *exchange model*. At its core is the concept of the government's granting Solidere, the private company it established, new land assets to be reclaimed from the sea. This committed the company to a costly 10-year program of sea-defense works and the environmental clean-up of wartime uncontrolled landfill—domestic waste and the rubble of destroyed buildings scarring the downtown waterfront. The transfer of new development land in exchange for financing infrastructure costs for the entire city center was defined in the company's formation Decree. *Infrastructure* included not only the streets and utility networks, but also public spaces, archeological excavations, sea defense and reclamation works and the re-housing of some 40,000 refugees, occupiers of abandoned downtown properties in the aftermath of the civil war. The regeneration of Beirut's war-damaged city center, perhaps the most important of Lebanon's post-war reconstruction commitments from the viewpoint of recovering Beirut's role and position in the region, has therefore been carried out without public funding.

A second important component of Solidere's formation Decree was the prerequisite that a Master Plan, together with its special regulations, must be completed and approved by relevant public authorities before the company could be formed. Given the powerful position the company would hold, including roles usually undertaken by public agencies, it seemed that a special form of Master Plan would be needed: one that was flexible in land use, encouraging the emergence of a contemporary, 24-hour active, residential and mixed-use city center available to all; one that was not so restrictive in its planning controls that it risked stifling investment; one that offered a variety of development opportunities arising from the natural assets of a waterfront site; and one that would protect the public interest, specifically in the provision of extensive public space and essential public and cultural facilities, preserve and restore identified heritage fabric and, with absolute transparency, limit development rights to a defined maximum by parcel and in total.

Market-Responsive Master Plan Mechanisms

Breaking Away from Uniform Height Controls

Several aspects of the Master Plan and its regulations differ markedly from Lebanon's standard, French-based zoning plans. These allocate blanket exploitation ratios, allowing Built Up Areas (BUAs) of five times the plot area, throughout the central zone of Beirut. This comprises the city center and contiguous districts, including Gemmayze, signposted as a *quarter of traditional character* of midrise buildings and two-storey Levantine villas of heritage and architectural value. Without adequate legal protection, much of this historic fabric is disappearing fast, due principally to zoning regulations that permit 10- to 12-storey development. The remnants that survive will be thanks to the commitment of landowners who value their heritage, rather than any planning or conservation policies of the state.

The City Center Master Plan was conceived very differently (Figure 5.1). Although the same legal right of exploitation at 5:1 on net development land was acknowledged, giving a total of 4.69M m^2 for the whole city center, a great variety of maximum building heights, from two to 40 storeys, were mandated in the plan. A limited number of highrise buildings, identified at carefully selected locations of townscape value, were essential to compensate for area losses in zones of restored, lowrise fabric.

Preserving Heritage Fabric, Streets and Views

In preparing the Master Plan the first task undertaken was to identify all surviving buildings to be preserved for restoration, and known or anticipated archaeological sites to be protected. Any uncovered remains were subject to a special UNESCO protocol and Lebanon's existing regulations administered by the Ministry of Culture. Two hundred and ninety-one buildings were identified for preservation, in surveys covering some 900 surviving structures, raising the number by almost 2.5 times that identified in previous city center master plans.

The wide geographic spread of preserved buildings formed concentrations in the central Conservation Area and two former residential districts of Saifi and Wadi Abou Jamil. The pattern indicated the need to preserve and reconstruct many existing streets, radiating outward from the fine Haussmannian grid of the Conservation Area and themselves carrying the identity of former historical layers.

The preservation of existing and the creation of new streets modeled on the unique forms that Beirut had evolved, became a primary driver of the Master Plan. Over the past 30 years, since Jane Jacobs' writings and the demise of the Modernist era in city planning, the *street* has been rediscovered as public, social space and a key component in the city-making vocabulary. Beirut's city center Master Plan is a *street-based* plan of this new era.

Principal streets of Mediterranean cities often focus on views to the sea. Central Beirut offers a second visual opportunity—northeasterly views along streets and public promenades toward Lebanon's coastal mountain range. In the Conservation Area the two existing *streets-to-the-sea* of Maarad-Allenby and Foch emphasize the importance of these view corridors that, oriented perpendicular to the coast, also carry summer sea breezes deep into the hinterland. These two streets set up a modern, orthogonal grid on the New Waterfront. The grid terminates in Beirut's now citywide Corniche drive, with its final curve opening up views toward Mount Sannine across St George's Bay. This arresting view is also celebrated along the pedestrian street of the re-excavated Ottoman harbor wall and other, parallel or East-West streets that cross the city center.

Transposed to the west of the Serail ridge, the orthogonal grid also set the alignment of Park Avenue, on the central axis of the Grand Serail. From this hilltop vantage point height controls establish a view cone that fans out above rooftops and across the park to the Mediterranean. It mirrors the view cone on the east side of the city center, that splays out seaward along the Martyrs' Square corridor. This open axis to the sea, planned since 1908 and finally achieved a century later, signals the return of Martyrs' Square as Beirut's premier public space. Its strategic importance has been further enhanced by excavations to the north of the square revealing Beirut's ancient Tell, site of the Canaanite-Phoenician city.

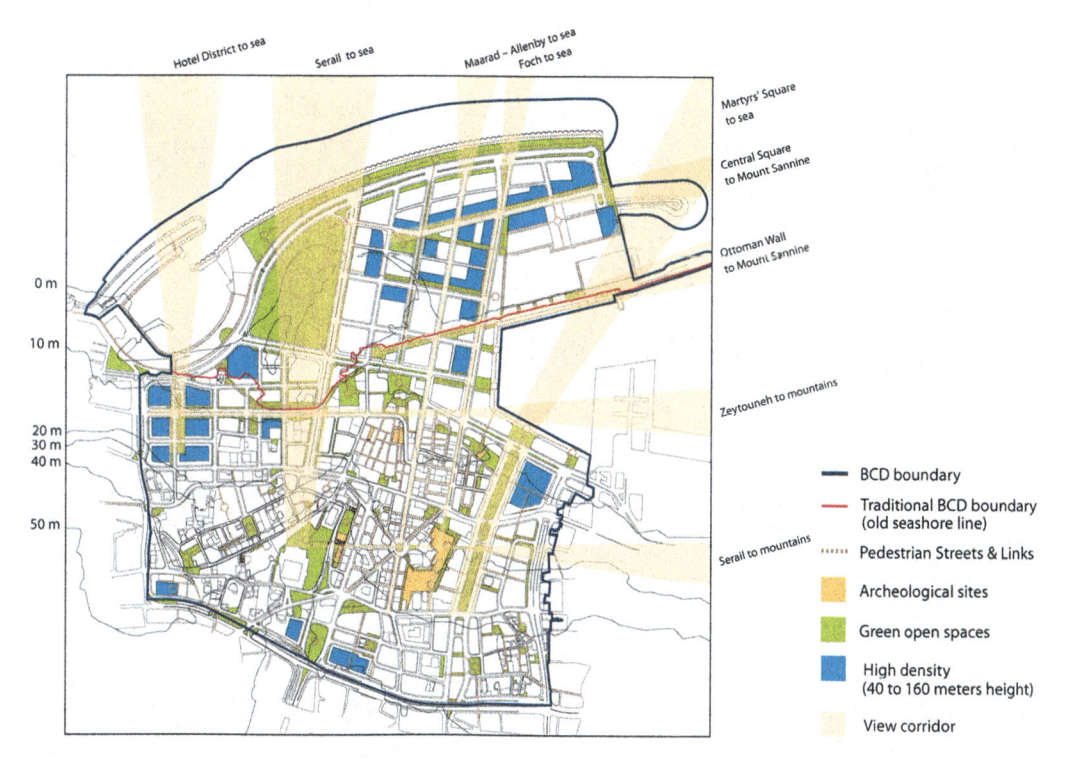

Figure 5.1   A new kind of Master Plan
Source: Solidere Archives.

Breaking Away from the Fixed Land Use Plan

The city center is conceived not as a single, homogeneous central district but as a cluster of city quarters or *Sectors*. Informed by natural boundaries in the topography, street pattern, neighborhood structure and concentrations of preserved fabric, the downtown comprises 10 separate *Sectors*, each with its own detailed plan and regulations. These define their widely differing characters and identities in terms of land use, built form and central, organizing features.

To encourage this variety of choice and mix the Master Plan excludes the traditional, fixed Land Use Plan. Subject to flexible, mixed-use policies defined in Sector regulations, land use is left as open as possible to suit end-user requirements. The process is intended to replicate over a much shorter time-span, the natural patterns and mix of long-term city development. Its success is in part dependent on the quality and professional skill of the investor-developers with whom Solidere deals: they must know their markets well and select appropriate sites and adjacencies for these uses to thrive.

This theme of essential flexibility is also embedded in the Master Plan regulations, which allow for the transfer of up to 10 percent of floorspace between Sectors. Future amendments are expected and four have already taken place, allowing strategic improvements to be incorporated.

Challenging Traditional Car-Based Transport Strategies

As in Beirut, urban highway Rings were built around the central areas of many cities during the 1960s and have threatened to sever their centers from the surrounding city. In Beirut Solidere has enhanced and substantially upgraded the Ring (Figure 5.2), tunneling through-traffic out of sight and making at-grade connections to serve traffic destined for the center.

Figure 5.2 **Upgrading and landscaping Beirut's city center Ring**
Source: Solidere Archives.

Significant differences have emerged in transport strategy between Solidere's vision for the city center and those of public authorities. With 30,000 new vehicles added every year to the national network, Beirut experiences frequent gridlock congestion. Lebanon, inexplicably, has the highest car ownership rate in the Middle East: some 100 cars per 1,000 population higher than Saudi Arabia and 40 per 1,000 above that of Qatar, which generates the highest GNP per capita in the world.

Solidere's traffic model demonstrates an urgent need for Beirut to invest in citywide public transport to carry up to 30 percent of peak hour trips. The compelling reason for this is that there is now a permanent deficit of some 30 percent in available roadspace on the network to carry such excessive levels of car traffic. All major radials in Beirut lead to the center, and unless the city begins to invest in public transport, congestion at the core will be so great as to deter further investment. No effective public transport has yet been introduced and current ridership on the bus network is below 2 percent. The impact of serious congestion affects Beirut's entire urban economy.

Instead of investing in modern public transport, current efforts of the authorities focus on resurrecting outmoded highway plans with severe disruptive impacts, and constructing free-flow grade separations at major intersections throughout the city, funneling ever more traffic onto the network. This strategy does nothing to reduce congestion—it simply moves it to the next intersection. New grade separation now under construction just outside the city center will soon bring excessive traffic flows to the Ring underpass and on into Martyrs' Square, whether destined there or not. This requires doubling the number of traffic lanes shown in Solidere's plan for the square and seriously compromising objectives to return active life to the most important, historic public space in Beirut.

Following the lead of most modern city centers today, Solidere's strategy has been to plan for and encourage investment in public transport, recommending modern bus-based rapid transit and planning for citywide routes to serve the central area. The Master Plan also aims to prioritize the pedestrian, diverting through traffic away from the center's internal streets and allowing these to serve access traffic. The Ring presents the opportunity to achieve this: at present 70 percent of movements on the main cross-streets in the city center are unnecessary through-traffic.

Another important planning objective is to expand the downtown's pedestrian-priority zone outwards from the historic core, linking directly into Martyrs' Square and across the Ring, perhaps cutting Rue Weygand and achieving a seamless north–south pedestrian connection from the Grand Theatre to the New Waterfront. Within 10 years up to two-thirds of the city center should be pedestrian-priority, much of it provided for in the Master Plan in the form of mandated cross-block easements. Such objectives—effective public transport, diversion of through-traffic and prioritization of the pedestrian—are part of a vision, generally accepted worldwide, for contemporary city centers. Sadly, in Beirut, where transport priorities of the public authorities remain stubbornly car-based, achieving these objectives seems a long way off.

Breaking Away from Traditional Envelope Controls

The need to preserve heritage fabric and street alignments, build new infill development to compatible scale and provide a very extensive public domain meant that a new form of regulatory plan was needed. What emerged was a 3D urban design plan with sufficiently well-defined building envelopes, so that precise BUAs can be calculated for every parcel, and mandated as maximum permitted rights in the site's Development Brief. A great deal of review and refinement of the Master Plan's massing scheme was necessary to ensure the total BUA for the whole city center, including all restored buildings, did not exceed 4,690,000 m^2—the limit for the city center, based on zoning rights at an exploitation coefficient of 5:1 on net development land.

The planning team's conviction to move away from a Modernist typology of object buildings, to a more contemporary, street-based urban design, was what made this possible. The lead was taken from several exemplary streets in the French Mandate historic core: Maarad, Allenby and Foch, where measured surveys revealed the urban design controls applied in the 1920s to the design and cross-sections of these fine streets. On many of the original buildings an upper-level setback floor had been added in later years, creating a streetwall section of building *base*, *body* and recessed *crown* that is unique to Beirut.

From these surveys a whole family of Streetwall Controls was created for widespread use throughout the plan (Figure 5.3), varying in scale from 20 m height for infill sites in the historic core, to a maximum 52 m height on certain frontages in the New Waterfront District. On many streets ground-level setbacks are mandated *build-to-line*, to add width and pedestrian space to the street and ensure all owners coordinate with their neighbors to build *joined-up architecture*, contributing to the making of the street (Figure 5.4). Where towers occur they are set back a minimum 9 m behind the streetwall, so that the scale and proportion of the street runs through. By applying the dimensional controls, together with building height and site coverage limits identified on the Master Plan, accurate BUAs can be calculated for any parcel.

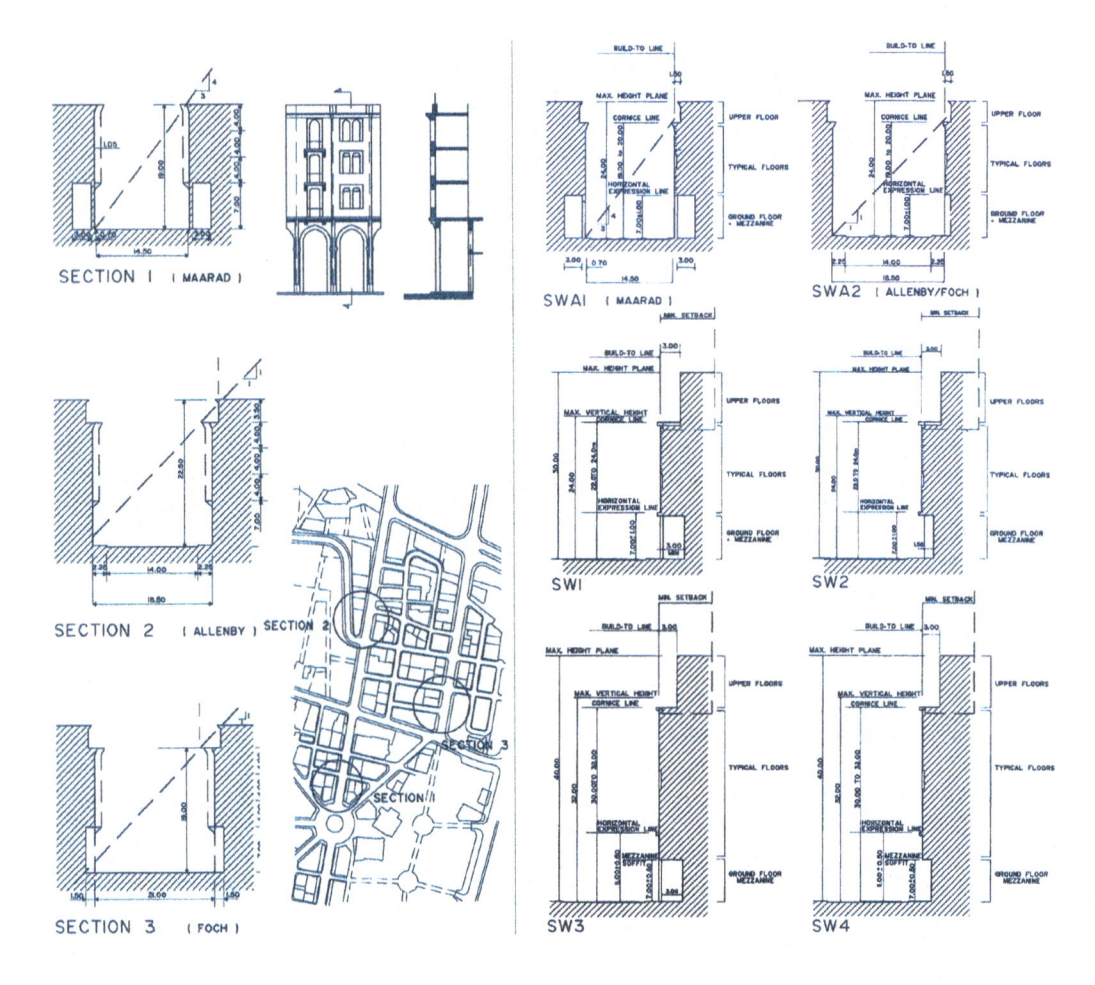

Figure 5.3   A family of Streetwall Controls to ensure the form and continuity of the street
Source: Solidere Archives.

The Master Plan calls for *build-to-line* frontage development on virtually all streets. Elsewhere in Beirut developers often make arbitrary setbacks, breaking the continuity of the street, as this enables them to increase building height and area. In the city center, however, maximum heights are indicated on all parcels, so that there is no real benefit to this kind of arbitrary setback. The plan encourages perimeter block development (building around the outer edges of a block) as the most efficient way to maximize BUA. The geometric efficiency of this form of development is demonstrated by a comparison of two existing, restored developments in the downtown. The Starco Center, a typical Modernist highrise complex of the 1960s that turns its back on the street, appears dense but in reality only delivers an exploitation of 3.5 times the plot area. By contrast, the Lazaria Center, built 10 years earlier, is in traditional perimeter block form with a central courtyard. It appears comfortably midrise, provides a shaded street frontage with generous sidewalks, and delivers the maximum permitted exploitation of five times the plot area.

This traditional form of massing, demonstrated in Saifi Village, is hard to beat (Figure 5.5a): it preserves the social space of the street, creates interior landscaped courts with mandated public access and, most importantly, maximizes floor area for a given height of development (Figure 5.5b). Relatively large areas of the plan contain restored lowrise buildings like Saifi Village, with new infill development mandated to be similar in height (6–7 storeys). This will clearly deliver less BUA than the 5:1 exploitation permitted in

Figure 5.4   Bank Audi Plaza: An exemplary streetwall building (Kevin Dash)
Source: © Lola Claeys Bouuaert.

Figure 5.5   Saifi Village
Note: (a) an internal courtyard view: vernacular architectural expression (Francois Spoerry); (b) northern extension: contemporary architectural expression (Allies & Morrison).
Source: Solidere Archives.

Gemmayze and resulting in 10- to 12-storey development. The exploitation achieved in Saifi Village is 2.8:1, and in Wadi Abou Jamil 2.5:1, demonstrating the need for highrise buildings somewhere in the downtown to compensate for these shortfalls below a target average of 5:1.

In planning, a conscious effort was made to reduce the number of towers to almost half the number shown on earlier plans for the city center. This was made possible through the efficiencies of street-based planning combined with perimeter block development. A total of 30 highrise sites were identified in the Master Plan, placed at locations of townscape value: as landmark towers at city center gateways, or forming a cluster in the previously established highrise zone of the Hotel District, overlooking the Beirut Marina. Twelve towers were located on the New Waterfront. Set well back from the Corniche and Park frontages, they form a central cluster of four with a further six towers overlooking the eastern waterfront, commanding views to sea and mountains. Two hero towers are located at the end of the Corniche on the northeast tip of land, framing spectacular views to Mount Sannine across the bay.

Market-Responsive Implementation Mechanisms

Re-Positioning Beirut: The Role of Star Architects and Competitions

Solidere has built up relationships with more than 300 consultants—local, regional and international—covering a wide range of expertise. Of greatest importance in achieving sought-after quality in public realm and building design are architects, urban designers and landscape architects. The company researches, prequalifies and selects these, continually updating its listings and sourcing new talent. Architects, in particular, are identified not only for Solidere projects, but also for those of other owners and developers, with the lists mandated in landsale contracts.

Let us briefly examine Solidere's rationale and criteria for selection of consultants, especially in relation to international architects. First, one of the main objectives of city center renewal is that of re-positioning Beirut, improving its status in the region and internationally after a long period of absence from the scene. Before the civil war Beirut played the role of global city of the Middle East, its center of business and banking, education, culture, healthcare and entertainment. In the hiatus it lost its pre-eminence, principally to the cities of the Gulf. Beirut now has to compete to regain something of its former role: applying the talents of star architects from across the world is part of a conscious strategy to achieve that.

Second, arising out of the kind of Master Plan we have in the downtown, there are broadly two main types of design challenge: that of reconnecting the city, re-making the street and the square and infilling damaged city quarters. For this we need a modest urban architecture of context and memory, and have found these talents among carefully selected local and international architects. The other type of design challenge is the landmark. Most obviously these are the signature towers of gateway, vista and orientation, but they can also be lowrise, place-making cultural buildings. Some of these will be the icons of the new Beirut, created by star architects including Moneo, Maki, Rogers, Foster, Hadid, Piano, Nouvel and Herzog & de Meuron.

There is a third, important criterion: Beirut is a cosmopolitan, trading city with a global diaspora and a long history of importing new ideas, creating an open, liberal culture where East meets West, making its architectural tradition rich and eclectic. Since medieval times Lebanon has imported new ideas, design and building techniques from France, Italy, Venice and more recently further afield, adapting these to climate, culture and lifestyle. Our objective is to extend this tradition—and this influences our search for architects. We do not want an architecture of the globalizing world: Dallas meets Dubai. We look for architects who respond to context and the cross-cultural eclecticism of Beirut, continually adapting new ideas to suit place and climate, creating new, sustainable, twenty-first-century architecture of the region.

Solidere's first exposure to design competitions was the 1994 UIA international open event for the Souqs of Beirut. The brief was purely architectural, with a strong note of nostalgia implied by the plans and photo records of the pre-war Souqs. Three hundred and fifty-seven entries were submitted and no winner announced, but three broadly different design approaches were recognized and rewarded. This was a fortunate outcome: it would have been wrong for a single architect to design what was, in effect, a whole city quarter. Nevertheless, in Solidere's first year of operation, the competition put the spotlight on Beirut and created a good deal of

Figure 5.6 The Garden of Forgiveness: Still waiting to be realized (Gustafson Porter)
Source: Solidere Archives.

international interest. Four architects and three landscape designers have been involved in the Souqs as since built or now in design: Rafael Moneo, Kevin Dash, Valode et Pistre and Zaha Hadid; and for the public spaces, Olivier Vidal, Martha Schwartz and the Portuguese designer, PROAP.

Solidere has since, in 2004, run one other major urban design ideas competition for the Grand Axis of Martyrs' Square, won by the Greek team of Agorastidou + Noukakis out of 270 submissions. However, extended delays of more than 10 years to the public authorities' launch of bids for construction of the parking structure beneath the square continue to hold up delivery of the public space and development around the square. Solidere has also assisted the Ministry of Culture in undertaking a UIA open design competition for Beirut's House of Arts and Culture, located on a city center site provided by the company.

Solidere prefers to undertake limited design competitions, with up to six carefully selected participants, for both landscape and architectural projects. Landscape projects seem prone to delays over contested public space—the Garden of Forgiveness (Figure 5.6) has been held up for 12 years for reasons beyond Solidere's control, following a successful design competition won by Katherine Gustafson in 2000. Other projects have been delayed, frequently by archaeological concerns. The results of recent competitions for the Waterfront Park and Khan Antoun Bey Square in the Souqs remain unannounced.

Competitions for building designs have been more successful and Solidere encourages other developers to follow this route. In 2009 Solidere moved back into real estate development, targeting the opportunity sectors of retail, hotel and hospitality, serviced apartments and high grade office. The company's objective was to create new markets in central Beirut and build the best projects in the Middle East, recognizing that this could only be achieved through the competition process. Winners for the Grand Theatre competition were Richard Rogers and Anoushka Hempel; for offices, Fumihiko Maki; mixed-use retail, hotel and spa, Peter Marino; and serviced apartments, Cruz y Ortiz. These projects are all currently on hold, due to the adverse conditions now prevailing in Lebanon.

Attracting Investment: Catalyst Projects

Over the past 15 years Solidere has built up valuable experience in delivering consistent quality in the public domain, restoration and new development. The company is both land developer and real estate developer. One of its main tasks and financial obligations is to deliver all infrastructure works within the city center, including land reclamation and sea defenses, streets, utility networks and public space, handing them over to public authorities on completion. To defray these substantial costs Solidere must sell improved land to other investor developers.

The company's policy is to undertake not more than 20 percent of the real estate development itself, focusing on catalyst projects that will attract investment by others as well and create new markets in the downtown. Examples include Saifi Village, stimulating a new residential market in the downtown, and the Beirut Souqs, bringing with it high street retail in a pedestrian environment in the surrounding historic core. In its dealings with many other developers a key concern of Solidere is how to ensure consistent quality. The main concern is that of protecting asset value: one project that fails to meet standards of design or quality of material finishes can have a significant negative impact on the whole.

Controlling the Quality of Development

Restoration and Development Briefs have been produced for every building or parcel in the city center. Concerned with external fabric only, Restoration Briefs specified accurate reinstatement of buildings of *heritage and architectural value* and the limits of acceptable alterations to *other* category buildings.

Development Briefs for new projects carried out by third party developers specify Master Plan massing and regulatory requirements together with many other conditions. All projects must be submitted to Solidere for design approval at a minimum of three identified stages. The Municipality's Building Permit cannot be granted without Solidere's prior approval of both the permit file and material finishes. Each project must appoint a Technical Controller to approve structural, building services, fire safety and other technical aspects of the design. While remaining advisory on projects elsewhere in the city center, all developments on the New

Waterfront District will be required to meet specified sustainability and energy conservation guidelines. Key requirements in these Development Briefs are linked to the contracts of sale, making them legally binding on the developer.

Raising the Quality of the Public Domain

A high quality, extensive public domain remains one of Solidere's top priorities in the implementation of the project. It changes perceptions, creates self-financing value and has become one of the main attractions of the downtown. Comprising green spaces, streets and engineering infrastructure, the public domain extends to just under half the total land area. A much higher proportion than elsewhere in the city, the intention being to create a strong, pedestrian-friendly public attraction and natural meeting-point in the downtown.

Beirut is a very dense city with little significant public space, with the exception of the active social arena of West Beirut's Corniche promenade. Within the bounds of municipal Beirut, outside the city center there is only some 40Ha of green public space, by any standard an extremely low ratio. The city center (10 percent of Municipal Beirut) will almost match this, with some 38Ha of green space in the form of 60 parks, squares and pedestrian promenades, thereby providing close to half the city's public space. Some of the area, including the Garden of Forgiveness site, remains in private ownership, but has been mandated by Decree, *non aedificandi* publicly accessible green space. The public quaysides, boardwalks and waterside terraces, provide some four times the area of the existing Corniche promenade over its entire length around the Beirut peninsula.

These green spaces also integrate the main archaeological sites of the city center, the boundary of which encloses the entire extent of known, urbanized Beirut from the Bronze Age settlement of 3,200 years ago until the 1830s. All key historic sites, heritage buildings and quarters will soon be linked on a Heritage Trail that circuits the Conservation Area. It will start and end at a new City History Museum, located on the ancient Tell immediately north of Martyrs' Square and accessed directly from it.

When all is built, public space will undoubtedly be one of the success stories of the city center, bringing substantial public assets to Beirut. During the making of the Master Plan, prior to the formation of Solidere, we felt the need to redress the city's grave shortage of green space, gradually increasing the downtown's public domain from some 38 percent to almost half the total land area. The Mediterranean city expresses its civic and cultural life in its promenading public spaces. West Beirut's seaside corniche was the only such space in the city, so why not link it through to the downtown and make its destination there, combined with a new City Park and almost 60 other squares, gardens, pedestrian streets and promenades? This is how the Master Plan emerged in the formation Decree.

Jewel in the Crown: The New Waterfront District

Beirut's renewed downtown has coalesced around the historic core, adjacent residential quarters, the city's former Hotel District and along the axis of Martyrs' Square. Next to be launched will be the city's New Waterfront District, where a model project of sustainable urban development is in the making (Figure 5.7).

The war years left the downtown foreshore scarred with 25Ha of uncontrolled landfill, largely domestic waste and the rubble of destroyed buildings. For 15 years there had been no municipal services operating in West Beirut. It has taken over 10 years and heavy expenditure for Solidere to complete this major land reclamation project to internationally acceptable environmental standards, re-excavating and breaking down materials, decontaminating methane-bearing waste to undersea bedrock level, and enclosing the new land within a sea defense caisson wall to meet 100-year storm criteria.

Beirut's new face to the Mediterranean, the New Waterfront District, has been through a long evolution since the over-roaded plans of the early 1990s. These proposed megastructure development within the port First Basin and 1970s-like urban highways, in tunnel and in decked cutting, traversing the city center and inevitably separating Beirut's historic core from the waterfront. The existing Master Plan still remains impacted by unresolved relationships with adjoining owners. Initially the First Basin lay within the city center boundary, offering the opportunity to connect the Corniche directly to the Ring. Although the First Basin

Figure 5.7   Massing model: The New Waterfront District (SOM)
Source: Solidere Archives.

was surplus to port requirements, the Port Authority objected, regaining control of the basin. The city center boundary was re-drawn along the edge of the quaysides and the situation remains unresolved: the port owns the water and Solidere owns the land around three sides of the basin.

The first Master Plan amendment affecting the waterfront was made in 1995, increasing the land area by 15Ha. The government instructed this change, as the planned reclamation contained insufficient development land to compensate Solidere for infrastructure costs, including those of increasing the public domain. The change was accommodated in SOM's 2003 Sector Plan for the waterfront, in which the disconnection of the Corniche, originally conceived as a continuous recreational drive through the city, was finally rationalized. The Beirut Corniche now terminates in a city center destination: the Eastern Marina and its leisure, entertainment and cultural activities, with its outer harbor and esplanade open to Beirut's most spectacular view toward the mountains.

The theme of the *greening* of the New Waterfront District, initiated by its 10-year process of environmental reclamation, will be taken forward in the development itself. Now under study are sustainability and energy conservation guidelines to be applied to development taking place here. A feasibility study has shown the potential for seawater cooling to substantially reduce air conditioning loads. Developers will be encouraged to implement this in their projects. The New Waterfront District is planned as a model project for sustainable urban development, with a target of 50 percent reduction in energy demand.

Meanwhile, the new infrastructure is now in detailed design, the reclaimed land backfilled to final levels, temporary roads constructed and the Corniche promenade open to the public. In the Beirut Marina, the boardwalk restaurants are open, attracting bustling weekend crowds and the Yacht Club is nearing completion. Several temporary projects have been constructed, including the Waterfront Exhibition Center, performance and nightlife venues. The first permanent projects are in design on waterfront and park-front sites, and the Eastern Marina is planned as Solidere's first catalyst development there, to be initiated as soon as positive market conditions prevail, attracting others to invest in new development around it. An international landscape design competition, held for the City Park, still awaits a decision identifying the winner.

Conclusions

Public Private Partnerships in some form have become the preferential option for large-scale urban development throughout the world. Without long-term, carefully contrived acquisition it is difficult for the private sector to obtain control over the large tracts of urban land necessary to undertake coordinated, comprehensive development. The public sector is no longer regarded as the sole agent for urban renewal. The most successful models are seen as those that bring together both public and private sectors in the mutual interest of inner-city renewal, brownfield redevelopment or new community building.

The public sector will generally provide strategic infrastructure and public facilities, using its powers of eminent domain to assemble land and its planning powers to control development. The private sector will generally contribute local technical infrastructure and some social infrastructure as well as investment capital, development expertise and an understanding of the market, together with the phasing and place-making skills essential to deliver a successful new urban destination. The mutual interest of public and private partners generally engenders a more efficient development process with fewer bureaucratic delays.

The Solidere PPP developed out of legislation enacted by the Lebanese government during the civil war, when the reconstruction of war-damaged downtown districts became a priority. The government had limited financial resources and its ministries, depleted by years of war, had insufficient administrative skill to manage large and complex urban projects. The legislation called for the formation of private real estate companies in which existing property owners would relinquish their property rights in exchange for controlling shares, with new minority shareholders providing the working capital to rebuild infrastructure and kick-start the renewal.

Rafic Hariri, Lebanon's first post-war prime minister, recognized the value of this idea and extended the legislation to cover the entire Beirut Central District, adding the incentive of future ownership by the real estate company of new land on the reclaimed area, making the whole project self-financing through Solidere. While brilliant in conception the legal framework also placed incentives on the company to create high land values, generating sufficient cash flows to defray its heavy infrastructure costs.

This led to creating new international markets in the retail and residential sectors, directed at a wealthy clientele, principally from the Gulf and Lebanese diaspora. While coinciding with the objective of repositioning Beirut as an international destination, the strategy has priced the majority of Lebanese out of the downtown residential market and given the city center a reputation as an enclave for the wealthy. This should not, however, be taken as evidence of failure: successful cities often evolve high-value downtowns seen, by contrast, as evidence of their success.

The unique complexities of the Beirut PPP, stemming directly from the post-war context of the downtown facing the Lebanese government, indicate the inherent difficulties of transferring such a model. Such a transfer was attempted—in the Jeddah Central District—but failed, because the political and landownership contexts there are so different. But the principal of combining public and private interests and capabilities is eminently workable and can be very creative. The secret is that each PPP must, by definition, be unique to the political, economic and social framework of the place. What is now taking place in Doha, Qatar can be described as a form of PPP. The city is investing massively in public transport: its Metro Master Plan incentivizes the development of District and Local Centers around subway stations. The private sector is already responding with plans for several such centers, creating transit hubs at higher densities than their surroundings. Within a matter of years Doha will begin adapting to a new, citywide neighborhood structure of conveniently located mixed-use centers, perhaps generating self-contained *quarters*, like the traditional Arab city.

While some may criticize Beirut's city center for apparent social failings, most would agree that the Master Plan and its unique regime of development controls has so far successfully delivered very high quality in both restoration, new development and the public domain. I believe it has also exposed some of the failings of existing zoning laws, as well as the imperative for Beirut to modernize its transportation strategy, thereby accommodating some of the more important needs of a contemporary city center.

The theme of this chapter: the *corporate discourse*, perhaps suggests that Beirut's city center Master Plan is designed to serve private interests. In fact the plan was devised within the constraints set by the public sector client, to protect the public interest. The urban design behind the plan is indeed market-responsive, but this does not mean it panders to private interests. Contemporary urban design must move beyond solely theoretical constructs, understanding and responding to natural economic pressures that exist in the city, ascribing for example higher values and densities to particular sites because of their location, views, accessibility and other physical assets. A good plan, by definition, will utilize urban design skills to create such sites as well as a great variety of others that offer different advantages and characters of place, appealing to a myriad of different interests. The outcome should be city-making of an intense variety created by many different stakeholders, much of it unforeseen by the planner—just like existing and historic urban places that we all admire.

Beirut's Central Area renewal is now approaching its halfway stage. Too early to pass judgment, it will no doubt pass through the rise and fall of several more economic and geopolitical cycles, bringing at times frenzied activity to the downtown: bustling Souqs, high street shopping, nightlife, cultural and recreational events at the premier visitor destination in Lebanon. At present the international residential market has stagnated and projects are on hold. Elsewhere in Lebanon the housing market is changing, with smaller units in demand. If this pattern repeats in the downtown, when recovery comes it should open up a welcome local market there, actively supporting downtown shops and services. Along with new parks, gardens and waterfront promenades there will continue to be an active program of festival and cultural events in the downtown, together with an ever widening range and mix of uses, including significant new employment opportunities. This bodes well for the future. I believe that in due time the Lebanese as a whole will assimilate the re-emerging center of their capital and make it their own, finally achieving a key objective of the Master Plan (Figure 5.8): while repositioning the city in its regional and international context it must also allow the Lebanese to rediscover their downtown's historic role as common ground and meeting point for all.

Figure 5.8   The Etoile: Beirut's meeting point in the downtown's historic core
Source: Solidere Archives.

Chapter 6
The Greening Discourse: Ecological Landscape Design and City Regions in the Mashreq

Jala Makhzoumi

Introduction

Cities in the Mashreq[1] are growing fast, harboring an increasingly large share of the population of these countries. It is estimated that by 2030, 90 percent of Lebanon's population, 80 percent of Jordan's population and 70 percent of Iraq's population will live in cities (UN-HABITAT 2012). Capital cities in the region shelter a growing portion of these countries' population, for example, 45.5 percent of Lebanon's population live in Greater Beirut. Cities in the Mashreq are also expanding spatially. The urban footprints of Beirut, Baghdad and Damascus have grown several times over from the historic, nineteenth-century cores, respectively, 375, 73 and 15 times (Figure 6.1). More significantly, the scale and pattern of urbanization has changed. "Regional agglomerations" and "urban growth corridors," the emerging trend,[2] is transforming not only the spatial and socio-economic structure of cities, but undermining the relationship of city and outlying region. Political instability is partly responsible[3] but also collapse of the welfare state, economic liberalization and partial integration into global systems. The rise of neoliberal politics is another influence, one that is widening the disparity between the rich and the poor. The spatial embodiment is a "segregated city" with exclusive, gated communities on the one hand and on the other informal, substandard squatter settlements. Excluded spatially, marginalized economically, the urban poor, rural migrants and internally displaced, appropriate open landscapes at the edge of the city and aggravate the environmental challenges.[4] Additionally, destruction of open landscape in the urban periphery diminishes opportunities for the encounter with nature at a time when urban population densities are increasing and the quality of urban living declining. Civil uprisings of the "Arab Spring" are in part a reaction to poor living conditions in cities and prevailing social injustices.

Accepting that the provision of jobs and affordable housing is a priority, measures to address the quality of the urban environment, though rarely mentioned, is equally important. Green areas are a key contributor to quality living and public health because they provide visual and spatial reprieve from the built fabric, opportunities for passive and active sports, a chance to encounter nature just as they enhance the urban microclimate, improve air quality and lower noise levels.

This chapter discusses urban green areas in the Mashreq vis-à-vis the scale and pattern of twenty-first-century urbanization. The narrow scope of prevailing conceptions and outdated planning practices is gauged against the global shift toward ecologically informed, environmentally sustainable and community inclusive urban greening.

---

1   "Mashreq," the Arabic reference for countries east of the Arab world, is used by UN-HABITAT to include Egypt, Iraq, Jordan, Lebanon, the Occupied Palestinian Territories and Syria.

2   Urban development corridors follow one of two models: mega urban region, for example, Damascus-Homs in Syria; or extended metropolitan regions, such as the Greater Cairo Region (UN-HABITAT 2012).

3   The Mashreq countries are home to 50 percent of the world's registered refugees, because of ongoing conflict in Palestine, Iraq and now in Syria. Refugees, internally displaced population, as a result of conflict in Palestine, Iraq and more recently in Syria, as well as rural–urban migration, place immense pressure on cities (UN-HABITAT 2012).

4   Unsustainable use of water is exacerbating water scarcity in a region that is predominantly arid. Based on data from 2000–2007, UN-HABITAT (2012: 61) warns that countries in the Mashreq use 88 million cubic meters annually, exceeding the total 80 million cubic meters of renewable water supply available. Unregulated energy use, air pollution and solid waste dumping are similarly repercussions of rapid urbanization in the region.

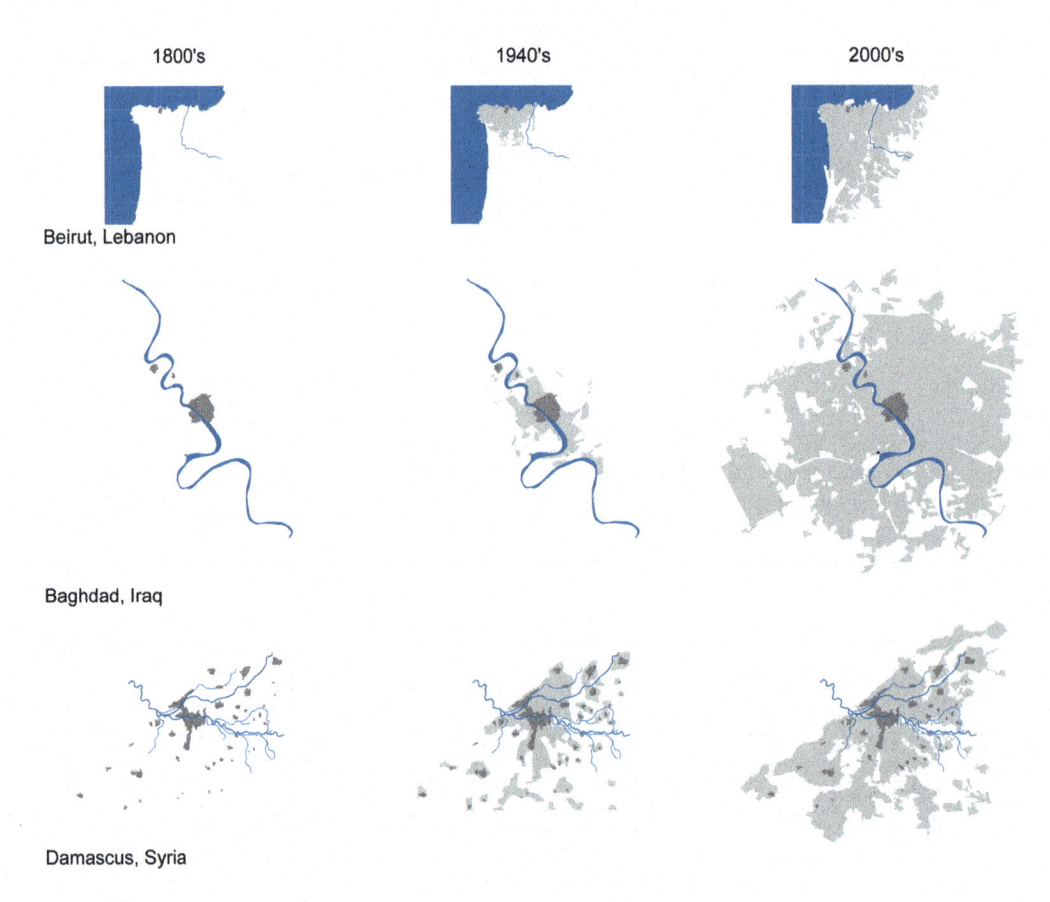

Figure 6.1   The rapid expansion of three cities in the Mashreq
Note: 5 × 5 kilometer grid.
Source: Author.

Urban Green Areas: The Core–Periphery Predicament

The discourse of urban green areas[5] in the Mashreq is problematic. On the one hand, is a limited understanding of green areas by local authorities and the public at large that is shallow and formal, equating green areas with the municipal park. Municipal parks undoubtedly serve inhabitants of the inner city, however, they are ineffectual at the metropolitan scale. Nor can new city parks be established considering rising land values in the city. Also problematic is the prevailing perception of the character of green areas, which is dominated by landscape aesthetics of a Western, naturalistic park, characterized by large expanses of lawn, ornamental shrubbery, scattered trees and free-form water bodies (Figure 6.2).[6] This idealized landscape disregards environmental limitations and water scarcity in the region and is at odds aesthetically with the regional

---

   5   In this chapter, "urban green areas" include: (a) publicly owned/managed green areas, for example municipal parks and traffic related green areas; (b) semi-public green areas, for example university campuses, cemeteries, housing estates, that offer limited public accessibility; and (c) privately owned green areas that enhance cities visually and environmentally, for example urban agriculture. Public open spaces, city squares and small plazas can also be included, but lie outside the focus of this chapter.
   6   Dominance of the naturalistic style can be traced to the earliest municipal parks established under Ottoman or colonial rule or shortly after independence. Park al Sa'doun and Hadiqat al Umma in Baghdad are examples, Hadiqat al Jala'a and later Hadiqat Teshreen, designed by Kenzo Tange in the 1960s, in Damascus and the new design for the Pine

landscape of the Mashreq (Makhzoumi 2014). Additionally, a limited understanding of green areas precludes innovative conceptions that draw on the landscape specificities of the Arab city.[7]

Furthermore, the discourse of green areas and public spaces in the urban core is changing. Neoliberal politics is increasingly transforming the public domain in capital cities into exclusive, commercially driven and monitored landscapes (Fawaz 2009; Daher 2013). The urban realm, notes Harb (2013), is giving rise to "informal" open spaces, appropriated and managed by local communities. Informal use is also associated with natural features, along the coastal landscape in Beirut, rivers and agricultural landscapes in Damascus and Saida, and similarly temporary use of vacant spaces in the inner city. No matter how successful, however, informal open spaces and gathering places are limited in the role they can play; they cannot compensate for the scale of urban expansion.

Complementing the discourse of green areas in the urban core is that of urban peripheries. "Peripheral landscapes" embrace the unstructured, nebulous landscapes at the edges of the city, held in reserve for future urbanization. "Peripheral" is not just a geographical reference, that is, in relation to the urban core, but embraces as well natural landscapes whose value lies in their development potential and/or because they are likely to raise property values. Another term used to define urban peripheries is "urban hinterland," a reference to the predominantly rural landscape of the city region.[8] Thousands of hectares of publicly owned open landscapes and fertile agricultural lands in the periphery are appropriated by informal settlements and/or development of upmarket gated neighborhoods (Figure 6.3).[9]

Whether informal or formal, the expanding footprint of the city is incrementally destroying valuable peripheral landscapes and undermining the ecology of the hinterland. Urgency to meet the needs of a growing urban population is partly to blame but also technological advances that have enabled a dismissal of natural resource limitations and regional ecological determinants.

The regional impact of urban growth in the United States became evident as early as the 1930s. Pioneers such as Benton Mackay and Lewis Mumford urged that the city region is recognized as a geographic and ecological system. Researchers continue to caution against urban sprawl and advocate policies for the management of urban growth boundaries (Anas and Pines 2008; Nelson and Moore 1996). The repercussions of unregulated urban growth "would destroy both the hinterland and the city unless controlled" (Pincetl 2006: 248). Many conservation planners advocate the preservation of nature in the hinterland "for both its scientific and moral importance," priorities that are absent from traditional land use planning concerns and tools. The "ecological footprint"[10] of cities is one measure to assess the growing impact of cities on the immediate and distant hinterland in terms of water consumed, land used and waste discharged. Indirectly, the measure raises awareness of the shortcomings of an insular approach to planning cities in the twenty-first century, of disregarding the urban ecology and neglecting natural processes that sustain the city.

Forest in Beirut in the 1990s. The Western city park model served as a prototype partly because the idea of a park was new but also because parks were a key component in the campaign to "Westernize" Mashreq cities.

7 As an example, the scope of the "landscape" in the Damascus 2030 master plan as defined by the Governorate of Damascus includes public parks, traffic related green areas, street verges and medians, sports and cemeteries. The author successfully argued that the scope is broadened beyond green areas in the city to include Mount Qassioun, the Barada River and the Ghouta agricultural landscape to serve as greening components of a scale that can serve Greater Damascus (Khatib and Alami, lead consultant, Makhzoumi, landscape planning consultant).

8 It is worth noting that the idea of urban hinterland is evolving toward greater complexity because of the scale and pattern of urbanization in the Mashreq, which is increasingly blurring the distinction between city and region.

9 Development of peripheral landscapes varies considerably from one city to another depending on landform and other physical constraints such as water bodies. In Damascus, for example, informal settlement in Muhajireen along its northern boundary and Mezza upmarket residential enclave to the east are approximately at equal distances from the historic core. Amman's expanding footprint sees the development of high-income residential neighborhoods Shmeisani, Abdoun and, more recently, Fheis, further and further away from the historic core. In contrast, peripheral landscapes south of Beirut, the formalized al-Dhahiya and the planned peripheral settlements in Baghdad, Madinat Al Sadr, Shu'la and Jamila, are all low-income.

10 The "ecological footprint" is an indicator that measures the impact of human activities on the planet's ecosystem in terms of the area of biologically productive land and water required to produce the goods consumed and to assimilate the wastes generated predominantly by cities, http://wwf.panda.org/about_our_earth/teacher_resources/webfieldtrips/ecological_balance/eco_footprint/ [accessed: February 4, 2014].

Environmental and ecological concerns aside, the exceptional natural and cultural diversity of the regional landscape in the Mashreq is embodied in the urban hinterland (Figure 6.4). Geomorphological heterogeneity makes for diverse climatic sub-regions that evolved over time to form a mosaic of habitats and ecosystems. Historically, people adapted to the diverse landscape setting through a range of land management routines, be they silvicultural, agricultural and/or pastoral, and through different modes of existence, sedentary and nomadic. Landscapes of the Mashreq as such embody the co-evolution of people and environment and constitute a valuable landscape regional heritage (Makhzoumi 2014).

Outdated urban planning practices, or the absence thereof, are in part responsible for the incremental loss of green areas in the urban core and periphery and for undermining the urban landscape heritage. Heritage conservation in the city is exclusively of architecture and the built urban fabric. Valuation of the landscape heritage, whether natural or cultural, is rarely a consideration. The fact that landscape architecture is an emerging profession in the Mashreq has allowed prevailing misconceptions of urban greening to continue uncorrected, hindering the potential contribution of a landscape framing of city and region in the Mashreq.[11] Collectively, these limitations result in a blinkered outlook in planning, preventing environmentally and culturally sustainable urban greening.

To summarize, the discourse of urban greening in the Mashreq is at an impasse because cities:

- Concede to the necessity of "urban greening," but continue to think in terms of the municipal park.
- Champion sustainable development in policies and legislation but fail to address the environmental and ecological impact of urban growth.
- Search for distinctiveness, and want to reclaim their identity, but refuse to look beyond the city, or to acknowledge the natural heritage of the city.

Urban greening in the Mashreq therefore should necessarily expand beyond the limits of the city to incorporate urban peripheral landscapes and the hinterland because they are the only remaining open lands of a scale comparable to the magnitude of urban expansion in the region and because they embody the landscape heritage of cities. At a time when cities of the Mashreq are rapidly losing their character, homogenized by globalizing influences, the visual particularity and distinctive landscape character of the urban hinterland is an invaluable asset.

Figure 6.2   The Western image of parkland landscapes dominates the conception of green areas in cities of the Mashreq (view of Al Jalaa Park, Damascus, Syria)

Source: Author.

---

11   See Makhzoumi (2014).

The Greening Discourse 69

Figure 6.3 View of the homogenized urban landscape of Amman, Jordan, the hilly terrain barely perceptible

Source: Author.

Figure 6.4 The diverse landscape of the urban hinterland in the Mashreq

Note: Clockwise from top left: coastal agriculture, Saida; date palm orchards, Karbala; pastoral landscape, Erbil; Ghouta agricultural enclave, Damascus.

Source: Author.

Shifting Paradigms of Urban Greening

With the growing awareness of ecology and sustainable development, urban greening strategies are increasingly concerned with the protection of "nature" inside cities and in their proximity (Harrison and Davies 2002; Kendle and Forbes 1997). River valleys and streams, coastal cliffs and beaches, sand dunes and marshland are gradually being recognized as urban wildlife habitats and managed to prioritize urban biodiversity. In this context, "nature" serves as an umbrella for reconceptualizing open spaces and protecting the natural and cultural landscape heritage of the city.[12] Prioritizing nature and green areas in the city has given rise to a range of strategies and concepts. As an example, "infrastructural landscapes" is one approach whereby transportation corridors (streets, railways, services) are designed as amenity landscapes (Benedict and McMahon 2006). Adaptive reuse of existing urban landscapes is another approach that aims to safeguard urban natural and rural landscapes at the urban, regional and national scales. In "Toward a Strong Urban Renaissance," the Urban Task Force argues for the reuse of "brownfield"[13] land instead of developing valuable greenfield sites; 70 percent of new development in 2005 was on brownfield land compared to 56 percent in 1997.[14] "Community gardens" and "urban agriculture" are also gaining ground as an approach to greening in the developing world but equally in Europe (Viljoen et al. 2005) (Figure 6.5).

The underlying rational to these approaches is twofold. The first concedes to the principle of "multifunctional landscapes" (Brandt and Vejre 2004), namely, incorporating more than one use/service within the same landscapes, for example nature conservation and tourism, infrastructure and amenity (Figure 6.6). The second premise expands the function of urban green areas beyond the conventional strictly aesthetic toward landscapes that are interactive and informative, places of pleasure but also for learning about environmental sustainability and nature in the city.

Alongside changing conceptions of urban green areas is a shift in the assessment of urban living away from strictly quantitative measures, for example economic, social and environmental, toward qualitative indices that are more closely aligned with the benefits of green areas and nature in the city. "Quality of life," for example, is a concept that is used as a measure of overall wellbeing, "the emotional quality of an individual's everyday experience" (Diener and Suh 2000). "Liveability" is another concept defined as the ability of the city to maintain and improve its viability and vitality (Balsas 2004; Zako 2014). At the global scale, Mercer's Quality of Living survey uses a total index based on 10 categories,[15] two or more of which relate directly or indirectly to urban green areas, for example "natural environment," "public services," "recreation."

Of direct relevance to urban green areas is the standards set by the World Health Organization (WHO). In its concern for public health and liveability in cities, the WHO cautions that the inhabitants of cities should enjoy the privilege of everyday contact with nature without having to make any special effort or journey.[16] Implicit to its argument is the need to safeguard nature in the city in all its forms for its own sake but also because it contributes to wellbeing. Accessible and experienced, natural landscapes mobilizes urban inhabitants to take stewardship and protect nature in practical ways. According to the WHO, every city should provide a minimum of 9 m^2 of green area per capita.[17] Cities the world over are aspiring to meet these standards, some have exceeded the benchmark, for example Beijing (66 m^2/capita), Barcelona

---

12 Abu Dhabi Urban Planning Council pioneers the protection and integration of peripheral landscapes in a desert ecology. In the "Plan Abu Dhabi 2030" (UPC 2010), "desert sand belt," "desert fingers" and coastal mangrove forests are recognized as natural landscape heritage of the city. "Plan Al Ain 2030" acknowledges and protects equally the natural landscape, Jabal Hafeet, and the cultural landscape heritage, five oasis and traditional agriculture in the urban core (UPC 2011).

13 Terms coined in the early 2000 to imply abandoned, underused and/or economically obsolete urban real estate. Whereas brownfield land implies sites that were previously industrial or commercial that can be upgraded, greyfield land comprises large asphalt areas associated with these sites.

14 Urban Task Force, Towards a Strong Urban Renaissance, http://www.urbantaskforce.org/UTF_final_report.pdf [accessed: December 12, 2013].

15 http://www.mercer.com/press-releases/quality-of-living-report-2012 [accessed: January 20, 2014].

16 http://www.who.int/en/ [accessed: February 1, 2010].

17 http://whqlibdoc.who.int/trs/WHO_TRS_297.pdf [accessed: February 1, 2010].

(18.1 m²/capita) and Istanbul (10 m²/capita). Cities in the Arab Mashreq are generally low on this standard. Beirut has less than 1 m²/capita, Damascus 2 m²/capita and Baghdad 3.19 m²/capita. The low green area index in Arab cities is partly the outcome of the limitations discussed earlier that are common to cities in the developing world.

Figure 6.5 Productive community garden in downtown Frankfurt
Source: Author.

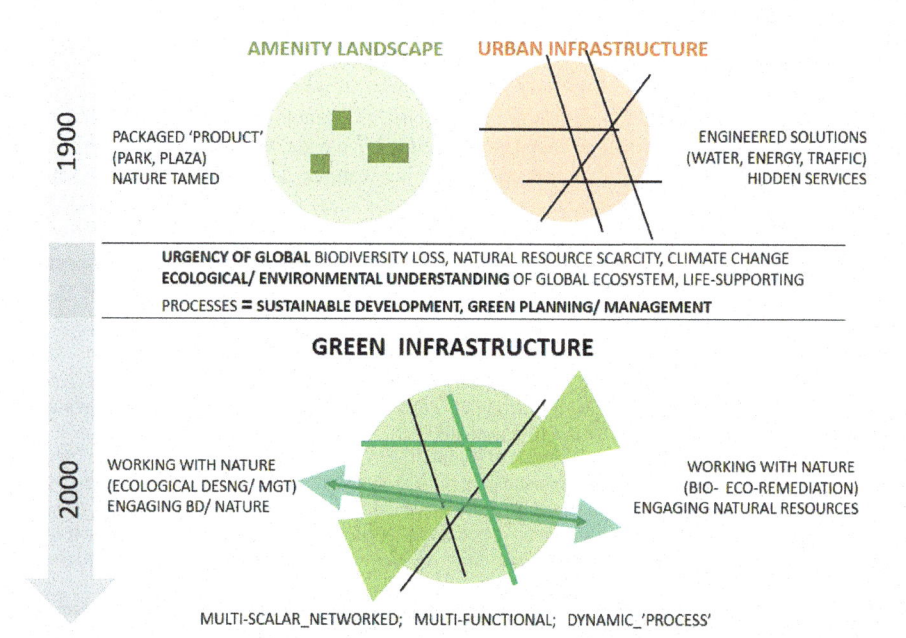

Figure 6.6 From city park to infrastructural landscapes, representation of the shifting paradigm in urban greening
Source: Author.

Ecological Landscape Design: A Holistic Framework for Urban Greening

The meaning of "landscape" has evolved since the 1950s from a restricted meaning implying "scenery" toward a holistic, expansive meaning that is culture- and place-specific. As a result, there has been a gradual surge in the use of "landscape" in urban planning and design,[18] recognition of its potential in international legislation[19] and its adoption by global organizations.[20] The close association between ecology, natural resources and landscape, growing awareness of sustainable development and the role of the ecological sciences is another factor encouraging use of "landscape." The European Landscape Convention (ELC) is the first initiative at the international scale advancing use of the term.[21] Calling for the recognition of "landscape" in legislature to enable development of "landscape policies dedicated to the protection, management and creation of landscapes," the ELC advocates "participation of the general public and other stakeholders in the creation and implementation of landscape policies." The equal emphasis on "protection" and "creation," "public participation" and "legislature" reflects clearly the potential of a landscape framework to affect socially and environmentally sustainable long-term planning.

Building on the holistic, expansive concept of landscape and informed by landscape ecology, the methodology of ecological landscape design (Makhzoumi and Pungetti 1999) is proposed as a flexible framework for urban greening.[22] Ecological landscape design, it will be argued, has the potential to produce a layered reading of the urban Mashreq, one that embraces the spatial overlap between natural and cultural components. As such, an ecological landscape design methodological framework is more likely to propose urban greening strategies that are contextualized, integrative of the history and responsive to the specificities of cities in the region (Figure 6.7). The framework was applied to secure a holistic reading and write future greening scenarios in two projects: the Saida Urban Sustainable Development Strategy (USDS); and Baghdad Comprehensive City Development Plan (CCDP).[23] Selection emphasizes the differences in the ecological setting and landscape character of the two cities and because of the urban planning methodologies adopted in each project.

The following is a summary profile of both projects, followed by a comparative analysis of the application of ecological landscape design principles that underlie the greening strategies proposed for each city.

Saida USDS: Summary Profile

The city of Saida (110,000 inhabitants), is the third largest city in Lebanon after Beirut, the capital, and Tripoli. The exceptional landscape setting is of a coastal city imbedded in a wide, verdant plain. The urban ecology is typically Mediterranean, landform and hydrology its defining features. The coastal plain, 7 kilometers long, 1–2 kilometers wide, is of sedimentary, calcareous soil that is ideal for citrus cultivation. Foothills of the Mount Lebanon Range define the eastern limits, punctuated by rivers and seasonal watercourses that flow from the mountains in a westerly course to the Mediterranean. The Awali and Sainiq rivers respectively mark the northern and southern limits of Saida Municipality. Further, seasonal watercourses ensure an abundance

---

18 For example "landscape Urbanism" (see Mostafavi and Najle 2003; Almy 2007).

19 The European Landscape Convention (ELC). The ELC defines "landscape" as an "area, as perceived by people, whose character is the result of the actions and interaction of natural and/or human factors" (see http://www.coe.int/t/dg4/cultureheritage/Conventions/Landscape/ [accessed: August 2011]).

20 The International Union for the Conservation of Nature (IUCN) introduced "protected landscape" to its protection categories, recognizing the value not only of pristine nature but also of human made/managed ones (http://www.iucn.org/about/work/programmes/gpap_home/gpap_biodiversity/gpap_wcpabiodiv/gpap_landscapes/ [accessed: February 2, 2014]).

21 The ELC defines "Landscape" as an "area, as perceived by people, whose character is the result of the actions and interaction of natural and/or human factors" (see http://www.coe.int/t/dg4/cultureheritage/Conventions/Landscape/ [accessed: August 2011]).

22 The flexibility and efficacy of the methodological framework of ecological landscape design has been demonstrated through a range of application in the Mashreq, for example in the conservation of bio-cultural diversity (Makhzoumi et al. 2012), in acknowledging rural heritage (Makhzoumi 2014, 2009), in post-war recovery (Makhzoumi 2010) and in contesting the right to landscapes (2011).

23 The author was ecological landscape planning consultant to both projects: appointed by Saida Municipality as part of the team commissioned to prepare the Saida USDS; and by Khatib and Alami for the Baghdad CCDP.

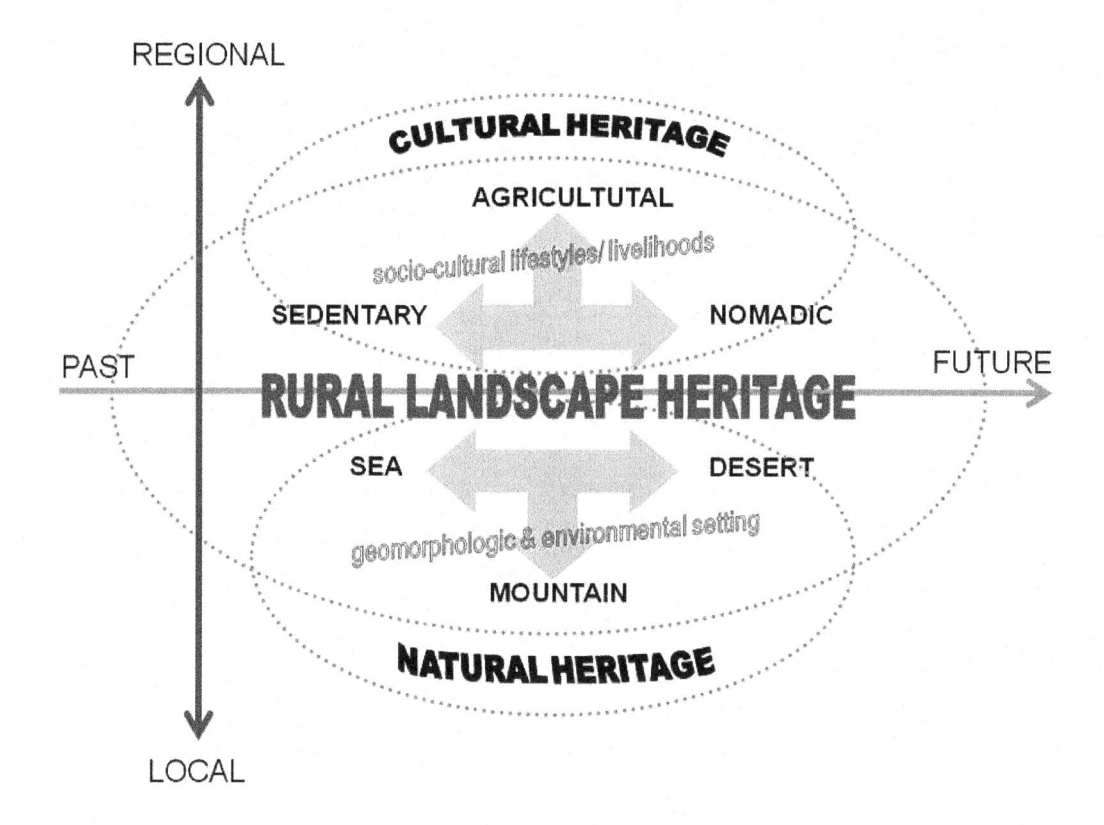

Figure 6.7 The spatially dynamic and temporally expansive ecological landscape planning framework provides a layered reading of the diverse rural, regional heritage in the Mashreq (Makhzoumi 2014)

Source: Author.

of water resources for the city and for agriculture in the plain. The climate is typically Mediterranean with average annual temperatures around 19.5°C, rainfall in the winter and increasing air humidity in the summer.

The urban character is a rich palimpsest that includes ancient, medieval, Islamic and contemporary urban overlays. At the center is the historic urban core, the archeological land-fort and sea-fort and the harbor. The strong relationship between city and sea has been the hallmark of the city since Phoenician times, securing trade and maritime livelihoods. Up to the 1940s the urban footprint was confined to the walled city, the surrounding coastal plain intensively cultivated, predominantly with citrus and other fruit trees. The earthquake of 1954 caused extensive damage to the historic city, encouraging some extramural expansion. The Israeli invasion in 1982 triggered another wave of urban expansion and renewed municipal planning activity in the mid 1980s. The maritime boulevard, completed in the late 1990s, cut the city off from the sea spatially, ecologically and in the perception of the inhabitants.

Saida today suffers many ills. The urban environment endures inadequate urban infrastructure, shortages in the supply of energy, dumping of sewage into the watercourses and solid waste in a coastal site forming a prominent hill south of the historic city.[24] The city bears the weight of the Ain Al Helwa Palestinian camp, the largest in Lebanon, its population and that of the adjacent Mie w Mie camp make up 42 percent of the total

---

24 The new sewage treatment plant south of the historic city which became operational in 2013 can process sewage collected from the rivers in the summer only. In the winter the sewage flows into the sea. A solid waste sorting plant is in the pipeline.

74   *Urban Design in the Arab World*

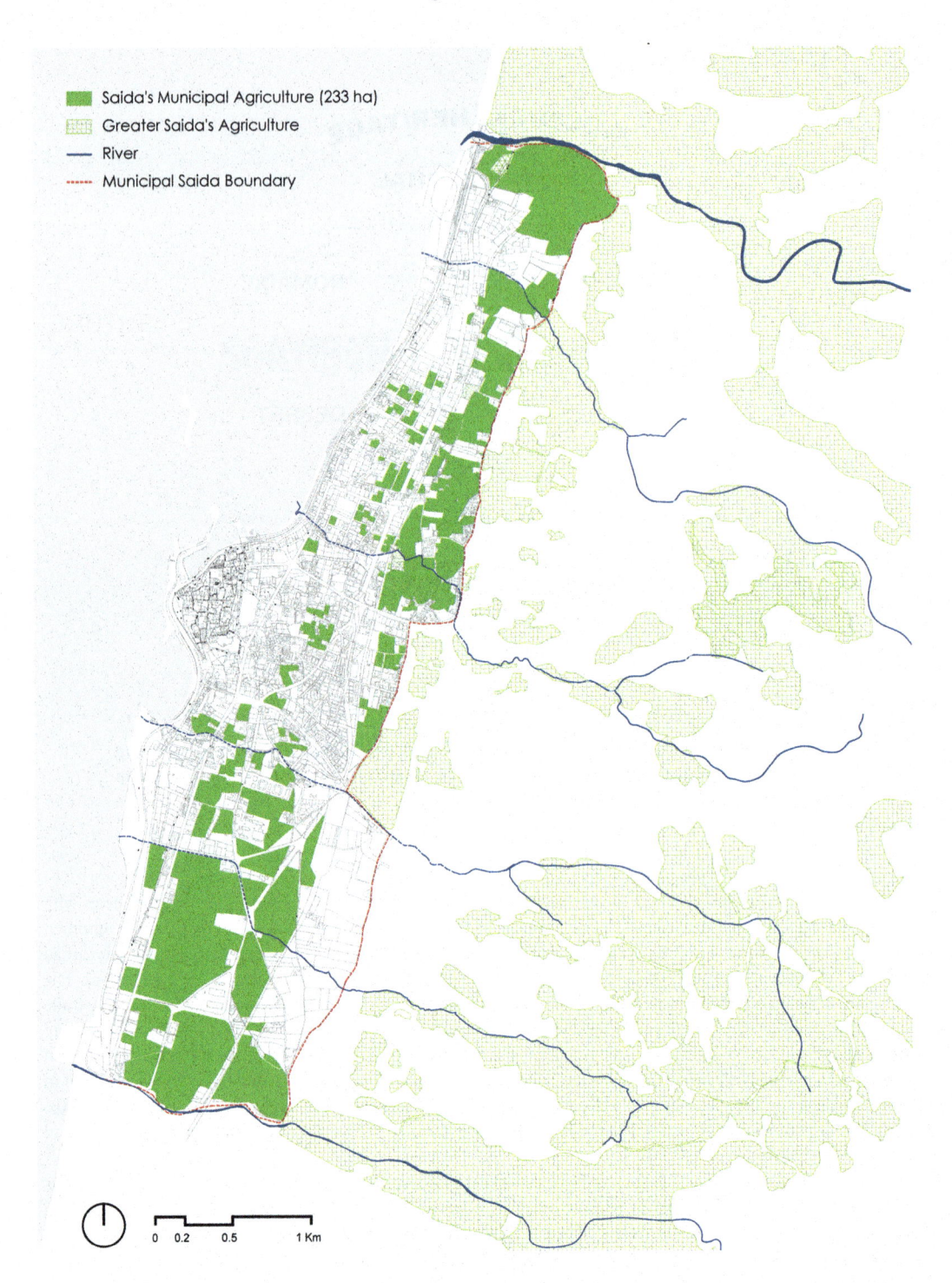

Figure 6.8   **Agricultural land comprises 33 percent of the municipal area of Saida**
Source: Author, Saida USDS Phase I Report.

municipal population. A large portion of the inhabitants fall in the minimum wage bracket, 37 percent, and 46.3 percent of the residents live under the poverty threshold. Economic development is slow, land pooling and speculation by a handful target what remains of open/agricultural lands.

Green areas in Saida are limited to planting of road medians and roundabouts. The maritime boulevard is the most prominent public open space stretching along the municipal waterfront. Land has been allocated for Saida's first municipal park, which is a matter of pride but ineffectual in addressing the needs of marginalized communities. Historically, Saida was famed for its *basateen*, the citrus orchards that were accessible to all, green space of scale and productive landscape that was valued as a heritage of the city. Today, the agricultural landscape has shrunk in size, fragmented into smaller parcels, but nevertheless, it constitutes more than one-third of the area of municipal Saida[25] (Figure 6.8). Traditionally, orchards and river shores met the recreational needs of the inhabitants: family outings, *seyran*, targeted cafés along the Awali River and the *basateen* and the *Qanaya*, the elaborate Ottoman irrigation network that continues to sustain agriculture south of the Awali River. Channelized and in places built over, rivers and minor watercourses have been degraded, their role reduced to collecting sewage. The memory of Saida's natural heritage is eroding just as the landscapes are themselves incrementally destroyed. The historic core continues to be viewed as the exclusive heritage of the city.

The USDS Project, a collaboration of MedCities, the European Neighborhood Policy Instrument and Cross Border Cooperation (ENPI-CBC), aims to develop "a strategic framework of inter-regional cooperation between EU and ENP neighbors." The focus is on "the promotion of sustainable development and social cohesion of Mediterranean cities through networking and use of Urban Sustainable Development strategies (USDS)."[26] The underlying aim is local capacity building, engaging and enabling local communities as active partners in urban development. Saida Municipality appointed a team of consultants, commissioning them to develop the USDS vision and strategic framework.[27] The interdisciplinary expertise of the consulting team was a key asset to the project.

The urban greening challenge for the Saida USDS was to demonstrate that a landscape framing of environmental and ecological concerns not only spatializes them but also addresses social concerns, provision of amenity green spaces, and cultural dictates, protecting the landscape heritage.

Baghdad CCDP: Summary Profile

Situated in the geographic center of Iraq, Baghdad with an estimated population of 6.133 million is the second largest city in the Arab world after Cairo. The urban landscape setting is dominated by the Tigris River that meanders through the city constrained by natural levees and a predominantly flat flood plain, mainly of sand, silt and clay (Khatib and Alami 2012). The urban hydrology includes a network of irrigation canals fed by the Tigris, the Qanat al Jaish flood-relieving canal and the Diyala River, a major tributary that marks the eastern limits of the city. The climate is dry, and intensely hot in the summer, and bitterly cold in the winter, temperatures dropping to freezing. Dust storms have been more frequent in the last decade due to the shrinking area of agricultural lands. Cultivated date palms are a prominent feature of the riverine landscape, a sustainable agro-ecosystem tolerant of excessive water and high temperatures.

Baghdad city dates to the eighth century, established as the capital to the Abbasid dynasty, prospering into a city of one million a century later. Historically, the urban morphology was, and continues to be, shaped by the Tigris River, which serves as the spine to the historic core, east and west of the river, respectively, *Rusafa* and *Karkh*. Expansion north and south of the historic core started during the Mandate and early years of statehood with the introduction of gridiron streets, roundabouts and municipal gardens.

---

25 The area of Saida municipality is 745 hectares, of which 449 hectares, 60 percent, constitutes the urban footprint, built-up and associated open spaces.
26 http://www.usuds.org/documents/10180/10830/USUDS+Brochure.pdf/4b0bades5-2e56-438f-a95e-6586409 ccef8 [accessed: January 2, 2014].
27 Team members: Local Economic Development, Social Structure and Urban Governance: Jad Chaaban, Ilina Srour and Kanj Hamade; Cultural Heritage and team leader: Howayda Al Harithy; Urban Infrastructure: Omar Abdulaziz Hallaj and Giulia Guadagnoli; Landscape Environment and Ecology: Jala Makhzoumi and Salwa Sabbagh.

The flat terrain allowed for the detached-house typology with relatively large plots. City planning was a well-established state practice in Iraq, legally upheld and implemented by a strong, centralized government. Baghdad has had a series of master plans. The one proposed by D.A. Doxiadis in the early 1950s had perhaps the greatest morphological impact because of the metropolitan scale, orthogonal street layout and satellite neighborhoods proposed. The Poleservice master plan in 1967 with updates are presently active pending completion of the CCDP.

Repercussions of the Gulf War, sanctions and the American invasion in 2003 have fundamentally transformed the demographic, spatial and economic structure of the city. With a weak state and political instability, there have been failures in upholding urban planning regulations contributing to considerable deterioration of the urban fabric. Unplanned population growth, internally displaced refugees, inadequate urban infrastructure, namely energy supply, sanitation, storm water and sewage collection, combine to undermine the quality of life in the city. Shortage in housing supply, estimated at 400,000 dwelling units, inadequate road and transportation network, are also contributing factors. Environmental quality has been compromised. Air quality is extremely poor because of traffic and local industries, the river polluted by dumping of raw sewage effluent and soil contaminated by hazardous waste (Khatib and Alami 2012).

Despite these failures, the overall character of Baghdad is of a spacious and green city. Streets are wide and well-planted, roundabouts spacious and house gardens everywhere. The city boasts a number of large parks, two established in the late 1980s on river islands, north and south of the river. The Abu Nuwas river boulevard is a wide profusely planted corridor east of the Tigris with restaurants and amenity gardens (Figure 6.9). The historical role of the river as an amenity corridor has been undermined by the lack of security and civic unrest. Dominant spatially, valued as an open landscape of scale and as a living ecosystem, the full potential of the river for urban greening is yet to be fulfilled. Another threatened landscape are date palm orchards, expansive up to the 1970s, incrementally destroyed by streets and buildings. Large date palm orchards today have receded to enclaves in the extreme northern and southern limits of the city, on both sides of the Tigris.

The CCDP was commissioned by the Mayoralty of Baghdad, the client. The aim was to examine urban planning and design issues and develop an integrated development plan for the city in 2030. The project duration was three years, 2010–13, embracing four phases: baseline report identifying status and trends; alternative development plan strategy outline; draft CCDP and action plan; final CCDP plan and implementation guidelines.

Figure 6.9 **View of the Abu Nuwas River Corniche green corridor**
Source: http://commons.wikimedia.org/wiki/File:Baghdad_Red_zone.jpg (image by Robert Smith via Wikimedia Commons) [accessed: December 12, 2013].

The Discourse of Urban Greening in Saida and Baghdad

The ecological landscape design framework adopted for both projects builds on three key principles. The first prioritizes on environmental sustainability and safeguarding ecological integrity, for example, in conceptualizing marine and riparian landscapes. The second reaffirms landscape connectivity by networking green areas spatially, to ensure continuous and safe non-vehicular movement, that is, pedestrian and cyclist, throughout the city. Landscape connectivity is also a necessary component of urban biodiversity conservation. The third principle upholds the concept of multifunctional landscapes through hybridized greening strategies, for example protecting riparian ecosystems as amenity corridors, upgrading and branding urban agriculture to animate the urban economy and support local livelihoods.

A comparative assessment of the greening strategies for the Saida USDS and the Baghdad CCDP projects, is herein presented. The focus is on four cross-cutting, mutually inclusive themes: (a) the ecological context and the potential of landscape to reconnect city and hinterland; (b) the spatial context and the shift from park to a network of green areas; (c) landscape heritage and local distinctiveness; and (d) the planning framework and community engagement.

(a) The Ecological Context: Reconnecting City and Region

A landscape approach expands greening strategies so they integrate urban peripheries, uncover forgotten ecological processes and capitalize on natural resources. And while rivers and watercourses are a key geomorphological feature and living urban ecosystem in both cities, urban agricultural landscapes are an important, multifunctional green space; the former a natural urban heritage, the latter a cultural one. In both cities, protecting rivers corridors as a multifunctional greenway was a key greening strategy. Although protected by Lebanese law, watercourses in Saida, with the exception of the Awali River, are threatened by urban encroachment and sewage dumping. Some, like the Barghouth and Qamli, are extremely degraded, which explains the prevailing negative perception of watercourses by the inhabitants of Saida. The focus of USDS framework on environment and ecology ensured that the health of riparian ecosystems was a priority. The landscape approach on the other hand served as a means of contextualizing, that is, spatializing environmental strategies, by conceptualizing them as multifunctional amenity corridors. In Baghdad, the scale of the Tigris posed a different challenge. The landscape strategy as such was twofold: to reintegrate the river spatially and programmatically; and to develop the river as an ecological corridor by reconfiguring the hydrology, managing embankments as wildlife habitat and by enhancing native plant communities. And because river morphology and ecology transcend urban limits, incorporating them into greening strategies serves to reconnect city and hinterland.

(b) The Spatial Context: From Park to Network of Green Areas

The phenomenal growth of cities in the twenty-first-century Mashreq dictates a twofold approach: to respond to the scale of spatial expansion; and to increase the per capita green area. Developing a network of green areas is a key greening strategy in both projects. Networks are formed by identifying potential landscapes components, both natural and cultural, and conceptualizing them as a whole to ensure a spatially expansive distribution that is accessible to all parts of the city, and as such socially inclusive. In Saida, the landscape concept embraces watercourses, the coastal waterfront and the abandoned railway corridor, conceptualized collectively as a blue–green network that covers the municipal area and beyond (Figure 6.10). In Baghdad the green area network includes the Tigris River spine and existing canals as connectors, rehabilitated streets to prioritize on pedestrians and cyclists, existing and proposed district parks (Figure 6.11). In both cities, networks increases the per capita green area allocation, from 3.2 m^2/capita to 7.42 m^2/capita in Saida, and from the existing 3.19 m^2/capita to 12.8 m^2/capita in Baghdad. Beyond quantitative measures, green networks ensure safe, quality urban landscapes that enhance urban liveability.

78 *Urban Design in the Arab World*

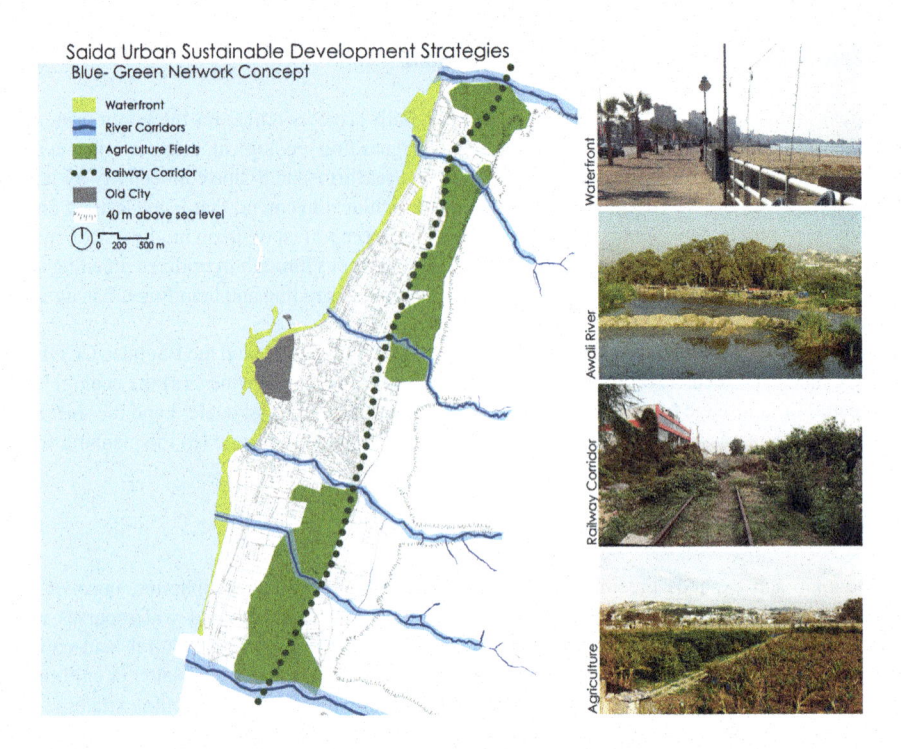

Figure 6.10 Saida USDS conceptual model of the green–blue network
Source: Author.

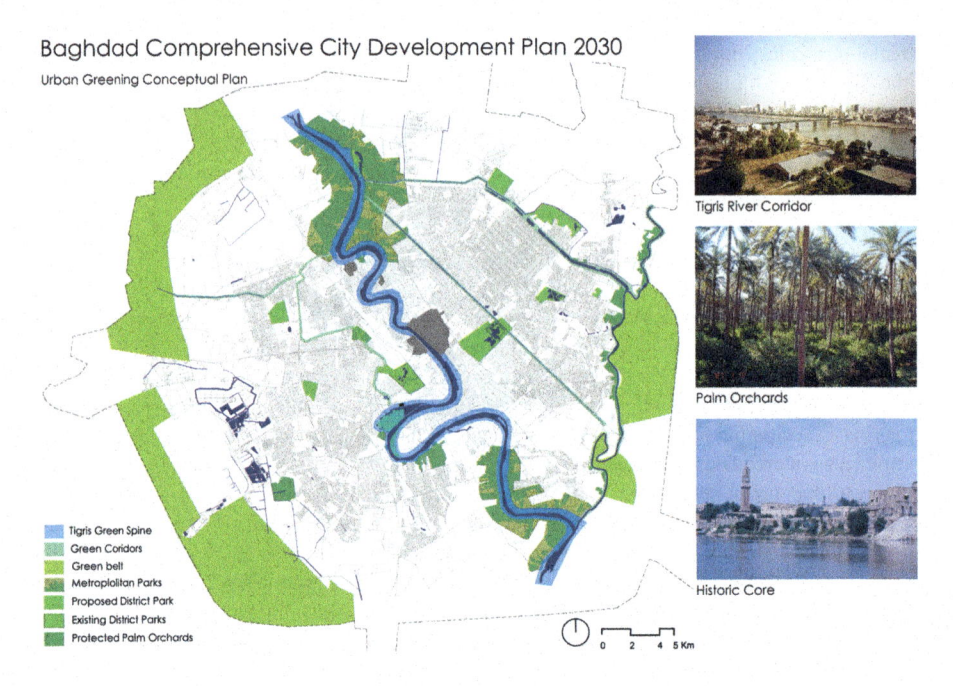

Figure 6.11 Baghdad CCDP landscape master plan
Source: Author.

(c) Urban Distinctiveness: Reclaiming the Urban Landscape Heritage

The shift away from generic municipal parks toward existing natural and cultural landscape features is a means for reaffirming urban distinctiveness while reconnecting city and region. Incorporating rivers and watercourses, and similarly urban agriculture, whether citrus orchards in Saida or palm groves in Baghdad, is more likely to counter homogenizing processes in both cities. The challenge of incorporating agriculture is at once economic and legal. Blanket protection is not feasible. Rather protection should target strategic locations, apply planning tools for pooling and re-appropriation of land uses. Further, traditional agricultural practices should be updated through sustainable long-term management strategies, alternative marketing and branding to ensure that they are economically feasible, that they combine amenity and productivity. In Baghdad, a distinction is made between protecting mature date palm orchards along the Tigris north and south of the city and new agricultural landscapes that fall within the greenbelt proposed by the CCDP along the western edges of the city. And though both are important components of greening, the significance of the former lies in its being a cultural heritage, while the latter's role is environmental, namely improving the urban microclimate and sheltering from dust storms.

(d) The Planning Framework: Engaging Local Communities

The well-established state planning apparatus in Iraq continues to rely on land use zoning that is based on in-depth analysis of existing conditions as a basis for predicting future trends. The process is time consuming; the reality on the ground would have changed by the time the data is gathered and analyzed and a master plan proposed. Although the Baghdad CCDP is an attempt to provide strategic interventions on transport and land use, the client was eager that it serves to update the Poleservice master plan. In contrast, the methodological approach of the Saida USDS proceeds from a rapid overall reading, strategic analysis to identify cross-cutting issues that need to be addressed through a vision and strategic framework for development. Just as significant, is the emphasis of the USDS on a participatory framework that engages local communities, NGOs and civil society representatives under the umbrella of Saida municipality throughout all phases of the project. And although both approaches rely on a range of disciplinary experts, the ongoing interaction among the team of experts and, between them, the municipality and local players in the USDS is an embodiment of transdisciplinary planning (Tress et al. 2003) (Table 6.1). In contrast, the "interdisciplinary" planning framework for the CCDP is more conventional.

Table 6.1 Greening components of the Saida USDS exemplify transdisciplinarity by breaching the disciplinary boundaries of environmental resources, ecological systems, livelihoods, and amenity and landscape heritage

Transversal # 2	Environmental health	Socio-economic benefits	Landscape heritage	Amenity, quality living
Watercourses	Integrity of ecocorridor	Tourism, irrigation	Natural and cultural	Greenways
Sea/coastline	Ecotone management	Fishing, tourism	Natural and cultural	Waterfront
Agriculture	Sustainable/organic	Livelihoods, branded marketing	Cultural, Qanaya	Agri-tourism
Green/open spaces	Sustainable management	Quality living	Archeology, cemeteries	Green–blue network

Conclusion

The discourse of urban greening in the Mashreq, this chapter has argued, endures the limitations of a narrow understanding of urban greening that draws on prevailing misconceptions of "landscape" whereby greening is equated with urban "beautification." Obsession with a static, scenic and outdated image of Western parklands in turn undermines the rich diversity of landscapes in the urban hinterland. Urban greening strategies should necessarily be compatible with the scale and pattern of urbanization in the Mashreq to overcome the repercussions of a blinkered focus on the city that fails to consider the hinterland and region beyond. Drawing on the Saida USDS and Baghdad CCDP projects, the chapter demonstrates the potential of ecological landscape design as a framework for conceptualizing greening strategies that are expansive *temporally* to include past narratives and future aspirations and expansive *spatially* to respond to the scale of twenty-first-century urbanization and embrace the continuity from inner city to peripheral and hinterland landscapes.

Shifting paradigms in urban economics is increasingly supportive of the expansive outlook to urban greening proposed here. The concept of "city-regions," argues McCann (2007), is becoming central to the formation of post-national economies. The author suggests that "the contemporary fusion of these two discourses," "city-region" and "urban livability," is more likely to address the predicament of twenty-first century cities, for example, "the politics of income inequality, housing provision, gentrification, service provision and environmental policy, among others" (McCann 2007: 192). In other words, a broader framework for conceptualizing urban greening is supported by the new economic model.

The challenge of urban greening in the Mashreq depends as well on a participatory framework. In this context, Pincetl argues the necessity of alternative governance, where "top-down planning policies, seen as intrusive and insensitive to local contexts" are replaced by "bottom-up approaches involving complex and numerous stakeholders responding to specific, local land issues" (Pincetl 2006: 254). Still, outdated, top-heavy planning dominates Mashreq countries, for example in Iraq, failing to engage the public as active stakeholders, prioritizing instead land use zoning and production of a "master plan." At the other extreme is a country like Lebanon with a frail state and rudimentary urban planning capabilities.[28] And although Lebanon's civic society is extremely active, ready and willing to participate in a range of issues, political instability and the confessional setup of state agencies are considerable obstacles. In Iraq, on the other hand, the role of civil societies has been negligible under the Saddam dictatorship and equally absent during American occupation. Recently, however, civil societies in Iraq have been more active in voicing their criticism of declining urban living standards. One author sees civil society as the only hope in Iraq to combat rampart corruption within state agencies that cripples development in cities and throughout Iraq (Al-Ali 2014).

We have argued elsewhere that "landscape" can serve as an enabling platform for public participation because it broadens the debate on public rights to embrace intangible social and cultural values associated with nature and landscape scenery (Makhzoumi 2011). Urban green areas, whether a city park, a river or coastal landscape, can serve to mobilize local communities to take part as active partners in greening the city. And because landscape is admired and valued by all, professionals, administrators and lay people, it is more likely to spearhead the discourse of public rights in the face of neoliberal trends in the Mashreq (Makhzoumi 2011). Lebanon's civil society is vociferous on public rights, specifically in the context of public spaces and green areas.[29]

Cities in the Mashreq are growing fast, their landscapes homogenizing just as rapidly. At a time when they desperately seek to reclaim their identity and reaffirm their distinctiveness, neoliberal politics is promoting urban development that relies on generic design solutions, favoring them because they have been tested and proven in other places. Ironically, the very appeal of neoliberal models for development "lies in their effectiveness regardless of the particularities of place" (Christopherson 1994: 409). This accounts in part for the growing sameness in cities in the Mashreq, as does a continued infatuation with the form and character of cities in North America and Europe and, more recently, Dubai.[30] The urban landscape image associated

---

28 To compensate for the absence of effective urban planning, for example, Beirut Municipality with technical support and funding from the La Region Ile-de-France launched several projects that impact urban greening, some directly, for example the "Liaison Douce" (see http://idf-beyrouth.com/?q=content/projet-de-liaison-douce/ [accessed: January 29, 2014]).

29 Lebanon has over 6,000 registered civil society groups that demand their rights to public spaces and state lands, coastal, riverine and forestland. Apart from media coverage, their concerns are rarely taken into account (see http://www.greenline.org.lb/ and http://www.beirut.com/l/16341, also a consortium of NGOs pooling their resources to green their city http://beirutgreenproject.wordpress.com/about/ [accessed: March 13, 2014]).

30 The dazzling urban character of Dubai with its high-rise towers amidst spacious green areas is increasingly serving as the embodiment of Westernization, a model cities in the Mashreq aspire to emulate from Erbil to Damascus.

with these Western models, blinds these cities to the beauty and distinctiveness of the outlying region. Recognizing the value of hinterland landscapes, protecting and incorporating them into future development as such has the potential to reaffirm urban visual distinctiveness and re-anchor cities of the Mashreq in the surrounding region.

References

Abu Dhabi Urban Planning Council. 2010. Plan Abu Dhabi 2030. Urban Structure Framework Plan. Available at: http://www.upc.gov.ae/abu-dhabi-2030.aspx?lang=en-US [accessed: March 13, 2015].

Abu Dhabi Urban Planning Council. 2011. Al Ain City 2030. http://www.upc.gov.ae/abu-dhabi-2030/al-ain-2030.aspx?lang=en-US [accessed: March 13]

Al-Ali, Z. 2014. *The Struggle for Iraq's Future: How Corruption, Incompetence and Sectarianism have Undermined Democracy*. London: Yale University Press.

Almy, D. 2007. *On Landscape Urbanism*. Austin: Center for American Architecture and Design.

Anas, A. and Pines, D. 2008. Anti-Sprawl Policies in a System of Congested Cities. *Regional Science and Urban Economics* [online], 38(5), 408–23. Available at: http://dx.doi.org/10.1016/j.regsciurbeco.2008.05.001 [accessed: February 14, 2014].

Balsas, C. 2004. Measuring the Livability of an Urban Centre: An Exploratory Study of Key Performance Indicators. *Planning, Practice & Research* [online], 19(1), 101–10. Available at: http://dx.doi.org/10.1080/0269745042000246603 [accessed: February 14, 2014].

Benedict, M. and McMahon, E. 2006. *Green Infrastructure: Linking Landscapes and Communities*. Washington, DC: Island Press.

Brandt, J. and Vejre, H. 2004. *Multifunctional Landscapes: Theory, Values and History*. Southampton: WIT Press.

Christopherson, S. 1994. The Fortress City: Privatized Spaces, Consumer Citizenship, in *Post-Fordism: A Reader*, edited by A. Amin. London: Blackwell Publishers, 409–27.

Daher, R. 2013. Neoliberal Urban Transformations in Arab Cities: Meta-Narratives, Urban Disparities and the Emergence of Consumerist Utopias and Geographies of Inequalities in Amman. *Urban Environment* [online], 7, 99–115. Available at: http://www.vrm.ca/EUUE/Vol7_2013/EUE7_Daher.pdf [accessed: February 14, 2014].

Diener, E. and Suh, E. (eds) 2000. *Culture and Subjective Well-Being*. Cambridge, MA: MIT Press.

Fawaz, M. 2009. Neoliberal Urbanity and the Right to the City: A View from Beirut's Periphery. *Development and Change* [online], 40(5), 827–52. Available at: http://onlinelibrary.wiley.com/doi/10.1111/j.1467-7660.2009.01585.x/abstract [accessed: March 13, 2014].

Harb, M. 2013. Public Spaces and Spatial Practices: Claims from Beirut. *Jadaliyya* [online]. Available at: http://www.jadaliyya.com/pages/index/14710/public-spaces-and-spatial-practices_claims-from-be [accessed: February 14, 2014].

Harrison, C. and Davies, G. 2002. Conserving Biodiversity that Matters: Practitioners' Perspective on Brownfield Development and Urban Nature Conservation in London. *Journal of Environmental Management* [online], 65(1), 95–108. Available at: http://dx.doi.org/10.1006/jema.2002.0539 [accessed: February 14, 2014].

Kendle, T. and Forbes, S. 1997. *Urban Nature Conservation: Landscape Management in the Urban Countryside*. London: E & FN Spon.

Khatib and Alami. 2012. Baghdad CCDP, Final Phase II Report, January 2012.

Makhzoumi, J. 2008. Interrogating the Hakura Tradition: Lebanese Garden as Product and Production. International Association for the Study of Traditional Dwellings and Settlements, Working Paper Series, 200, 50–60.

Makhzoumi, J. 2009. Unfolding Landscape in a Lebanese Village: Rural Heritage in a Globalizing World. *International Journal of Heritage Studies*, 15(4), 317–37. Available at: http://dx.doi.org/10.1080/13527250902933793 [accessed: March 13, 2014].

Makhzoumi, J. 2010. Marginal Landscapes, Marginalized Rural Communities: Sustainable Postwar Recovery in Southern Lebanon, in *Lessons in Postwar Reconstruction: Case Studies from Lebanon in the Aftermath of the 2006 War*, edited by H. Al Harithy. London: Routledge, 127–57.

Makhzoumi, J. 2011. Colonizing Mountain, Paving Sea: Neoliberal Politics and the Right to Landscape in Lebanon, in *The Right to Landscape: Contesting Landscape and Human Rights*, edited by S. Egoz, J. Makhzoumi and G. Pungetti. London: Ashgate, 227–42.

Makhzoumi, J. 2014. Is Rural Heritage Relevant in an Urbanizing Mashreq? Exploring Discourses of Landscape Heritage in Lebanon, in *The Politics and Practices of Cultural Heritage in the Middle East: Positioning the Material Past and Contemporary Society*, edited by R. Daher and I. Maffi. London: I.B. Tauris, 233–51.

Makhzoumi, J. and Pungetti, G. 1999. *Ecological Design and Planning: The Mediterranean Context*. London: E & FN Spon, Routledge.

Makhzoumi, J., Talhouk, S.N., Zurayk, R. and Sadek, R. 2012. Landscape Approach to Bio-Cultural Diversity Conservation in Rural Lebanon, in *Nature Conservation—Patterns, Pressures and Prospects*, edited by J. Tiefenbacher, 179–98. Available at: http://www.intechopen.com/articles/show/title/landscape-appro ach-to-bio-cultural-diversity-conservation-in-rural-lebanon [accessed: February 14, 2014].

McCann, E. 2007. Inequality and Politics in the Creative City-Region: Questions of Livability and State Strategy. *International Journal of Urban and Regional Research* [online], 31(1), 188–96. Available at: http://onlinelibrary.wiley.com/doi/10.1111/j.1468-2427.2007.00713.x/abstract [accessed: February 14, 2014].

Mostafavi, M. and Najle, C. 2003. *Landscape Urbanism: A Manual for the Machinic Landscape*. London: Architectural Association.

Nelson, A. and Moore, T. 1996. Assessing Urban Growth Management Policy Implementation: Case Study of the United States' Leading Growth Management State. *Land Use Policy* [online], 13(4), 241–59. Available at: http://dx.doi.org/10.1016/0264-8377(96)84555-8 [accessed: February 14, 2014].

Pincetl, S. 2006. Conservation Planning in the West, Problems, New Strategies and Entrenched Obstacles. *Geoforum* [online], 37(2), 246–55. Available at: http://dx.doi.org/10.1016/j.geoforum.2005.05.001 [accessed: February 14, 2014].

Tress, B., Tress, G., Van der Valk, A. and Fry, G. 2003. *Interdisciplinary and Transdisciplinary Landscape Studies: Potential and Limitations*. Wageningen: Delta Series.

UN-Habitat. 2012. *The State of Arab Cities 2012: Challenges of Urban Transition*. Available at: http://www.unhabitat.org/pmss/listItemDetails.aspx?publicationID=3320 [accessed: February 14, 2014].

Viljoen, A., Bohn, K. and Howe, J. 2005. *Continuous Productive Urban Landscapes: Designing Urban Agriculture for Sustainable Cities*. Amsterdam: Elsevier.

Zako, R. 2014. *Liveability Issues and Housing in City Centres: Towards a Micro-Scale Understanding of their Dynamics*. PhD dissertation, University of London.

PART II
The Hybrid: Blurring Boundaries between Design Disciplines

Chapter 7
Cultural Infrastructure for the Margins: A Machinic Approach to Nahr Beirut

Lee Frederix

Introduction: Occupying the Margins

In broadening the definition of infrastructure to include social and cultural networks within the city, this chapter[1] takes inspiration from recent Western models of landscape analysis in addressing a case study of the marginal territories of contemporary Beirut. Attempting to investigate both socio-economic and spatial aspects of marginality, the work conceptualizes the Nahr Beirut [*Beirut River*], not as an environmental entity, but as an edge condition and as the potential site for operational strategies in the development of a *cultural infrastructure*. The work posits that the countercultural contingent of Beirut's art community, by definition relegated to the social margins, could be accommodated within the physical margins of the city and that a cultural infrastructure, an active network catalyzing the rehabilitation of the city's derelict peripheral spaces, could help to revitalize the role of art in contemporary Beirut.

Global Precedents

In major metropolitan areas, there is a long tradition of artists appropriating abandoned industrial space and derelict buildings. Witness the examples of Greenwich Village in New York, Montmartre in Paris and Soho in London—or more recently, DUMBO, quai de la Seine, and the eastern docklands. And it is precisely the artistic character of those formerly marginal neighborhoods that aided in the gentrification process and later made them some of the most desirable addresses in each respective city. Also at an urban scale, there are several conceptual precedents for the rehabilitation and adaptive reuse of post-industrial brownfields for the benefit of artistic and cultural practices. Projects for both the Parc de la Villette and for Freshkills are prime examples, and those schemes will be discussed as models for this current project; other examples include the King's Cross railyards, Downsview, and the Greenwich peninsula. But these types of projects have thus far only been considered in highly developed, post-industrial urban contexts. Perhaps a similar process of urban reclamation is also possible in cities of the developing world; this current project aims to test that hypothesis by experimenting Western paradigms of urban renewal and reclamation in the unique context of contemporary Beirut.

Local Appropriation

Post-industrial reclamation is only just beginning to happen here in Beirut; since this research was undertaken several art-related spaces that complement the proposed framework have appeared within the suggested study area. But these developments are unfortunately being spearheaded by capitalist ventures in what amounts to an appropriation of the margins by the mainstream art "establishment." Besides new construction and the conversion of former industrial buildings into luxury lofts, a few high-end commercial interests have already moved in.[2]

---

    1 Based on the author's MArch thesis with a concentration in Landscape Urbanism (Frederix 2010).
    2 These include the local branch of European art gallery Sfeir-Semler, the Ashkal al Alwan Homeworks project, and the Beirut Art Center, funded by global financial corporate structures.

> Now there is no choice but to invent something new ... In places where destruction has and is still forcing the issue, the time to do so is short. The forces of reaction, as cynical and self-serving as ever, are eager to fill the void left by a destruction that they themselves to a large degree have caused. (Woods 1997: 27–8)

The localization of the mainstream art "establishment" within the study area validates its choice as an appropriate location for the implementation of a full-fledged enclave of cultural practice. But these venues should only be considered as a wake-up call for marginalized artists, a catalyst for initiating action toward the proposed cultural infrastructure.

Goals of the Study

The majority of the work written about contemporary Beirut has been deeply rooted in established and pragmatic modes of urban discourse, including economic fallout, population displacement, or master planning proposals. With the exception of academic ventures such as theses (Frem 2009) and urban design studio projects, none of the work uncovered in the research for this project has truly applied experimental investigative models into the Beiruti context. Therefore, the current project aims at providing an unconventional method of looking at the city, investigating ignored emerging theoretical practices, and offering alternative mapping schemes of Beirut's margins, all through the lens of Landscape Urbanism.

In an attempt to identify a method appropriate for addressing the marginal territories of post-war Beirut, a Landscape Urbanism approach seems a logical choice. As the field has emerged in recent years, its defining prototypical projects have dealt overwhelmingly with leftover interstitial spaces and gaps in the urban fabric, that is, marginal spaces. Although the informal qualities of this unique type of space defy traditional urbanist models of understanding, this chapter does not suggest abandoning conventional urban analysis, but instead will explore the applicability of emerging Western methodologies from the forefront of urban investigation in decidedly non-Western circumstances.

The aim then is to utilize Landscape Urbanism to accommodate the socio-cultural aspect of marginality within the physical/geographic margins of the contemporary city. Instituting horizontal surface strategies will unlock variation and flexibility, open-ended strategies capable of addressing any number of interacting systems and processes (Corner 2003: 60). In this way, the work attempts to explore, within the spatial margins of contemporary Beirut, the conception of a *cultural infrastructure*, one intrinsically linked to the future development of the marginalized art community. It is hoped that an alternative approach to reading the urban condition through the machinic mapping of Beirut's marginal landscape will add to our understanding of the complex urban processes at play in the developing world.

Defining the Margins of Contemporary Beirut

Before attempting to formulate a new strategy for addressing contemporary Beirut's marginal conditions, it stands next to identify what those margins are and to link them to urban circumstances in order to define a specific context in which the proposed concepts and methodologies could apply.

The Socio-Cultural Margins

As a consequence of ongoing conflict and the ensuing economic crisis, artistic and cultural activities in Beirut currently play a diminished role within the life of the city. Despite the existence today of an active cultural scene, large portions of the city's art community have effectively been marginalized, with no access to institutional backing. Beirut's emerging artists are relegated to the role of marginal figures, struggling for opportunities and exposure, and frustrated by a lack of financial or logistical support. The limited and elitist gallery system caters to a dwindling art market, with the current economic situation discouraging "risky" investments, leading to a conservatism in artistic taste and production.

Beirut's edge-dwellers are already accustomed to creative re-adaptation in everyday life and must maintain a critical attitude in order to force the issues at hand. A truly novel modus operandi and lifestyle appropriate to changing conceptions of society is beginning to emerge and requires continued struggle in order to allow the people of the edge to determine their own place within the boundaries of contemporary Beirut. Unfortunately, this type of action is also hindered by a general lack of organization or cooperation among Beirut artists. A large number of younger, independent artists are struggling to gain access to a tiny number of exclusive cliques. Without a true sense of community, many artists are relegated to an existence on the periphery of the cultural scene.

The Physical Margins

The term *community* inherently implies a shared spatiality. In order for any real sense of artistic community to develop in Beirut, there is a need for well-defined space for meeting, discussion and action. Currently, studio and exhibition spaces available to the budding artist are extremely limited. Fortunately, Beirut is a city of voids, gaps in the urban fabric that are a direct result of the above-mentioned political and economic crises. Two decades after the war's end, there is a huge quantity of forsaken warehouses, empty lots, abandoned industries and vacant buildings. Artists should see these spaces of the physical margins as opportunities: emptiness that could be filled, collapse that could be rebuilt, communities that could grow.

The Geographical Margins

The easternmost municipal edge of Beirut is defined by the Corniche El Nahr region (Figure 7.1). In the years preceding the civil war, the river's floodplain became a hub of light industry and logistical support, with easy access to the port and to the country's internal rail system. During the war years, emigration from the city reinforced the boundary between urban and suburban. Nahr Beirut, once the threshold of the city, became the margin, the empty edge, neither belonging to the city proper nor to the new "safe" areas. It was close but far, city but not, urban but empty.

These days, the area can still be considered the edge of the city, but occupies a very different role. As a socio-economically depressed Armenian enclave, it stands as a separate community from the Beiruti mainstream. The region hosts various support services associated with manual labor, including electrical supply, auto mechanics and carpentry shops, resulting in a noisy and dusty environment. Despite the re-emergence of some light industries and a low-end retail sector serving local residents, this area of the city has been relatively slow in post-war recovery and has thus been further relegated to urban marginality.

Reconceptualizing Marginality in Contemporary Design

In stark contrast with the Modern tendency to criticize the alienating quality of the modern city, the work of experimental architects John Hejduk and Lebbeus Woods—though very different stylistically—are both attempts at usurping established cultural norms and empowering the marginalized within the city. Building on the sense of personal autonomy, mobility and choice adopted in their work, this chapter also embraces the condition of marginality as one of many inevitable complexities of the contemporary city, an idea that can be traced back to the writings of Baudelaire and, more poignantly, Walter Benjamin.

Writing about Paris in his *Arcades Project*, Benjamin (1999) discussed a series of allegorical characters that typified various outsiders of modern culture, including the gambler, the prostitute, the rag picker, the dandy, and most importantly, the flâneur. Through him, Benjamin was illustrating an example of how the outcast might feel comfortable within the modern city, a cue borrowed from Baudelaire:

> For the perfect flâneur ... it is an immense joy to set up house in the heart of the multitude, amid the ebb and flow ... To be away from home, yet to feel oneself everywhere at home; to see the world, to be at the center of the world, yet to remain hidden from the world—such are a few of the slightest pleasures of those independent, passionate, impartial natures. (1986: 9)

Through the eyes of the flâneur, Benjamin was beginning to examine the urban condition from a point of view unfamiliar to the literary world of his contemporaries and to question the established roles of various societal positions. According to Graeme Gilloch, he was seeking "to empower the marginal and oppressed" (1996: 15) and seems to be the first to advocate alternative and even subversive practices in the urban domain. The flâneur's sense of autonomy and freedom from constraints allowed him to dissociate from the crowd while finding comfort in its anonymity. Thus the margins become "the hiding place of modernity, the haunt of the bohemian and the fugitive" (Gilloch 1996: 142) and the "asylum for the reprobate and prescript" (Benjamin 1999: 446).

From therein, the flâneur was afforded a coherent vision, knowing the city in ways others cannot: "Indeed, for Benjamin, it would seem that the dispossessed and despised occupy a privileged position within the domain of knowledge. They have access to a vision of society that is dereifying and critically negating" (Gilloch 1996: 15). From this "privileged position," the flâneur developed a moral responsibility to react against what he saw as the ills of modernity. Anthony Vidler (1992) agrees that among the characteristics of marginality is an inherent critique of social norms from a point of view deeply embedded within a given culture, but with the objectivity of an outsider.

Benjamin's flâneur has inspired later generations to build upon a marginal position in order to propose new modes of living within the city, new ideas of belonging, and if not embrace urbanity, then at least to accept its inescapable role in our lives. In Paris of the 1960s, for example, the Situationists International developed the *dérive*, a flâneur-like wandering described by the group's leader Guy Debord as "a mode of experimental behavior linked to the conditions of urban society" (Knabb 1981: 56). Through their dérives, the Situationists proposed new methods of mapping the urban fabric that challenged traditional municipal and legislative boundaries. Their new maps of Paris were based instead on mental and experiential qualities associated with various neighborhoods that could only have been gathered during the dérive.

Even more recent are the aforementioned Hejduk and Woods. Hejduk developed a *vagabond architecture*, a series of mobile architectural elements that travel from city to city, from culture to culture, never becoming a permanent part of the urban condition, always looking on critically from a self-imposed distance (Vidler 1992). These structures take the forms of "houses" for various allegorical figures of cultural relevance. They are insistently provocative to the urban unconscious in a way that "transforms the city ... into an autocritical artifact" (Vidler 1992: 210). Woods on the other hand designs for heterarchal cities, focusing on the individual outside of defined political and social structures. He argues that "it is more ethical to actively propose new ways and conditions of living in which one can personally believe" than to follow those that one considers "outmoded and regressive" (1992: 11–12). He proposes spaces for the "people of crisis," those who cannot or will not fit in, and whose inventiveness, spontaneity and acuteness of perception are critical for contemporary urban survival (Woods 1997).

Woods's people of crisis, like Benjamin's flâneur, are trying to establish new modes of living within the city, modes which are appropriate to new ways of thinking, and new ideas of belonging: "There is a fundamental difference between being alienated in the city and choosing to be isolated. The latter makes alienation unlikely" (Woods 1992: 11). If those who chose marginality as an existential condition can in fact be accommodated within the physical margins of the contemporary city, it remains then to outline a framework for investigating those margins, one by which the unique conditions of the contemporary city can begin to be clarified. This work proposes that framework could be Landscape Urbanism.

Conceptual Background: Landscape as Infrastructure

In writing the article that helped to forge the identity of the field of Landscape Urbanism, James Corner (2003) specifies infrastructure as one of the five conceptual frameworks that this discipline must necessarily address. He specifies: "Landscape Urbanism implants new potential in a given field through the orchestration of infrastructural catalysts—infrastructures that perform and produce, or exfoliate effects" with the intention "to liberate future sets of possibility—cultural as well as logistical" (2003: 60). Infrastructures, as matrices of horizontality, are intended as permissive systems, as opposed to the prescriptive approaches of traditional urban design or planning. And it is this open-ended nature that gives Landscape Urbanism a critical advantage in approaching the changing conditions of contemporary urban ecologies and geographies.

Since its inception Landscape Urbanism has been developing a new set of tools for analysis that have already proven successful, especially in international competitions that "proposed landscape as the basic framework for an urban transformation of what had been a part of the working city, left derelict by shifts in economies of production and consumption" (Waldheim 2006: 40). Well-known projects for the Fresh Kills and Downsview competitions and, more importantly, two entries for the Parc de la Villette competition, conceive of the landscape as the primary mediating device between public space, infrastructure and unknown future possibilities. At la Villette, projects by both Rem Koolhaas and Bernard Tschumi broke down the site through the imposition of artificially created organizational systems, attempting to reveal unconventional elements and their relationships within a given field. Tschumi's winning scheme focuses on *event* and *program*, instead of formal and stylistic concerns, using the landscape as a medium "to order programmatic and social change over time, especially complex evolving arrangements of urban activities" (Waldheim 2006: 40–41). Equally compelling is the submission of Koolhaas, which addresses this same variable nature:

> [D]uring the life of the park, the program will undergo constant change and adjustment ... The underlying principle of programmatic indeterminacy as a basis of the formal concept [that] allows any shift, modification, replacement, or substitutions to occur without damaging the initial hypothesis. (Koolhaas 1998: 921)

These projects, by accommodating flexible, non-hierarchical strategies for horizontal infrastructure, have become prototypical models for the field of Landscape Urbanism as a whole, and more particularly for this current study.

Methodology: Investigating the Margins

Complementing conventional processes of landscape analysis, the methodology applied in this work takes a second look at Beirut's margins through the lens of Landscape Urbanism, placing "the emphasis on urban processes ... to construct a dialectical understanding of how [spatial form] relates to the processes that flow through, manifest, and sustain it" (Corner 2006: 28). While not attempting to replace traditional analysis, it is hoped that an alternative approach will enrich the understanding of conditions on the ground, at the same allowing newer methods to be tested in a context quite different from that for which they were originally conceived.

Loosely inspired by the work of several pioneers in the field, specifically Ian McHarg, Tom Turner and Kevin Lynch, assessment of a given site through the overlaying of various area maps, landscape plans and site characteristics in thematic layers facilitates a preliminary landscape understanding and diagnosis. This approach has proven effective for conventional landscape evaluation as it relates to traditional landscape architecture and urban design; however, it relies on static and constant components and techniques. Its perceived shortcomings lie in its inability to incorporate into the analysis what Charles Waldheim (2006) refers to as "the temporal mutability and horizontal extensivity of the contemporary city." He argues that the established models of investigation have proven "inflexible in relation to the rapidly transforming conditions of contemporary urban culture" (2006: 37). Out of this critique has arisen Landscape Urbanism, a new paradigm of inquiry for the postmodern city.

By "shifting attention away from the object qualities of space (whether formal or scenic) to the systems that condition the distribution and density of urban form" (Corner 2006: 28) this current study seeks to embrace constantly changing processes and to recognize accidents and inconsistencies within existing urban systems. But because the various analytical approaches have differing origins, concepts, underlying frameworks and defined purposes, their synthesis requires constant re-analysis, questioning and development. Like the field of Landscape Urbanism itself, its accompanying paradigm should be open-ended, indeterminate and responsive:

> [C]ontemporary landscape urbanism practices recommend the use of infrastructural systems and the public landscapes they engender as the very ordering mechanisms of the urban field itself, shaping and shifting the organization of urban settlement and its inevitably indeterminate economic, political, and social futures.
> (Waldheim 2006: 39)

In an attempt to add to the growing body of knowledge of this nascent field, the final phase of this project makes use of the pioneering theories laid out in the seminal volume published by the Architectural Association and edited by Mohsen Mostafavi and Ciro Najle (2003). By proposing to incorporate traditionally unmappable forces such as permeability, dissolution, intensities and accumulations, a *machinic* analysis of the landscape plans results in a more responsive, heterarchal, process-based framework.

According to Guattari, the *machinic* is necessarily "linked to procedures which deterritorialize its elements, functions and relations to alterity" (1995: 9). As such, a machinic analysis of the landscape serves to dissociate its systems from traditional formal and programmatic qualities. It should not be surprising then, that the subsequent mappings do not present the recognizable urban forms or landmarks usually associated with the study area. On the contrary, the methodology of this project predictably results in highly abstract schematics and non-prescriptive diagrams, in the words of Eisenmann, "not subordinated to the laws of resemblance or utility and not producing conceptually stable form-objects" (2007: 57).

This approach makes use of an alternative mapping of the site based on the innovative method of *systemic simulation* as proposed by Najle (2003). In this method, intangible relationships and processes at work within a given landscape are incorporated into the analysis in order to create a more indeterminate approach to landscape intervention. In Najle's own words: "The relationship between problems and solutions can thus be treated loosely, yet with precision, keeping differentiation open and complexification pliable. Rather than strategizing by decision-making, systemic simulation catalyzes tendencies, intensities, probabilities, feasibilities, and impacts by iteration management. It abandons direct control and governs by loops" (2003: 63).

Applying the Methodology: Landscape Analysis at Corniche El Nahr

The investigation focuses on a section of the river frontage approximately 350 meters in width and 3 kilometers in length with the river itself as the eastern boundary. The western floodplain includes a diverse selection of land uses and urban landscape types including an active industrial zone and a dense residential area, locally known as Beddawi. The study area stretches inland, following the Nahr Beirut to the point where it ceases to form the administrative boundary of the capital, easily recognized as the site of the abandoned railyards and their surrounding warehouse district (Figure 7.1). Unifying (or dividing) the study area are several principal circulation corridors, including a section of the Beirut-Jounieh highway, the Pierre Gemayel Corniche, and Emile Lahoud Avenue, a relatively recent highway that parallels the river, linking the coastal highway to points further up the river valley. This district is a major threshold for commuters, with bridges crossing the river and connecting Beirut to Bourj Hammoud, Sin el Fil, and all of the northern suburbs.

Due to its location and role as a major entry point to the city, the Corniche El Nahr area has suffered greatly from rampant but poorly planned development, typical of the Lebanese coastal zone. A conventional process of landscape analysis defines a series of diagnostic issues, which can be roughly categorized into four principal themes: vehicular, pedestrian, environmental and aesthetic. Once the landscape issues have been identified, a clear reading of problems facing the area began to highlight zones of overlap. These action areas, where intervention would bring about the maximum positive impact, were determined to be highly unsustainable and to face significant threats from continuous unchecked development. But because of its implicit "inability to offer coherent, competent, and convincing explanations of contemporary urban conditions" (Waldheim 2006: 37), conventional analysis here reaches its applicable limits.

Figure 7.1   The study area: Beirut's geographical margins
Source: Author (based on Google Earth Image 2009).

Machinic Analysis of Corniche El Nahr

Applying a machinic approach to the Corniche El Nahr offers a more indeterminate and open-ended attitude to the reading of the initial landscape plans. It is important to note here that the proposed readings are not a pre-described process, but rather a series of suggestions. Each type of plan has specific goals, possibilities and levels of applicability. Before drawing up a given landscape plan, certain insightful decisions concerning its use must be made according to project needs and existing site conditions. This intuitive aspect is clarified by Makhzoumi and Pungetti, who state that the planner must consider "the rationality of the outer world, but also neglected intangible relationships of the inner world" (1999: 195).

The resulting analytical diagrams described below, *Articulations of Network and Territory* (Figure 7.2), are intended as prototypical, by no means exclusive nor prescriptive. The machinic processes of Landscape Urbanism are by nature mutable and capricious, with further experimentation anticipating countless variations in descriptive articulations of circumstance.

Lateral Clustering

Landscape types and associated land uses exist in relatively continuous longitudinal sections throughout the study area. Transversal sections, on the other hand, reveal heterogeneous conditions that impede the traditional reading of the surface. Regular lateral segmentation of the site allows for alternative processes of analysis, and is extended to mark out a rectilinear datum, used for schematic cataloging. Therein, the clustered distribution of various systems throughout the site can be documented. In this particular iteration, the chart emphasizes networks of transportation, voids in the urban fabric, topographic anomalies and pedestrian accessibility. Such cataloging allows for a better understanding of how certain systems are related across newly homogenized zones of activity (Figure 7.2a).

Temporal Sedimentation

Surface accumulation, incorporating built form, infrastructure networks and transitory bodies, reflects the area's changing socio-economic role within the capital. Tangible remnants of inconsistent growth patterns over time are diagrammed according to the interplay of collisive sites and bundled densities of land uses. An accrual of logistical matrices, each one rendered obsolete when superseded by a more highly efficient model, creates a vectorial complexity that serves to both isolate and interconnect territories of shared identity. Here the elements have been extruded into three-dimensional form in order to emphasize the significant volumetric accumulation throughout the area. From this volumetric treatment emerges pockets of comparable densities, themselves punctuated by the presence of residue from each successive (but now archaic) system (Figure 7.2b).

City as Body

Rethinking the landscape as a living, changing system provokes metaphorical comparisons to physiological and biological systems, which in turn engenders unconventional forms of critical reassessment. A defunct rail system, for example, is viewed as an essential component of the internal structure of the site and also as a network for the conveyance of information. This comparison is translated allegorically as a spinal column, the core element of both the skeletal and nervous systems. Fibrous neuron receptors pervade the body, extending impulses outward to collect environmental stimuli and to transmit appropriate reflex actions. Reversing the metaphor creates a symbolic representation of a public transport corridor used as a link among sites of cultural importance (Figure 7.2c).

Descriptive Associations

Intimate knowledge of the area begets an awareness of community, and consequent perceptions of neighborhood identities can begin to be diagrammed. Within this matrix of localities, existing nodes of cultural activity within the study area are designated. Employing the lateral segmentation outlined above, we can begin to understand their distribution and clustering. In stark contrast to the mainstream's perception of the area, a rich palimpsest of urban culture is revealed, though not exclusively artistic. In addition to art-related spaces, the diverse components serve also ethnic, social and educational niches within the community, all of which can be considered as an integral part of the proposed cultural infrastructure (Figure 7.2d).

Cultural Infrastructure for the Margins 93

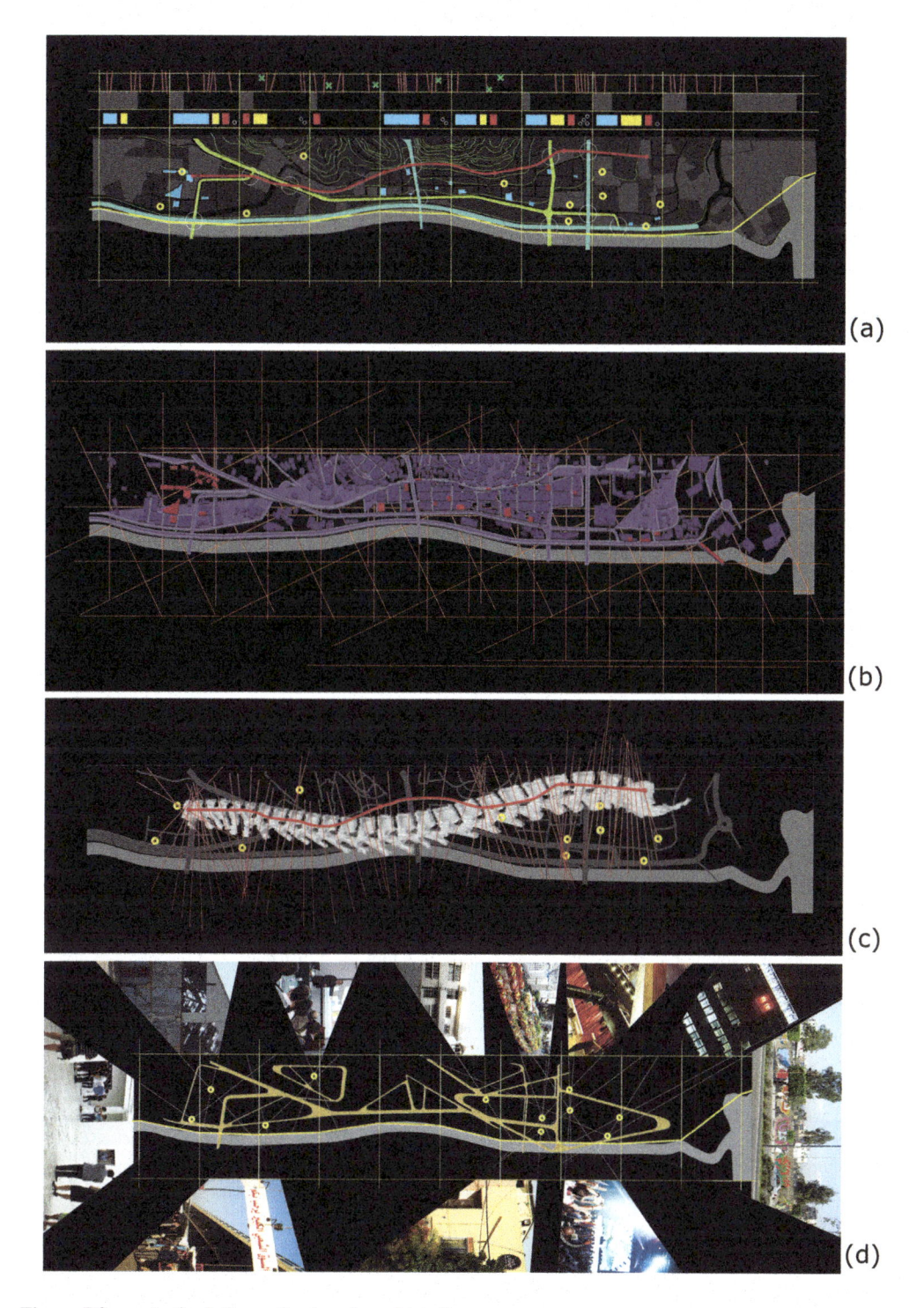

Figure 7.2 Articulations of network and territory
Note: (a) lateral clustering; (b) temporal sedimentation; (c) city as body; (d) descriptive associations.
Source: Author.

Accommodating Marginality: Implementing Cultural Infrastructure

By injecting the flows and modulations of the city into the stratifications of landscape diagnosis, the machinic analyses begin to fabricate new symbiotic networks among the abiotic, biotic and cultural elements of the landscape. The resulting intervention strategies, dubbed *synthetic ecologies*, become the basis for the new types of surface advocated by Landscape Urbanism: horizontal, infrastructural and machinic, and serve as illustrations of what Eisenmann calls "a matrix of forces, a condition of becoming which uncovers potential attributes of space covered up by the formal" (2007: 67). Though the drawings may seem highly unorthodox, the method of representation is completely in line with Guattari's view of the machinic, with Eisenmann's architectural *détournement* of that idea, as well as with academic projects recently published under the heading of Landscape Urbanism.

> The new human landscapes created at the boundaries of the formerly known are those that increase the possibilities of choice among those people who find (or need to place) themselves on or against those boundaries. These landscapes may seem startling, even irrational, but they are nothing if not extensions of reason. (Woods 1997: 13)

These *synthetic ecologies* maps described below (Figure 7.3) are again inspired by the work of Najle. But the surface and systemic conditions of the Corniche El Nahr differ greatly from those he originally investigated. In order to test the applicability of these processes in the context of Beirut's urban landscape, the criteria have been altered and the terminology adapted to the distinctive territorial conditions of the study area. In other words, although the machinic processes themselves are not site-specific, the local applications and resulting strategies are generated by the particularities of the Corniche El Nahr region.

Virtual Catchment System

The contemporary equivalent of industrial run-off, operational data flows out from various sites within the reprogrammed surface toward the river basin. A virtual catchment network composts the pulses like so much organic waste, redirecting them back into alternative nodes within the system to be reprocessed, thereby optimizing determinate production and minimizing indeterminate eco-contamination (Figure 7.3a).

Collective Distribution Network

Vectoral space among potential locales of development is textured through a system of triangulation, defining an envelope of continuity across otherwise isolated gaps in the urban field. A volumetric treatment additionally engenders contiguity among collective spaces and allows for a top-down distribution of resources to derelict sites (Figure 7.3b).

Reconstructive/Invasive Procedures

Building on the *city as body* metaphor from above, connective tissue is retrofitted arthroscopically into an aging and weakened skeletal/structural system, reinvigorating the body, renewing flexibility in movement, and rejuvenating the elasticity of nodes of the operational network. The resulting systems are better capable of managing saturation and fluctuations through improved resilience (Figure 7.3c).

Irrigating across Identities

Perceived neighborhood identity is clustered around nodes of operation and meshed with existing infrastructures. A process of extrusion and infill creates a synthetic programmable surface of collectivity. The horizontality of the resulting system canalizes resources and logistical networks through a strategy of linkage to irrigate the field with operational logics of potential (Figure 7.3d).

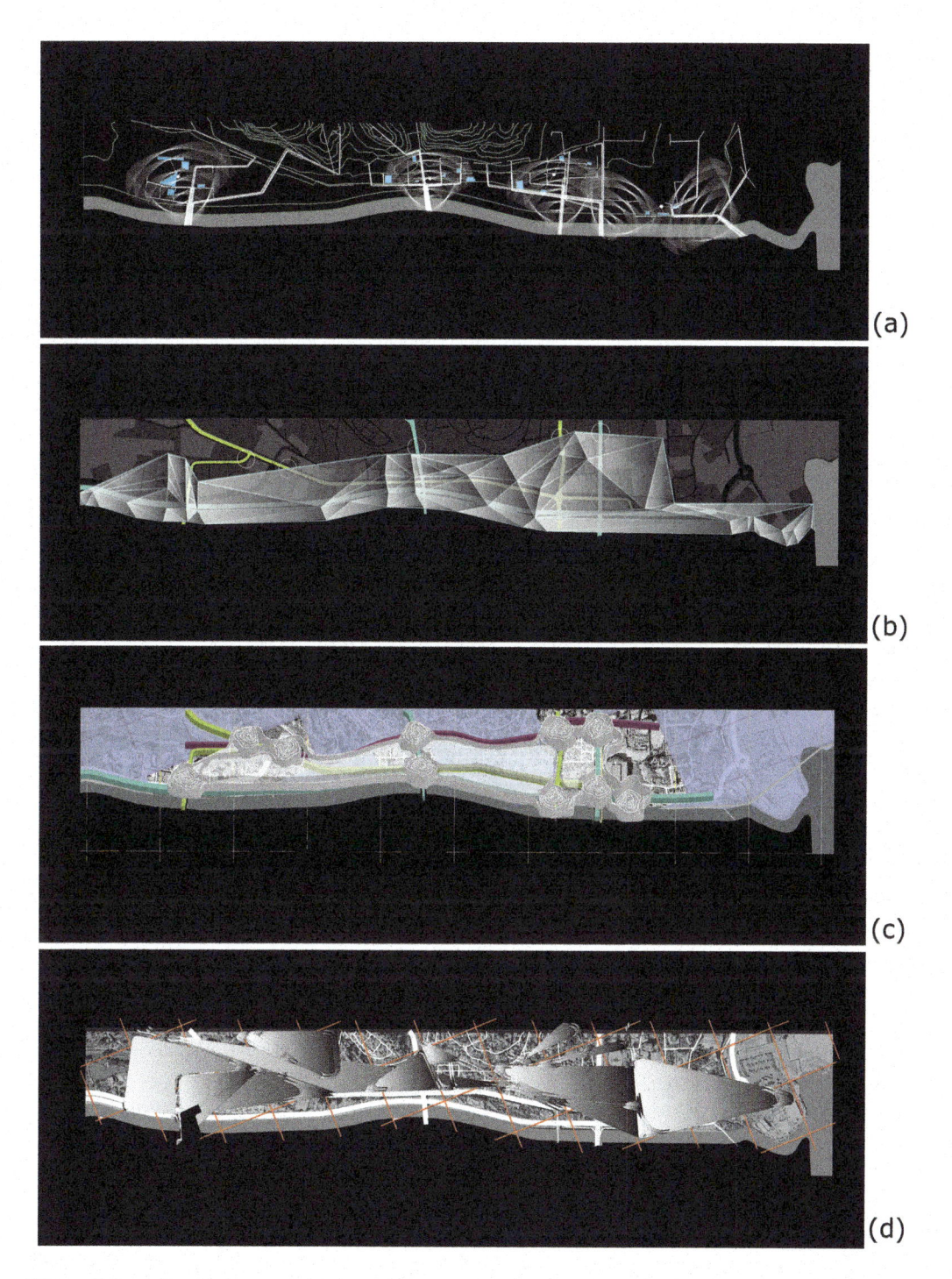

Figure 7.3 Synthetic ecologies
Note: (a) virtual catchment system; (b) collective distribution network; (c) reconstructive/invasive procedures; (d) irrigating across identities.
Source: Author.

Conclusions

The programming of these surfaces remains intentionally vague, with no definitive solutions prescribed. Instead, horizontal structuring functions as an open-ended strategy that provides the setting for a wide range of future activities, whether formal or casual, organized or spontaneous. It is precisely this type of indeterminate nature that confirms Landscape Urbanism as an appropriate tool for addressing marginality.

Nontraditional mapping provides an alternative understanding of the urban landscape, and although the project does not provide concrete answers to the myriad of problems facing Beirut's marginal spaces and communities, it *has* attempted to pose a new series of questions about the role of the study area within the city, to investigate urban space as a fertile ground for change, and to propose experimental models for rethinking the landscapes of uncertainty.

The (de)programmed surfaces proposed in this project should act as a catalyst for the development of the cultural infrastructure along the city's boundaries. But the forms, typologies and operating systems of this type of landscape modulation do not allow for the strict prescription of design interventions. Instead the work simply opens the range of possibilities, permitting what Rem Koolhaas refers to as the 'irrigation of territories with potential' (1998: 969). Whatever the final physical form of the Beiruti marginal landscape, the open-ended strategies proposed herein, and not conventional prescriptive schemes, should help to allow the relevant actors to proceed from within, themselves acting as catalysts for activating the synthetic ecologies of these new genre urban landscapes.

References

Baudelaire, C. 1986. *The Painter of Modern Life and Other Essays*. New York: DaCapo.
Benjamin, W. 1999. *The Arcades Project*. Cambridge, MA: Belknap Press of Harvard University Press.
Corner, J. 2003. Landscape Urbanism, in *Landscape Urbanism: A Manual for the Machinic Landscape*, edited by M. Mostafavi and C. Najle. London: Architectural Association, 58–63.
Corner, J. 2006. Terra Fluxus, in *The Landscape Urbanism Reader*, edited by C. Waldheim. New York: Princeton Architectural Press, 21–33.
Eisenmann, P. 2007. Processes of the Interstitial, in *Written into the Void: Selected Writings 1990–2004*. New Haven: Yale University Press, 50–71.
Frederix, L. 2010. Reclaiming Beirut's Marginal Landscape: Cultural Infrastructure as Urban Catalyst. MArch Thesis. Notre Dame University, Faculty of Art, Architecture, and Design.
Frem, S. 2009. Nahr Beirut: Projections on an Infrastructural Landscape. MS Thesis, Massachusetts Institute of Technology, Department of Architecture.
Gilloch, G. 1996. *Myth & Metropolis*. Cambridge: Polity Press.
Guattari, F. 1995. On Machines. *Journal of Philosophy and the Visual Arts*, 6, 8–12.
Knabb, K. (ed.) 1981. *Situationist International Anthology*. Berkeley: Bureau of Public Secrets.
Koolhaas, R. 1998. *S, M, L, XL*. 2nd Edition. New York: Monacelli.
Makhzoumi, J. and Pungetti, G. 1999. *Ecological Landscape Design and Planning*. London: E & FN Spon.
Mostafavi, M. and Najle, C. (eds) 2003. *Landscape Urbanism: A Manual for the Machinic Landscape*. London: Architectural Association.
Najle, C. 2003. System, in *Landscape Urbanism: A Manual for the Machinic Landscape*, edited by M. Mostafavi and C. Najle. London: Architectural Association, 63–75.
Vidler, A. 1992. *The Architectural Uncanny: Essays in the Modern Unhomely*. Cambridge, MA: MIT Press.
Waldheim, C. 2006. Landscape as Urbanism, in *The Landscape Urbanism Reader*, edited by C. Waldheim. New York: Princeton Architectural Press, 35–53.
Woods, L. 1992. *Anarchitecture: Architecture is a Political Act*. New York: St. Martin's Press.
Woods, L. 1997. *Radical Reconstruction*. New York: Princeton Architectural Press.

Chapter 8
Architectural Urbanism: Proposals for the Arab World

Sam Jacoby

The argument to unify the planning and design of cities gave birth in 1960 to a new academic field with practical orientation: urban design. The aim of the first urban design program at the Harvard Graduate School of Design was to combine a systematic conceptualization of the urban with its physical design by bringing together the disciplines of architecture, landscape architecture and city planning (Tyrwhitt 1962). Half a century later, this ambition seems largely replaced by a marketing-friendly beautification of failed or new urban plans, and the vague term *place-making* has become a popular excuse by urban designers to justify their involvement. Yet the importance to understand cities in their multi-scalar realities and simultaneously in conceptual and practical terms has remained, or even become more urgent with relentless urbanization. To consider this challenge not as the management of different disciplines but as the possibility of a cross-disciplinary framework raises the question of a shared knowledge. And architecture, having an established body of knowledge concerned with the theory, analysis and design of built form, offers a rational entry into the questions of what this shared knowledge could be.

Architecture's modern disciplinary knowledge principally originates from the abstractions afforded by typal reasoning, a primarily conceptual and systematic thinking, and typological reasoning, the diagrammatic and analytical resolution of formal models.[1] Essential to making this typo-diagrammatic knowledge available to the multi-scalar city is the premise that architecture does not only exist as a specific object at one scale, but as a generic possibility at many scales. If urbanity then can be said to emerge significantly from the synthesis of *fundamental types*—buildings and urban armatures critical to a city's formation—type can be defined as a specific spatial, socio-cultural and political product that as much derives from the city as it organizes its abstract idea, whereas typology enables the translation of generic into specific practice-driven and structural solutions. Therefore, both type and typology are interrelated and necessary to conceptualize, design and manage an urban plan, and suggest a concurrent reading of the city at different scales. With this, an analysis of the common organizational and structural diagrams of type, its *formative diagrams*, becomes critical to make typology translatable and operative to design. The methodology of typal and typological reasoning is grounded in architecture's disciplinary knowledge and, once extended to the scales of the city, can be termed *architectural urbanism*.[2]

In the following, the chapter develops what kind of project and research is associated with, or arises from, typological and architectural urbanism by discussing proposals for the Arab world by students from the Architectural Association's Diploma School and Projective Cities program.

The relations of fundamental types and their formative diagrams to an urban plan are revealed by an analysis of the church type and the urban history of Rome in Italy, which was significantly structured by the erection of more than 400 churches. In their study, Marcin Ganczarski and Yuwei Wang analyzed the Catholic church type based on the correlation of emitter and receiver—the spatial organization of altar, from which the service is led, and nave, where the congregation gathers for worship—which is prescribed by liturgical rules

---

1 This knowledge emerges from the eighteenth-century normative discourse in France. Of importance are the conclusions by Antoine-Chrysostome Quatremère de Quincy, who in his entry "Type" in the *Encyclopédie méthodique: Architecture* of 1825 argues for a new basis of architectural theory, and J.-N.-L. Durand's *typological* design method propounded in the *Précis des leçons d'architecture données à l'École polytechnique* (1802–5).

2 Compare with the concept of typological urbanism, dominant type and deep structure by Lee and Jacoby (2007, 2011).

and determines the orientation and relation of building elements, their structure and decoration and the use of void and light. The church is paradigmatic in its spatialisation and tectonic expression of social and political intentions. Marcin subsequently related the type study to the urban development of Rome. During the Roman Empire, the Aurelian Wall demarcated the open fields surrounding Rome as belonging to the city. Erected in the third century, the wall anticipated and defined the future growth of the city and its urbanity. While this idea of the city initially depended on an arrangement of common Roman armatures—important political and trade routes, forum, thermae, aqueduct, amphitheater and temple—beginning in the eighth and lasting to the fourteenth century, a radical transformation occurred. With rising Christianization, Medieval Rome witnessed the construction of churches at the crossing points of main roads. Each node defined a unified religious inner and secular outer space, the communal church and piazza, even if the church spatially, functionally and symbolically dominated the piazza. This created a legible network of streets and radial growth points around which urban blocks began to form. While in following periods, urban densification still employed the insertion of new churches, the intimate medieval relation of street-to-void organized by the piazza eventually failed; and the eighteenth-century piazza became effectively a transitional space that equally belonged to a local and urban scale. The piazza, which until then functioned as an exterior "holding" area for the sanctity of the church, became progressively secularized and evolved into a fundamentally different kind of public space—with the church gradually acting as a landmark or element subservient to the piazza (Figure 8.1).

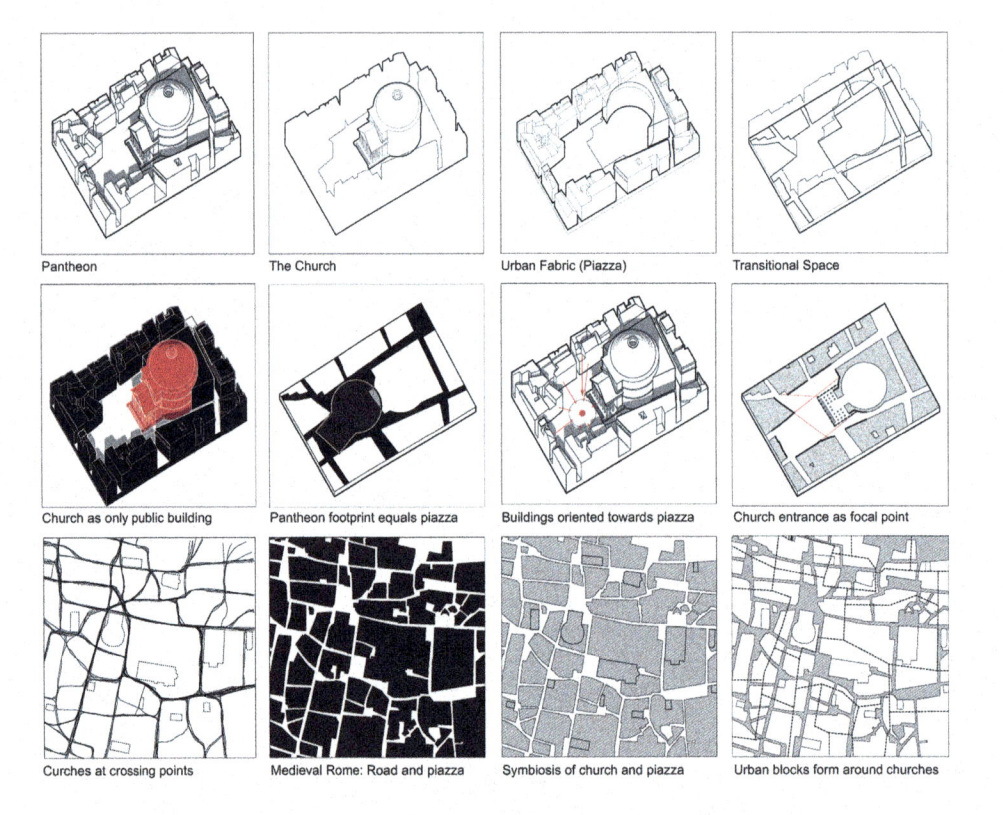

Figure 8.1 Marcin Ganczarski, changing relations between the church and piazza in Rome
Source: Projective Cities, Architectural Association 2012.

Architectural Urbanism

The transformation of the piazza was the result of urban rationalization, which gave birth to the fifteenth-century Renaissance Street that cut open existing, dense fabric and connected points of proposed significance where no urbanity yet existed. This created urban lines and restructured the city through a series of scenographic processions. But its aim was also to realize an urban concept of the public realm and express papal power. The new hierarchy depended on a basilica system, largely envisioned by Pope Sixtus V in the late sixteenth century, which established an urban circulation that made the fabrics around each church secondary parts to the whole. When in the nineteenth century the Italian nation-state formed, the Unitarian boulevard completed the process of rationalizing and secularizing the city, and streets became more than regulators of circulation by emerging as formative urban and public elements (Figure 8.2).

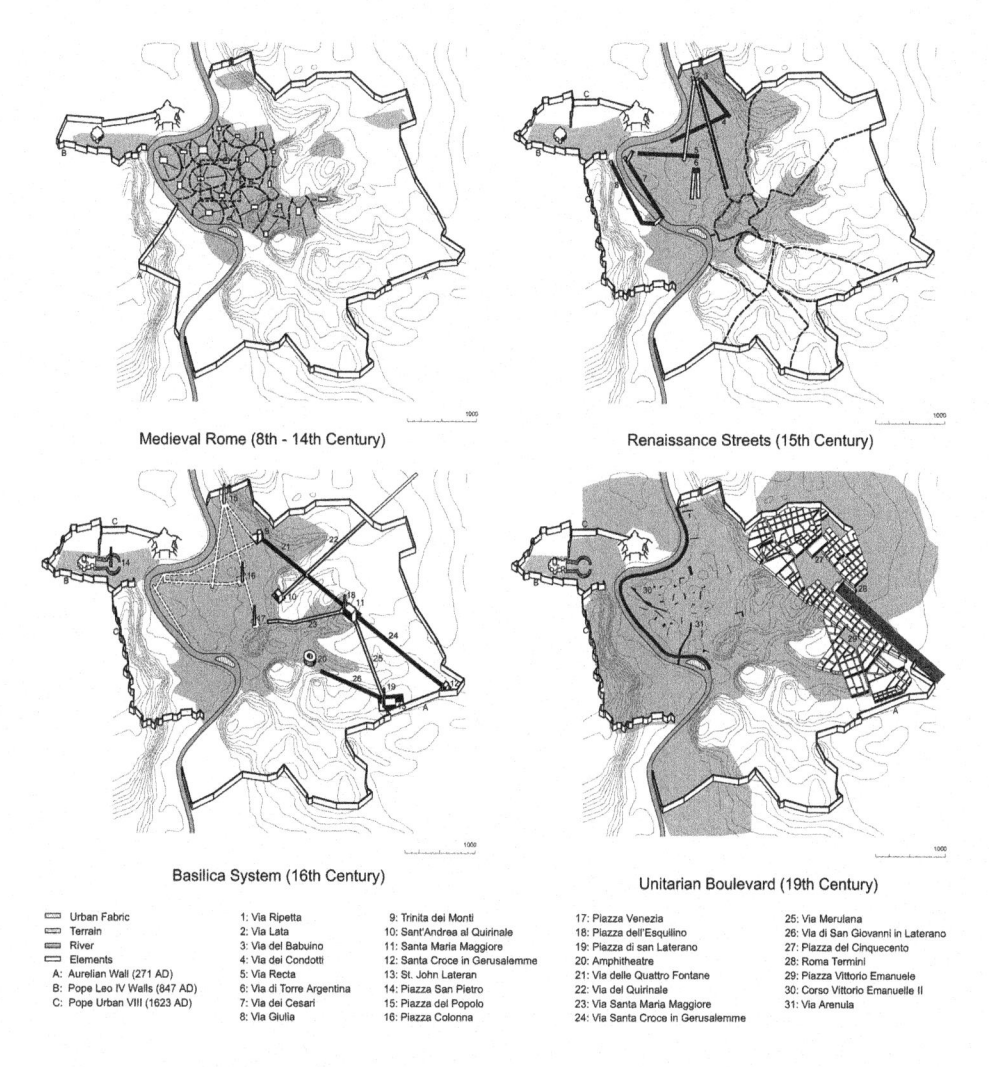

Figure 8.2   Marcin Ganczarski, urban transformation of Rome
Source: Projective Cities, Architectural Association 2012.

The analysis of the church type and the urban restructuring of Rome suggests that fundamental types are not fixed in their spatial and social meaning but transform and have over time a changing effect on the formation of the urban plan. The study of type and typology reveals the synergies between architecture and city, and makes them available to analysis. However, this analysis is not only instrumental to studies of the past, and one of the aims of architectural urbanism is to make it useful to current problems of design and planning. While the spatial transformations of Rome bears witness to a long process of urban rationalization and secularization, during which new public spaces emerged previously not imaginable or possible, parallels exist in the current problems faced by Makkah in Saudi Arabia. Comparable to Rome, its unique urban character is defined by it being a center of pilgrimage, yet its urban problems relate to the planning of a secular city.

The necessity on the one hand to manage a vast number of pilgrims, and on the other the difficulty to balance temporary infrastructural demands with a sustainable social and economic urban model, are the starting point for the project *The Holy City and Its Discontents* (2008) by Deena Fakhro. Makkah al-Mukarramah is host to one of the world's largest gatherings of humanity, when once a year around three million devout Muslims fulfill their duty of the fifth pillar of Islam: the Hajj. To facilitate the Hajj (and peak of the Umrah), the provincial city requires an enormous amount of infrastructure. With 90 percent of the modern pilgrims arriving by air, and cheap air fares the cause of an extraordinary increase in numbers, the airport in Jeddah is de facto the gateway to the city and its infrastructural weakest link. It has to deal with four million single visits over a period of two months. But the otherwise regional airport, along with other Hajj infrastructures that pilgrims depend on to complete the required ritual acts, is for most of the year redundant. These infrastructures are consequently an economic burden, with Saudi Arabia spending each year billions of US dollars to construct and maintain them.

These predicaments provoke the project to combine the economy of Makkah with regional ambitions to establish a globally competitive and Islamic knowledge economy—reducing dependence on a seasonal service industry. The feverish drive to build a new economy is evident in the projected total spending on planned developments around Makkah exceeding US$100 billion.[3] The project therefore sees the annual 90 percent underuse of Jeddah airport as an opportunity to reduce infrastructural redundancy and integrate the plans for a new King Abdulaziz International Airport with that for a knowledge economy and modern Islamic education. Following a type study of circular airports and historical Islamic universities, a hybrid model, part airport and university, is proposed. During the peaks of pilgrimage, which coincide with academic holidays, it works as an airport, while at all other times it functions as a university.

The project also questions the current development plans for a knowledge economy around Madinah and Makkah, as they are primarily based on generic campuses and business districts in tabula rasa sites. In response, three strategically located airport–universities in the valleys of Makkah are envisioned that re-establish three historically important gateways into the city from Jeddah, Madinah and Taif. This disperses incoming pilgrim flows and eases congestion, while defining a limit to the urban sprawl and restoring the ancient significance of the pilgrim's journey by heightening the experience of religious procession already on arrival to the Holy City.

For the proposed design, type studies of the Islamic university and circular airport are instrumental to develop a new organizational and spatial model. The traditional Islamic university, for example the Al-Azhar University in Cairo, the oldest still functional university in the world, was established in the early 970s as a *madrasa* and formed around an earlier founded mosque. The complementarity between a center of learning and religion, the *madrasa* and mosque, which function as an urban and public node within a dense fabric often enclosed by a limiting city wall, is typical for the historical Islamic university and city.[4] The regular distribution of classrooms around a central courtyard and mosque nevertheless creates an internal hierarchy of varied building elements with programs layered around a single core which, despite a radial arrangement, establish a clear urban orientation (Figure 8.3a).

---

3 These include a US$7 billion Knowledge Economic City in Madinah, the US$86 billion King Abdullah Economic City, a US$10 billion King Abdullah University of Science and Technology, and the US$3 billion Um Al-Qura Economic City in Makkah.

4 For example the sixteenth-century *Çoban Mustafa Paşa Complex* or Sokollu Mehmet Paşa Complex in Istanbul.

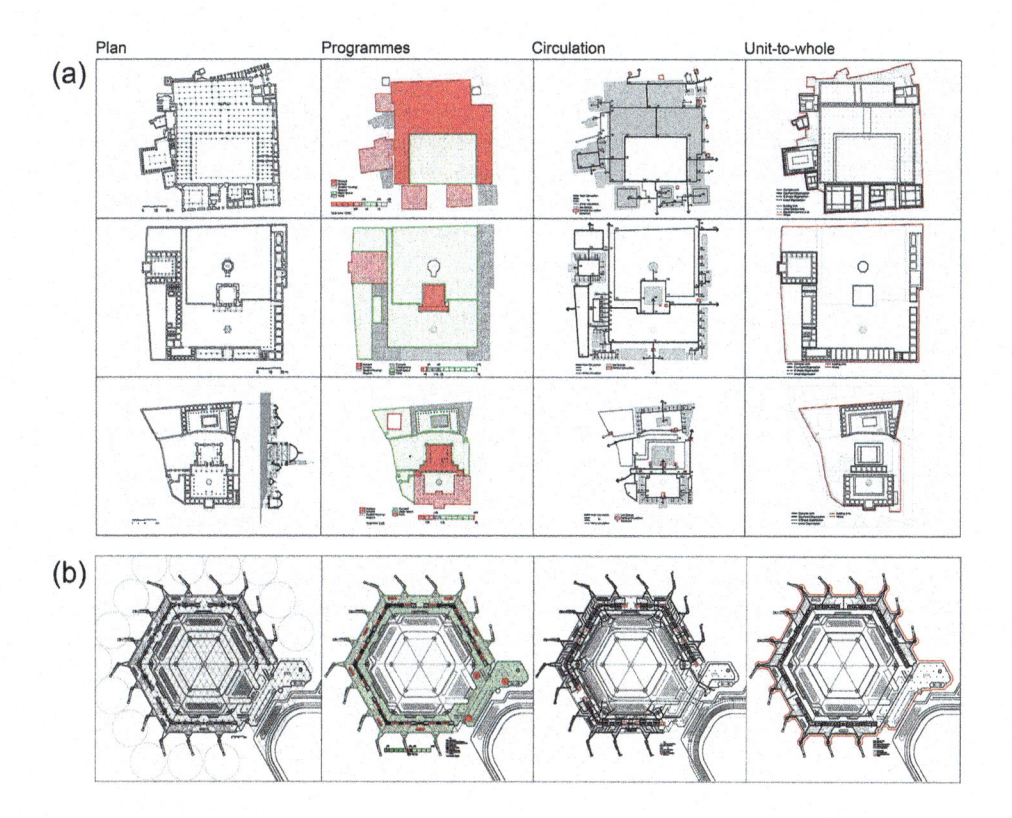

Figure 8.3   Deena Fakhro, typological analysis
Note: (a) the Islamic University: Al-Azhar Mosque (Cairo, 988), Çoban Mustafa Pasa Complex (Turkey, 1523) and Sokollu Mehmet Pasa Complex (Turkey, 1571); (b) Tegel Airport (Berlin, 1975).
Source: Diploma Unit 6, Architectural Association 2008.

In comparison, the circular airport, such as Charles de Gaulle's Terminal 1 in Paris and Berlin Tegel, has two distinct directions and layers, the airside and landside, but no meaningful organizational hierarchy or variation in its building units (Figure 8.3b). Tegel's efficient circulation between airside and landside is separated by a thin security threshold, as the airport is a vestige of a glamorous age of aviation, whose model is today economically redundant with airport operators making their profit from shopping malls inserted into an enlarged security zone.

Yet, organizational diagrams common to the two types allow a typological transformation of the airport by overlaying a mosque-school (Figure 8.4). The hybrid has at its center a mosque, encircled by the airport, with the landside facing the mosque and the airside located on its outer periphery. They form between them a thickened security buffer that during peak times, when functioning as an airport, becomes the arrival and departure area, and after programmatically switching to a university, reveals a cellular network of public and semi-public spaces in which classrooms and university facilities are grouped around internal courtyards. The mosque and airport ultimately form a new urban core and the university acts like a *walled city* through which future growth is controlled.

For the detailed design of the airport–universities (Figure 8.5), the project uses the peak demand of 20,000 daily passengers per airport to determine the number of airport gates, and the student population of 10,000 to calculate the growth limit of each university. But in order to emphasize the building's orientation to Makkah and, more importantly the Kaaba, the donut-shaped *aerotropolis* is off-centered and articulates an urban direction. The entrance to the airport–university opens into a large space evocative of a hypostyle hall, while the undulating ground floor level creates an open, public ground with its highest and central point marked by the mosque. From the distribution ring enclosing the central courtyards and mosque, the airport gates are accessed via spiralling ramps, and a double tier of structural arches lift the building above the public ground to permit direct access from the outside. Between these arches and along the circulation ramps that cross the inner courtyards, the airport services and facilities are inserted, with passengers in their circular movement through the building echoing the processions of the Hajj.

After the programmatic switch to the university, the building's organization changes from one regulated by security to one structured by a sequence of internal courtyards and transversal secondary circulation. The airport with efficient linear connections converts into a campus, and to the occupants meandering through the courtyards a differentiated, interior fabric with public and academic activities is revealed—a fabric familiar from the traditional Arab city. Then the mosque is not just an orienting landmark but also an activator of the public ground. With the airport–universities restoring important city gateways and maintaining the historical limits and legibility of the Holy City, they reinstate an ancient relationship between gateway and city, and pilgrim and pilgrimage.

The project for Makkah demonstrates how through an abstraction of formative diagrams, typologies can be analyzed but also transformed and projected. However, the study of types also reveals a tension between their conceptualizations, one speculative and typal and the other material and typological, which simultaneously operate at architectural and urban scales. For that reason, design is always both a theoretical and specific investigation of build form, through which the city is considered as an architectural project and architecture as a project for the city. Thus two interrelated methodologies can be posited. One concerned with the study of fundamental types through the analysis of their formative diagrams and relations to the urban plan; and another that speculates on a typological transformation in order to project a diagram of the city.

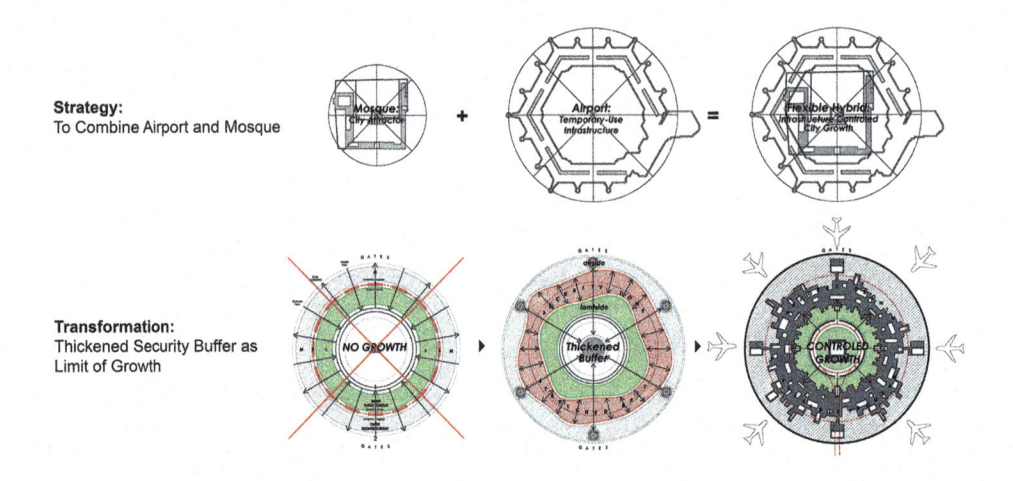

Figure 8.4 Deena Fakhro, typological transformation of the airport to an Islamic walled city and university

Source: Diploma Unit 6, Architectural Association 2008.

Architectural Urbanism 103

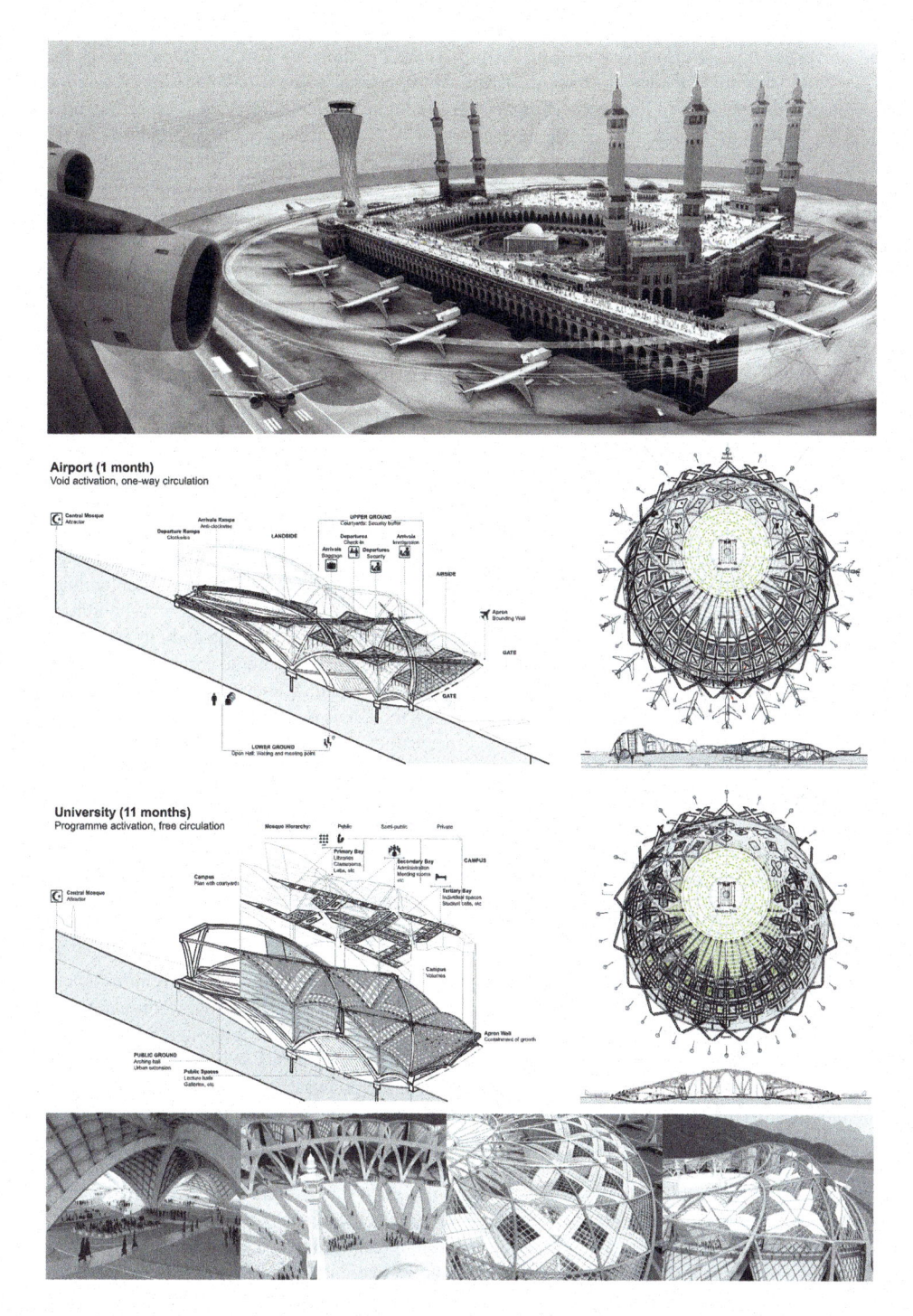

Figure 8.5   Deena Fakhro, airport–university in Makkah
Note: Collage (top); programmatic switch from airport to university showing typical fragment and upper ground floor plan (middle); 3D views (bottom).
Source: Diploma Unit 6, Architectural Association 2008.

The university type is also considered in the project *Re-Framing the City: A Monument of Radical Neutrality* (2009) by Fadi Mansour, however not as an *aerotropolis* but *univerCity* (Figure 8.6). The difficulty to conceptualize the meaning of the public and public spaces in the contemporary city is especially apparent in Beirut, as provisions commonly considered the responsibility of the state are surrendered to private initiatives and investment. Challenging this condition, the project argues for the former void of the Green Line to be transformed into a public infrastructure under the auspices of the Lebanese University, the only public institution for higher learning in Lebanon. Despite observing that in Beirut all territories are marked and occupied by political and religious factions, demarcated during the Lebanese Civil War from 1975 to 1990, the project posits the Green Line as the last neutral, if abandoned, ground that separates East and West Beirut. Taking the American University of Beirut (AUB) as a paradigm of how an academic institution is able to operate without factional allegiances and offer a refuge for public debates by maintaining a (privatized) neutral void, the proposal is to strategically transform the Green Line into a city-campus that will seed a multiplicity of public activities and attract different constituencies.

Although the city can be read as a series of material and immaterial boundaries and divisions, the Green Line as a void and the AUB as a gated enclave are examples of a public realm that challenges conventions. The AUB supports the argument that education offers a new functional public space in Beirut and that different private stakeholders and constituencies play an important role in their provision and maintenance. This radicalizes the concepts of neutrality.

The design of the city-campus derives from a study of mat-buildings, which in their conception as part city and part building are prototypical models indexing both the material specificity of architectural design and the infrastructural possibilities of an urban fabric. This lends itself to the project's ambitions of an architecture capable of establishing a large-scale public infrastructure in a city that has none. The mat-building is an urban form with a horizontal low-rise expansion in which interior space, landscape and city are interlaced and organized by a unifying system of repetitive modules. Accordingly, a structural system deriving from the unit of the Venice Hospital project by Le Corbusier of 1965 is developed. After analyzing its planar pinwheel organization around a vertical structural shaft, Le Corbusier's module is transformed into a three-dimensional spiral that acts as the superstructure of the proposed megastructure and the different layers of circulation through the city and campus. Two pinwheels extending in different directions are superimposed—with a tall, narrow spiral inserted into a short and wide one—in order to avoid a stacking of program and circulation. The four arms of the lower spirals are connected and articulated as storey-high structural beams with in-between spaces triangulated and cross-braced to form an undulating thickened platform filled with university programs. Similarly, the taller spirals form an upper, programmed platform for the campus, creating above it an open, and below it a covered, landscaped deck accessible to the public. These decks are the incubators of public program and invite different stakeholders to partake in an urban redevelopment under the protection of the institutional campus.

The building system, composed of inverted conical modules of different sizes, covers an entire city quarter. Scattered along the former Green Line, the spirals connect the two elevated campus platforms and the public landscapes with the street level. Along the raised landscapes, the megastructure frames views of the city and remaining scarred urban tissue. These destroyed and abandoned war remnants are rehabilitated, annexed or maintained as monuments to the recent past. The structures of the proposal strategically touch the ground in building plots destroyed by the civil war and provide spaces for new public programmes at street level. Above it, the campus platforms appear as a thin, hovering slab that forms a continuous and raised new Green Line. Pathways stitch existing and proposed structures and public programs, with the porous platforms creating urban fragments linked by voids through which natural light reaches the ground and enters into the campus.

Composed by layers of circulation and volumetric modules, the campus is envisioned as a double "High Line"; and reinforcing the edges of the Green Line, it reinterprets the void characterizing the territory as a sectional condition. Arguing for political and social autonomy as conditional to academic institutionalization, the city-campus converts a former zone of conflict into a neutral and mediating section in which public exchange and coexistence that otherwise could not exist becomes possible. The proposal maintains the significance of the void but transforms it into a permanent monument formed by collective urban spaces.

Similar to the city-campus, the project *From City of Capital to Capital City* (2013) by Yasmina El Chami examines the idea of coexistence in Beirut by exploring the potential of architecture to shape and acquire

Architectural Urbanism 105

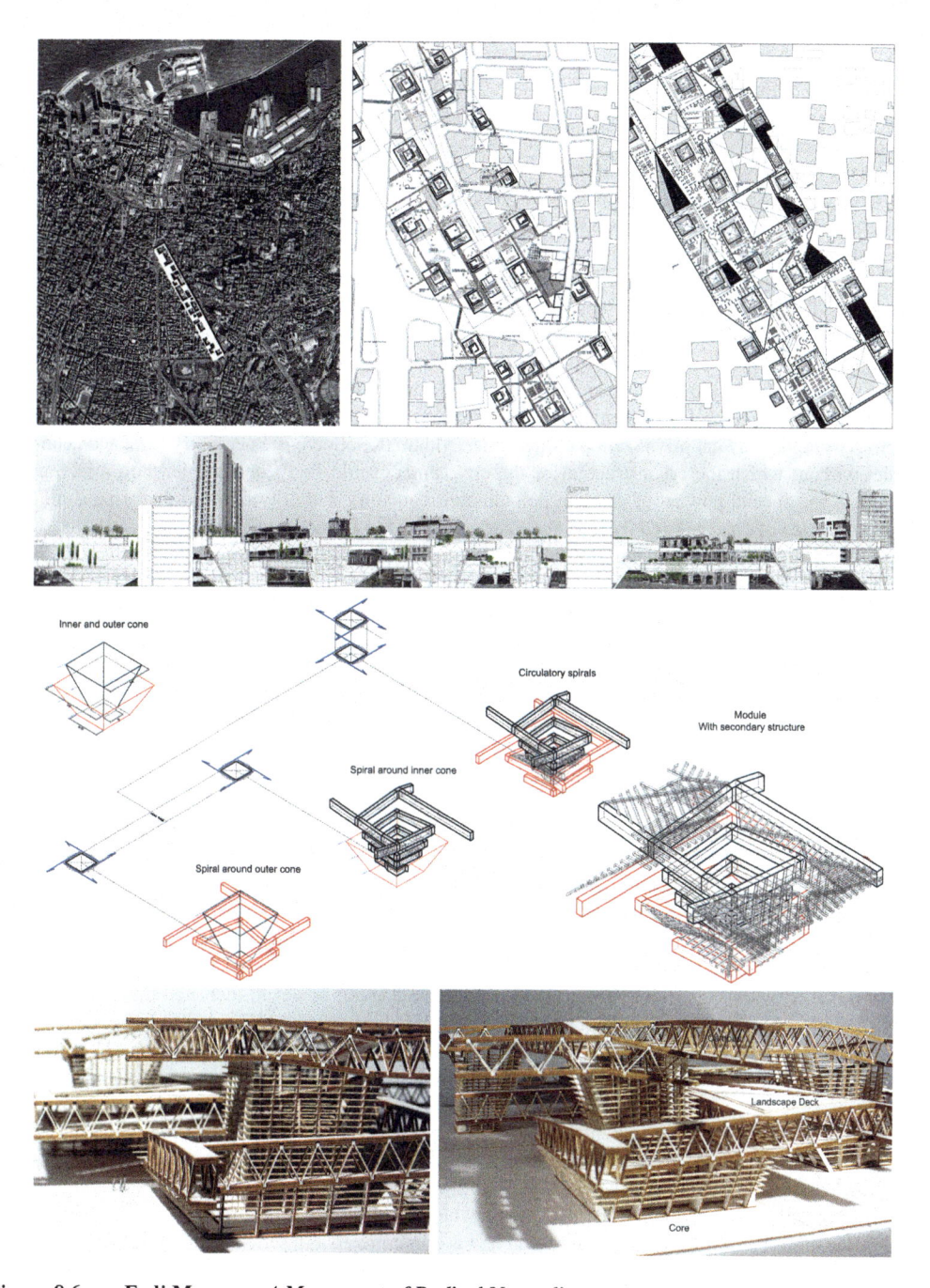

Figure 8.6 Fadi Mansour, *A Monument of Radical Neutrality*
Note: Collage and ground and campus plan (top); site section (below); typical structural module (middle); fragment models (bottom).
Source: Diploma Unit 6, Architectural Association 2009 (collage based on Google Earth image).

political agency. Specifically, it looks at the role of architecture in the construction of the capital city and questions its ability to either form or signify the state. This is particularly problematic in Lebanon, a weak state that—20 years after the civil war—is still coming to terms with sectarian divisions and political corruption (Figure 8.7a).

Given the state's failure to form a Lebanese statehood, the project argues for a reversal of the architectural notion of nation building—commonly seen as the project of the capital city itself. The premise for this reversal is the understanding of two related processes, the *symptom* and the *symbol*, as representational dimensions of power in the architecture of capital cities (Sonne 2003). Political power can be examined after the fact, as a symptom of specific policies or rules, or before the fact, as an intentional projection of the identity and ideology of a state. This distinction is important to understand the idea of the capital city not as symbolic urban gestures but as spaces of negotiation and decision-making in which the state is not an abstract entity but actively forms and sustains a shared political identity. Power thus obtains spatial reality when it is symptomatic and obtains a precise spatial articulation that productively frames societal and political relations. Consequently, the project criticizes the masterplan of Beirut's city center by the real estate management company Solidere, as it effectively proposes a total privatization of the center. Although Solidere is a necessary legal and economic construct without which the reconstruction of the city center would be inconceivable, the project argues that not only the special powers of eminent domain and regulatory authority but also the responsibility to reconstruct an idea of citizenry and collectivity were transferred to the company by the state.

The site of the proposal is along the east of Martyrs' Square and surrounding archaeological sites at the eastern edge of the city center, a tabula rasa created by the civil war but equally by Solidere's post-war extensive site clearance. Martyrs' Square is the oldest civic center of the city, was a battlefield during the war and today is still a significant place for political rallies (Figure 8.7a). Deliberately compromised in its urban and political significance by Solidere's plans, this counter-project reclaims the square's role as a primordial civic space. Observing Solidere's commercial strategy and zoning for exclusive private housing, a complementary series of public, institutional and educational spaces is proposed, which are to re-establish an active participation of the state in the supposedly private–public joint venture in order to form a new common ground that functions beyond sectarian identifications and class distinctions.

Based on an analysis of the city center through its dominant (domestic) type—the Lebanese central hall—a transformed type operating at both urban and architectural scales is proposed (Figure 8.7b). The central hall type is exemplary of a finely calibrated relationship between private and public spheres and embodies a familial and patrimonial structure of Lebanese society, with its typological evolution reflecting urban and social changes. While the original introverted type represented the social diagram of a society formed around the individual family unit, its orientation toward the street in the Ottoman period signified a new social exchange in which the relation between the individual and society became important. The transformation of the central hall to an office building during the French mandate era, however, indicated that the individual unit had lost its meaning as an urban structure and was replaced by a modern French form of urban planning that aimed for large-scale rationalization. This loss of structural significance was completed by Solidere's reduction of the central hall to a façade and the introduction of a larger urban grain that could fulfill the requirements of generic offices and corporate investment (Figure 8.7a).

Opposing this form of development, the project understands the possibility of the political in a new secular city center as dependent on a synthesis between the domestic sphere of the individual and a public space of coexistence. A relationship between citizens and society that is explored through the design of the central hall type. Notions of family and patrimony, which underlie the still ongoing political conflicts, no longer define this relationship. Instead, the central hall is reinterpreted as a series of individual frames, which through repetition form larger, articulated spaces. These typological transformations respond to urban and architectural constraints, creating several hierarchical and scalar transitions between the unit of the individual and the public city. The transformations exploit the type's structure by translating load-bearing walls as a differentiated and directed column grid. The abstraction of the central hall type into a series of twisting and thickening walls allow formal articulations that range from a column and arch to a wall with different porosities. This permits the preservation of specific views across Martyrs' Square and creates differentiated enclosures and multi-directionality both in plan and section. Through an accumulation of frames and building units, and by enlarging the distance between structural walls, differently sized (public) programs

Architectural Urbanism 107

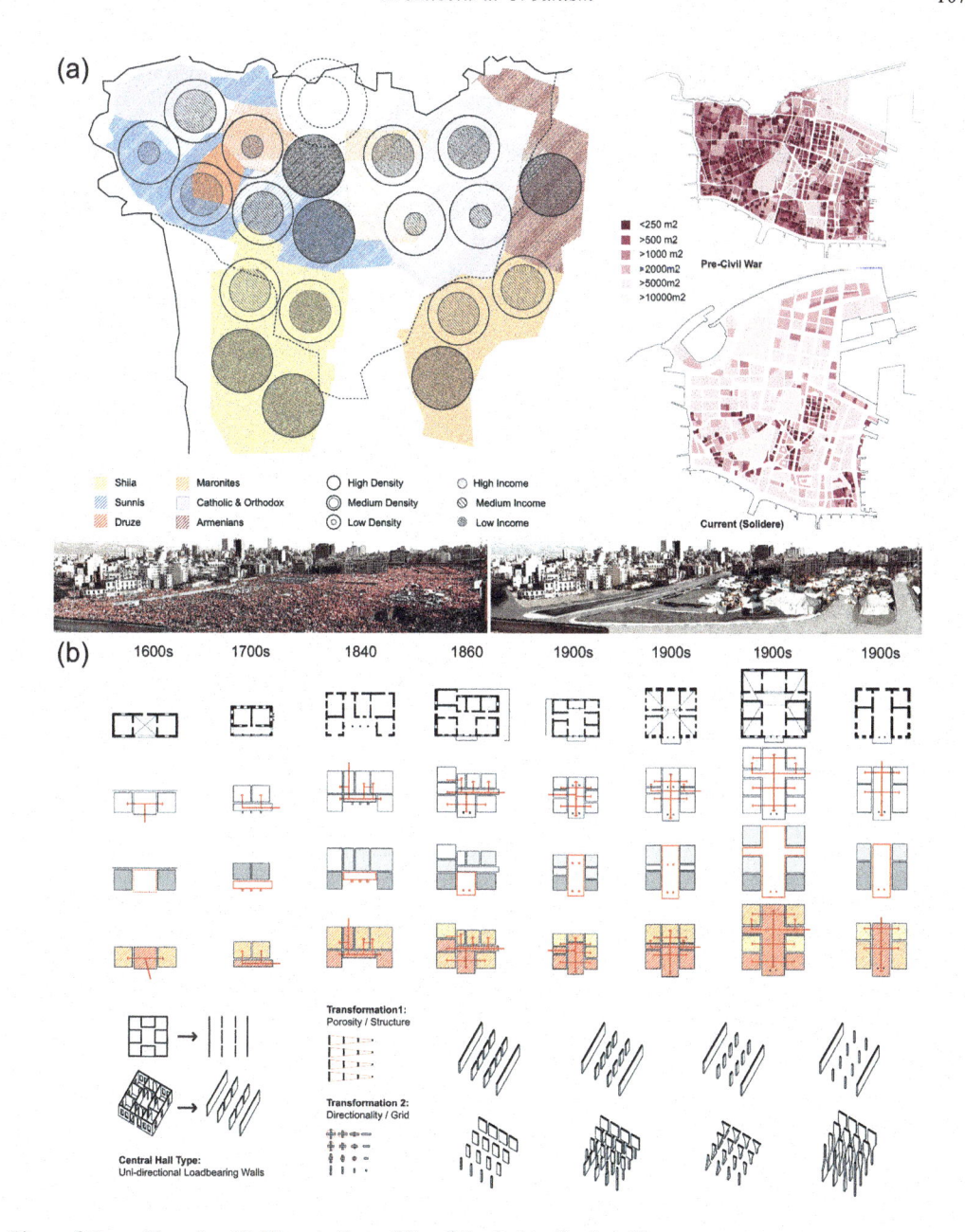

Figure 8.7   Yasmina El Chami, *From City of Capital to Capital City*
Note: (a) sectarian enclaves in Beirut after the civil war (top) and change of urban fabric after Solidere (left); anti-Syrian protest in 2005 following the assassination of Rafic Hariri, and pro-Syrian occupation in 2006–8 of Martyrs' Square (below); (b) the central hall type: historical analysis and typological transformation from central hall to directional frame.
Source: Projective Cities, Architectural Association 2013.

can be accommodated. Thus the typology becomes a structural model through which urban and architectural hierarchies, and porosities and directions that frame public and political life within the specific context of the site, are realized. This typological reasoning is the formal basis to rethink the capital campus as a multi-scalar relationship of institutional, urban and private spaces and their embedded social exchanges.

At the urban scale, the area around Martyrs' Square is an important entry and transition point between the highway at the edge of the city center and the Garden of Forgiveness, a large archaeological site that severs the square from the reconstructed area around the French Place de l'Etoile. The urban strategy of the proposal (Figure 8.8a) therefore introduces in addition to the existing south–north axis from the square toward the Mediterranean Sea an east–west axis. This produces a layered urban fabric around Martyrs' Square, which consists of underground car parking and vehicular access, a new public ground at the level of the archaeological sites that forms a plinth and through its east–west orientation links the proposal with the Etoile conservation area, the Tell of Beirut, the Garden of Forgiveness and the small-scale urban fabric to the east. The top of the plinth is at the level of Martyrs' Square, which forms an upper ground level with a south–north orientation and is defined by first a layer of public programs and then a layer of institutional, educational and administrative functions. Above this is the private housing required by Solidere's masterplan and its economic strategy (Figure 8.8c).

The main proposed building mass around Martyrs' Square is divided into three strips, with a central public spine running parallel to the square and forming two neighborhoods, one related to the highway and Gemmayzeh beyond and another facing the square and the historic center (Figure 8.8b). The central spine responds to surrounding buildings, archaeological sites and existing streets by creating open spaces and pedestrian links. At the lower and upper public ground level, a series of perpendicular souqs are inserted that connect the levels of the archaeological sites and Martyrs' Square, while following the existing complex topography. The new souqs contain the most public spaces and programs, and pedestrian access to the residential and institutional programs above. Following the direction of the souqs, the three urban strips are most porous along the square and public spine. The largest and fully enclosed programs, for example auditoriums, theaters and exhibition spaces, are placed in the center of the strips to maintain porosity at the edges. Thus, the central hall exists both at the neighborhood and block scale, with each block consisting again of three parallel strips with a large street or public space in its center.

The transition from the public ground to the institutional, educational and administrative levels above, which are arranged around voids opening to the public ground below, creates a change of orientation toward the sea and is enabled by twisting the structure. Whereas the institutional spaces are organized along central corridors aligned with a south–north direction, the educational spaces are oriented perpendicularly and face interior courtyards or the spine and square. Finally, institutional and educational spaces are separated from the top layer of private housing by another shared but less public level. This is mainly accessible to residents and marks another directional shift with an east–west orientation. The clusters of residential units are in turn oriented toward the north–south visual corridors, in order to provide double aspect viewing of the sea from the central hall housing.

The project understands the idea of the central hall as the most "public" space within a private environment at different scales. At the city scale, when forming a larger public realm, it informs the urban plan, the neighborhood and the block, but at an architectural scale it defines the building and finally the unit itself. This gives the articulation of public spaces hierarchy and differentiation. The public spine and square hereby create the most important relationships between the individual strip and the block, the individual block and adjoining blocks and the spine and finally between the spine and the square. Thus, the *symptomatic* is interpreted through the central hall type as a singular form capable of realizing through its strategic deployment across scales, a future diagram of the city. The *symbolic* then only exists when the whole is completed, when associations between individuals, individuals and institutions, and institutions themselves result in a new public formation: that of the state. This understands the contemporary capital city less as an administrative center than as a concentration of human capital and knowledge. Through a typological reasoning, the project acquires the specificities of architectural language and is thus able to overcome the distance between the symptomatic and symbolic—which relies on a formal representation. Type becomes an alternative to language in the search for a state and a national identity. However, this also implies that the conception of the capital city can never be purely symptomatic or symbolic.

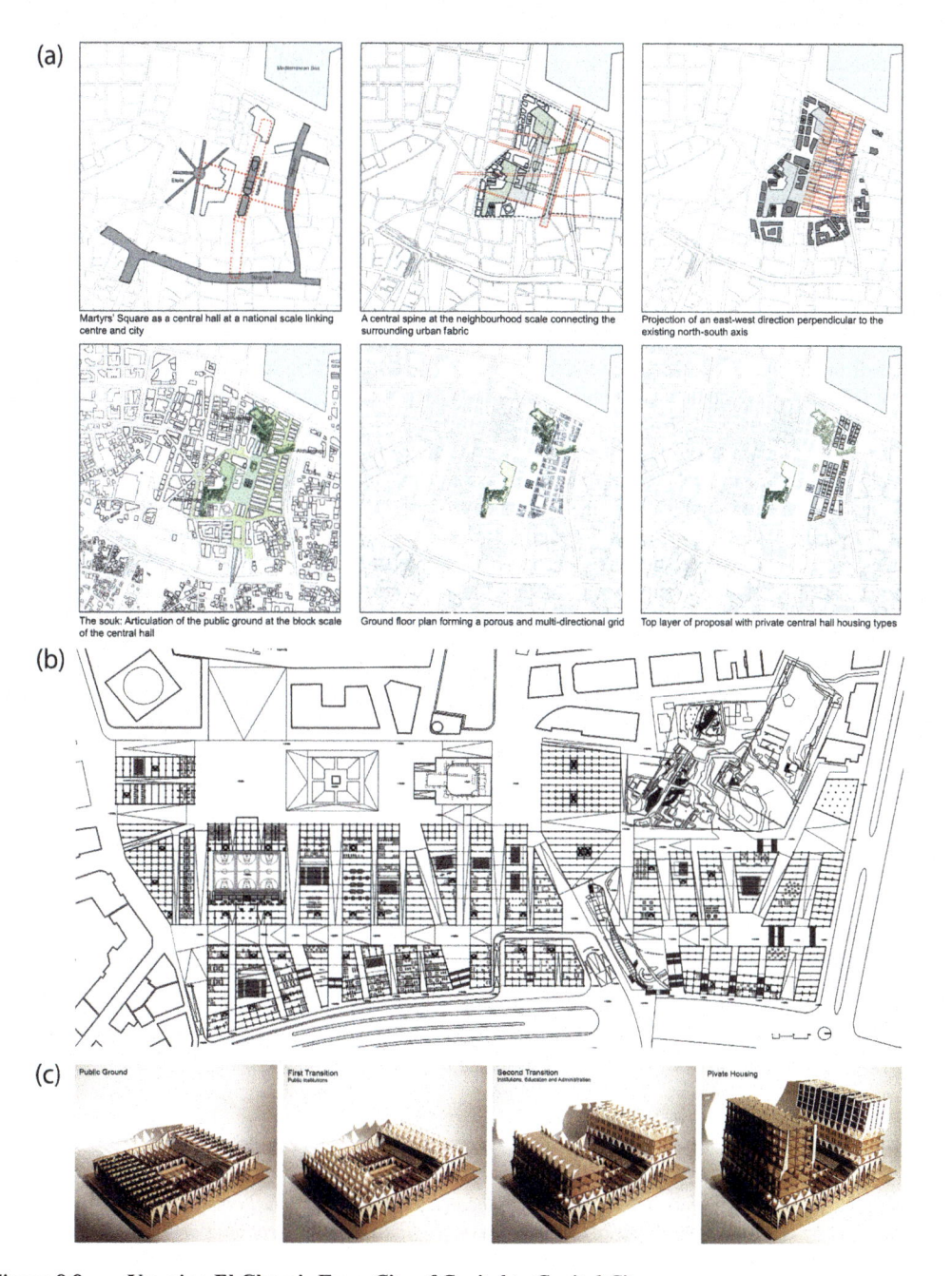

Figure 8.8 Yasmina El Chami, *From City of Capital to Capital City*
Note: (a) urban strategy and central hall at multiple scales; (b) ground floor as porous fabric linking square and the city; (c) urban massing model showing layering of typical fragment.
Source: Projective Cities, Architectural Association 2013.

In conclusion, having studied the life of built form through typal and typological reasoning, several observations can be made. Type is fundamentally autonomous of function and scale, and its organizational or structural thinking precedes formal realization. This does not mean that architecture and city have no qualitative or quantitative difference but that type and typology offer an understanding of how their layered and multi-scalar relations are conceived and regulated. Thus, form is not a direct product of type but rather its diagrammatic possibility.[5] While type is always implied in a design, often by unconsciously comparing or classifying the formal objects under consideration, type remains irreducible to a design method or an instance. Although we rely on received forms and established norms transmitted by typological knowledge, we are free to fulfill or reject them. In fact, invention requires by definition their disintegration. Type's significance is consequently its analytical potential and the possibility to reflect on principles of formation that connect invention to disciplinary reasoning. Accordingly, we can understand Antoine-Chrysostome Quatremère de Quincy's distinction between type and model, which is critical to the first construction of an *architectural system* at the turn of the nineteenth century, as necessary to formulate an idea of architecture, but also as continuously concretized and challenged by the development of models.[6] Therefore the analysis of types should not just consider the formative diagrams or syntactic-tectonic organization of build form, but ought to critically assess the physical, cultural and socio-political context in which they exist, in order to make architectural urbanism relevant to the contemporary city.

While a typal and typological reasoning is methodologically general, it becomes specific when considering a particular context, such as Makkah and Beirut. At least within the contexts of the three discussed projects, the need for a secular city with a sustainable social and economic future emerged. Through this we can propose new public realms and specific constituencies, imagine stakeholders and reason for their maintenance. The important process of urban transformation from a religious to a secular city was exemplified by Rome, but raises, as the project by Yasmina for a capital city proposed, a more fundamental and difficult question that urban planners and designers should address in the context of the contemporary city, that of the rather symptomatic than symbolic. Type and typology offered to all three projects a different framework to conceive the symptomatic. Aldo Rossi thus referred to type as the "analytical moment of architecture," from which the knowledge and possibility of new spatial and collective realities derive, adding that they are "readily identifiable at the level of urban artifacts" (1982: 41). In other words, a rethinking of types is a means available to architectural urbanism to consider a shared, disciplinary knowledge and synthesize architecture, landscape architecture and city planning.

Acknowledgement

None of the work discussed in this chapter would not exist without the insights and dedication of students, or the vital contribution by my former colleague Christopher Lee. My project descriptions rely on those by their authors. Especially Yasmina El Chami and Fadi Mansour provided me with texts that I used at times verbatim.

References

Durand, J.-N.-L. 1802–5. *Précis des leçons d'architecture données à l'École Polytechnique*. Paris: Author. Translated by D. Britt 2000. *Précis of the Lectures on Architecture with Graphic Portion of the Lecture on Architecture*. Los Angeles: The Getty Research Institute.

Lee, C. and Jacoby, S. (eds) 2007. *Typological Formations: Renewable Building Types and the City*. London: AA Publications.

---

5 This diagrammatic practice is anticipated by J.-D. Le Roy in *Les Ruines des plus beaux monuments de la Grèce* (1758) and advanced in Durand's methodological understanding of genre in his *Précis*.

6 As Quatremère states in his dictionary entry *Type*: "the word *type* presents less the image of the thing to copy or imitate completely, than the idea of an element which must itself serve as a rule for the model" (Younés 2000: 254).

Lee, C. and Jacoby, S. 2011. Introduction: Typological Urbanism and the Idea of the City. *Architectural Design* [online], 81(1), 14–23. Available at: http://onlinelibrary.wiley.com/doi/10.1002/ad.1184/pdf [accessed: July 19, 2013].

Rossi, A. 1982. *The Architecture of the City*. D. Ghirardo and J. Ockman (trans.). Cambridge, MA: MIT Press.

Sonne, W. 2003. *Representing the State: Capital City Planning in the Early Twentieth Century*. Munich: Prestel.

Tyrwhitt, J. 1962. Education for Urban Design. *Journal of Architectural Education* (1947–1974) [online], 17(3), The Architect and the City. The 1962 AIA-ACSA Seminar Papers Presented at the Cranbrook Academy of Art, Part II (December 1962), 100–101. Available at: http://www.jstor.org/stable/1424105 [accessed: August 25, 2013].

Younés, S. 2000. *The True, the Fictive and the Real: The Historical Dictionary of Architecture of Quatremère De Quincy*. London: Papadakis Publishers.

PART III
The Operational: Bridging Boundaries between Research and Practice

Chapter 9

Aleppo 2025 City Development Strategy: A Critical Reflection

Ali Saad and Thomas Stellmach

Preface

As part of the Aleppo Urban Development Project, a joint undertaking by the Aleppo municipality and German Technical Cooperation (GIZ),[1] this chapter discusses the spatial strategy of the project (Figure 9.1) that aimed at articulating a long-term vision for sustainable development at a city scale. The study, carried out by the firm Uberbau,[2] acknowledged the existing dynamics shaping the city as the base for defining future spatial qualities and for steering urban development. It proposed the reorganization of the existing spatial structure based on Aleppo's socio-economic and environmental potentials in order to ground the future strategy in the reality of the city. The work resulted in a final report, the urban spatial component of the Aleppo City Development Strategy (CDS) that was delivered in February 2010 (Saad and Stellmach 2010). A major contribution of this German–Syrian cooperative effort was transparency in decision-making and a flexible strategic approach—as opposed to another masterplan—in order to target a dominant culture of over-regulation that had proven to be non-operational given the overwhelming informality of Aleppo's growth.

This chapter is intended as a critical summary of the initial report organized in four sections. The first section develops the overall approach to the study. The second section explains the main findings of the urban analysis. The third section outlines the five thematic concerns related to sustainable growth on which the whole study was based, and a final section concludes.

It is worth noting that the work was developed before the eruption of the tragic events in March 2011 that led to the ongoing civil war in Syria; accordingly most of the facts mentioned in this chapter are based on this period. Due to the lack of clear information at this stage, it is very difficult to give any precise statement on the city's actual or future situation beyond the widely accepted fact that it is being devastated. Nevertheless this chapter will conclude with a careful assessment of the legacy of the urban spatial vision in relation to a future reconstruction of the city by asking what the main spatial challenges will be in a post-conflict Aleppo, and in what ways the Aleppo CDS could be relevant to the reconstruction process.

From Masterplan to Sustainability Strategy

The key challenge of the CDS was to bridge between the ambitions of the municipality, GIZ, and the other stakeholders. For a successful implementation of the spatial strategy it was considered paramount to enable cooperation across the academic, private and public sectors, that is, a research-based approach that encouraged the joint development of ideas (Figure 9.2). Horizontally linking the understanding of these sectors—commercial experience with academic knowledge—is the only way to achieve continued sustainable

---

1 The Aleppo Urban Development Project promoted sustainable urban management and development. The Aleppo City Development Strategy (CDS) process was co-funded by the Cities Alliance (2006), the Deutsche Gesellschaft für Technische Zusammenarbeit (GTZ), and the City of Aleppo. Besides an urban spatial component, it also integrated other sectors, such as local governance, urban economy and service provision. The GTZ has since merged with two other public development agencies and was renamed the Gesellschaft für Internationale Zusammenarbeit (GIZ) in January 2011. This new appellation will be used throughout the chapter.

2 Berlin-based Uberbau is the practice of Ali Saad and Thomas Stellmach that specializes in research-based strategic urbanism and architecture, http://www.uberbau.eu.

Figure 9.1   The visual landscape of Aleppo
Note: Aerial perspective of the Aleppo Vision for 2025 (above); panoramic view of Aleppo from the Citadel (below).
Source: Uberbau/GIZ 2010 (based on Google Earth Image 2009) (above); Uberbau/GIZ 2010 (below).

development beyond the horizon of an electoral period. Uberbau was able to achieve this link due to its position acting at the intersection between a "think tank" and a "consulting practice" with experience in both urban spatial research and the realization of large-scale urban projects.

Uberbau's approach toward the Aleppo CDS consisted primarily of understanding and visualizing existing local interests, aims and conditions through the analysis of aerial maps, demographic development and the existing ratified masterplan. Based on principles of participation, phasing, space reservation, layered decentralization, integrated mobility and the introduction of public spaces of various scales, the study proposed the reorganization of the city based on its existing structure and socio-economic as well as environmental potentials. An integral part of the study and consultation process was to introduce the urban spatial structure to the stakeholders via a diagrammatic set of illustrations, layer by layer—green spaces, water network, industrial centers and transport systems. This graphic isolation and simplification of layers enabled a new interpretation of the existing masterplan and led to a set of clear conclusions about key issues and characteristics (see as examples Figure 9.3 and Figure 9.6f). Uberbau's research-based approach produced analytical outputs, which could then be confronted with the initial brief. It also enabled a comparison between existing conditions in Aleppo and best-practice examples and urban spatial principles from other global cities, some of which had the potential to illustrate development perspectives for Aleppo's future.

Aleppo 2025 City Development Strategy 117

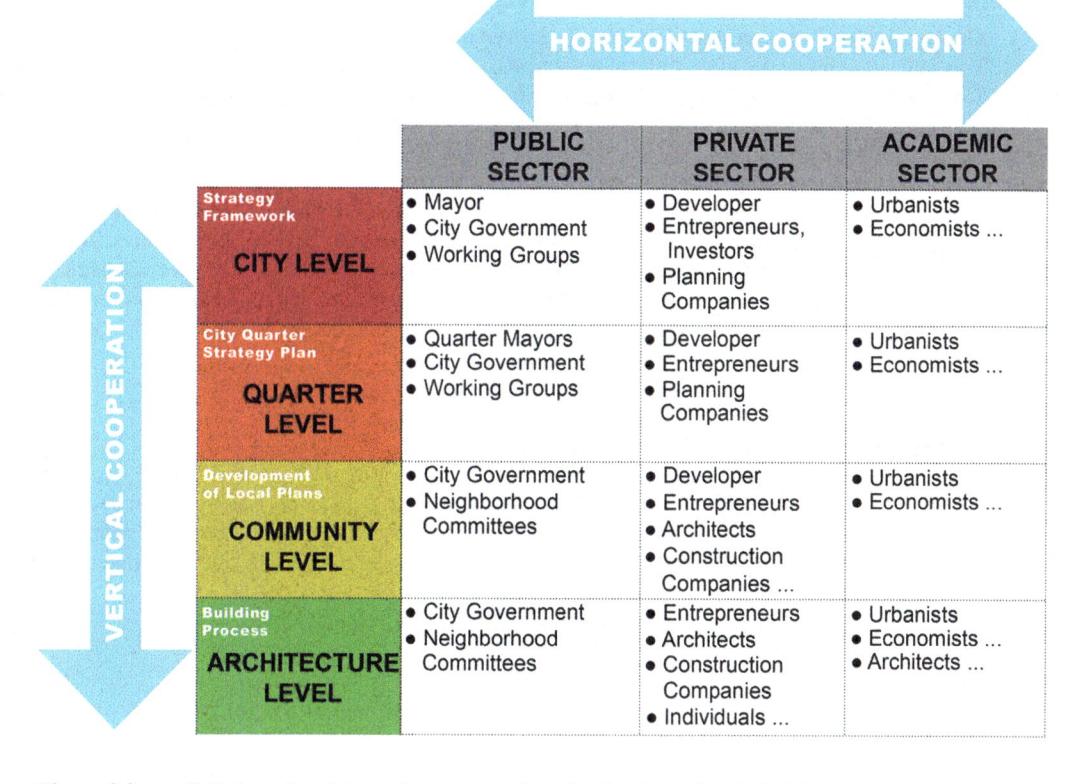

		PUBLIC SECTOR	PRIVATE SECTOR	ACADEMIC SECTOR
Strategy Framework **CITY LEVEL**		• Mayor • City Government • Working Groups	• Developer • Entrepreneurs, Investors • Planning Companies	• Urbanists • Economists ...
City Quarter Strategy Plan **QUARTER LEVEL**		• Quarter Mayors • City Government • Working Groups	• Developer • Entrepreneurs • Planning Companies	• Urbanists • Economists ...
Development of Local Plans **COMMUNITY LEVEL**		• City Government • Neighborhood Committees	• Developer • Entrepreneurs • Architects • Construction Companies ...	• Urbanists • Economists ...
Building Process **ARCHITECTURE LEVEL**		• City Government • Neighborhood Committees	• Entrepreneurs • Architects • Construction Companies • Individuals ...	• Urbanists • Economists ... • Architects ...

(HORIZONTAL COOPERATION ↔ ; VERTICAL COOPERATION ↕)

Figure 9.2 Collaboration integration across planning levels and stakeholder sectors
Source: Uberbau/GIZ 2010.

In contrast to past approaches of Western modernist planners who often tried to impose their own values onto cities in developing countries,[3] Uberbau tried as much as possible to avoid influencing or defining the objectives of Aleppo's development from the perspective of a foreign practice. Uberbau rather decided to employ the Local Agenda 21 (LA21),[4] a document dating from 2009 in which the working groups of Aleppo's city council enumerated the critical issues facing the city in its near future. Based on those issues, Uberbau used eight social, ecological, economic and cultural benchmarks for sustainable development in Aleppo, the first six of which are particularly relevant for the spatial plan of the city:

1. Green atmosphere, sustainable clean air preserved by a conscious society.
2. Reaching a sustainable, economically developed society.

---

3 See for example the case of the Indian New Town Rourkela, planned by the German Krupp Company in the 1950s. While Krupp's team tried to impose Western ideas of modernization—such as a highway, single family housing and car-free public spaces—onto a rural society, the local population adapted these ideas to local patterns of use for example by subdividing unused public space into rice fields (Saad 2005).

4 The "Local Agenda 21" (LA21) is an action program based on the United Nation's Agenda 21 presented at the Earth Summit 1992 in Rio de Janeiro. Its implementation was intended to involve action at international, national, regional and local levels. Some local authorities have taken steps to implement the plan locally, as recommended in Chapter 28 of the original document, upon which the Aleppo LA21 was based. Also see the Agenda 21 website of the United Nations: http://www.unep.org/Documents.Multilingual/Default.asp?documentid=52 [accessed: August 22, 2013].

3. Preserving and reviving heritage to consolidate the individual's belonging to the environmental and cultural surroundings.
4. Organizing illegal settlement to become well-serviced residential areas.
5. Preventing the emergence of new illegal settlements.
6. Ideal social and economic status for better life with identity.
7. Improved solid waste management.
8. Improved water management.

The fact-based analysis, the adoption of the LA21 principles, and the reinterpretation of existing planning efforts were carried out in close collaboration with the GIZ, the municipality and key stakeholders. These became the basis for a spatial vision and strategy for Aleppo that was accepted as valid by all involved parties, resulting in a flexible, strategic plan that was able to involve different groups and to react to the changing context of a rapidly growing Aleppo. This strategic approach also reconnected the ambitions of the current masterplan with the local economic and social realities.

Towards an Urban Spatial Strategy

Before introducing ideas for the future, one must understand the present and past developments that have led to the contemporary situation. What is particular about Aleppo? Are there any features that set it apart and can help guide future development? Below are summarized the findings of the analysis of the existing urban structure of Aleppo in combination with socio-economic factors.

Urban Spatial Characteristics

Aleppo is situated in northern Syria, about 100 km east of the Mediterranean coast and 50 km from the Turkish border. The climate is arid-continental with hot summers, and the location of the city marks the beginning of a dry desert steppe extending toward the east, interrupted only by the Euphrates river corridor at a distance of 70 km from the city. The city is located along a north–south valley containing the riverbed of the Quweik within a network of smaller settlements of mostly agricultural character (Figure 9.4). The river passes the old city center in the form of a partly tunneled, manufactured waterway fed by a pipeline that carries over water from the Euphrates. In the very center of Aleppo, the Citadel stands out as a landmark built on a partially artificial mound. Topographic changes are mostly mild, but there are a few higher points in the city that allow for vistas. These geographic conditions have generated several urban spatial issues that characterize the city today.

Demographic Pressure

Aleppo's demographic growth poses fundamental challenges regarding infrastructure, society and ecology that a development strategy for any similar fast-growing metropolis must face. At the time that the Aleppo CDS was being elaborated, the city was under enormous pressure, with estimated annual growth projected at about 2.7 percent annually over the next 10 years. This would add 1.2 million people to Aleppo's population over that period, resulting in a projected total of 3.6 million inhabitants in 15 years.

Compact Urban Form

In spite of its rapid growth, Aleppo is a surprisingly compact city with virtually no sprawl. This compact urban structure opens up a wide range of opportunities for future sustainable development in the areas of transportation, infrastructure and the integration of living and working spaces. All this despite the fact that approximately 50 percent of today's population lives in informal settlements (Wakely 2009: 8) with varying degrees of legality, and despite the fact that buildable land is widely available. This density also results in a city with a recognizable boundary, a clearly readable transition from countryside to city.

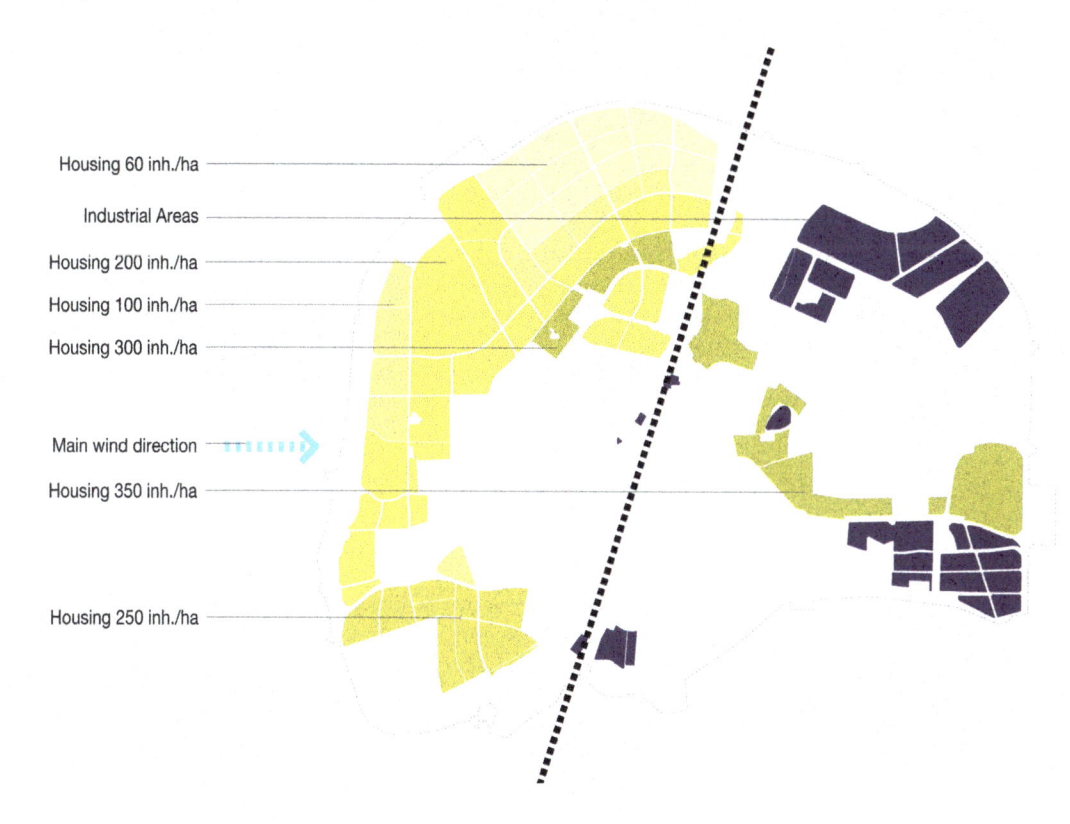

Figure 9.3 East–West disparity of residential areas and allocation of industry in the East
Source: Uberbau/GIZ 2010 (based on 2010 Masterplan, Municipality of Aleppo).

East–West Divide

The city is socially divided into an eastern and a western part, aggravated by a new industrial area that is being laid out at the northeastern periphery of the city (Figure 9.3). The north–south rail tracks that run along the riverbed on a four-meter high embankment form a physical barrier that further marks a functional and social rift. The western part hosts upper class sub-centers and residential neighborhoods with direct connections to Turkey and Damascus, while the airport, industries and a majority of informal settlements are located in the east. Prevalent western winds carry cool air from the coast and mountains, further contributing to an uneven distribution of richer and poorer areas.

Social and Functional Mix

Aleppo's social and functional structures are highly intermixed, a feature that considerably raises its potential of social and economic sustainability. Established around the second millennium BCE (Busquets 2005: 41), the city is one of the oldest continually inhabited places on the planet, and due to its strategic position at the crossroads of various ancient trade routes, it has been culturally influenced by an extraordinary amount of outside forces. This has resulted in a strikingly multifaceted local community; nearly 70 percent of Aleppo's inhabitants are Sunni Muslims, mainly Arab, but there are also Kurds, Assyrians/Syriacs, Bosnians, Bulgarians, Chechens, Circassians, Kabardins and Turkmens. Furthermore Aleppo has the largest Christian community in the Middle East after Beirut. And even though only a handful of Jewish citizens still live in Aleppo, the properties and houses of the Jewish families who left the country were not sold after the migration and remained under the protection of the Syrian government. This ethnic, religious and social plurality is still notable in the city structure today; each city quarter has a distinct role and quality and, despite being relatively homogeneous typologically, the functions and atmosphere vary widely. Many areas feature a well functioning mix of uses brought about by economic factors rather than through regulation—or in fact in spite of regulation.[5] This dense diversity of uses is mostly observable in *mature* neighborhoods, while more recent and future developments tend more toward monofunctionality.

Any vision for Aleppo necessarily must take these heterogeneous features as a starting point and work with them to open up multiple opportunities for the development of the city—economically, spatially, politically and socially—which yet remain unexploited. It needs to implement a coherent structure that makes these potentials perceivable and accessible. The spirit of diversity needs to be maintained throughout the future development of the city, and technocratic tendencies toward homogenization need to be discouraged.

Aleppo 2025 Urban Spatial Strategy

The current Aleppo masterplan is ambitious; it more than triples Aleppo's urbanized area to a total of 463 km^2 to be implemented before 2025 (Figure 9.4). Its structure consists of five concentric highway rings and radial axes that connect the city center to the countryside, with the two outermost rings yet to be executed. The concentric figure is also incomplete; its southeastern segment is missing due to agricultural land use and the political delimitations of the municipality. The plan provides extensive area for low to medium density residential development in the west, while allocating relatively little for high-density residential development in the poorer east. Despite the higher densities, much less green space is provided in the east than in the west. The new industrial city relocates polluting industries from the rest of the city into the east. Large areas designated as buildable land mostly lie in productive agricultural areas. As mentioned earlier, in adopting the LA21 as a benchmark for evaluating the masterplan, large discrepancies were uncovered, stemming from a lack of awareness of the specific urban qualities and problems of the city. Additionally a lack of vision limited the masterplan to a reactive role, unable to keep up with the fast pace of reality. Accordingly, the planning process needed to be amended with tools that would encourage participation and help to anticipate and steer development by incorporating a less rigid, more strategic approach. This was especially urgent considering the fast population growth and the slow five-year ratification cycle of the masterplan.

The Aleppo 2025 Urban Spatial Strategy was conceived as a framework that uses the mentioned urban characteristics of the city as the point of departure for strategic and sustainable development. It incorporates a vision of Aleppo as a compact, mixed and polycentric city, while outlining an organization based on the city's existing urban structure and potentials. In contrast to an existing culture of over-regulation that stands in contradiction to the informal character of much of Aleppo's urban development, it accepts the existing forces of the city and steers them to secure future qualities. While the masterplan fixes quantities, the Strategy acts as a complementary tool in the discussion of the city's qualities (Figure 9.3). The Strategy is structured along the five themes of Growth Management, Mobility, Establishment & Distribution of Open Spaces, Conservation and Modernization, and Managing Informality, with each of these themes responding to multiple LA21 targets. The Aleppo 2025 Urban Spatial Strategy was then summarized and turned into concrete steps for action and suggestions for inception projects, with the main recommendations for the ongoing Aleppo 2009 masterplan revision process incorporated into a synthesis map (Figure 9.7).

---

5 For example vegetable shops, street trading and office spaces in residential areas are often in violation of zoning regulations, but continue operating due to personal relationships or bribery.

Aleppo 2025 City Development Strategy 121

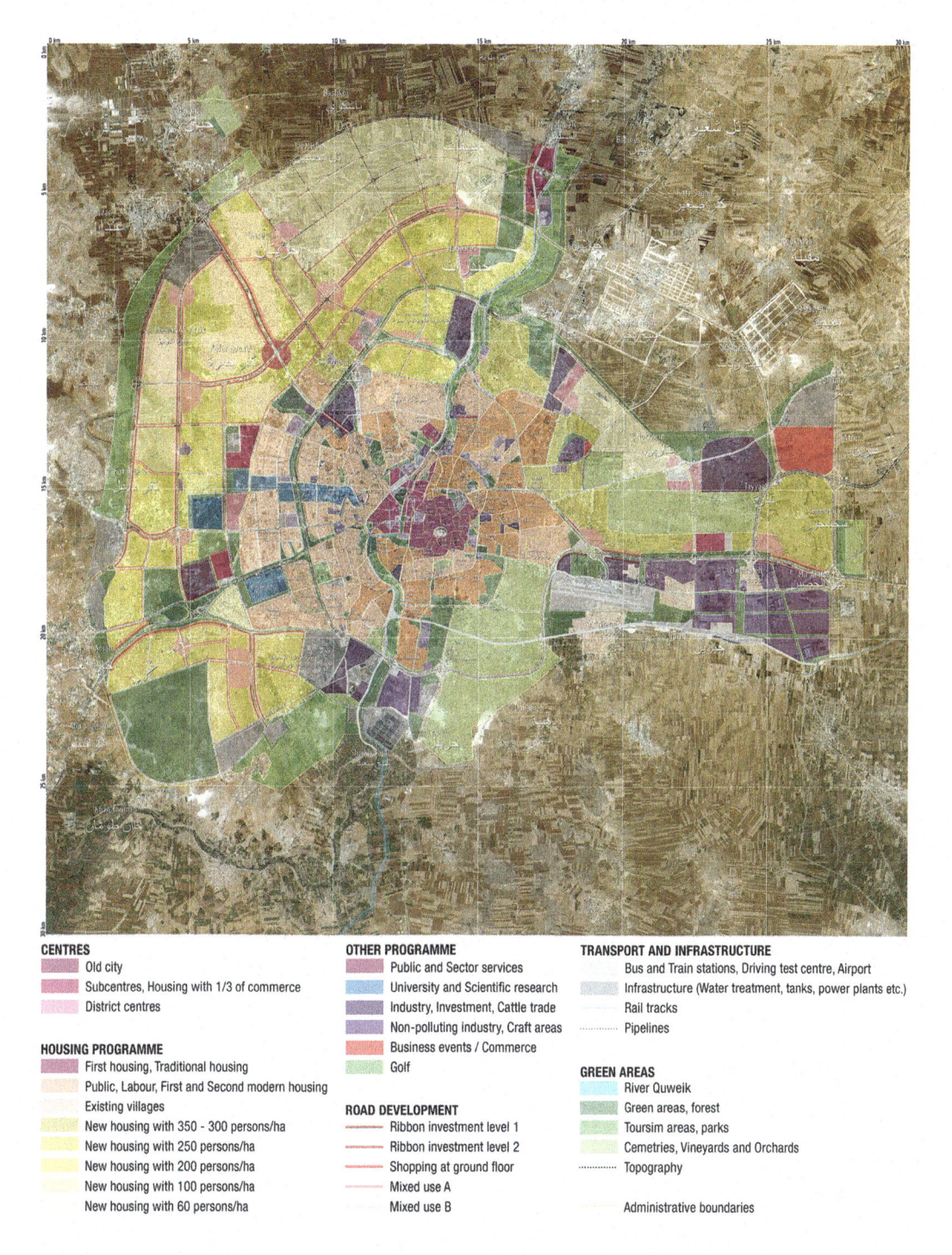

CENTRES
- Old city
- Subcentres, Housing with 1/3 of commerce
- District centres

HOUSING PROGRAMME
- First housing, Traditional housing
- Public, Labour, First and Second modern housing
- Existing villages
- New housing with 350 - 300 persons/ha
- New housing with 250 persons/ha
- New housing with 200 persons/ha
- New housing with 100 persons/ha
- New housing with 60 persons/ha

OTHER PROGRAMME
- Public and Sector services
- University and Scientific research
- Industry, Investment, Cattle trade
- Non-polluting industry, Craft areas
- Business events / Commerce
- Golf

ROAD DEVELOPMENT
- Ribbon investment level 1
- Ribbon investment level 2
- Shopping at ground floor
- Mixed use A
- Mixed use B

TRANSPORT AND INFRASTRUCTURE
- Bus and Train stations, Driving test centre, Airport
- Infrastructure (Water treatment, tanks, power plants etc.)
- Rail tracks
- Pipelines

GREEN AREAS
- River Quweik
- Green areas, forest
- Toursim areas, parks
- Cemetries, Vineyards and Orchards
- Topography

- Administrative boundaries

Figure 9.4 The Aleppo masterplan superimposed on the existing city showing the large scope of the planned project

Source: Uberbau/GIZ 2010 (based on Google Earth Image 2009 and 2010 Masterplan, Municipality of Aleppo).

122 Urban Design in the Arab World

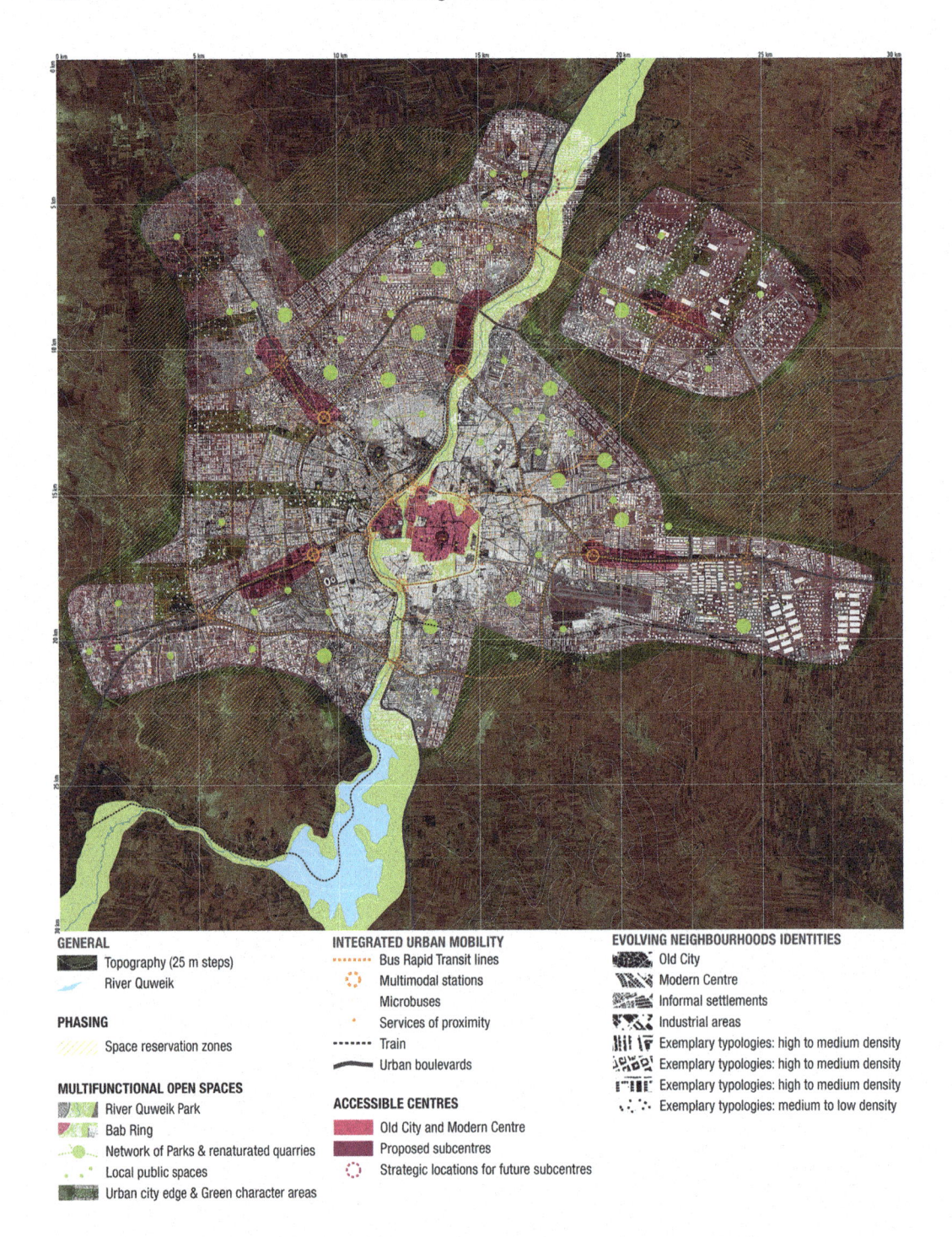

GENERAL
- Topography (25 m steps)
- River Quweik

PHASING
- Space reservation zones

MULTIFUNCTIONAL OPEN SPACES
- River Quweik Park
- Bab Ring
- Network of Parks & renaturated quarries
- Local public spaces
- Urban city edge & Green character areas

INTEGRATED URBAN MOBILITY
- Bus Rapid Transit lines
- Multimodal stations
- Microbuses
- Services of proximity
- Train
- Urban boulevards

ACCESSIBLE CENTRES
- Old City and Modern Centre
- Proposed subcentres
- Strategic locations for future subcentres

EVOLVING NEIGHBOURHOODS IDENTITIES
- Old City
- Modern Centre
- Informal settlements
- Industrial areas
- Exemplary typologies: high to medium density
- Exemplary typologies: high to medium density
- Exemplary typologies: high to medium density
- Exemplary typologies: medium to low density

Figure 9.5 Illustrative map of the Aleppo Vision 2025 outlining the spatial strategy
Source: Uberbau/GIZ 2010 (based on Google Earth Image 2009 and 2010 Masterplan, Municipality of Aleppo).

Growth Management

> LA21: "Reaching a sustainable, economically developed society."
> "Ideal social and economic status for better life with identity."

The spatial structure of the 2009 masterplan reinforces the existing physical and mental imbalance between west and east and does not appear to be in line with the LA21 goal of achieving social sustainability. The proposed dwellings for 2,515,000 citizens before 2025 appears largely overestimated when bearing in mind the expected population increase during that period, particularly given the low density of the expansion areas in the west (Figure 9.5). The large increase in available buildable land could lead to a speculation bubble, and certainly to dispersed and sprawling developments that weaken the compact nature of the city.

The Strategy proposes to support Aleppo's growth along the main thoroughfares that are already the backbone of the city's current development (Figure 9.6a). Along those routes, higher densities and a more business-oriented programmatic mix should be concentrated. Away from the thoroughfares the landscape is pulled into the city, preserving the precious landscape and offering flexibility for future transformations of the city. To avoid the loss of existing characteristics—the clear contrast between city and countryside, the compactness and programmatic mix of Aleppo—for the sake of market-driven opportunistic development, a step-by-step development of Aleppo was proposed (Figure 9.6b). The results should not only describe a desired state for the year 2025, but also should address how Aleppo is to evolve toward that state.

The Strategy proposes concentric growth areas, phased through at least two development stages—three in case of high development pressure—spanning a total of 15 years. This incremental development, starting with areas close to the city core, will ensure controlled growth patterns that maintain the particular qualities of Aleppo. To allow for more precision and adaptation to changing trends, each phase should be continuously evaluated every five years according to the existing rhythm of masterplan implementation. Within each phase, networks of logistic and social infrastructure—that is, schools, roads, electricity, water and sewage—should be developed prior to the development of the residential plots.

Given the over provision of buildable land in the masterplan, the Strategy proposes to reserve large areas of this land for later development, retaining current land use for the immediate future (Figure 9.6b and Figure 9.7). This means maintaining productive agricultural areas in the north, preserving the culture–historic agricultural landscape in the west and south, and forming a green buffer zone between Aleppo and the new industrial zone in the east. This land reserve of areas with high natural and climatic value guarantees easy access for citizens to recreational and productive areas from within the administrative boundaries of the city. In case more space for city development is needed in the future, some of these areas could serve for the next phase of city expansion.

The current spatial model of one center hosting all administrative, economic and cultural services of the city has reached its limits, leading to congestion and extravagant real estate prices. Aleppo already features a set of various small sub-centralities with individual character, often linked to a specific economic base unique to the city, such as production, education, commerce, food, electronics or entertainment. These existing, emerging or possibly dormant specialized centralities may not yet have developed identities as strong as the Old City, but opening up a process of development and modernization could help them consolidate and generate economic development. The Strategy proposes to rigorously decentralize the city by supporting the development of new sub-centers in direct proximity to existing and planned transport nodes, at the intersections of the ring roads, and along the main thoroughfares (Figure 9.6d). This linkage between dense centers and transport infrastructure planning can yield large social and economic benefits due to high accessibility and provision of services, as witnessed in similar international cases.[6]

As mentioned above, the masterplan proposes large areas of low-density housing in the west, with smaller areas of high-density housing in the east. The Strategy recommends overcoming this socially undesirable imbalance by implementing a wider range of typologies in the different development areas, that is, the introduction of high-density typologies in the west as well as middle-class typologies in the east (Figure 9.6c). This should initiate a long-term process of change in the perception of Aleppo's east side as an undesirable

---

6 For example the urban developments along Curitiba's BRT line or Tokyo's Yamamote Line.

124 *Urban Design in the Arab World*

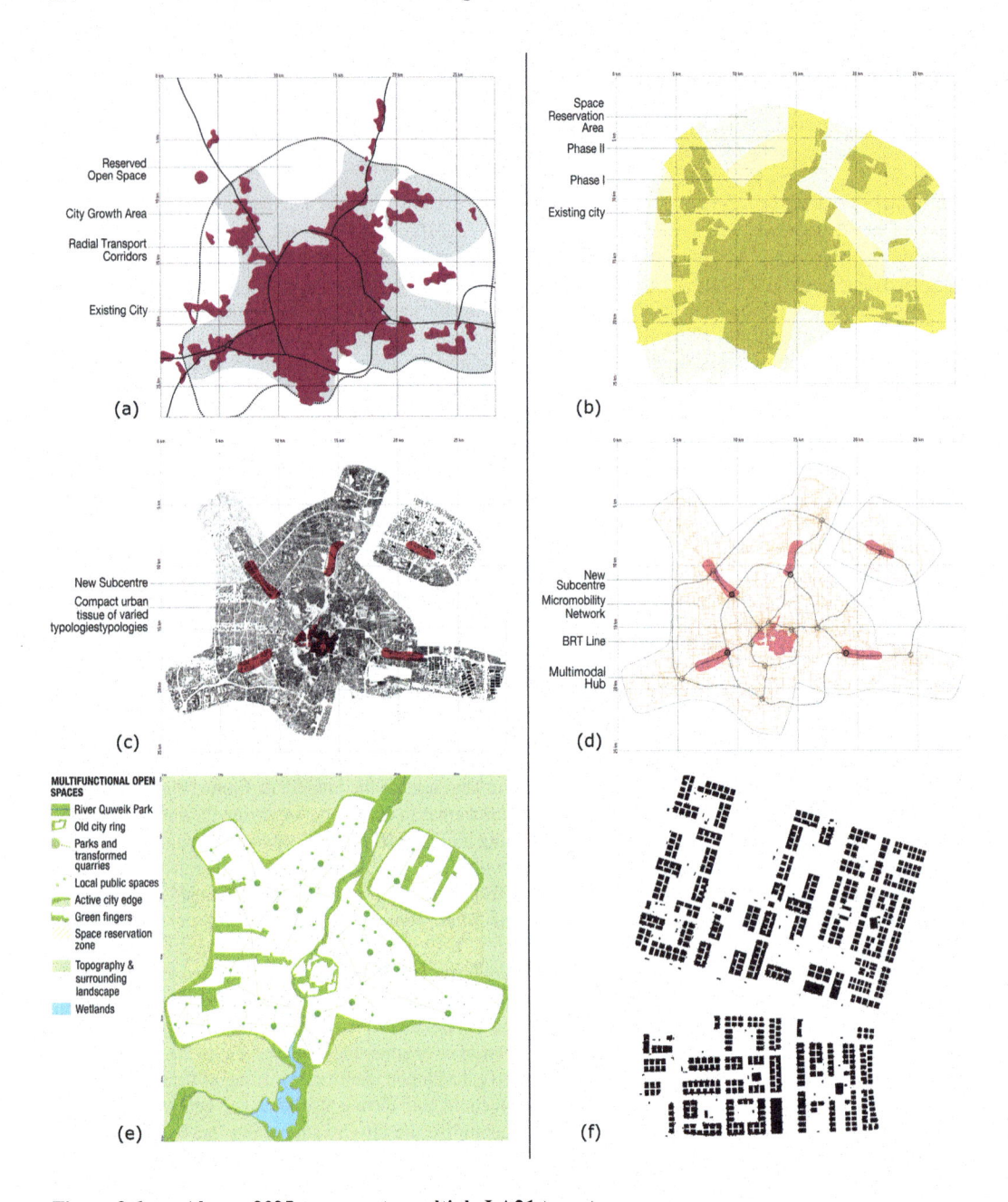

Figure 9.6   Aleppo 2025 response to multiple LA21 targets
Note: (a) Aleppo's development along main thoroughfares; (b) proposed growth phases; (c) proposed dense urban structure; (d) proposed mobility system; (e) proposed open space system; (f) the spatial homogeneity of the western areas.
Source: (a–e) Uberbau/GIZ 2010; (f) Uberbau/GIZ 2010 (based on GIS Model, Municipality of Aleppo 2009).

Aleppo 2025 City Development Strategy 125

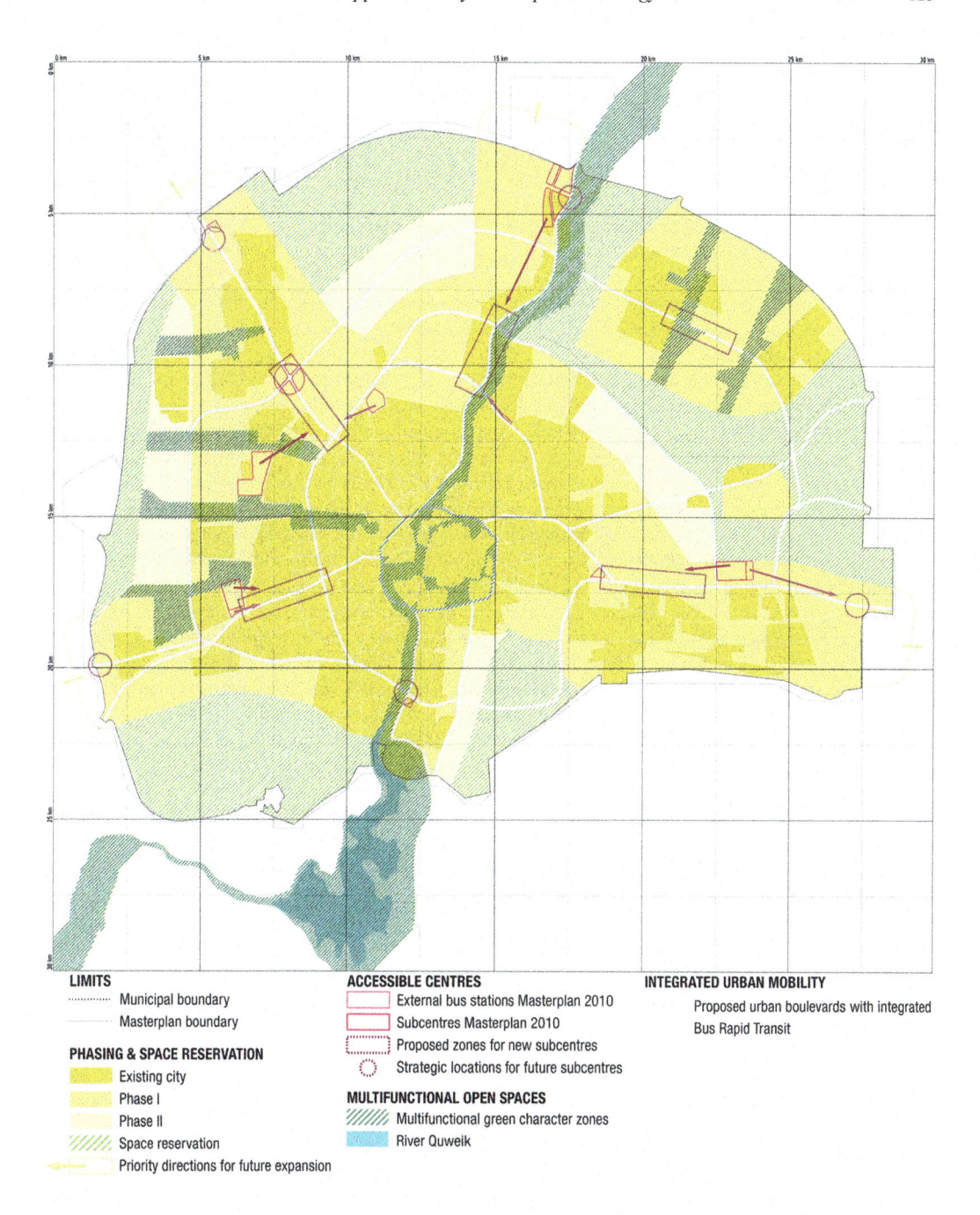

Figure 9.7   Map that summarizes Uberbau's proposed amendments to the masterplan
Source: Uberbau/GIZ 2010.

area of the city, optimistically acknowledging that newer generations in the east can raise their income levels. It should be equally possible for lower-income individuals to live closer to potential workplaces in the west, avoiding inconvenient travel distances.

Mobility

> LA21: "Green atmosphere, sustainable clean air preserved by a conscious society."
> "Reaching a sustainable, economically developed society."

The masterplan is clearly car-oriented. There is no prescription for public transport, with the large amount of low-density areas leading to increased car use, infrastructure needs, maintenance costs, energy consumption and ultimately air pollution.

As a first step toward more ecological means of mobility, the Strategy proposes reorganizing the current public transport system to relieve the city's dependence on individual transport. It proposes the implementation of a public high-speed Bus Rapid Transit (BRT) as a macro-mobility system. A BRT system has advantages for Aleppo in terms of relatively low maintenance costs, easy implementation—existing transport lanes can be adapted—and the pre–existing knowledge among public transport personnel of a bus network. The system should be established on the already over-dimensioned main roads designated in the masterplan. Located at the new sub-centers, the BRT stations should be well integrated and offer an easy transition between various transport modes—car, bus, pedestrian, taxi and minibus—and will attract investments in the vicinity of multimodal train stations (Figure 9.6d). The combination of high-speed transport facilities at urban nodes of high density would not only lead to greater efficiency in the transport system, but could also have positive effects on public transport affordability and revenue, contributing to the financial viability of the entire system.

In order to cater to the middle and low-density neighborhoods, a reorganization of the existing minibus system is proposed to shuttle citizens from their houses to the nearest BRT station. Minibuses running on fixed routes should stop next to local landmarks, such as convenience stores, linking transport to daily routines and creating new points of local identity and social interaction. Another option could be minibuses on-demand that could be called for citizens with individual needs, for example families or the disabled.

Establishment and Distribution of Open Spaces

> LA21: "Green atmosphere, sustainable clean air preserved by a conscious society."
> "Ideal social and economical status for better life with identity."

There is currently a lack of good public, open and green spaces within Aleppo. The masterplan also shows no effort to create ventilation or biodiversity corridors within the city and does little to preserve existing fertile areas within the masterplan boundaries. The Strategy proposes the establishment of different types of multifunctional open spaces (Figure 9.6e):

1. *Active city edge*: a band of recreational urban programs is proposed along the edge of the city, reinforcing the clear contrast between city and countryside and activating the periphery of the city for recreational uses.
2. *Green fingers*: transversal green corridors with no or low density construction should connect city and countryside, ensuring good ventilation and providing larger recreational areas close to the citizens.
3. *Quweik Park*: a new city park is proposed along the Quweik riverbed, transforming the current mental and physical border between east and west into a social interface for all citizens and a biodiversity corridor running north to south through the city.
4. *Old City ring*: a sequence of small parks, squares and green boulevards is proposed around the Old City as an active public transition zone between the Old City and the rest of Aleppo.

5. *Graduated public space network*: at the city level, a sequence of larger squares and streets linked to specific programs should be placed at strategic locations to underline the main city functions. At the neighborhood level, major efforts are proposed for the implementation of intimate public spaces, especially in the east.

Conservation and Modernization

> LA21: "Preserving and reviving heritage to consolidate the individual's belonging to the environmental and cultural surroundings."
> "Ideal social and economic status for better life with identity."

Aleppo has a great asset in the recently refurbished Old City, a world famous cultural monument. Besides exceptional pieces of cultural heritage including the souqs, the Citadel, the districts of Al Medina and Jdeideh, its striking quality lies in its authenticity as a living and inhabited organism. But authenticity is a sensitive issue, threatened by either museumification or "Disneyfication." Through the process of renovation, the rise of real estate prices, and fading local economies, traditional ways of living and working, as well as established forms of social organization, are being challenged.

To preserve its social and physical heritage, Aleppo has to evolve by carefully balancing modernization and conservation; local economies have to adapt to new times and new opportunities. The Strategy proposes supporting existing efforts to establish Aleppo as a destination for cultural tourism in collaboration with the inhabitants of the Old City by creating a larger touristic network through public spaces, transport, guidance, communication systems, as well as the provision of programs that carefully integrate tourist activity in the Old City.

In contrast to the city's rich heritage, the new living quarters in the west appear spatially and programmatically homogeneous and sometimes lack character (Figure 9.6f). Their layout has adequate density and high flexibility in itself, but the use of a standard typology needs to be more specifically adapted to local conditions, such as topography and immediate urban context, as well as being able to react to changing conditions. Accordingly, a wider range of residential typologies is desirable to accommodate changing markets, new lifestyles, and inhabitants of all income levels. A process of deregulation should be initiated that would allow for the introduction of innovative typologies and floor plans. This would lead to more flexibility and diversity in the use of existing typologies and would better suit socially balanced neighborhoods, eventually contributing to a sense of identity that each quarter could develop with its own unique mix of program and people.

Managing Informality

> LA21: "Organizing illegal settlement to be well-serviced residential areas."
> "Preventing the emergence of new illegal settlements."

While recently planned neighborhoods offer good technical and civic infrastructure, they sometimes lack a lively character. Informal settlements face the opposite situation; their unregulated character results in a close spatial relationship between working and living that often engenders a close-knit social fabric and a heightened sense of identification of its inhabitants with their environment. Unfortunately, the masterplan does not include any information on those settlements, despite the targets of the LA21 and the profusion of informal settlements in Aleppo. In fact, the proposed fifth ring road, which would run across open land at the city edge, is expected to have the effect of encouraging even more informal building activity.

The retroactive establishment of a framework of policies that would legalize informal settlements, train their inhabitants to build their houses safely, and establish basic infrastructure are recommended as among the most important measures. The examples of Sao Paulo, Medellin and Caracas prove that such measures can be successful and that an upgrading of informal settlements can be a sustainable alternative for the provision of low-cost housing.

An Assessment of the Aleppo CDS Process

Early on in the CDS process, an important question arose: is the masterplan still an adequate tool, or should it be substituted with a more strategy-oriented approach? The CDS supplied an answer to the immediate need for a more flexible and integrative approach to planning, starting by realistically assessing the existing conditions, understanding development trends, and from there, steering and guiding the development of the city in an inclusive way. It did not provide a plan, but rather established both principles and a process that should prove useful beyond the 2025 scope of the project.

However, the masterplan is still necessary as an important tool for implementation with a defined legal meaning, delineating ownership boundaries and construction plots. But it cannot serve as the sole planning instrument in a fast-developing context with decisions made by multiple parties. More conceptual representations of development scenarios are a better tool for involving the public, and for facilitating communication and decision-making already in the early planning stages, with a process-oriented approach potentially leading to a legally binding plan. Over time, this type of process could ideally establish itself at various scales and could be repeatedly employed in a permanent cycle of revision and adaptation to reflect the changing realities of the environment. In the long run, this would institute a permanent ongoing intellectual reflection by the public and experts about their built environment.

The entire Aleppo Urban Spatial Strategy process was positively received by both local and international partners, in part because it realistically assessed the conditions of the existing city and did not exclude politically undesirable—but nonetheless crucial issues—from the analysis. This was made possible by coupling foreign experts with local counterparts, thus ensuring ownership by the client, the municipality of Aleppo. At the same time, the opinions of the foreign experts allowed for addressing delicate topics, often difficult to breach by members of the local community. Foreign experts did not only bring their knowledge to support the local planning processes, but also acted as facilitators. The fact that urban planning was used as an entry point within the larger CDS process and that "soft" factors were introduced into the decision-making process also had a positive impact. Since the process used to develop the CDS was iterative, frequent discussions managed to link the expectations of the client, the knowledge of local experts, and the ideas and capacity of the foreign experts. The very spatial "hands-on" approach to consultancy meetings using maps, sketching paper and pens supported the exchange of ideas and helped avoid misunderstandings within the group. In this spirit, the final document extended the usual scope of a CDS report by making it more accessible through the inclusion of supporting illustrative graphics and project references.

During the entire process, the inclusiveness of the project—the participation for example of local community leaders in the CDS Midterm Forum—marked a major positive change in the approach to planning in Syria. Furthermore, strong public involvement in various events and workshops was encouraged through a communication strategy using the slogan "*madinatuna*" [our city], transmitted through a clear graphic language.[7] Finally, the specific issues of Aleppo were questioned as part of a larger framework of urban issues that face many other cities in the region, offering a certain potential for being replicated.

Despite its positive reception, the project ultimately failed to be even partially implemented, most likely because of the resistance of powerful landowners. The Strategy questioned the over provision of developable land, which was apparently driven by speculation interests. Uberbau's clear recommendation to reduce the amount of developable land would have reduced the potential profitability of many properties, probably rendering the public ratification of the amendments to the masterplan impossible. Later in 2010, some of the local actors involved in the Aleppo spatial planning process were detained and questioned concerning illegal land speculation. In an atmosphere of such uncertainty, it very quickly became politically undesirable to be involved with Aleppo's spatial planning in any way, bringing the process to a standstill up until the current civil–political crisis emerged.

---

7 See http://madinatuna.com/en [accessed: August 22, 2013].

The Aleppo CDS and the Syrian Civil War

In light of the ongoing destruction and violence in Syria, and particularly in Aleppo, it seems in retrospect grotesque to write so optimistically in describing the potential of that city. Individual actions of the citizens of Aleppo today are concerned with sheer survival, while political factions focus on garnering political and military strength. It is difficult for us to understand the current situation in Aleppo, even more so to speculate on its future development. We do know that the historic souq has been burned down, that the minaret of the Umayyad Mosque has been destroyed, and that many areas—most notably the informal settlements—have been devastated.

Looking forward, the main spatial challenges in a post-conflict Aleppo will certainly be the restoration of the basic services and infrastructure. A precondition for the restoration of other urban functions is to re-establish and maintain a working transport infrastructure and to establish a street grid in new development areas—including in the temporary refugee camps that often develop into permanent settlements. But working within a partially destroyed urban organism poses very different challenges to NGOs and international agencies than working in the countryside. Meticulous cooperation with the staff rebuilding the remaining infrastructure is of paramount importance. Access to food and employment will allow for the eventual long-term establishment of an urbanized structure. The management of refugees and returning families flowing into the city after the conflict will also be a key challenge; the provision of shelter and the resolution of conflicts within contested areas will be critical. It is to be hoped that this will create a chance for the empowerment of decentralized neighborhood initiatives, and that informal settlements will lose their stigma through structural assistance from governmental and/or international agencies. If not managed properly, the lack of shelter, disputes over ownership, and the influx of refugees could acerbate the divide between the privileged and the disadvantaged, leading to continued conflicts.

Despite the above risks, the potentials and values as described earlier in the chapter are inscribed into the socio-cultural and spatial DNA of the city, and are permanent enough to still be relevant once the current conflicts have abated. As the spatial strategy is based on these lasting characteristics, it is likely that the legacy of the Aleppo CDS can be of use for a future reconstruction of the city. Also a certain mode of urban cohabitation has become part of the common cultural memory and will therefore continue. One can only hope that the city's multicultural, ethnic and religious richness can continue to coexist in the peaceful manner which was so unique to Aleppo within the greater context of the Middle East.

References

Busquets, J. (ed.) 2005. *Aleppo: Rehabilitation of the Old City*. Cambridge, MA: Harvard Graduate School of Design.
Cities Alliance. 2006. *Guide to City Development Strategies: Improving Urban Performance*. Washington: The Cities Alliance.
Saad, A. 2005. Rourkela—Das Doppelleben einer Indischen New Town. *archplus*, 185, 30–33.
Saad, A. and Stellmach, T. [Uberbau]. 2010. *Aleppo Diverse Open City—An Urban Vision for the Year 2025*. Final Report. Berlin/Eschborn: Uberbau/GTZ. Available at: https://dl.dropboxusercontent.com/u/376106/_persistent/100205%20Uberbau%20Aleppo%20Diverse%20Open%20City.pdf [accessed: August 22, 2013].
Wakely, P. and Abdul Wahab, R. 2009. *Informal Settlements in Aleppo: Rapid Profiles of all Informal Settlements in Aleppo*. Final Report. Aleppo: GTZ and Municipality of Aleppo.

Chapter 10
Community-Based Design as Mediator between Academia and Practice: The Case of Souq Sabra, Beirut

Rabih Shibli

Introduction

Souq Sabra is one of Beirut's most popular markets, stretching from the neighborhood of Tariq el Jdideh on the southern edge of municipal Beirut to Al Rihab roundabout in the adjoining southern suburbs (Figure 10.1). Attracting a diverse population of refugee camp residents, expatriate temporary workers and lower income inhabitants from across the city, Souq Sabra is a thriving market although informally managed and poorly maintained. Its *Saha* [main square] stretches across the boundary between the two municipalities of Beirut and Ghobeiri, blurring the responsibility for public improvement and maintenance. To address the poor conditions of the open spaces within the souq, the Center for Civic Engagement and Community Service (CCECS) at the American University of Beirut (AUB), partnered with the Hariri Foundation for Sustainable Human Development (HFSHD), conducted a community-based design study with a team of students in consultation with both community representatives and local merchants. The chapter is a reflection on my personal experience as an active faculty member of the team and considers the processes and outcomes of this study, looking at community-based design both as an intervention tool that provides a viable alternative in the absence of state development plans and municipal services, and as a pedagogical tool that constitutes a mediating platform between design education and practice.

The chapter starts by introducing the academic and administrative position of the CCECS in terms of its ideological and operational framework and the respective roles of key stakeholders—the university, the community, and the donor/partner agencies—in articulating and implementing community-based projects. Through the description of the Souq Sabra study, the chapter seeks to demonstrate how learning and service were integrated, leading to a sustainable initiative that impacted positively on the local community. More specifically, it shows how the students were presented with a challenging opportunity to engage in participative design, and consequently, to develop a plan of action that led to implementation. Generalizing from this case study, the conclusion outlines the necessity of institutionalizing Community Based Learning (CBL) as a pedagogical framework for addressing the pressing concerns of underdeveloped areas in Lebanon and the Arab region.

Academic Context

In the aftermath of the 2006 war between Israel and Hezbollah, students and faculty members from the Architecture Department at AUB were heavily involved in relief and reconstruction efforts under the auspices of the Reconstruction Unit at the Department of Architecture (Al-Harithy 2010). Shortly after, and "in response to the humanitarian crisis in North Lebanon at the Nahr el Bared Camp,[1] a group of faculty and students from the AUB and other institutions initiated the Nahr el Bared Relief Campaign" (AUB 2007). It became

---

1 Between May 20 and September 7, 2007, a fierce battle between the Lebanese Army Forces and the militarized fundamentalist group Fatah el Islam resulted in the termination of the latter and the destruction of the camp.

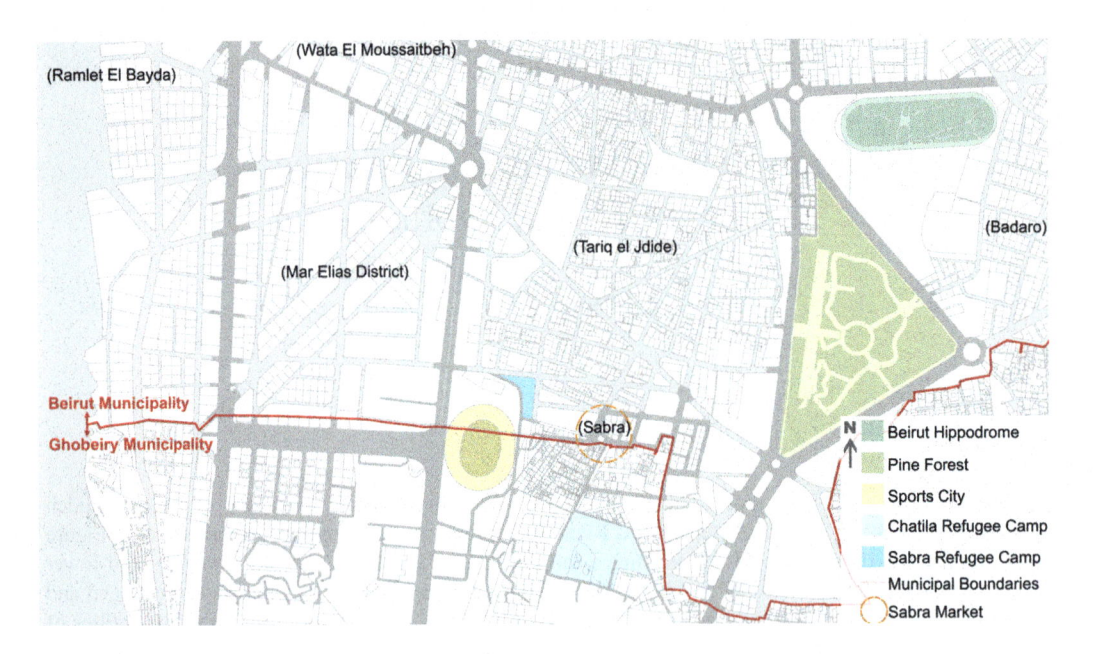

Figure 10.1 Map demarcating the main landmarks surrounding the area of intervention
Source: Author.

clear by then that there was a pressing need for AUB to acknowledge and harness its community's growing involvement in civic issues. Accordingly, the CCECS was founded in 2008 with the following mission:

> The Center for Civic Engagement and Community Service (CCECS) aims to develop a culture of service and civic leadership within the AUB community and provide opportunities for AUB students, faculty, and staff from all backgrounds to study and respond to social and civic needs. The Center identifies, integrates, and supports university-wide community initiatives, thus upholding AUB's mission of service towards its community. (AUB and OIRA 2008: 69)

The Community Development Projects Unit (CDPU) was established as a division of the CCECS with a mission to initiate and support community-based research and development projects constituting the instructional link between various academic departments, donor agencies, NGOs and the municipalities. Since then, the CDPU has been leading various initiatives nationwide, including: the upgrade and landscaping of Karem el Zaytoun pedestrian trail, an originally Armenian lower income neighborhood in Beirut in 2008–9; the rehabilitation of the water reservoir of Marwaheen, a village in South Lebanon on the border with Israel in 2009–11; the construction of an Urban Agriculture Training Center (Figure 10.2) in Ain Al Helwa Palestinian Refugee Camp in Saida in 2011–12; and the recent implementation of hygienic facilities in Syrian Refugees' Collective Shelters in 2013–15.

Conceptual and Operational Framework

In each case, the above grassroots projects have been developed and implemented with the full participation of local inhabitants and user groups. This process begins by securing consensus on a general theme, and develops by incorporating local knowledge and molding the support of political stakeholders. Although clearly structured, the methodology of the work is highly flexible to accommodate the fluidity of various situations on the ground and is founded on a few guiding concepts. *Developmental planning*, as defined by Bollens, "seeks to integrate traditional spatial planning with social and economic planning, as well as

Figure 10.2 A 3D model of the Urban Agriculture Training Center in Ain Al Helwa
Source: Author.

to include a participatory process aimed at empowering the marginalized" (2012: 56). Next, *participatory design* leads to socially responsive projects. Because informal urban settlements function mostly according to *'urf* [local customs] with limited adherence to written state codes, operating in such areas requires in-depth understanding of local practices and local knowledge. Local involvement in the decision-making and implementation processes stimulates innovative ideas in terms of technical operations and resource management. Finally, *strategic intervention* targets short-term interventions with an immediate impact meant as a catalyst that induces complementary initiatives by the community itself.

These guiding concepts are rendered operational through the dynamic interaction among stakeholders, bringing together the university, a partnering donor and the community, all framed by the municipality as the legislative and legitimizing public agency (Figure 10.3). Their successful interaction is dependent upon the following criteria from each respective participant:

a. *Academic commitment*: community-based projects require strong commitment from the associated faculty members to the institution's public engagement mission. This process emphasizes "shifts from individual faculty, courses, and curricular redesign to collective faculty culture" (Beere et al. 2011: 120). Accordingly, syllabi become operational briefs that are progressively amended as civic engagement unfolds, and learning to learn in unstructured environments becomes a necessary measure to acquire negotiation and problem-solving skills.
b. *Social responsibility*: implementing projects on "sensitive" sites is subject to repercussions caused by exceptional factors that necessitate greater effort, an elastic timetable and supportive funding. An essential part of the challenging process is a partnering donor, fully aware and understanding of onsite operations, who dedicate a team of their own to work hand-in-hand with the university and the targeted communities.
c. *Local receptiveness*: residents of marginalized communities are often skeptical about outsiders, especially when mapping, photographing and interviewing. Informing local stakeholders on the objectives of the study usually alleviates suspicion and changes the mood into a warm and welcoming one. Working within a receptive context is key to engaging local groups in designing and managing meaningful projects. However, there are groups who are unwilling to participate in any form of civic engagement due to traumatizing experiences, covert activities or monopolizing resources. Weak or denied access to research sites yields hollow projects with minimal impact on the targeted communities.

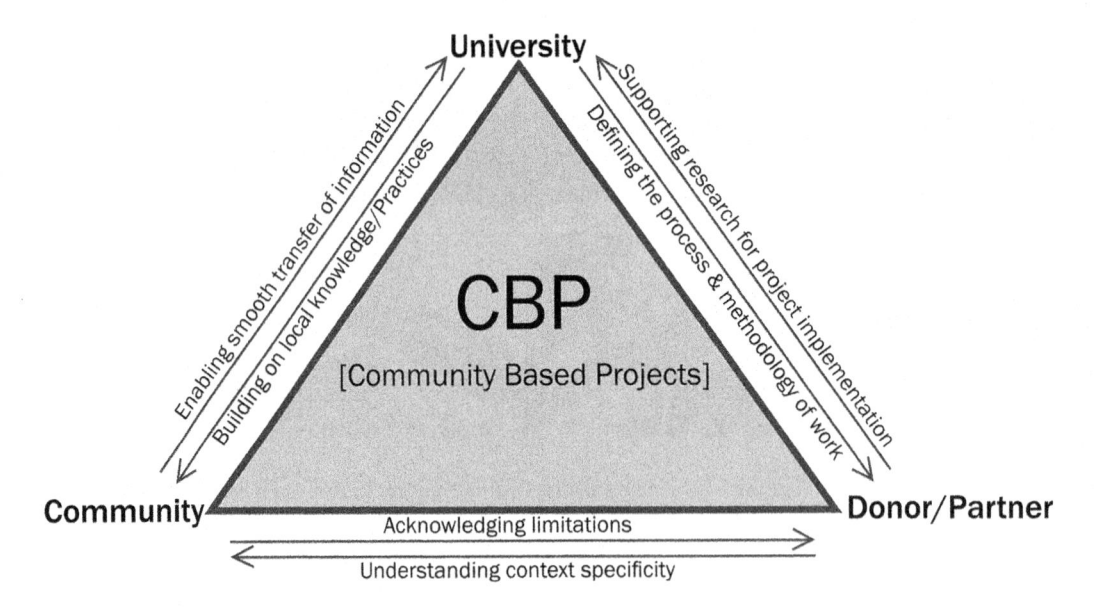

Figure 10.3 Schematic representation of the operational framework enabling the implementation of Community Based Projects

Source: Author.

Administrative Context

In the case study of Souq Sabra presented in this chapter, the abstract operational framework outlined above took tangible form through the following three stakeholders:

a. American University of Beirut (AUB): for the research and implementation study, the CCECS coordinated with three departments: Landscape Design and Ecological Management (LDEM), Civil and Environmental Engineering (CEE) and the Health Promotion and Community Health (HPCH). The designated site was tackled as a final-year project by one student in LDEM and four others in CEE, in addition to five graduate students in HPCH who focused on issues related to health and hygiene hazards.
b. Hariri Foundation for Sustainable Human Development (HFSHD): a dedicated team was fully engaged in the project development and implementation phases. The Foundation's strong ties with the local community, notably in the Sabra area, and their awareness to the complexities inherent in the field were instrumental to the community consultation process and later to the project implementation.
c. Sabra Market Street Committee: established based on a request from CCECS and the influence of HFSHD to present the locals' views and facilitate the tasks of our researchers. The Committee's input was instrumental in determining the strategic design intervention and the smooth implementation of works.

Through HFSHD, the Souq Sabra upgrading project received funding from the United Nations Development Program (UNDP) under a wider initiative entitled "Youth Mobilization and Development in Beirut and its Suburbs" encompassing the two neighborhoods where the Hariri Foundation was already strongly established, Sabra and Karem el Zaytoun. Due to the absence of state departments entrusted with developmental planning and projects, municipalities represent the only legal bodies issuing the required permits to secure the implementation of Community Based Projects.[2] As such, Beirut and Ghobeiri municipalities were directly involved in legitimizing Sabra project as both shared jurisdictions over the northern section of the market. At the time of implementation, coordination among the respective municipalities were at their weakest due to the rift in the Lebanese politics following the 2005 assassination of former Prime Minister Rafic Hariri and the July 2006 War.

Physical and Spatial Context

Early images and maps of Beirut during the French Mandate show the Sabra area as a garden suburb filled with fig, cactus, pine and orchards. During the early 1940s this area was zoned by French urbanist Michel Ecochard as the city's "respiratory lung" (Ghorayeb 1998: 109), a vision transformed by the arrival of successive waves of Palestinian refugees, rural migrants and foreign laborers (Ghorayeb 1998). Currently Sabra neighborhood is inhabited by competing groups, each securing a zone with access to the street market known as Souq Sabra. Operations in the market area started with the opening of butcher shops along the *Saha* [main square] when the Karantina slaughterhouse situated in the vicinity of Nahr Beirut [*Beirut River*] became inaccessible with the outbreak of civil war in 1975. The lucrative business was eventually diversified and today Souq Sabra is one of Beirut's busiest street markets, informally appropriated by retail shops and street vendors. Within this market, forged CDs and pornography are sold next to electronic devices, vegetable, fish and poultry products. It is located in the southern periphery of municipal Beirut adjoining the Sports City complex and cuts across a zone of informal settlements and two Palestinian camps, Sabra and Shatila (Figure 10.4).

The Souq is the main source of livelihood for the various groups of the neighborhood whose control over each segment of the street is supported by influential parties and street-lords. From the entrance to Al Rihab up to *Saha* Sabra, posters and slogans are flown and plastered on walls to define territories. These overwhelmingly reflect the "geo-politics" of the space, with Syrian workers and supporters of the Amal Movement active around the Ghobeiri entrance,[3] the Dom community appropriating the stretch facing Hey el Gharbi,[4] Palestinians opening shops along Sabra Refugee Camp, and the Future Party[5] supporters controlling the *Saha* that is defined by the meat market. To further complicate the politics of the space, the *Saha* that demarcates the northern entrance of the Souq falls under the jurisdiction of two rival municipalities (Figure 10.5), specifically Beirut (with strong March 14th support) and Ghobeiri (with strong March 8th supporters). Weak coordination between the two authorities contributes to the insalubrious conditions within the *Saha* and its vicinity, where sewage floods the streets, the slaughtering of livestock is carried out in the open air, and solid waste is poorly managed and accumulating daily.

Spatially the *Saha* is a 500-square-meter space connecting the market to three roads extending toward Tariq el Jdideh. Geographically it sits at the lowest elevation within its context, collecting the watershed from the hilly terrain between the Beirut Arab University and the Sports City. The existing infrastructure within the Sabra neighborhood consists of an old combined system dating back to the late 1950s that underwent some rehabilitation works in the year 1993 along primary roads surrounding the Souq. During the dry season, the existing system takes on only wastewater and is adequate for collecting the flow. During the rainy season, however, flooding is a frequent occurrence in the Souq, as the network gets overloaded with both storm and

---

2   According to the Municipal act, Decree-law no. 118 Article 1 states that "the municipality is a local administration exercising, within the scope of its work, the powers entrusted thereto by the law. The municipality shall hereby enjoy legal personality as well as financial and administrative independence."

3   Amal is a Lebanese political party headed by Speaker of the House Nabih Berri. It is a core constituent of the March 8th Movement, an alliance of political parties that was formed in the aftermath of the assassination of former Prime Minister Rafic Hariri.

4   "The Dom communities are commonly mistaken as Bedouin, and while they are distinct groups with very different histories and cultural practices, both are minority groups in Lebanon and face similar issues in terms of marginalization and discrimination from majority communities. They are commonly referred to, derogatorily, as the Nawar" (Das and Davidson 2011: 267).

5   Future Party is a Lebanese political party headed by Saad Hariri, son of the former Prime Minister Rafiq Hariri, and is one of the core parties that make up the March 14th political alliance.

136   *Urban Design in the Arab World*

Figure 10.4   An aerial image locating landmarks and clusters in Sabra neighborhood
Source: Author (based on Google Earth Image 2013).

Figure 10.5   Photograph of Souq Sabra showing the Ghobeiri and Beirut municipally boundary lines coinciding along the market street
Source: Author.

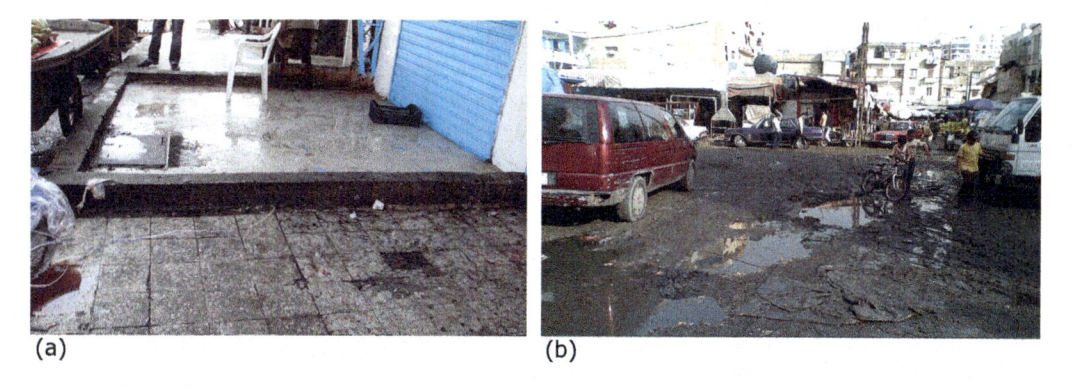

Community-Based Design as Mediator between Academia and Practice 137

Figure 10.6 Photographic documentation
Note: (a) an elevated curb aimed at stopping the infiltration of flooding sewers; (b) photograph of the flooded *Saha*.
Source: Author.

Figure 10.7 Market dynamics
Note: Handcarts wrapped to protect the displays when street vendors are away (above), various types of sheltering devices (middle left), in-house garbage collection using the "custom made" trolley (middle right), spatial organization of handcarts in the street (below left), and a shop owner connecting electrical wire to the main grid (below right).
Source: Author.

wastewater. Detailed studies were prepared in the mid-1990s, yet works have been halted due to concerns raised by the Ghobeiri municipality, claiming their inability to endure excessive workloads. Locals believe that political tension is the main reason hindering the implementation of a new piping system and, in anticipation of a slow resolution, have improvised basic methods to curb the infiltration of water into their shops and residences (Figure 10.6a).

Market Dynamics

During the first field visit, we noted an over-crowded market where merchants and street vendors appropriate every available space that is not cluttered with rubbish or broken wooden carts. Cargo trucks enter the market at dawn, after which cars are only allowed for residents' emergencies as the Souq functions as a "pedestrian friendly" street. Handcarts are positioned to allow for a linear flow along the market while leaving enough space for shoppers to interact with vendors. Awnings protect shops from inclement weather and demarcate their appropriated territory onto the sidewalks, while umbrellas serve the same purposes for street vendors. Plastic sheets are extended across streets from balconies, sheltering shoppers from both rainstorms and the heat of the sun. During the night, projectors illuminate wide stretches along every shop and street vendors fix fluorescent tubes to the umbrella stems to showcase their vegetables. Access to services is highly informal; electric wires and water hoses are tapped to the main networks, and regular outages are resolved by resorting to power generators and water supplied by trucks. The *Saha* itself serves as the Souq's service area; where cargo trucks, generators and water tanks are positioned. Local informal garbage collectors use trolleys framed on bicycle wheels to carry meat leftovers toward Sukleen bins;[6] the odors that emanate from those bins required their positioning in open land 500 meters from the *Saha* (Figure 10.7).

According to the initial agreement signed between our partner and the funding agency, upgrading had to tackle the part of the Souq under the jurisdiction of Beirut's municipality, but municipal boundaries are blurred within the market's congested streets and the rundown conditions are the same on both sides. Merchants' sectarian and political affiliations determine clearer boundaries, and political sway held by the Future Party around the *Saha* guided the choice of that area as the main location for works. The area also acts as a portal to a portion of Sabra market that stretches toward the edges of El Dana Mosque, 200 meters inside the Ghobeiri boundaries. This segment is an L-shaped street with 15 informal butcher shops located on the corner of the *Saha*, a tin-sheet-covered vegetable market along the sides of the mosque, and street vendors occupying the rest of the street and sidewalks that front 22 retail and grocery shops. Rental fees are relatively high in the market, ranging up to 500 USD/sqm. Protection money is paid to *abadayat* [strongmen] who secure the street, and the *khuwwa* [extortion fees] range according to the location of shops and handcarts and the type and quality of products sold.

Participative Urban Design Process

The multidisciplinary background of the AUB students had a significant impact on their readings of the informal landscapes and the definition of their roles in the envisioned process for change. Community Based Learning (CBL), defined by Furco and Holland as the process of enabling students to "engage in activities that enhance academic learning, civic responsibility and the skills of citizenship, while also enhancing community capacity through service" (2004: 27), was determined as the overarching paradigm of researchers. Learning to work in unstructured environments was key to the development of an in-depth understanding of contested territories. Advanced critical thinking grew out of operating in the field with students actively engaged with local inhabitants. These readings became the basis for defining—and later assessing—the following course outcomes: defining a clear problematic, developing a comprehensive narrative/argument, and setting a sustainable vision for change. Accordingly, the syllabi became operational briefs that were progressively amended as the process unfolded. During the first stage of research, students conducted fieldwork as one group. Following each visit, findings were thoroughly reviewed and discussed, and reflections determined

---

6   Sukleen is a private company in charge of waste disposal and waste treatment of Metropolitan Beirut.

the requirements of the next steps. The final result was a comprehensive analysis that enabled the researchers to draw on their expertise in urban landscape, infrastructure and community health fields. The site was then divided according to the three disciplines, with students continuing the coordination that proved so valuable in the development of their projects.

Data Collection

Students started their research work by examining the available literature that shed light on the area, and by collecting data from the engineering firms that had prepared infrastructural drawings for the Council for Development and Reconstruction (CDR). Soon after conducting the initial field visits, research revealed major discrepancies within the material at hand. Accordingly, reliable data had to be gathered directly from the site, a matter that entailed intensive fieldwork (Figure 10.8). Merchants and street vendors stated their suspicions regarding the collection of information, which they feared could be improperly used by newspapers or TV reports to stigmatize the neighborhood, or by the *darak* [police] and *mukhabarat* [intelligence] to raid and arrest wanted figures. Three of our team members were held captive for three hours in one of the butcher shops for taking pictures of the meat market. Within this cautious environment, trust-building was a prerequisite to any fieldwork. Accordingly, we advised HFSHD, which has significant political influence in the area, to setup a local committee representing shop owners, street vendors, residents and concerned stakeholders as a coordination mechanism. This committee mediated between our team and the locals in order to clarify the scope of our research and define our objectives. A liaison figure was named from the committee to escort our teams during site visits and familiarize them with the market's shop owners and street vendors. In this way, the process was smoothed out and the market became a welcoming zone for the researchers.

Investigating the daily practices and the management of activities was essential to setting a design proposal that aligned with the market's unique dynamics. Field research depended on three primary collection methods: (a) surveying—open- and closed-ended forms conducted with local stakeholders and shoppers; (b) mapping—preparing detailed drawings of the existing physical condition in the market (Figure 10.9); and (c) sampling—collecting indicators related to waste management. Following each round of surveying,

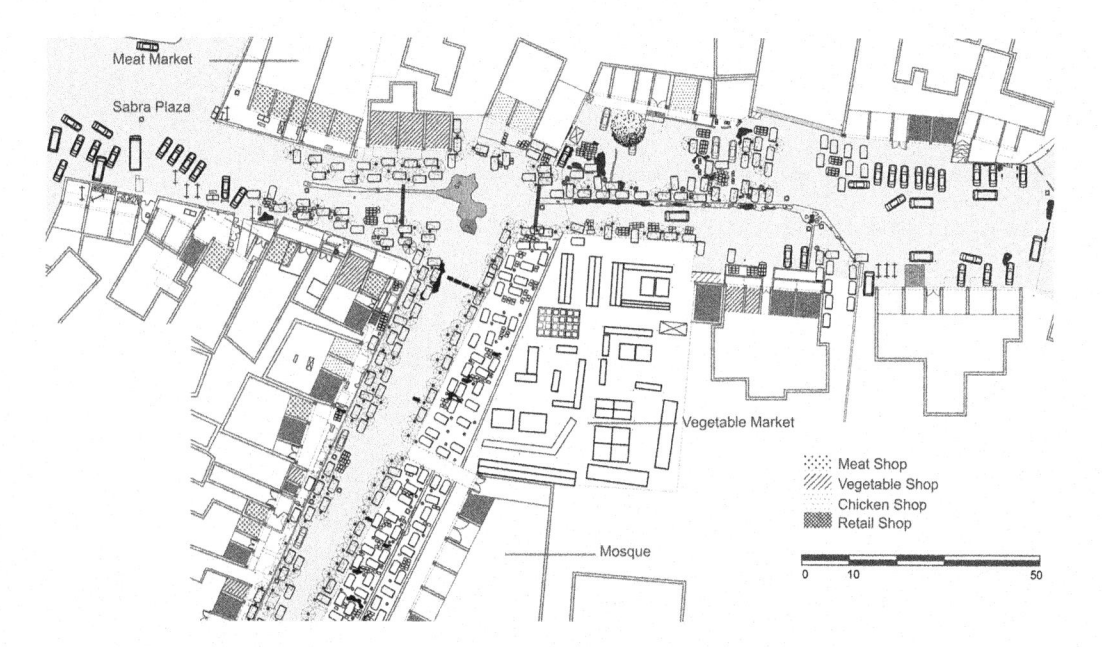

Figure 10.8   Map as prepared by AUB students on Souq Sabra
Source: Author.

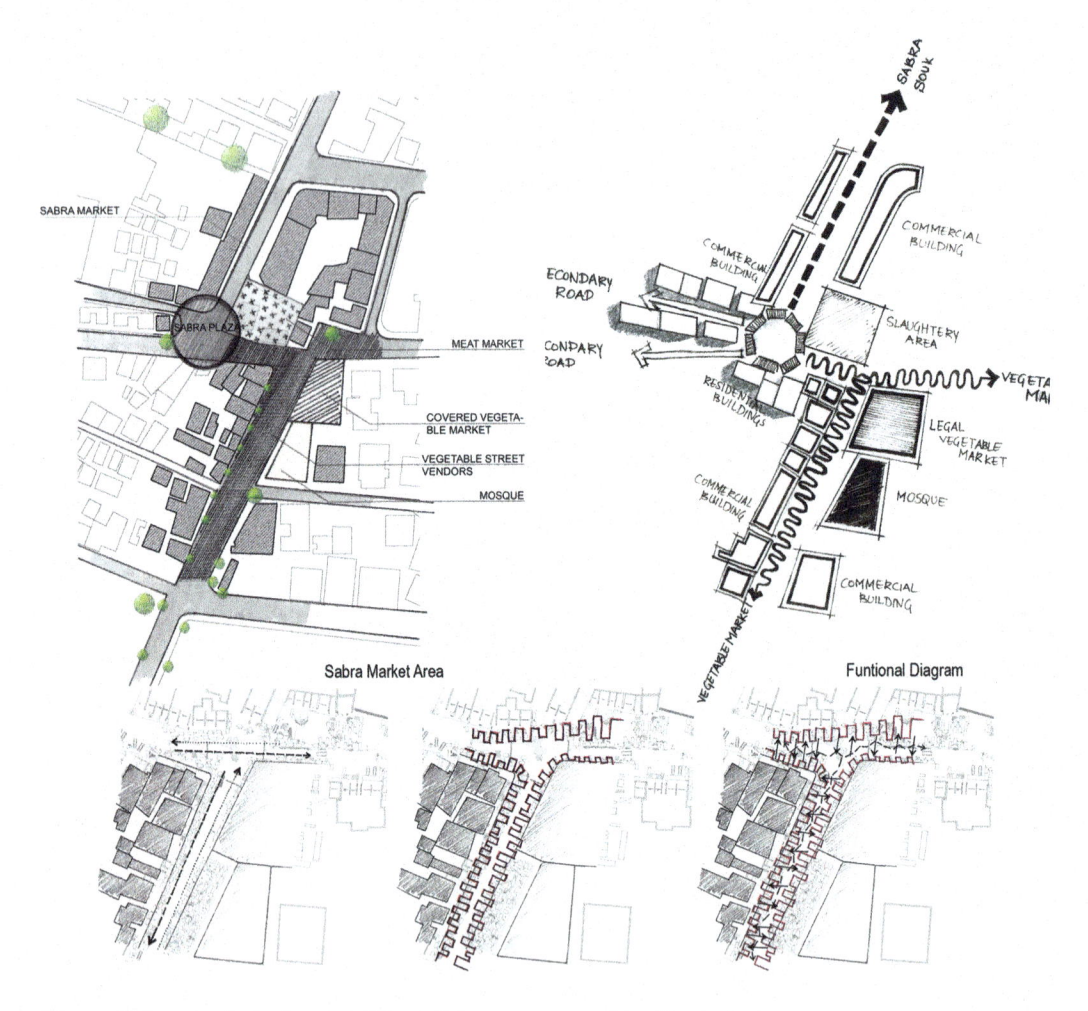

Figure 10.9 Analytical maps of Souq Sabra as prepared by the students
Source: Author.

mapping and sampling, students met and discussed their findings, and adjusted their research accordingly. The acquired data determined the Souq's key structural elements to be space organization, circulation patterns, service delivery, garbage collection, rental procedures and working shifts.

Design Vision

Execution drawings had previously been prepared to implement a roundabout with a few trees planted in its center in an attempt to define the northern entrance of the market (Figure 10.6b). Our team argued to postpone this action plan, preferring to save the allocated money for a more significant intervention. Upon viewing video where street vendors claimed that a "roundabout will be used as an additional space by peddlers," and two butchers unabashedly expressed their intent to "chop down the trees and use the logs for barbeque," our partner was convinced to the change in the initial plans.

Our overall objective was to instead design a project that was gleaned from local elements, responsive to merchants' concerns, feasible to implement, and adequate as a platform for further development. Steel plates and randomly elevated curbs, used by shop owners and residents to block the infiltration of water

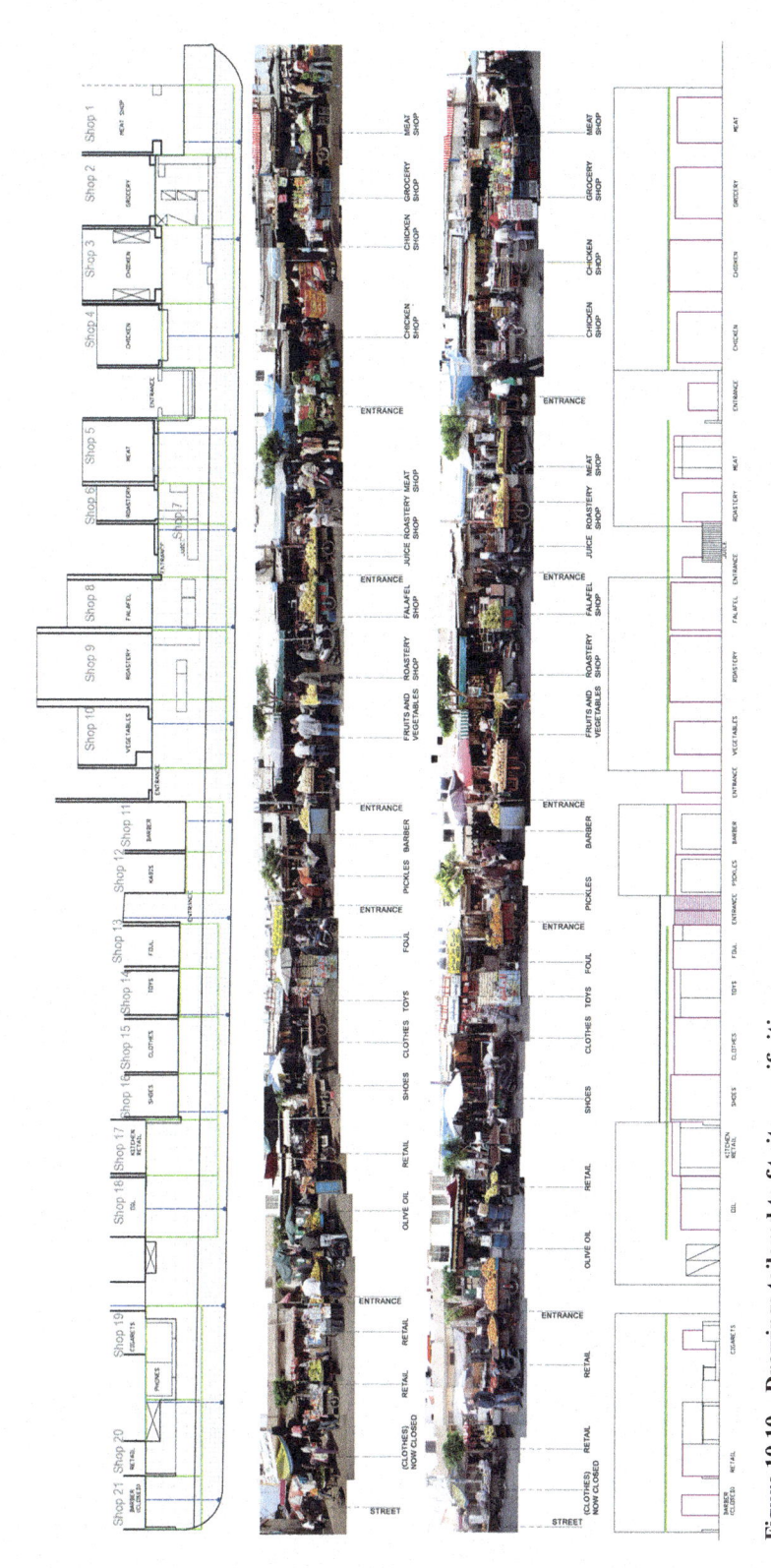

Figure 10.10 Drawings tailored to fit site specificities
Source: Author.

and sewers, provided inspiration for the design vision. We developed a proposal for market upgrading and spatial organization based on the *Water Breaker* concept, a slogan we used to promote the project. A cross-section with an elevated curb, uniform sidewalk, lighting poles, stone cladding and adjustable canopies would unify the allocated segment, curtail water infiltration and begin to define a base plan for market organization. Blueprints and 3D models were thoroughly discussed and a mockup was built on site in order to gain approval. The committee favored the idea and expressed their enthusiasm for the implementation of a project that would tackle the issue of flooding. Together we decided to choose the stretch of 22 retail and grocery shops as the site for implementing the first phase of works (Figure 10.10).

Having reached consensus with the local committee on the work plan, we had to secure the permission of the concerned municipalities. In a separate meeting with Beirut and Ghobeiri mayors, both voiced their opinions on "slum clearance" as being the best-fit scenario for Sabra neighborhood. During those meetings, our proposal was presented as a simple, short-term solution that would not conflict with the municipalities' plans for the area. Soon after an informal approval was granted, works were launched and carried out during the night at hours of relatively low traffic in the market. The simple model defined in the first phase of design was necessarily more complex when applied on the ground; the design had to be tailored to meet the requirements of each shop owner and street vendor within the defined stretch, as illustrated by the following anecdote:

> I got a phone call from the contractor implementing works in Souq Sabra asking me to immediately come on site; 'Abo Senan, the owner of the chicken-snacks, kicked out all workers from the Souq and is threatening us to never come back.' It didn't make sense. The guy has always been cooperative and eager to see the project done, something really bad must have happened. I went directly to Sabra, Abo Senan was furious ... at best disappointed. With a high-pitched voice he asked me 'what gives you the right to change my sunshield?' The committee decided on having a unified system, I answered. 'Well, the committee can raise blue banners as much as they like; blue ruins my business. The yellow sunshield I have reflects perfectly on the roasted chicken; a blue one will make them look sick,' said Abo Senan.[7] Afterwards, Abo Senan and the committee reached a middle ground, red sunshields![8]

Conclusion

The Sabra Project presented CDPU's methodology *to bridge the divide between theory and practice*. CDPU coordinated community meetings, ensured the students safe access to sites, and followed up on all implementation procedures. The in-depth understanding of the project benefitted from the students' varied educational backgrounds, while the students, who were teamed in groups, were given the opportunity learn in an unstructured environment and developed advanced critical thinking skills through operating in the field and engaging with local inhabitants (Figure 10.11). The defined learning outcomes of (a) defining a clear problematic; (b) developing a comprehensive narrative/argument; and (c) setting a sustainable vision for change, can be recapitulated by the following *three R's*:

a. Reflection: in the form of papers, PowerPoint presentations, or pinups, students documented their observations reflecting the impact of each site visit. This process conveyed personal attitudes and values that underwent notable changes with the students' growing involvement in developing site narratives.

---

7 It is worth noting that supporters of rival political parties in Lebanon use color codes to manifest their loyalties. For example, green is used by Amal supporters, blue by Future supporters, yellow by Hezbollah supports, orange by Free Patriotic Movement supporters, and so on.

8 This is an excerpt from a conversation between the author, the contractor and Abo Senan, a shop owner in the Sabra market.

Figure 10.11 AUB students in action
Note: Presenting their findings to HFSHD team (left), presenting the design proposal to the council of Beirut municipality (middle), and interviewing a garbage collector from Sukleen (right).
Source: Author.

b. Reciprocity: this implies equal transfer of knowledge between researchers and the partnering NGOs, stakeholders and communities. Each student had to closely follow up with a focal person who had in-depth knowledge on the area of study, and who was acknowledged by the local inhabitants. Community representatives attended class presentations and were engaged in active discussions, ensuring reciprocity in the learning process.
c. Responsibility: Community Based Projects enabled students to learn in unstructured environments where they gained significant negotiation skills. Students' field hours and active engagement with community groups gave researchers a real feel for the dynamics of chaos that govern areas that are "out of control." Many students took the debate outside the confinement of academia and participated in public discussions on progressive issues.

The success of the projects led by the CDPU in various underprivileged locations across the Lebanese territory, where the lack of technical and financial resources and weak governance exacerbate impoverishment, highlights the necessity of replicating our experience and expanding academic involvement in Lebanon. Community Based Learning (CBL), which challenges mainstream thinking and passive learning, should be incorporated into curriculum development, a process that would require an academic infrastructure that introduces, supports, adopts and recognizes CBL as an effective source for generating and contextualizing theories. Results can be reached through initiating the following steps:

a. Recruiting CBL faculty members: each department needs to solicit one or more faculty members with a main objective of fully integrating CBL into teaching methodology and course learning outcomes. The faculty member needs to have a developed spirit of teamwork, to be able to link between theory and practice, to believe in the core values of community service, and to inspire students to become actively engaged in the process of change.
b. Establishing civic engagement centers: the role of the center is to connect with all university departments, faculty members and student groups in order to establish a collective academic culture regarding community based courses and initiatives. The center will also serve as a junction between the university and community representatives, ministries, NGOs and the like. When a long-term commitment on a certain community project is needed, the center will ensure smooth flow of works and accountability on deliverables.
c. Opening a chapter for CBL alumni: CBL instills students with great passion to seek public good. The highly politicized grounds that exist outside the confinement of academia can easily overwhelm a new graduate's program for change. An alumni chapter targeting these community-sensitive graduates would allow for sustainable interaction and exchange of expertise with faculty and students and could provide the facilities needed to present their work and their vision in a liberal environment.

Outcomes and Postscript

The locals' involvement in the design process paid off during the implementation of the project and its maintenance afterwards; they felt complete ownership. In April 2013, two years after execution, I went on a site visit to inspect the area. Souq Sabra was much busier than what I had usually experienced as a result of the influx of Syrian refugees fleeing the civil war. In the crowded street, the upgraded section of the market was commendably maintained; none of the urban furniture had been vandalized, all streetlights were working, and the trees planted had not been chopped down. As a second phase of the project, CDPU aims at extending the upgrading project toward further sections of the street, developing better arrangement for handcarts, and tackling the issue of organic waste management (Figure 10.12).

Figure 10.12   Pictures taken of Sabra market before and after the implementation of works
Source: Author.

References

Al-Harithy, H. (ed.) 2010. *Lessons in Post-War Reconstruction: Case Studies from Lebanon in the Aftermath of the 2006 War*. London: Routledge.
American University of Beirut [AUB]. 2007. EMERGENCY RELIEF-Nahr El-Bared Relief Campaign. *AUBulletin Today* [online], 8(7). Available at: http://staff.aub.edu.lb/~webbultn/v8n7/article28.htm [accessed: May 11, 2012].
AUB and Office of Institutional Research and Assessment [OIRA]. 2008. *Fact Book 2007–08* [online]. Available at: http://www.aub.edu.lb/oira/Documents/FB200708.pdf [accessed: February 20, 2012].
Beere, C., Vortuba, J. and Wells, G. 2011. *Becoming an Engaged Campus: A Practical Guide for Institutionalizing Public Engagement*. San Francisco: Jossey-Bass.
Bollens, S. 2012. *City and Soul in Divided Societies*. London: Routledge.
Das, R. and Davidson, J. 2011. *Profiles of Poverty: The Human Face Of Poverty in Lebanon*. Beirut: Dar Manhal Al Hayat.
Furco, A. and Holland, B.A. 2004. Institutionalizing Service-Learning in Higher Education: Issues and Strategies for Chief Academic Officers, in *Public Work and the Academy: A Guidebook for Academic Administrators on Civic Engagement and Service Learning*, edited by M. Langseth and W. Plater. San Francisco: Anker/Jossey-Bass.

Ghorayeb, M. 1998. The Work and Influence of Michel Ecochard in Lebanon, in *Projecting Beirut: Episodes in the Construction and Reconstruction of a Modern City*, edited by P.G. Rowe and H. Sarkis. Munich: Prestel.

Chapter 11
[Trans]Forming Nahr Beirut: From Obsolete Infrastructure to Infrastructural Landscape

Sandra Frem

Introduction: An Unplanned Obsolescence

During the twentieth century, infrastructures perfected monolithic, top-down solutions and embodied—above all considerations—efficiency, technology and standardization. Prevailing practices after World War II ensued a worldwide legacy of mechanized infrastructures: standardized drainage and flooding structures, canalized rivers, normalized public works, concealed water processes, and disconnection between natural systems and man-made systems. However, the twenty-first century witnessed unprecedented economic and ecological crises at a global scale, leading to the failure of such practices, and a need to shift to softer approaches to infrastructure.

Yet in Lebanon, the top-down attitude is still an enduring model for public works, providing Lebanese cities with a generation of outmoded infrastructures with no relationship to the public realm and natural systems. Local engineers and politicians still address roads, rivers, bridges and water treatment facilities as no more than technical containers that provide efficient delivery of services and flows, at the expense of existing ecologies. This one-sided utilitarian approach does not leave room in the design and execution of such structures for any cultural considerations beyond their performative aspects, exempting them from societal and ecological roles. This is evident in the state-led public works that channelled many Lebanese coastal rivers during the second half of the twentieth century as a flood mitigation measure.

Due to heavy engineering, the lower basins of rivers such as Nahr Beirut, Nahr Abou Ali, Nahr El Mot and Nahr Antelias mutated into isolated concrete entities with a lack of formal, social and ecological integration in the urban areas they cross.

With the wake of climate change, the Lebanese coast is currently witnessing a pressing urbanization, giving rise to major challenges: longer dry periods, chronic water shortages, lack of green recreational space, urban heat island effect, pervasive traffic, ecological degradation and urban fragmentation. Unplanned urban growth has cast major stress on the various infrastructural water systems that are required to perform more, and as a result, reach earlier critical thresholds of obsolescence. Disturbances such as anthropogenic pollution, river canalization and roofing radically transformed rivers intersecting dense urban areas into obsolete water infrastructures. Designed uniquely as flood mitigation tools, they proved unable to deliver other much needed functions, such as pedestrian friendly mobility networks, green open space networks, water harvesting and retention systems, stormwater and wastewater treatment and reclamation, in addition to water supply for irrigation and non-potable uses. On the hydrological level, the massive form of these concrete rivers has failed to adapt to intermittent water conditions across seasons; most of the year, they are no more than empty open-air sewers. During the wet season, and due to their hard materiality, they proved unequipped to filter and attenuate flooding and sedimentation like a fluvial riparian system would, leading to increased flooding risks, polluted watercourses and costly maintenance in removal of sediments.

Under such conditions, rivers need to be rehabilitated into multifunctional, soft and dynamic infrastructures, providing effective hydrological and transportation arteries, and at the same time, becoming ecological and cultural corridors that permeate their respective cities and communities. Taking these challenges as a departure point, this chapter elaborates a multidisciplinary approach and a transformative process on Beirut's canalized river—Nahr Beirut, where such issues intersect and are magnified. The chapter argues that infrastructural landscape is a relevant approach to addressing infrastructure in general and to reclaiming canalized rivers back to their cities in particular. Expanded at a territorial scale, the project shows how the proposed rehabilitation approach could apply to various cases of depleted coastal river systems, projecting them as performative networks of water and public space, and catalysts for new territorial ecologies on the Lebanese coast.

Zooming in on Nahr Beirut, the project details the proposed transformation, joining the concepts of infrastructure with public green space in the design of flood management, wastewater reclamation and water purification systems. The obsolete channel mutates into an ecological corridor that harvests water for the city and becomes an infrastructural landscape that takes a civic character while performing beneficial functions for the city, thus making it an affordable solution to adopt and maintain. Instead of a rigid masterplan, the adopted strategic planning approach is catalytic and open to constant input, allowing different scales of implementation, funding and engagement.

The chapter concludes by discussing implementation and the relevance of the used approach to contemporary urbanism in general and the Lebanese context in particular.

Approach: The Infrastructural Landscape

A Multidisciplinary Approach to Infrastructure

After staying outside the realm of debate, infrastructure has witnessed in recent years a renewed interest from the disciplines of architecture, urbanism and landscape. Following the rise and fall of massive/monofunctional infrastructures, cities needed new hybrid models capable of addressing complex factors like climate change, environmental degradation, resource harvesting, urbanization and social inequality. There is a growing awareness that such contemporary urban challenges can only be addressed properly in a multidisciplinary and multileveled approach. Indeed, the complexity of cities and the intricacy of urban and natural networks require a mix of tools and tactics rather than ideological grand visions of past urban models.

At this moment in history, the focus on infrastructural rehabilitation is a unique opportunity to blur boundaries between the disciplines of architecture, urban design, landscape, engineering and ecology, and work within an expanded field of practice. Rather than leaving this field to technical experts, designers should expand current understandings of infrastructure, by coupling infrastructural engineering with the performance of natural processes, and urban design strategies. Seminal publications (Graham and Marvin 2001; Corner 1999; Shannon and Smets 2010; Waldheim 2006; Mostafavi and Doherty 2010; Mostafavi,Najle and Architectural Association 2003; Stroll and Llyod 2011) and projects[1] have offered new interpretations, reclaiming the territory of infrastructure, and the technical processes as significant to design content. It is in such simultaneous discourses that the infrastructural landscape paradigm has emerged as a remedy to reclaim obsolete infrastructure.

In her seminal work titled *Infrastructure in the Ecological City*, Kathy Poole advocated for a new interpretation of common infrastructures in the city, allowing them to regain their civic and environmental significance (Poole 1998: 126–43). According to her, the city is composed of two main apparatus: the first is the natural systems, which are the original and enduring spatial, temporal and climatic components that engage cultural entities. The second is the infrastructural systems such as sewers, streets, water supply, waste disposal and electricity, which constitute the structure, the function and the dynamics of a city. Both systems form the *built natural infrastructure*, the cultural infrastructure of the city. Indeed, I argue that infrastructural landscapes are constructed ecosystems that complement existing watersheds, and at the same time become catalysts for new ecologies and economies in the city. As an integrated solution to the seemingly independent problems of water and infrastructure, infrastructural landscapes also encompass social, spatial and environmental benefits by creating site-specific identities to obsolete infrastructure, and allowing communities to re-appropriate territories of water to the city.

However, for the landscape to become infrastructural, we need a deep knowledge of the interrelation between infrastructural, ecological and urban systems (Stokman 2008: 36–45). Consequently, it becomes essential for urban designers to expand their knowledge in processes traditionally delegated to other disciplines, such as ecological consequences of hydrology, drainage, sewage treatment and solar technology

---

1   The work of OMA, Fields Operation, West 8, Stoss LU, Stan Allen, to name a few.

and road construction. It is within such a multidisciplinary ground that we can start rethinking the design and role of infrastructure in a holistic and non-linear manner.

Infrastructural Landscape as Public Space

To expand further our understanding of the infrastructural landscape, it is essential to revisit two key moments in the history of infrastructural development: Frederick Law Olmsted's Emerald Necklace in Boston and Baron Haussmann's Grand Axes in Paris, uncovering the civic role these infrastructural landscapes had in the nineteenth-century city's development.

Indeed in nineteenth-century Boston, what started as problem-solving approaches to the issues of sanitation and public health in the deteriorated marshes of the Charles River soon expanded to include larger social issues. In his proposal for the Emerald Necklace, Olmstead embedded transportation networks, flood and drainage engineering, purification wetlands and ecological restoration into the creation of a public park system, which to-date still benefits the citizens (Zaitzevsky 1992).

In the case of nineteenth-century Paris, the infrastructural development led by Haussmann exceeded pure rationalism and economics to offer civic benefits which engaged the public sphere. Between 1852 and 1869, Haussmann's reshaping of Paris comprised a new system of sewage infrastructures that improved urban sanitation conditions, and gave rise to a new public order and social consciousness among Parisians. Like the boulevards and the promenades of Paris, sewers were used as a linkage to reconnect the city to its citizens (Saalman 1971). Unlike the American apolitical experience, Haussmann reinvested Paris's infrastructures with a radical political vision, while keeping the ability and sensibility to address both the technological rationality and the emotive considerations about the city–nature relationship.

Learning from such experiences as our cities are becoming denser, it is essential to concentrate public works efforts on upgrading sanitary and ecological networks and at the same time reverse a system of urban green spaces for recreational purposes.

Adopting the Infrastructural Landscape approach is particularly relevant to developing cities which generally cannot afford privileged landscaped parks and gardens or expensive infrastructural systems, and in which open spaces are usually pressured by private development. In such cases, designers should utilize the basic need for infrastructure as potentially the only generator of public green space that is otherwise diminished by private development. In the case of Lebanese cities, typically suffering from underdeveloped water networks, scarce water resources and limited public budget, it is essential to highlight how infrastructural landscapes could constitute affordable solutions, specifically for the dual benefit of providing ecological water management and spreading the amenity of public green space throughout the city.

Revealing Processes

In the contemporary city, infrastructure has increasingly been rendered invisible and technical. As Antje Stokman mentions in her article, *Water Purificative Landscapes*, cities are increasingly dissociated from the organization of their hydraulic system, erasing the visual and spatial logic of their urban watershed. Centrally controlled and mostly invisible water infrastructure systems have disconnected urban land-use from the logic of the watershed as well as people's experience from the ecological processes of the landscape. Underground networks of water pipes and sewage are replacing smelly and dangerous open watercourses, this being considered a major progress in the field of engineering and urban planning. Water problems are solved by engineers in a technical and preferably invisible manner, allowing urban and landscape designers the freedom to focus on aesthetic and spatial design issues of the urban layout—producing arbitrary and exchangeable designs that detach from their immediate surroundings and render their cities prototypical (2008: 51–61).

Here, I second Stokman and Poole who argue that infrastructural landscape can unearth and make visible the hidden systems of hydrology, energy, waste and biology, exposing their latent potential by making them meaningful in substance and physical presence.

Indeed, it is essential for an infrastructural landscape to work in tandem with the natural ecologies and breed new public consciousness among citizens by revealing the processes of the conjoined natural and urban systems that cater to their cities.

However, it's crucial that this revelatory act does not become purely symbolic. As counterexamples, many structures like trees on boulevards and fountains become simple natural features that are completely detached from the original ecosystems. As such, to prevent the infrastructural landscape from becoming mere urban furniture, its formal expression should reveal first and foremost its functionality and the processes embedded within both the natural and urban systems.

Hybrid Networks rather than Centralized Technical Solutions

In her paper "Affordable Landscapes," Elisabeth Mossop re-questions the relevance of centralized technical solutions to urban water management problems, and argues for a new approach (2005: 13–23). Indeed, some the key issues of dense urban regions are underdeveloped drainage and purification water systems. In such agglomerations, planned water infrastructure like piping, technical treatment and water reclamation fall short in front of the intense pace of urban development. This entails deficient water management, leading to high levels of water pollution and hygienic problems. These issues are exacerbated in arid regions that suffer from chronic water shortage. In such cases, the lack of water supply and sewerage services leads to pervasive groundwater subsidence and contamination of water tables.

As a remedy, public administrations and international organizations invest considerable budgets on massive centralized facilities like—in the case of Lebanon—wastewater treatment plants.[2] However such structures often do not operate properly due to deficient piping networks. Due to their large catchment areas, they require considerable energy loads, large spatial footprint, and bigger risks in case of failure. In addition, they minimize the possibility of local water reclamation, due to the considerable pumping required for redistribution.

Addressing the described challenges, Mossop considers that it is crucial for city-makers, designers and planners to develop hybrid networks of small infrastructures involving both human and natural processes, rather than completely replacing ecological processes with centralized, expensive and technically controlled systems. Through infrastructural landscapes, obsolete spaces develop, in time, an integrated mechanism of positive transformation at the city-level and become appropriated by neighborhoods in order to counter the mainstream arena of exclusive transformation driven by highly centralized official strategies and market pressures.

Project[3]

Territorial Approach to Coastal Lebanese Rivers

Home to two-thirds of Lebanon's population, the issue of water supply on the Lebanese coast is central to the region's future. The challenge posed by water scarcity in such a region has recently become acute, as demand has exceeded supply by three times. Existing public/private initiatives do not bridge this deficit (Yamout and El-Fadel 2005: 791–812). In an already established crisis of climate change and increasingly longer drought periods, relying on primary sources such as rainfall and water tables is no longer sufficient. This poses an urgent need to resort to secondary sources like water reuse and reclamation. Recognizing water as an increasingly valuable resource in the future, the project rethinks the hydrological role of coastal rivers in that light. At the territorial scale, it proposes to transform coastal rivers into a network of living systems that harvest water for the coast, by treating and reclaiming all of the coastal region's stormwater and wastewater (Figure 11.1a). Treated water will be redistributed through the rivers to their respective cities, creating closed water loops that meet future water demand.

---

2   The CDR has planned to treat the sewage of more than 50 municipalities in the Metn, plus the capital's sewage water in a large treatment facility that will occupy what is currently a natural sandy beach on Bourj Hammoud waterfront (Ministry of Environment/LEDO 2001).

3   The project expands on the author's master's thesis (Frem 2009).

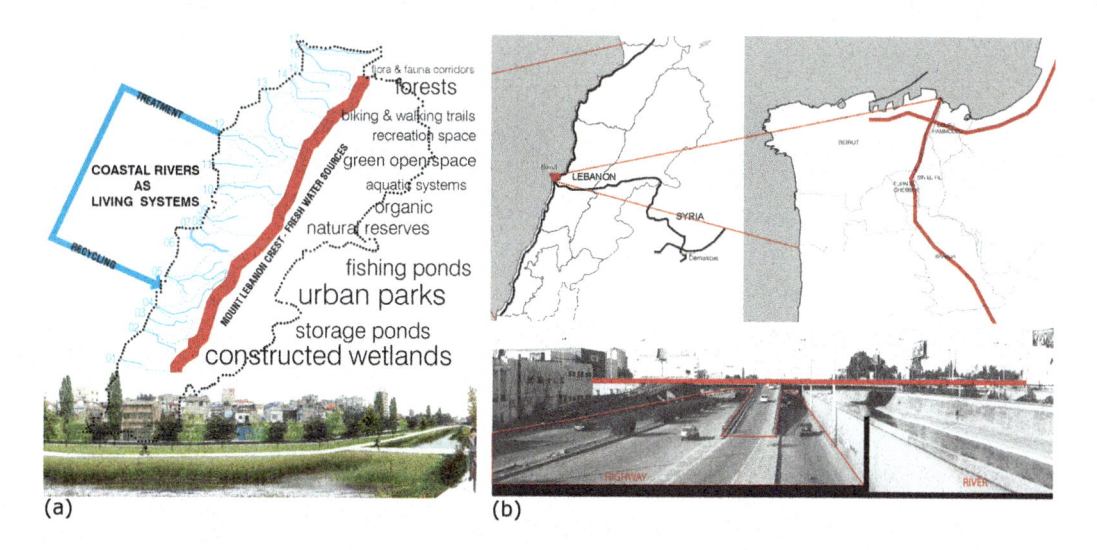

Figure 11.1 Coastal rivers in Lebanon

Note: (a) rivers as living systems: by 2050, the Lebanese coast will turn into a living system that treats and recycles 100 percent of its own water through its 17 coastal rivers; (b) Nahr Beirut: nexus of regional transportation flows.
Source: Author.

Coastal rivers as living systems will also spread the amenity of open green space throughout their respective cities, and recreational areas that improve the quality of urban life. In addition to their sustainable water system, these landscapes will become microclimatic corridors that reduce significantly urban heat island effect (UHI) and air pollution.

The project elaborates further on such approach while zooming in on Nahr Beirut as a case study.

Trans [Forming] Nahr Beirut

It would be difficult to find a site in Beirut more challenging than its river. Nahr Beirut sits at the center of the Beirut Metropolitan Region and forms in its lower basin the common boundary to six different municipalities (Figure 11.1b). The river occupies a strategic location that coincides with the intersection of Lebanon's two national highways, acting as a space of connection for millions of commuters, and at the same time, a space of separation in the city. The channeled part of the river crosses different morphologies separating the valley from the waterfront within a very short distance of 6 km before draining in the Mediterranean Sea. The Nahr district currently contains the last consistent open green space in the city, given the abundance of post-industrial sites and rail yards around the river. It is currently one of the most coveted zones for speculative private development in Beirut (Figure 11.2).

After its canalization, Nahr Beirut evolved into an over-engineered corridor of transport and water. It suffers from an intermittent flow that has declined its public image as an urban river, multileveled pollution (Rizk and Adjizian-Gerard 2000–2001), a latent risk of flooding,[4] and an isolating road infrastructure that prevents pedestrian activity (Figure 11.3). The ecosystems of its upper basin and the estuary at its tip became permanently fragmented since its channeling. The urban form of the canal acts as an abrupt boundary to all adjacent neighborhoods, restricting visual and physical access.

---

4 The river channel is dimensioned in all its profile variations to contain a flow of 1,100 cubic meters per sec, while maximum flood limit for Nahr Beirut is 1,571 cubic meters per second (Fawaz and Zein 1965: 24–36). As such, the canal form is dimensioned below the maximum flow that could occur, but much above the normal flows that does not exceed 10 m^3/sec in the wet season.

152 *Urban Design in the Arab World*

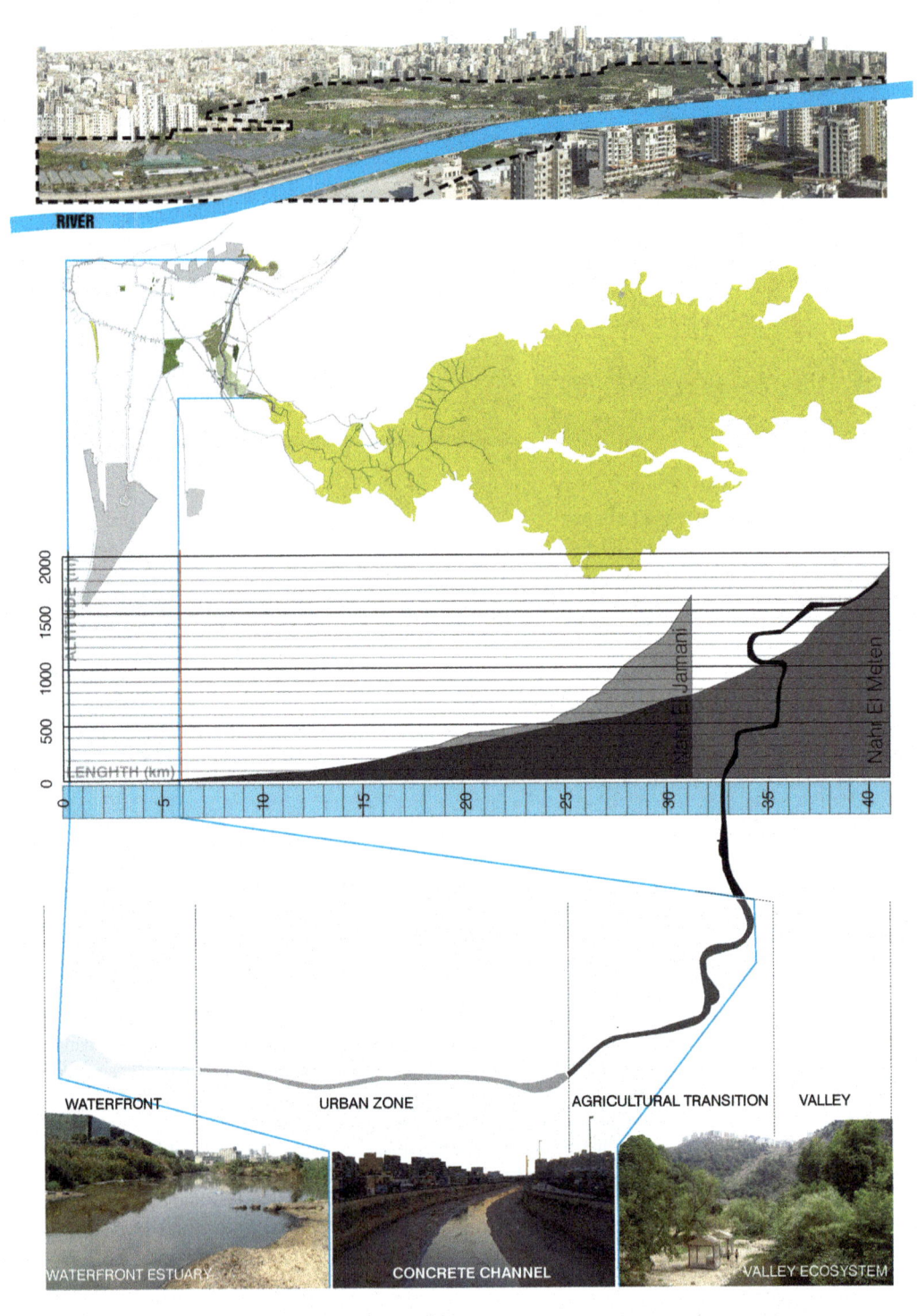

Figure 11.2 Morphologies of Nahr Beirut, which show the river district as the last open space in Beirut

Source: Author.

Figure 11.3 Intermittent flow cycles of Nahr Beirut, its different pollutants, and the appropriation of its infrastructure as public space

Note: Top, middle and bottom respectively.
Source: Author.

Beyond the obvious water, ecological and traffic problems, the Nahr area and Beirut in general suffer from a severe lack of public green space.[5] To add to this fact, exclusive governance in Beirut imposes selective access to the city's few public spaces, transforming its urban nature into a privilege rather than a right and repressing the common culture of using public green spaces for recreational purposes. To make up for such lack in the river district, the Nahr communities are appropriating and using interstitial spaces like the underbelly of bridges and leftover parcels near the river channel for public markets and improvised playgrounds (Figure 11.3). Projecting an infrastructural landscape on Nahr Beirut lies in embracing these communal practices in a more inclusive manner.

In such a context, the project proposes the transformation of Nahr Beirut into an infrastructural landscape that combines water reclamation and mobility systems with opportunities for public space, all embedded in an open space landscape framework (Figure 11.4). This physical mutation is achieved through the deployment of multifunctional water systems along Nahr Beirut that treat independently stormwater and wastewater; using microorganisms, aquaculture, mollusks (snails and oysters) and plants (Figure 11.5). Through two ecological systems—living machines and wetlands—treated water will be harvested, stored and reused by the city, creating a closed water loop that caters for 70 percent of Beirut's non-potable water consumption (Yamout and El-Fadel 2005: 791–812) (Figure 11.6). Countering the top-down approach of a massive technical intervention, the proposed water systems are networks of small-scale living systems that operate environmentally at the city scale. These systems join their performative functions with recreational landscapes on top of them, thus presenting economic and social incentives to create public green spaces along the river.

Living machines are ecological treatments that use microorganisms, aquatic and wetlands processes to treat wastewater naturally. Local living machines will reclaim 40,000 m^3/day of wastewater for Beirut (Ministry of Environment/LEDO 2001), supplanting the mega-treatment plant projected by CDR on the waterfront and allowing local reclamation.

The first type, *living machines* (Todd et al. 1995), treat wastewater (Figure 11.6) by combining localized wastewater treatment plants for the first two steps of treatment with constructed wetlands and fishponds deployed around the river for the final treatment. Public programs overlay the final treatment structures, such as wetland parks and communal platforms at the location of fishponds (Figure 11.7).

The second type, *wetlands* (Todd et al. 1995), are constructed landscapes that clean stormwater and urban runoff using biological processes (Figure 11.8). In this case again, storage structures can take a variety of design forms (dry wells, off-stream reservoirs, infiltration beds and diversion ponds), allowing public programs to happen on top of them: pedestrian and bike trails, playgrounds, communal agriculture and fresh water fish lakes. Sediments traps are deployed near construction factories, allowing the latter to clean them regularly in return for free sand and gravel. In addition to storing water for the dry season, the key benefit of this system is to act as a flood mitigation apparatus; decanalizing the river, replacing the high channel walls with lower banks and opening the river corridor to the city (Ocean Arks International 2009).

Locally situated in the upper and lower basin of the river, the different living systems are more thus easily upgraded and controlled, allowing local water reuse for the respective municipalities. As a result, they require less energy loads (GHG emissions) because treating and pumping water in a single centralized location is energy intensive. With embedded piping and linear wetlands, the river infrastructure is used to link the different systems together and to redistribute the reclaimed water to the municipalities as an alternative water supply. In addition to treating urban runoff, the linear wetlands provide the ecological and pedestrian continuity of the river corridor, expanding to become a wetland park and estuary at the waterfront, and reaching out to connect to other green spaces in the city (Figure 11.9).

The mobility systems propose better transversal access to/between Nahr Beirut banks through pedestrian bridges (Figure 11.10) and an improved longitudinal mobility through a new public transport line, city shuttles and pedestrian trails (Figure 11.11). Infrastructural manipulations propose to rethink key intersections, by using the footprint of redundant ramps, channel walls and empty lots to expand the riverbanks when possible and make room for the river (Figure 11.12).

---

5 Beirut has one of the lowest ratios of accessible green space per person which equals less than 0.5 square meters per person (Beyhum 1996: 13–16).

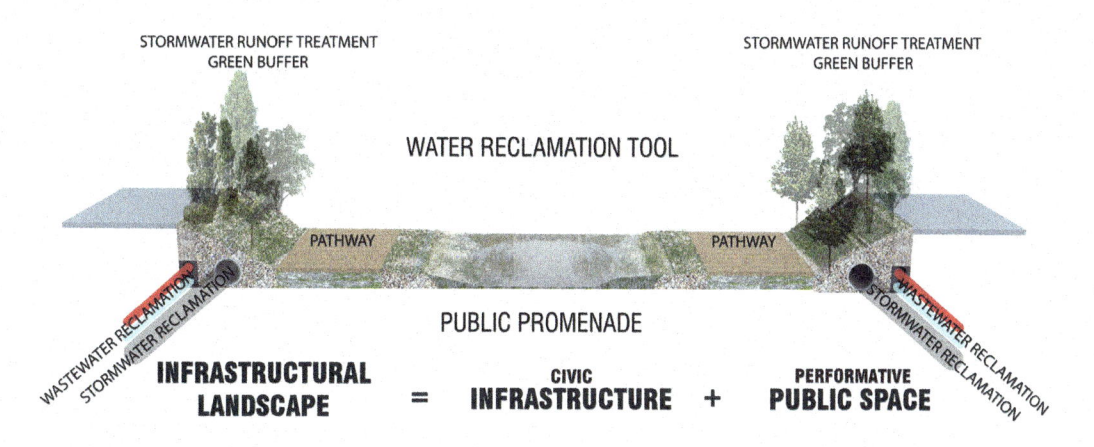

Figure 11.4 The infrastructural landscape: The river as a civic and performative landscape
Source: Author.

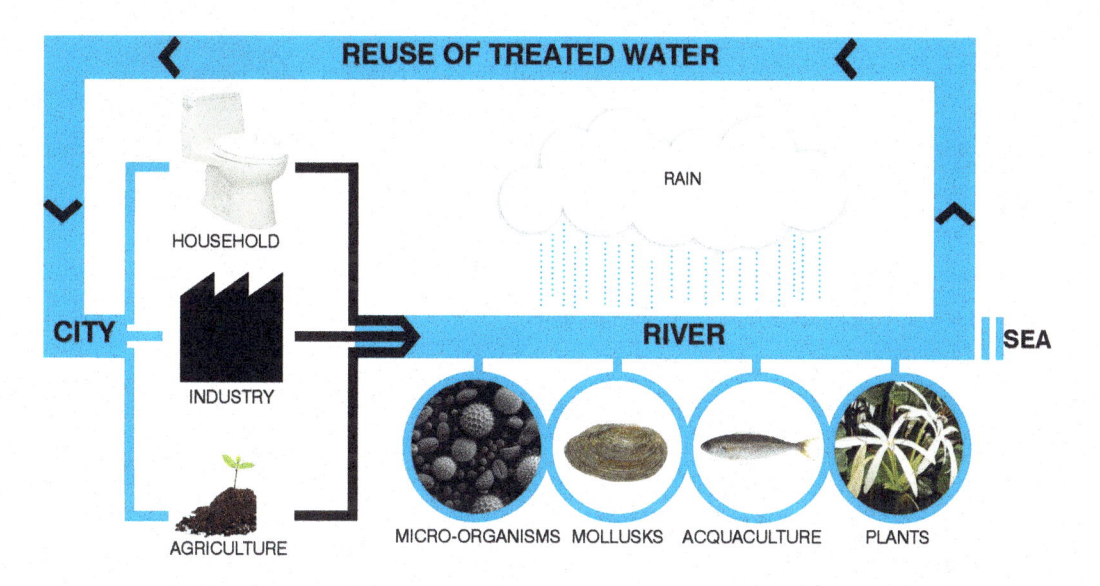

Figure 11.5 Nahr Beirut will treat the city's water using micro-organisms; treated water will be given back to city and will cover 70 percent of its non-potable needs
Source: Author.

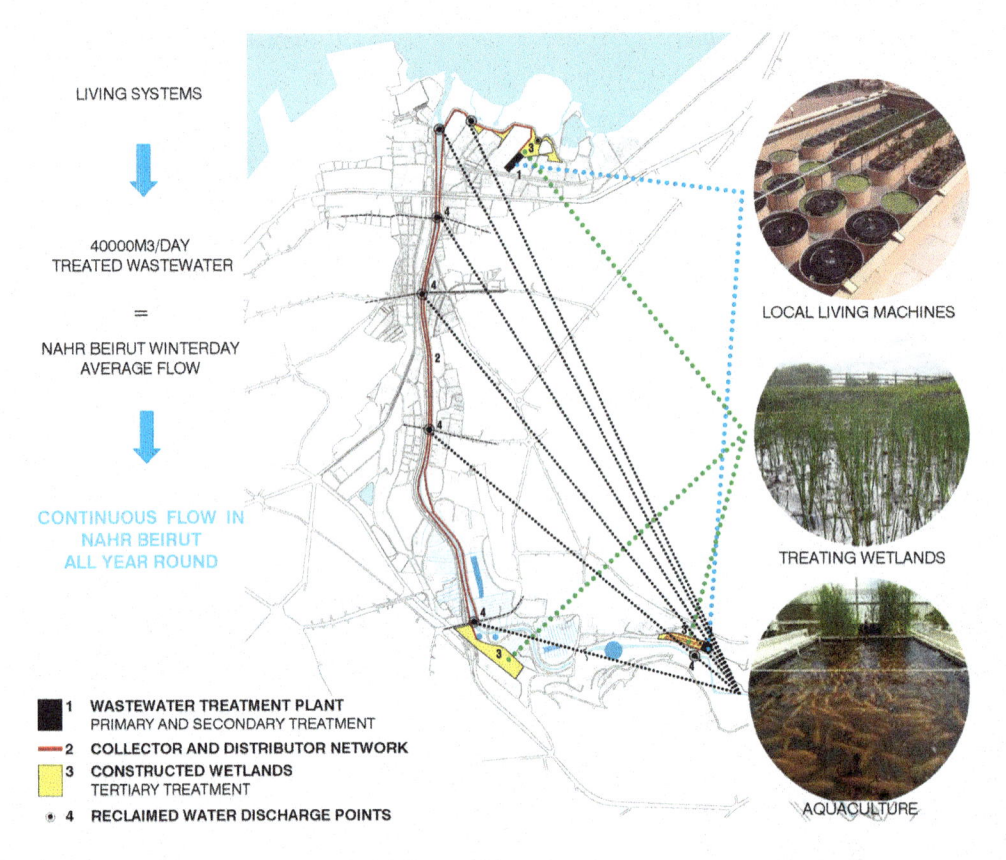

Figure 11.6   Living systems type 1—living machines
Source: Author.

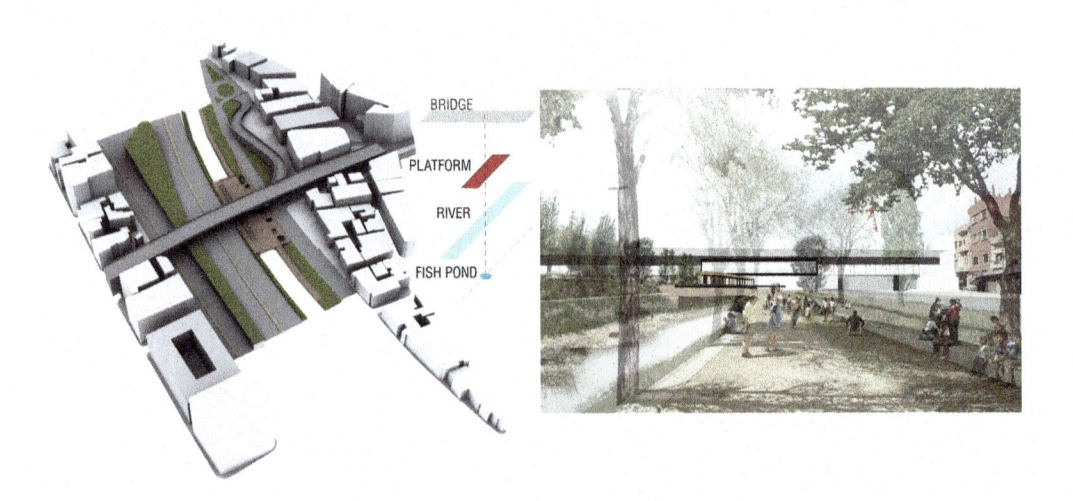

Figure 11.7   Case study of the Nabaa platform
Note: At this instance, a public platform overlays the river linear wetlands and aquaculture fishponds forming the last step of wastewater treatment.
Source: Author.

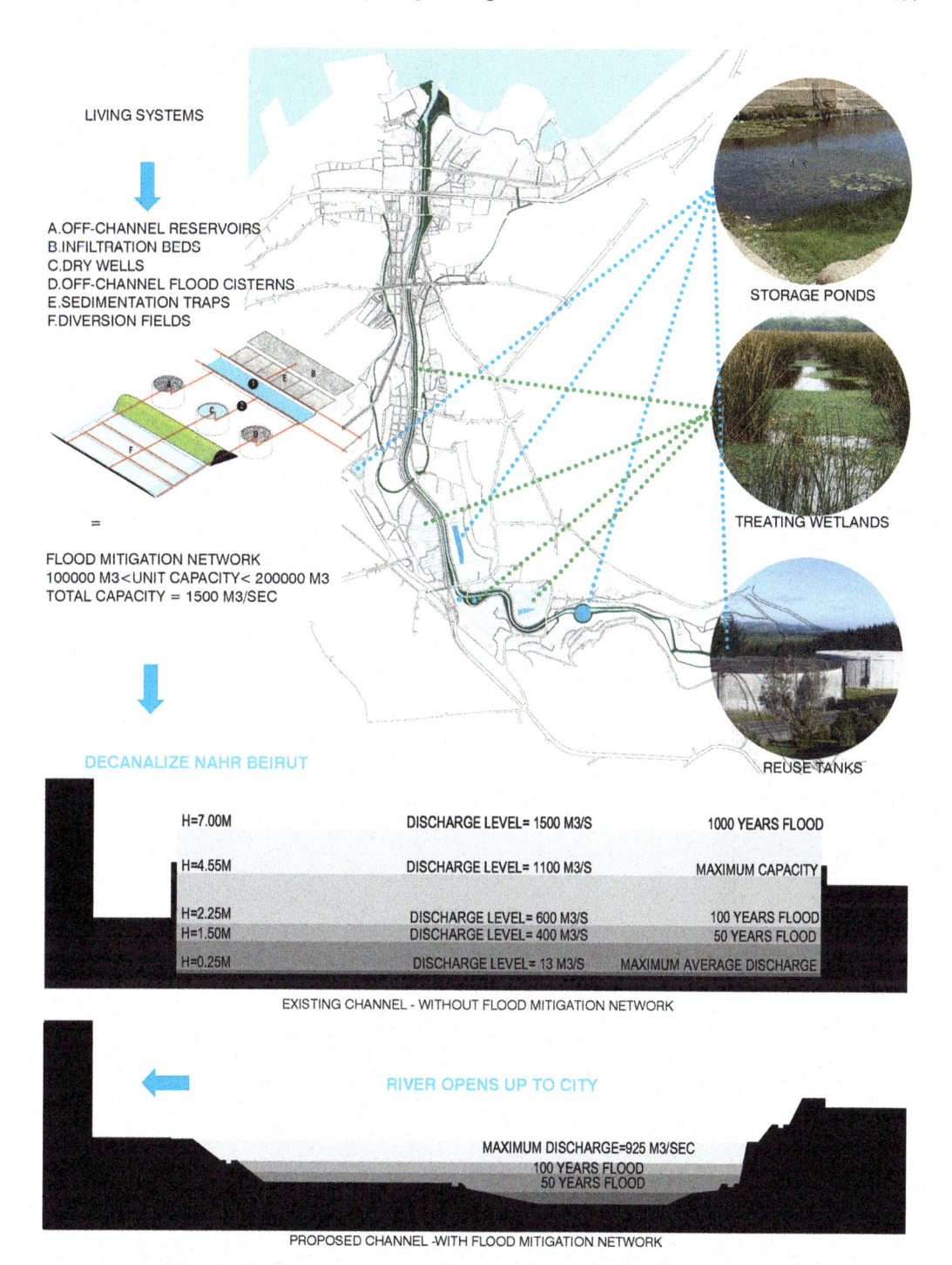

Figure 11.8 Living systems type 2
Note: Constructed wetlands will biologically filter and clean stormwater and urban runoff. Stormwater living systems will act as a flood mitigation apparatus.
Source: Author.

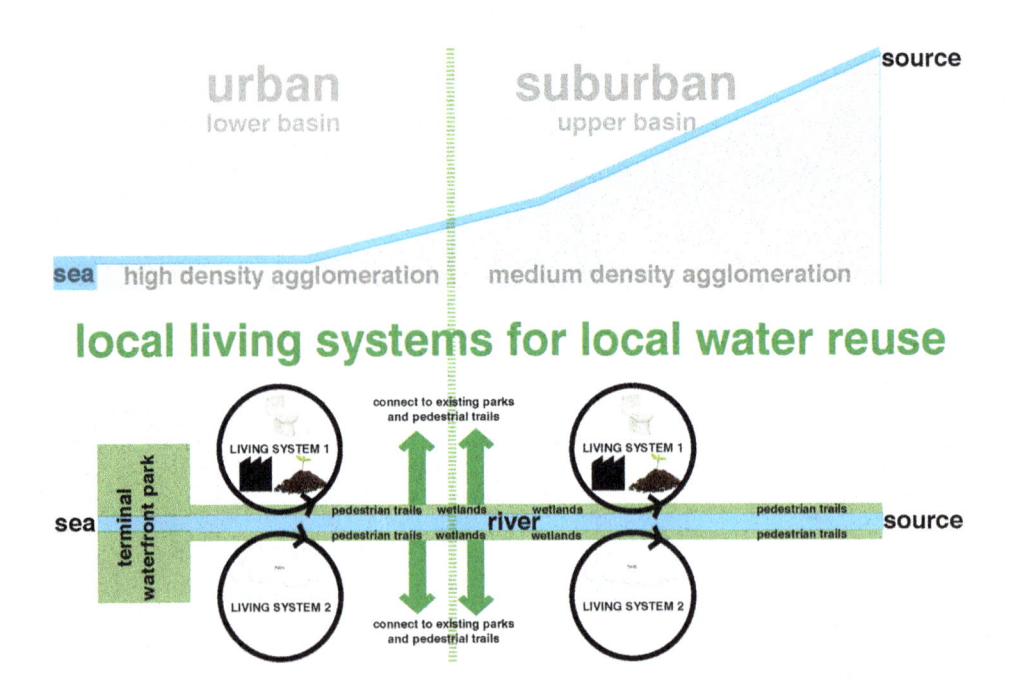

Figure 11.9 Sectional and plan diagram of the river as a connector
Note: Nahr Beirut links decentralized living systems, green space and natural–urban networks. Local living systems allow local water reuse.
Source: Author.

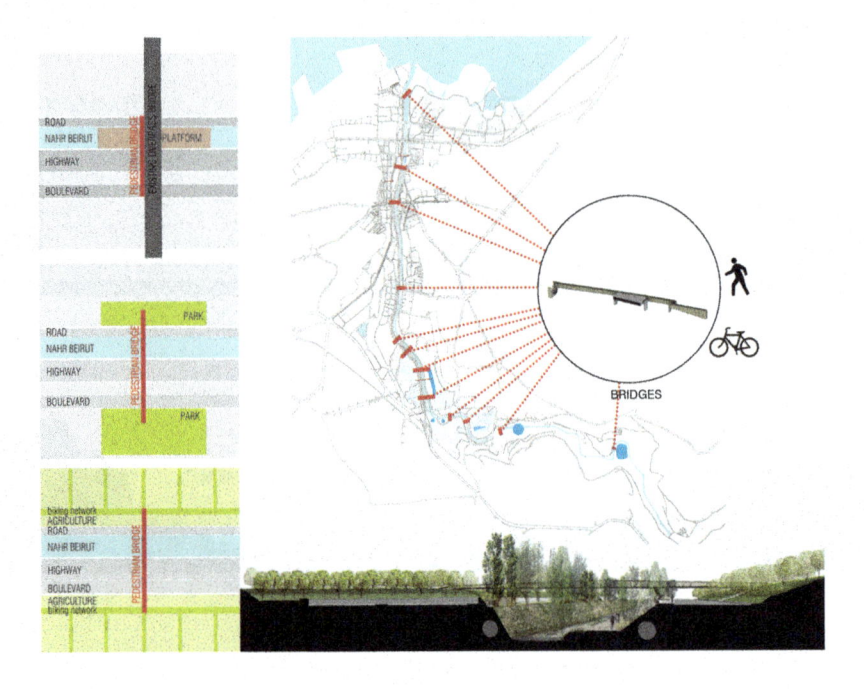

Figure 11.10 Transversal bridging typologies
Source: Author.

[Trans]Forming Nahr Beirut 159

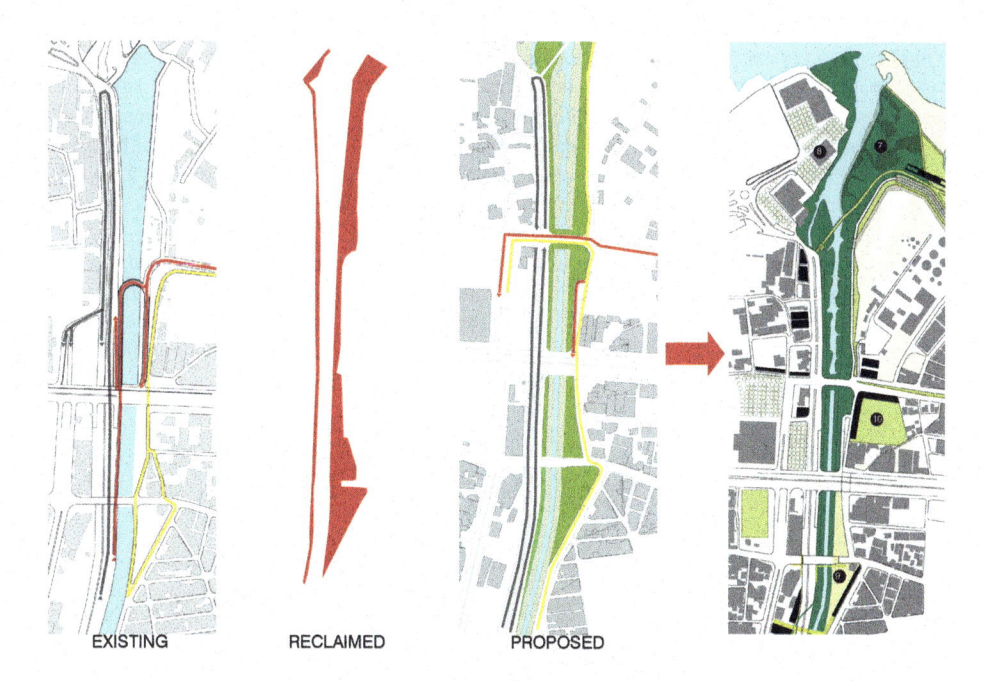

Figure 11.11 New pedestrian friendly mobility networks around Nahr Beirut
Source: Author.

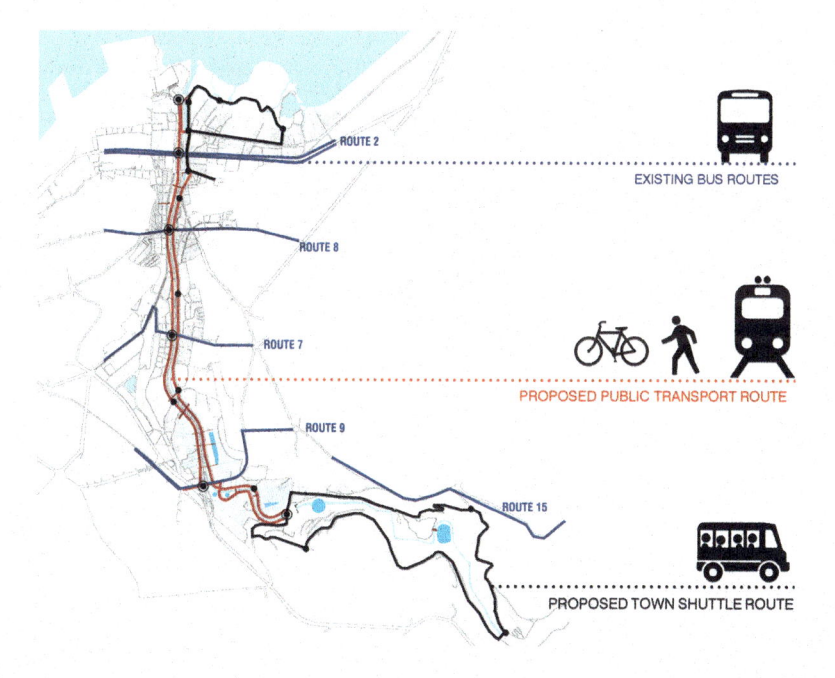

Figure 11.12 The decanalization of the river has rendered some of the ramps and bridges going over the former canal walls obsolete
Note: Their footprint is used to widen the area of the banks and create public space.
Source: Author.

The public space system draws on the various morphologies of the infrastructural landscapes to provide a variety of spatial typologies, including: a major wetland park at the waterfront; urban parks at the old rail yards; pedestrian trails at the location of old rail tracks and within the new river promenade; expanded banks at the location of obsolete ramps, community institutions and linear parks, pedestrian bridges, bikes networks, playgrounds overlaying the water system, and communal platforms comprising fishponds—the last step of water treatment (Figure 11.13). The above-mentioned typologies are strategically superposed to provide continuity of the river corridor.

In such approach, the territory of water infrastructure was reclaimed as significant to the city's open space design; the interrelations of the systems revealed the water purification processes in order to breed a new cultural consciousness (Figure 11.14). Through infrastructural landscapes, infrastructure takes a civic character, and public green space comes with incentives since it performs beneficial functions for the city, thus making it an affordable solution to adopt and maintain.

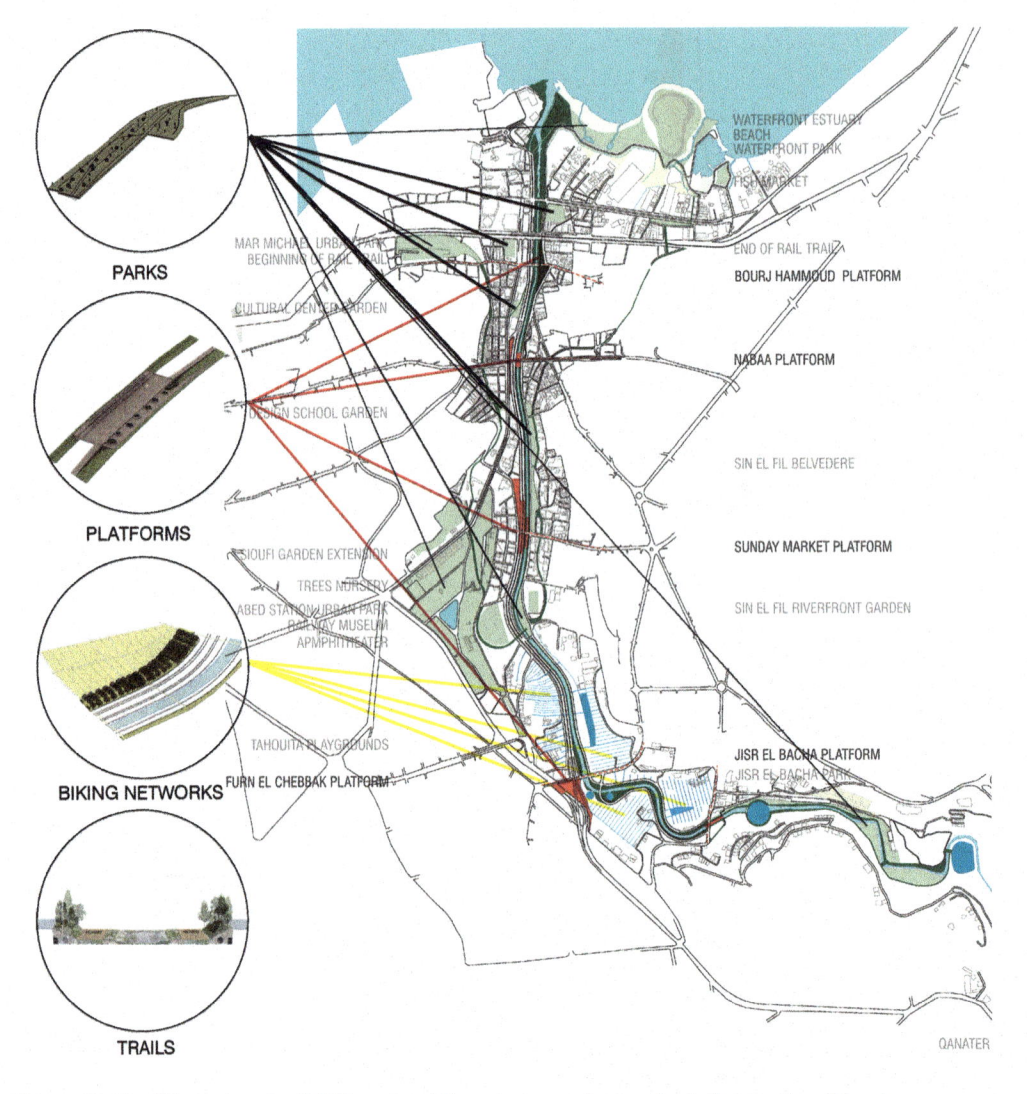

Figure 11.13 The network of different public spaces overlaying the infrastructural landscapes
Source: Author.

[Trans]Forming Nahr Beirut 161

Figure 11.14 **The river opens up to the city with linear promenades and terminal wetland parks that treat urban runoff**
Note: Water levels fluctuate across the year in the park depending on the city's need for reclaimed clean water.
Source: Author.

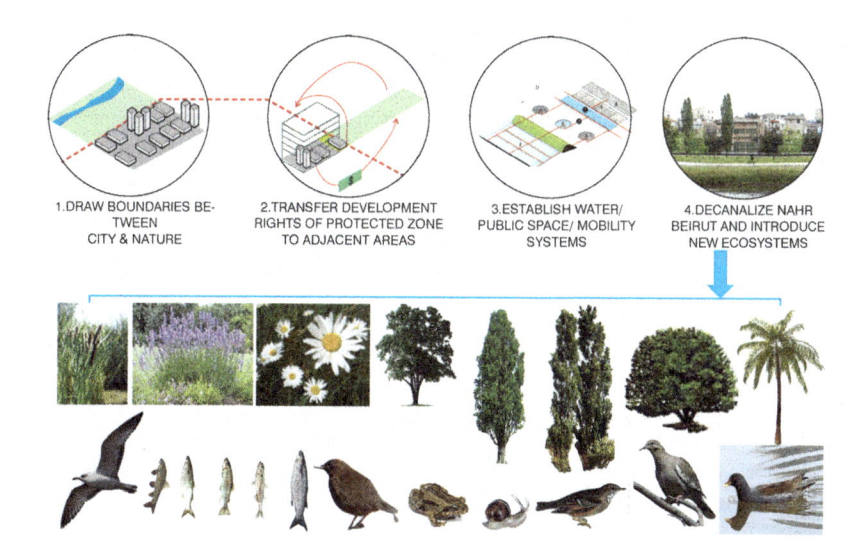

Figure 11.15 **Major phases for implementation: Space reservation, network establishment and introduction of public spaces, decanalization of Nahr Beirut**
Note: Potential phasing and implementation is measured by the gradual improvement of water, public space, mobility and ecology.
Source: Author.

Implementation

In a phased implementation process, measures for reclaiming water and enhancing its quality become the driving agent for rehabilitation. The process starts by: declaring the agricultural zone of the river as *nonædificandi*; transferring its development rights to other zones of the city in order to preserve this open space; deploying the water storage systems in this area; and, thus, reclaiming Nahr Beirut (Figure 11.15). In the intermediate phase, adjacent public spaces and riverfront developments are paced in order to incrementally re-link communities with Nahr Beirut. The design of public space by the river would adapt to the needs of adjoining neighborhoods. Under each major bridge, such public spaces would function as open hardscape plazas overlooking the river and embedding fishponds. In agricultural zones, public spaces would be a combination of bikes tracks, public groves and playgrounds. In urban areas, public space would function as customized community parks. The decanalization of the river comes as a last step after completing and activating the water treatment reclamation systems. By the end of each phase, water, public space, mobility and ecology improve gradually.

The implementation framework posits the design research as a starting point of any potential planning process. As opposed to regarding design as a final stage within a set planning framework, this design team instigates through this initial project a participatory framework of dialogue between the different actors: producers of space (private sector), regulators (public sector) and users (communities). The goal is to create—through such project—a platform for negotiation, which exists at the intersection of the different interests and priorities.

Conclusion

In addition to the site-specific issues it addresses, this project attempts to explore new attitudes in urban design: editorial, flexible and multidisciplinary. Such approaches are directly relevant to the lack of public funds, and scarcity of public space intrinsic to dense Lebanese cities, yet they need a stronger governance and bottom-up commitment in order to be concretized.

Editorial Urban Design

Only an *editing* attitude to existing infrastructures can result in a design that responsibly negotiates what to keep and what to give up in the existing context, and at the same times makes existing structures respond to contextual challenges. It is in this line of thought that the proposed intervention along Nahr Beirut reuses the river channel to connect a network of sizable structures with large-scale benefits.

Flexible Evolution

In line with its networked nature, the project is proposed as a flexible design framework rather than a masterplan. It is designed to be a trigger for negotiation and open to future optimization and input. Its implementation is envisioned as process-driven. However, such flexibility could be abused under the weak governance and speculative practices of local planning actors which could break the project in fragmented parts, thus missing its greatest potential which is to adopt an integrated city-scale approach. For this reason, flexibility must be met with more coordination in the planning and implementation phases to keep any future change relevant on the regional scale.

Multidisciplinary Design

Re-envisioning urban rivers as hybrid infrastructures offers the opportunity for a new interpretation of their role in Lebanese cities, redefining infrastructure's new values and purposes in contemporary urbanism, and allowing them to regain a multidimensional significance—performative, civic and environmental. In the case of Nahr Beirut, this reinterpretation is only possible through expanding the understanding of urban design across other disciplines; in order to incorporate the technical aspects of water and transport with public space. By reconnecting infrastructural systems to civic imagination, and human to natural systems, the project defines a new approach toward a more resilient infrastructure as a base for an ecological urban form.

References

Beyhum, N. 1996. Plan vert pour Beyrouth. *Urbanisme*, 291, 13–16.
Corner, J. 1999. *Recovering Landscape: Essays in Contemporary Landscape Architecture*. New York: Princeton Architectural Press.
Fawaz, M. and Zein, P. 1965. L'aménagement du Nahr Beyrouth. *Horizons Techniques du Moyen Orient*, 5, 24–36.
Frem, S. 2009. *Nahr Beirut: Projections on an Infrastructural Landscape*. MS Thesis, Massachusetts Institute of Technology, Department of Architecture.
Graham, S. and Marvin, S. 2001. *Splintering Urbanism—Networked Infrastructure, Technological Mobilities and the Urban Condition*. London: Routledge.
Mossop, E. 2005. Affordable Landscapes. *Topos*, 50, 13–23.
Mostafavi, M. and Doherty, G. (eds) 2010. *Ecological Urbanism*. Cambridge, MA: Lars Muller Publishers/Harvard GSD.
Mostafavi, M., Najle, C. and Architectural Association. 2003. *Landscape Urbanism: A Manual for the Machinic Landscape*. London: Architectural Association.
Ministry of Environment/LEDO. 2001. Waste Water Management. *Lebanon State of the Environment Report* [online]. Available at: http://www.unep.org/dewa/westasia/Assessments/national_SOEs/west%20asia/Lebanon/Chap15WastewaterManagement.pdf [accessed: January 10, 2009].
Ocean Arks International. 2009. *Restorer Technology* [online]. Available at: http://www.oceanarksint.org/about-us/services/restorer-technology/ [accessed: January 10, 2009].
Poole, K. 1998. Civitas Oecologie. Infrastructure in the ecological city, in *10 Civitas/What is City*, edited by T. Genovese, L. Eastley and D. Snyder. New York: Princeton Architectural Press, 126–43.
Rizk, H. and Adjizian-Gérard, J. 2000–2001. Identification des sources de pollution dans le bassin-versant du Nahr Beyrouth. *Géosphères, Annales de Géographies*, 21–1, 149–59
Saalman, H. 1971. *Haussmann: Paris Transformed*. 1st Edition. New York: George Braziller.
Shannon, K. and Smets, M. 2010. *The Landscape of Contemporary Infrastructure*. Rotterdam: NAi Publishers.
Stokman, A. 2008. *Water Purificative Landscapes—Constructed Ecologies and Contemporary Urbanism*. Kuitert, Wybe. *Transforming with Water*. Proceedings of the 45th World Congress of the International Federation of Landscape Architects IFLA. Wageningen: Blauwdruk/Techne Press, 51–61.
Stroll, K. and Llyod, S. 2011. *Architecture as Infrastructure*. Berlin: Jovis.
Todd, N.J. and Todd, J. 1995. Living Machines, in *Steering Business toward Sustainability*, edited by F. Capra and G. Pauli. New York: United Nations University Press, 163–77.
Waldheim, C. 2006. *The Landscape Urbanism Reader*. New York: Princeton Architectural Press.
Yamout, G. and El-Fadel, M. 2005. An Optimization Approach for Multi-Sectoral Water Supply Management in the Greater Beirut Area. *Water Resources Management*, 19(6), 791–812.
Zaitzevsky, C. 1992. *Frederick Law Olmsted and the Boston Park System*. Cambridge, MA: Harvard University Press.

PART IV
The Visionary: Crossing Boundaries between the Utopian and the Real

Chapter 12
Sites of Globalization: New Cities; Reflecting on the Dialectics between Designer and Client

Anne Marie Galmstrup

Urban design practice in the Gulf region has been witnessing in the recent decades a shift away from the regeneration of heritage districts to the creation of "new cities," strategically conceptualized by public authorities and private investors as part of the *world map* and a *global network* that emphasizes technological advancement and economic diversification. Such cities are often rooted in market strategies, and typically built on global visions that overshadow the local realities, sometimes driven by idealistic fascinations and manifested by utopian concepts that are far removed from what the users actually need.

In the past, the practice of urban design and planning was more focused on frameworks for urban expansion rather than on the creation of new cities; however due to the growing demand for instant cities, this ideology has been broken. To meet this demand, international design firms are being commissioned to contribute their global design experience to the region, which in many cases are resulting in a contrast between the two mindsets, that of the local client and that of the international firm. On one hand, the client is driven by a global outlook, favoring an image of futuristic forms and high-tech architecture, planned and built at once in their entirety. On the other hand, the designer is often guided by a fascination toward the local culture and context, making reference to the model of the traditional city, growing incrementally and adapting over time.

This chapter is based on my reflections as a practicing designer, trained in Copenhagen and London, living in the region since 2009, and an Associate Partner at Henning Larsen Architects, a Scandinavian practice established in 1959 and working in the Middle East for the last 10 years. Like most designers, I am interested in creating *place*, or providing a suitable spatial identity for a given activity. And I feel that this mutual misunderstanding at the level of the *strategic vision* poses a major hindrance to a fluid and effective design process. Despite the temptation to talk about design as a final outcome, I have chosen instead to focus on this dialectic between the client and the designer by conceptualizing their mindsets in terms of several underlying components. *Agenda* explores the different opinions of the designer and the client toward the economic, aesthetic and social goals of the project, and how they are negotiated towards a vision or an image. *Vision* considers how the above dual agendas are reflected in the client's futurist image versus the architect's traditional image for a project, with an emphasis on the formal/spatial models that each one uses as a reference. The chapter investigates how these dialectics can be explored through *approach* and reconciled through *process*. It is based on the premise that methods of mediation based on collaboration rather than negotiation can inform design decisions and allow for a shared vision. As such, the chapter serves as a reflection, from a design practitioner's viewpoint, on our role and responsibility to balance between our ideology and that of our clients in the development of instant cities, from the initiation of a strategic vision to the stage of implementation. To exemplify the premise, the chapter will focus on two of our office's *projects* in Riyadh, Saudi Arabia, both of which were intended, in my view, as investment ventures meant to diversify the kingdom away from a petroleum-based economy and the wish to move toward a more sustainable, knowledge-based society.

Projects

I still remember first arriving in 2008 from Damascus to Riyadh—from the Old City to the New City. Heading into Riyadh from the airport reminded me of my life in New Jersey, where streets are wide but lack pedestrian activity, and drive-in parking places are lined up along storefronts. As we approached the center, the city got slightly denser with a few towers dominating the skyline over this low built, spread carpet of a city, but there were still no people to be seen. This contrasted sharply with Damascus where, throughout the day, the streets were continuously full of people. At that time, our firm of Henning Larsen Architects had decided to set up an office in Riyadh to follow up the implementation of our masterplan design for the King Abdullah Financial District (KAFD), and we were booked into a hotel around the corner from the new office. Initially we planned to walk over, however our office manager at the time looked me straight in the eyes and said, "Please Anne, there are cars waiting for you outside." This incident illustrates one example of the prevailing attitude against walking versus driving and the given importance to the public domain. This is subsequently part of the reason I find our projects in Riyadh important to discuss and reflect on our approach to new cities.

Typically, new cities are conceived in terms of their spatial and thematic attributes. Spatially, they are categorized either as: a *city in a city*, a district built within the metropolitan fabric; or an *annex city*, extending outwards from the existing city but in direct proximity; or a *satellite city* as a physically independent entity. Functionally, the themes range from *economic*, *knowledge*, *environment*, *healthcare* and *entertainment*. As mentioned above, this chapter will refer to two of our firm's projects for Riyadh; the first is the King Abdullah Financial District (KAFD), an example of a *city in a city* with *economy* as its central theme, and the second is the Dirab, a *satellite city* that is *healthcare*-oriented, still at the conception stage of development.

The King Abdullah Financial District (KAFD) comprises 3.3 million square meters built-up area, and is currently under construction. The new city is following an implementation strategy with a five-year duration and is expected to become the largest sustainable development in the region, facilitating investment in the Kingdom and consolidating Saudi Arabia's position as the region's financial capital. The client is the local Public Pension Agency and Capital Market Authority and, since winning the international competition for the 160-hectare site back in 2006, our role has been to lead the masterplan design from the initial strategic concept through design development (Figure 12.1) and guidelines to the current aesthetic site supervision.

The design goal of the project is to unite the regional urban traditions with a contemporary metropolis, providing the Saudi capital with more public open space, a characteristic skyline, and a new sustainable landmark. At the heart of the district is the transformation of an arm of the Wadi Hanifa that traverses the area into a pedestrian streetscape. The district will become an active and attractive urban space comprising financial institutions, offices, residential and recreational areas, shops, restaurants, hotels, and conference, entertainment, educational and sports facilities. The district includes a unique public transportation system, featuring a monorail connecting the various areas of the district. Key buildings and monorail stations are linked by air-conditioned footbridges above street level, enabling walking distance to all meetings within the KAFD, quite extraordinary for Riyadh.

The second project we are involved in is the Dirab masterplan. Dirab Development Company is an emerging markets infrastructure development company with a focus on healthcare, biomedical R&D and sustainable design. It is developing a network of purpose-designed, ecologically efficient cities centered around children's hospitals and biomedical innovation hubs, driven by a desire to bring sophisticated biomedicine and increased prosperity to the target regions. The client is a joint private–public venture and our involvement has been in developing the concept masterplan.

The Dirab project is a low-rise masterplan of a 200-hectare site, 25 minutes south of metropolitan Riyadh (Figure 12.2). The site will include a major medical center, step-down facility, biomedical R&D facilities, and associated office and residential spaces. The project responds to the site's natural setting, dominated by sustainable elements that harness the natural resources surrounding the site, and inspired by the ancient villages and building typologies found in the Riyadh region, reinterpreted into an innovative oasis-like environment. The objectives of Dirab are community-based and are set to offer an attractive sustainable city to live, work and study in. The different functions of each space and its associated buildings have been combined to form an innovative setting for both world-class biomedical research and for lively neighborhoods filled with activity throughout the day and during the changing desert seasons. The masterplan suggests solutions for outdoor activity in a harsh climate, and pedestrians are given preferential treatment with the aim of encouraging use of the public realm.

Sites of Globalization 169

Figure 12.1   KAFD: Bird's eye view from the conceptual design stage and construction view in 2013

Note: Top and bottom respectively.
Source: Henning Larsen Architects.

Figure 12.2 Dirab: Bird's-eye view of the concept design
Source: Henning Larsen Architects.

The information included about the two projects draws on both our work at Henning Larsen Architects and interviews with two concerned stakeholders. Concerning the KAFD, I talked with Mr Louis Becker, partner and principal of international projects at Henning Larsen Architects. Although based in Copenhagen, he has frequently visited Riyadh since 2005 and has played a major role in the implementation of the masterplan. I also talked with Mr Drew Carr-Ellison, the foreign investor of the Dirab project in Riyadh, based in Istanbul. Mr Carr-Ellison is the COO of an investment firm with a strong agenda for building sustainable developments within local settings.

Agenda

One of the larger issues today is privatization, which has resulted in the compartmentalization of cities and their social demographics. Historically designers predominantly dealt with municipalities as clients for urban development; their emphasis was on spatial quality. The municipality had decision-making power and was thinking from a long-term perspective. I suppose there was less talk about return-on-investment and more about sanitation and quality of the public spaces, and on how the city could subsequently grow over time. From the outset time was allowed for the process of testing options in the existing urban fabric; frameworks for urban development were outlined for implementation to happen over a long time span. Cities had time to mature and were developed from *inside-out*.

The reality is different today; rapid urbanization and medium speculation has created a demand for instant cities that are not only about providing homes, but also reflects a shift toward investment strategies. The agenda has changed accordingly; it is no longer about public interest, but about rapid return-on-investment. Marketing strategies aiming at selling *lifestyles* are planned into the early design phases and urban design is about creating products for investors to buy into. As a result, urban designers today are more focused on time, creating cities quickly from *outside-in*, commissioned to single-handedly develop hundreds of thousands of square meters down to the balustrade details. But designing for cultures and in contexts where spatial qualities and values are different from your own upbringing and training means you have to research and listen, especially if you still retain an idealist view of masterplans as tools for social change and promoters of public good.

In our meeting, Mr Becker said, "We have a very limited timeframe of 5 years for the implementation of the King Abdullah Financial District." Within that, it was important for him to secure the public realm between the buildings of the KAFD, with the right mix of functions as an important consideration. The main challenges were in persuading the client to include a larger density than seen in Riyadh today, and that the Financial District should work as a city and not only as a business center. Mr Becker explained how the design team traveled with the client team around the world to look at examples of successes and failures in similar *new city* structures. An example was London's Canary Wharf where the initial high percentage of office space meant that the developers could not sell the spaces because buyers would not invest in an area where there was no cultural life outside of working hours. As a result, the initial KAFD functional agenda was modified to have a larger percentage of residential, cultural and educational functions. I would suppose that densifying the development was also a strategic move to ensure the urban feel of the district should it not be as populated as planned.

With respect to cultural agenda, I asked Mr Carr-Ellison, the client of the Dirab project, if his organization could foresee or had any wish for change within Saudi Arabia. "It is no life mission for us to change the Saudi culture with our project," he replied. "We want to provide the best of human advances in medicine and it is a personal choice to be in on the global advance." I asked him if their approach to projects in Saudi Arabia is different than it might be in a Western context, to which he replied, "I admire the strong identity and strength of the culture in Riyadh … we would not want to make a Taco Bell satellite like the American suburbs that have no identity."

Table 12.1   Agenda: New city versus maturing city

Agenda	Agent	Emphasis	Medium	Outcome
New city	Investor	Time	Marketing	Product
Maturing city	Citizen	Place	Municipality	Process

Vision

One of our office's inspirational images for the KAFD project included an old photo of a mud city on the outskirts of Riyadh (Figure 12.3a). Our client, on the contrary, imagined a contemporary image of a glass and steel high-rise downtown (Figure 12.3b). For me, this contrast reflected the stereotypical example of our first conversation with clients in the Arab world a decade ago—the foreign architect with a romantic fascination for the local setting versus the local client's wish for globalization.

Figure 12.3   Inspirational images for the KAFD project
Note: (a) historical Saudi town versus; (b) Canary Wharf.
Source: (a) Henning Larsen Architects; (b) Richard Wood.

What our international principal Mr Becker had envisioned was not literally a mud city, but an abstraction of the spatial qualities within that mud city. The relation between the height of the walls and the width of the streets should translate into shaded walkways, the origin of a vision of "the city of shade" as he had described. "I don't think our client team on the contrary literally wanted a glass and steel downtown highrise development, but the term was used as a metaphor for wanting to modernize their country," explained Mr Becker. The vision for the KAFD was to build a modern Saudi city; "the image I had in mind was the shadow, a reflection of how to live in extreme climate."

When asked to name his favorite city, Mr Becker replied "Probably an Italian city–Venice or Modena," noting that it was a bit romantic to choose classical cities, those where everything was not done in one go, and where there is a diversity of spaces to gather. In Saudi Arabia, people gather in malls and big centers, all new clean developments. "It is like taking the city to the dentist—you clean up everything in between. It is nice and shiny but the surprises disappear." Mr Becker continued that it was important to define a public realm in a country where this is hard to find. Within the KAFD, for example, it is essential to secure more of a vision of public space between the buildings (Figure 12.4a) and less of the buildings' formal design, and that despite the rapid implementation period of five years for 3.3 million square meters (Figure 12.4b). Accordingly, narrow crooked streets were envisioned for the design, encouraging the visitor to be curious about what lies around the next corner. Buildings would shade the streets, lowering the temperature of outdoor spaces by 6–8 degrees so that Saudis would be able to walk through the city despite the harsh desert climate. Furthermore, a plan for public transportation would keep the district car-free and optimize pedestrian area, steps that could almost be considered as revolutionary in Riyadh.

I was talking with Mr Carr-Ellison about the Dirab project, and I was curious to hear what a foreign investor in Riyadh had envisioned for a new city development in Saudi Arabia. "We like to call it a community rather than a city," Mr Carr-Ellison answered. The intention was to offer an attractive sustainable city to live, work and study in. "We see our vision more as a model of community which is seen working elsewhere outside Riyadh," he continued. I asked what his favorite city was and was puzzled when he chose Liverpool. He explained that he saw it as a non-commercial city with a strong sense of identity. "You can feel the souls of people in Liverpool—they have their own accent yet [they are] contemporary." I asked if their Saudi partner might have a different favorite city; he imagined the answer to be New York City, or maybe Knightsbridge.

Figure 12.4 **KAFD: (a) conceptual view from the main street; (b) construction view in 2012**
Source: Henning Larsen Architects.

Figure 12.5 Dirab: Views from the residential area
Source: Henning Larsen Architects.

I think the interesting difference is that the foreign investor talked about how people give a city its identity, whereas the Saudi investor's vision revolved around the abstract ideal of a Western model. Accordingly, I imagine that the local investor bought into the vision for the Dirab project as a sustainable community because he sees sustainability as a symbol of Western values. But common to both the local and foreign investor is that their answers reflected a way of living—a lifestyle—and that the chosen designers had to be trusted to gain the knowledge of the culture and context necessary to design their vision accordingly (Figure 12.5).

The issue of vision is linked to a mindset, manifested by images, and serving as a tool of mediation; it should not be misunderstood as a design concept for something local or global. The term *local* comes with an idealistic approach, grounded in the site-specific context and culture. *Global*, on the other hand, has to do with a desire for Western values. The dialectic here is that the local mindset is rooted in the user while the global mindset is rooted in economic development. This can be further understood to mean that the local mindset has the socio-cultural objective of wanting to create communal city space, and the global mindset is more about selling the plot, creating the city as commodity.

Table 12.2 Vision: From a global and local viewpoint

Vision	Agent	References	Visualization	Outcome
Global	Developer	Western models	Bird's-eye	Lifestyle
Local	User	Culture/context	Eye-level	Lifetime

Approach

Despite the limited implementation time allowed for new cities, one positive is that the clients of both the KAFD and Dirab invested in a masterplan, laying out the design of their land before plots or parcels were designed individually, thereby ensuring that attention would be given to the overall public realm. The essential challenge with many of these new city masterplans is that they are designed and constructed all in one go and, despite the correct programmatic mix, they have the same *tone* throughout, lacking that sense of place that comes with development over time. I personally find the overall framework and guidelines for the masterplans far more interesting than the visual and formal designs themselves. The interest in the masterplan lies in defining which parts would be fixed through design and which parts would be left for interpretation, able to mature over time through the intervention of different architects involved. Could this have been the approach of the Romans in importing their pre-planned structures despite the local context? Was there room for local growth and adaptation within these structures over time, or at least for locally sourced materials?

I suppose that my main concern is the immense number of schemes in which a single architect, as mentioned above, designs hundreds of thousands of square meters from concept to the finishing details with no room for interpretation; I can't help but wonder if the inhabitants will play a part in the maturing process of the design over time. Or has the rapid urbanization we are witnessing today killed the idealistic notion of community and compartmentalized our cities into neighborhoods which people inhabit simply because of their practicality or prestige, without a sense of belonging or social participation? Many designers literally reinterpret traditional urban form into new city structures in an attempt to maintain the *local look* of the place, while decision-makers often see investing in urban design as a quick fix for society—whether the masterplan is based on emulating traditional forms or demonstrating global progress. But neither of these considers the user of the place after implementation of the masterplan; instead the masterplan is seen as an instant product that is not designed from the inside-out. Our challenge as a profession is to accept that the typical idealistic notion of cities maturing over time is currently not realistic for instant cities. Instead, providing new design concepts for how these new instant cities might be allowed to grow and develop after implementation should become our professional objective.

Process

The demand and speed of urbanization in developing areas like the Gulf region allows little time for user involvement or collaboration. In societies where decisions can be long bureaucratic processes, budget-driven time schedules resign the designer to a state of limbo, constantly trying to negotiate decisions in order to move on and avoid redesigns, at the same time hindering any real attempt at client engagement. In many cases, images in the form of eye-catching perspectives are produced in an effort to create the semblance of a shared vision between architects and clients. Intended as shortcuts to gain precious time needed to solve design-related problems, they actually consume time that should instead be invested in *an initial open dialogue* between all involved parties, creating a shared vocabulary and a common understanding of design goals and limitations.

This brings forward the question: how important are images and rendered perspectives in bringing together the visions of the client and the architect during the design process? Common between both parties is the stated need for *the vision to sell the story*, whether from a design or sales perspective. However, the images we as designers have been producing most often over the last decade reflect more lifestyle visions than functional masterplans responsive to user needs, local practices or long-term appropriation by the inhabitants themselves. Although the atmosphere of usage of a place is essential, as expressed by Mr Becker above, the lifestyle images produced for marketing purposes today are in many cases overshadowing actual suitable design solutions.

Images of strategic dreams for cities a decade ago have become reality in many Arab countries today; drawings and rendered perspectives created for marketing purposes have actually been implemented. However, in many cases I still see an overall disconnect between design concepts that reflect the culture and context of the place and their actual implementation; perhaps the disconnect is due to concept implementation based on misinterpreted visions, a misinterpretation that could have been avoided by investing in the sharing of knowledge during the early phases of the design and by greater involvement of the design team with the client during all stages of the design process. Could the process-based approach of mature cities be part of the masterplans for new city construction in order to avoid the design of *product*? And could further collaboration be used as tool to mediate between the local and global visions?

Table 12.3   Process: From negotiation toward collaboration

Process	Approach	Emphasis	Medium
Negotiation	Outside-in	Prescriptive	3D renderings
Collaboration	Inside-out	Participatory	Shared vision

Concluding Remarks

Building on the above discussion of *agenda*, *image*, *masterplans* and *process*, a few key points stand out as initiators of further investigation.

Neo-Colonization?

As often mentioned in design literature since the 1980s, our cities are starting to look the same. With increased consumer power in emerging markets, are we forgetting the specific identity of our cities and cultures under the impact of globalization? To some extent, you can find the same major coffee chains and clothing brands in the city center of any capital and the same suburban living silos along the approach to most of our major cities. It would be easy to consider foreign designers working in the Arab world as a neo-colonial phenomenon, imposing global Western images onto non-Western cultures. However, at the beginning of the twenty-first century the reality is that many emerging market countries look to the "old culture cities" of the West for unadulterated inspiration. Emerging societies are searching to project a global identity abroad, looking to contemporary design as a quick fix instead of developing identity from within, that is, based on their own cultural and contextual settings.

Social Responsibility

Perhaps responsible designers can help to curb this trend away from the local; as Mr Carr Ellison noted: "We are contributing to globalization with our projects, but we work locally and invest much in finding the right local partners for each project, whether it is private investors, the government or architects." Although design may not be able modify the socio-spatial practices, it can set the stage for better communication and interaction between people. As such, design is a powerful tool that can have an impact on the quality of social exchange. Practicing architects often mistakenly think that they can "design their way through" by over-designing the project, down to the level of balustrade details. However, I believe that good design has to mediate between architecture as commodity and architecture as agent of social change, and this by reaching a shared mindset between the client and the designer with regards to the relevance of design and its impact on the users during the early stages of the project.

Shared Visions: Bridging the Gap between the Designer and the Client

Projects of the scale of KAFD and Dirab are typically joint public/private ventures. But there is a tendency in the region today for smaller scale masterplans to be run by private investors that often only take into consideration their own parcel and find it easier to communicate with one designer as opposed to coordinating between many. Investing to create a shared vision among a cross-disciplinary team at the initial design phases could perhaps be helpful in bringing the *maturing city* strategic method into the *instant city* projects. In my experience, the power of design lies in the initial collaborative process, where a shared vision is mediated among all involved parties from the beginning of the design process. This method of design, bringing the facts and visions to the table before anything is drawn, encourages both the trusting participation of all parties involved and customized sustainable designs. Furthermore, in complex societies it can be hard for an outsider (the foreign designer) to gain the access and trust required to understand in depth the needs of local users. It is therefore even more so essential for the foreign designers to step out of their idealistic fascinations and into the local setting in order to both design for the user and mediate between their clients and their own values. Accordingly the time is over for the fly-in, fly-out architects; foreign designers instead of only flying in for presentations, should be present on the ground in order to deepen their local understanding and allow for a true exchange, local designers should work to acknowledge their culture, and investors should invest time in dialogue. In this way, any initiative that creates dialogue is an essential methodology for undertaking and implementing a project. The power of urban design is in the participation process and not in the aesthetics.

Chapter 13
Sites of Worship: From Makkah to Karbala; Reconciling Pilgrimage, Speculation and Infrastructure

Robert Saliba

This chapter attempts to frame, from an urban design perspective, generic issues facing sites of worship and their host cities in terms of the pressures imposed by *pilgrimage, accessibility* and *real estate speculation*. Taking into consideration the specificity of sites and their regional significance, questions are asked at three complementary levels. Spatially, how to accommodate the increasing number of pilgrims and still protect the integrity of the historic and social fabrics? Symbolically, how to address and define both the tangible and intangible aspects of sacred heritage? Politically and economically, how to mediate between the agendas of various stakeholders, mainly the religious and political authorities? As an attendant concern, the chapter asks whether sites of worship belong to the global or local community. In this regard, is their development a concern primarily for their host country or for the Muslim world as a whole?

Although the chapter cannot claim to offer definitive answers to such complex and multilayered questions, it does aim to derive, through the critical examination of recent urban design competitions and ongoing studies, a reflective framework for considering the dialectics of conserving, developing and managing the growth of holy cities in relation to their sites of worship. To do so, it will reflect on several specific urban design projects related to key sites of worship in the Arab world: Yves Lion's development scheme for Jabal Omar in Makkah, Giuseppe Cinà's urban requalification of the Abu Hanifa Mosque in the Adhamiyah neighborhood in Baghdad; and the urban renewal of the Iraqi "holy shrine cities" of Kadhimiya, Najaf and Karbala by Dewan Architects & Engineers.

The purpose of analyzing and commenting on these case studies is less to critique than to illuminate existing best practices and innovative approaches to persisting and typical problems. The case studies were presented in an international conference, "City Debates 2012," organized by the author at the American University of Beirut on the theme of "Urban Design in the Arab World." At that event, the presentations on the Adhamiyah neighborhood and the Iraqi holy shrine cities were both part of a panel titled "Sites of Worship." Sateh El-Arnaout, Senior Urban Development Specialist in the MENA region at the World Bank, introduced the theme of the panel, commented on the interventions, and moderated the ensuing discussion.

The third presentation was by Yves Lion (also the conference's closing keynote speaker) who explained his urban design work in the Arab world, with an emphasis on his winning entry in Makkah's Jabal Omar competition. Further insights on the background of that competition were provided during discussions by Nezar AlSayyad, who served as the head of the competition jury. Primary information was also contributed by Abdelhalim Jabr, a collaborator of Yves Lion on the Makkah competition and other projects in the region.

For background on planning in Makkah and Madinah until the mid-1980s, the main source for the chapter has been Stefano Bianca's reflections on holy cities in his book *Urban Form in the Arab World—Past and Present*. Two theses also served as key references on the formation of Makkah's architecture and townscape and the issues facing the historical conservation of its Haram district: *Mekkan Architecture* (1988) by Sami Angawi; and *Conservation in an Islamic Context: A Case Study of Makkah* (1997) by El Sayed Touba.

The chapter also draws on field visits by the author to sacred sites in Baghdad during the 2010 International Conference on the Preservation and Rehabilitation of Iraqi City Centers at the Mayoralty of Baghdad and as a member of the Dewan Architects & Engineers Advisory Board working on the "urban renewal" of the holy cities of Najaf and Karbala. Additional information comes from press reports and online articles on recent developments related to sites of worship in the region, which include interviews with local stakeholders.

The chapter starts by outlining the generic attributes of sites of worship that will serve as a base for the analysis of the case studies. It concludes with a discussion of the key issue of agency, including the governance of sites of worship in differing regional contexts.

Framing Case Studies and Generic Attributes

In the contemporary Arab world, sites of worship have a dual connotation: on the one hand, they promote a unitary spirit of tolerance and devotion; on the other, they are sometimes sites of political confrontation and terrorist activity. In "holy cities" like Makkah or Karbala, sites of worship, due to their overwhelming significance, are perceived as places of transcendence and pacific encounter. Usually clustered in the city center and serving as prime destinations for religious mass tourism, they crystallize the identity of their host cities and condition these cities' physical and spatial structure. In contrast, sites of worship in "mosaic cities"—those with multiple religious affiliations, such as Baghdad or Beirut—are perceived as potential generators of local sectarian conflict. Spatially diffused, such sites still shape the cultural and political townscape, but they have a reduced impact on the overall dynamics of urban growth and infrastructure.

To investigate *the close relationship between sacred sites and urban development* I am primarily concerned here with holy cities. However, to bring forward their specificity, I will mention at times how their conditions differ from those in mosaic cities. Makkah and Madinah will serve as my primary sites of reference. Both cities have undergone extensive changes in the last two decades, and both exhibit a propensity to initiate and announce trends, later followed by other cities in the region. Conditions in Iraq's holy cities and pilgrimage sites will also be referred to. However, Iraq is presently in a postconflict, transition stage, and except for the organization of urban design competitions and the commissioning of master plans, no significant design work is currently underway in its holy cities.

I consider Jerusalem to be outside the scope of the present investigation due to its symbolic complexity and contested political status. As Peters (1986: 60–61) has argued:

> Mecca is a relatively straightforward urban case study, a city with a single and continuous tradition and an evolutionary development[. But] Jerusalem ... presents no such prospect of religious continuity. Its sacred charter has been written and rewritten by Jews, Christians, and Muslims in turn, and each new set of terms of the covenant was converted into the normal urban language of buildings and institutions ... From this perspective it might appear that we are dealing with not one but three Jerusalems.

There are three generic attributes of holy cities that are important to understand: *centrality*, *monofunctionality* and *seasonality*. In terms of urban design, it is particularly important to reflect on the implications of these in relation to four key issues: identity/legibility, physical and social infrastructure, public space, and private development (Table 13.1).

Table 13.1 Analytical urban design framework, with the generic attributes of holy cities expressed as columns (see Chapter 1 for further details), and key urban design issues as rows

	Centrality	**Monofunctionality**	**Seasonality**
Townscape identity and legibility			
Physical and social infrastructure			
Public space			
Private development			

Centrality and Townscape Identity

> Au début était le centre [At the beginning was the center]. (Yves Lion, City Debates 2012)

In "holy cities" of global significance, centrality has a double connotation. Broadly, it may be interpreted as the point of "spiritual convergence" of millions of worshippers throughout the world and the ultimate destination for fulfilling their religious obligations. In its narrower definition, however, centrality refers to the sacred precinct at the heart of the holy city where all rituals have to be performed in relation to sacred structures and spaces. In both senses, "symbolic centrality" shapes the worldview and "image of the city" of inhabitants and pilgrims. In urban design terms, it constitutes the anchor around which townscape legibility is articulated in terms of landmarks, paths, nodes, edges and districts. It also dictates the morphology of surrounding developments, as was evident in Makkah's recent Jabal Omar competition, where visual permeability toward the *Kaaba* [Sacred House] at the center of the Holy Mosque proved to be the decisive criteria in determining the winning entry.

In contrast to holy cities, mosaic cities exhibit a "business central district" where "places of worship" are at a par with places of finance, transportation and governance. Although self-evident, this distinction points to the radical changes occurring in the symbolic townscapes of holy cities. Intensive real estate speculation, capitalizing on religious tourism, is presently commodifying their formerly sacred townscapes. In particular, the ongoing construction of massive new service buildings and transport infrastructure is threatening to overpower the original visual prominence of their sacred landmarks (Figure 13.1).

Figure 13.1 Bird's-eye view of the clock tower in Makkah
Source: http://commons.wikimedia.org/wiki/File:Aerial_View_of_Abraj_Al_Bait_Under_Construction.jpg (image by Fadi El Benni of Al Jazeera English via Wikimedia Commons) [accessed: April 2, 2014].

Centrality and Transport Infrastructure

"Symbolic centrality" today implies "infrastructural centrality," whose purpose is to secure optimum accessibility to and within the holy precinct. As such, infrastructure is the prime shaper of the layout of holy cities, having the key roles of improving the fluidity of vehicular and pedestrian movement and ensuring the adequacy of public utilities and services during the short and congested pilgrimage season.

In the 1960s and 1970s secular as well as holy cities received the same engineering treatment, which stressed the accommodation of vehicular traffic through the construction of urban highways, multistory car parks and underground structures. In holy cities, a paramount issue was also how to manage the mass movement of pilgrims to and from the central Haram area. But improving accessibility resulted in additional congestion of the city center and severe conflicts between vehicular and pedestrian movement. Furthermore, as shown in the cases of Makkah and Madinah, ring and radial roads created infrastructural breaks that isolated sacred precincts from their historic context. This led to the decay of the peri-center zone, its development with sporadic high-rise structures, and the conversion of former pedestrian walkways to vehicular streets.

During the 1980s thinking about accessibility in holy cities evolved toward a more integrative approach, whose purpose was to limit vehicular access while stressing the role of public transport. Accordingly, holy cities were planned into concentric zones, with the sacred precinct surrounded by a low-traffic/pedestrian zone, in turn surrounded by successive ring roads aimed at diffusing radial traffic flows. Meanwhile, at the periphery, these plans called for temporary pilgrim villages, car parking structures, and stations for rapid transit where visitors could board shuttle trains to the center (Bianca 2000: 224–5; Touba 1997: 193).

During the last two decades, these recommendations by international and regional consultants have again been modified. In particular, plans for holy cities must now accommodate a more aggressive real estate development agenda focused on the immediate periphery of the Haram. The ever increasing number of visitors has also created a persistent pressure to expand the size of the Haram and its related open spaces, resulting in the clearing of large areas of the surrounding, nonreligious, historic urban fabric.

Centrality and Open Space

Until the middle of the twentieth century, most holy cities in the region grew organically around their sacred centers, with residential structures acting as an integrated edge. This meant that the local pattern of streets and open spaces extended right up to the walls of the sanctuary to service an adjoining, dense residential fabric (Figure 13.2). This pattern contrasted with the Western tradition, in which religious buildings generally stand apart as monuments fronting public squares. One reason for the difference is that mosques traditionally incorporated open space within their precincts as *enclosed prayer areas, space for religious and political gathering* and *havens for contemplation and seclusion from the surrounding urban bustle*.

Since the 1960s, however, with the progressive clearance of old residential quarters adjoining the central Haram (Figure 13.3), holy mosques have increasingly been treated as freestanding monuments isolated from their historic fabric. This process has not been confined to Makkah and Madinah; however, the case of Madinah is particularly extreme (the Prophet's Mosque has now been extended from 16,000 to 100,000 square meters and been surrounded by new plazas whose area now reaches 170,000 square meters). It has also occurred in other sacred locations, including Iraq's holiest Shia cities, Najaf and Karbala. In Karbala, the city's twin shrines have been linked by a wide linear space reminiscent of a nineteenth-century Haussmannian boulevard that has undermined the primacy of the city's medieval fabric. And in Najaf, a vast empty space has been carved out of the city's historic core to create a large square where hotels and commercial developments now face directly onto the western entrance of the Imam Ali Shrine (Figure 13.4).

It should be noted here that connecting pilgrimage focal points by linear spaces is a recurrent practice in the history of holy cities. A typical and often-cited example is the restructuring of Rome's medieval fabric by the Renaissance Pope Sixtus V. However, as explained by Sam Jacoby (see Chapter 8 in this volume), this eventually resulted in a fundamental change in the relationship between religious monuments and their adjoining open spaces [piazzas]. As he notes, while in medieval Rome the piazza had acted as "an exterior holding area for the sanctity of the church, [it] became progressively secularized and evolved into

Figure 13.2 Hierarchy of streets and open spaces in the vicinity of the Haram in Makkah, showing the historical encroachment of residential areas on the Haram edge
Source: Author (after Angawi 1988).

Figure 13.3 Map showing the clearance of the periphery of the Haram area in Madinah
Source: Author (after Bianca 2000).

Figure 13.4 Iraq's holiest Shia cities
Note: Karbala's twin shrines connected by a boulevard (above); Najaf's main square fronting the Imam Ali Shrine (below).
Source: Aerial views: Google Earth, 2013; oblique views: Dewan Architects & Engineers.

a fundamentally different kind of public space—with the church gradually acting as a landmark or element subservient to the piazza."

The same change may eventually affect the vast open spaces created around holy Muslim shrines from Makkah to Karbala. In recent master plans these areas are increasingly being designated as "plazas" or "piazzas," a Western concept of limited relevance to Arab–Islamic cities. As mentioned by Touba (1997: 108), for example, the Dar Al-Handasah study of Makkah in 1985 "recommended the demolition of homes and introduced piazzas around the Holy Mosque [named Al Haram Plaza], with no isolation between the houses and the Mosque itself. The consultant considered no alternative plan except to create these surrounding piazzas which resulted in an alien pattern for an Islamic city."

Although intended as open extensions for prayer, such spaces are also evolving into interface zones between the sacred precinct and its commercial periphery. In particular, since this is a strategic and highly profitable zone for prime religious tourist services and commerce, their edges are increasingly being allotted for private development.

Centrality and Private Development

With an ever-growing influx of pilgrims (presently 12 million visits per year for Makkah, with a projection of 17 million by 2025), land values around holy shrines will continue to increase. Areas of central Makkah today are estimated to be the most expensive real estate in the world. Left to market forces, a high-rise ring zone will no doubt emerge. This condition has been criticized as "toast-rack" and "concentric urbanism" in the popular press (Wainwright 2012) (Figure 13.5).

Already, central Makkah has been subdivided into vast tracts for the development of megaprojects. These envision construction of hotels, malls and cafés capitalizing on the adjacency of the Haram and strategic views toward the Kaaba. The same approach is being applied in Madinah, where the periphery of the Prophet's Mosque has been expropriated and subdivided into real estate plots. Investors are now vying to redevelop these into an upscale modern central district encompassing permanent and transient residential accommodations and commercial and service facilities.

Such projects raise the issue of public/private complicity in developing the periphery of the Haram and the impact such speculation will have on townscape identity and the sanctity of place. However, as argued by Peters (1986: 233, with reference to Kister 1972: 83–9), speculation has been a persistent phenomenon in Muslim holy cities, dating to their early days:

> The issue of public versus private space was raised early in Mecca. In the years immediately following the death of the Prophet hajjis apparently set up their tents in the still abundant open space close to the sanctuary and had acknowledged right to camp even in the courts of privately owned houses there. It was reportedly Caliph Mu'awiya who first began buying up the open land and building on it as well as investing in a great many already existing properties in Mecca. Mu'awiya's commercial and real estate policies, which must have greatly stimulated construction in the city, found little favor among some traditionalist Muslims who feared that what had always been a free privilege would be converted into a profit-making enterprise, a fear that was rapidly realized in the holy city.

Current megaprojects planned within and around the Haram districts of Makkah and Madinah may thus be seen as reflecting a historic controversy, contrasting two perceptions of pilgrimage—either as a "free privilege" or a "profit-making enterprise" (Figure 13.6). While holy sites are envisioned as spiritual havens that promote a sense of social equality between all believers, they have also always been places of trade and speculation focused on pilgrim-connected businesses. Thus, according to Peters (1986: 51), "If the haram, the sacred place, was the heart of the Holy City, pilgrims were its life-giving blood, and the network of economic and political arrangements that carried them to and from the shrine were its veins and arteries."

In essence, economic dependence on the single function of pilgrimage has always conditioned the types and spatial distribution of land uses in holy cities as well as the physiology and typology of their residential and commercial architecture.

Figure 13.5 High-rise ring zone in central Makkah
Note: The proposed "Urban Landing" and its ring of skyscrapers (left); clock tower in Makkah (right).
Source: Atelier Lion associés (left); http://en.wikipedia.org/wiki/File:Abraj-al-Bait-Towers.JPG (image by King Eliot via Wikimedia Commons) [accessed: April 2, 2014] (right).

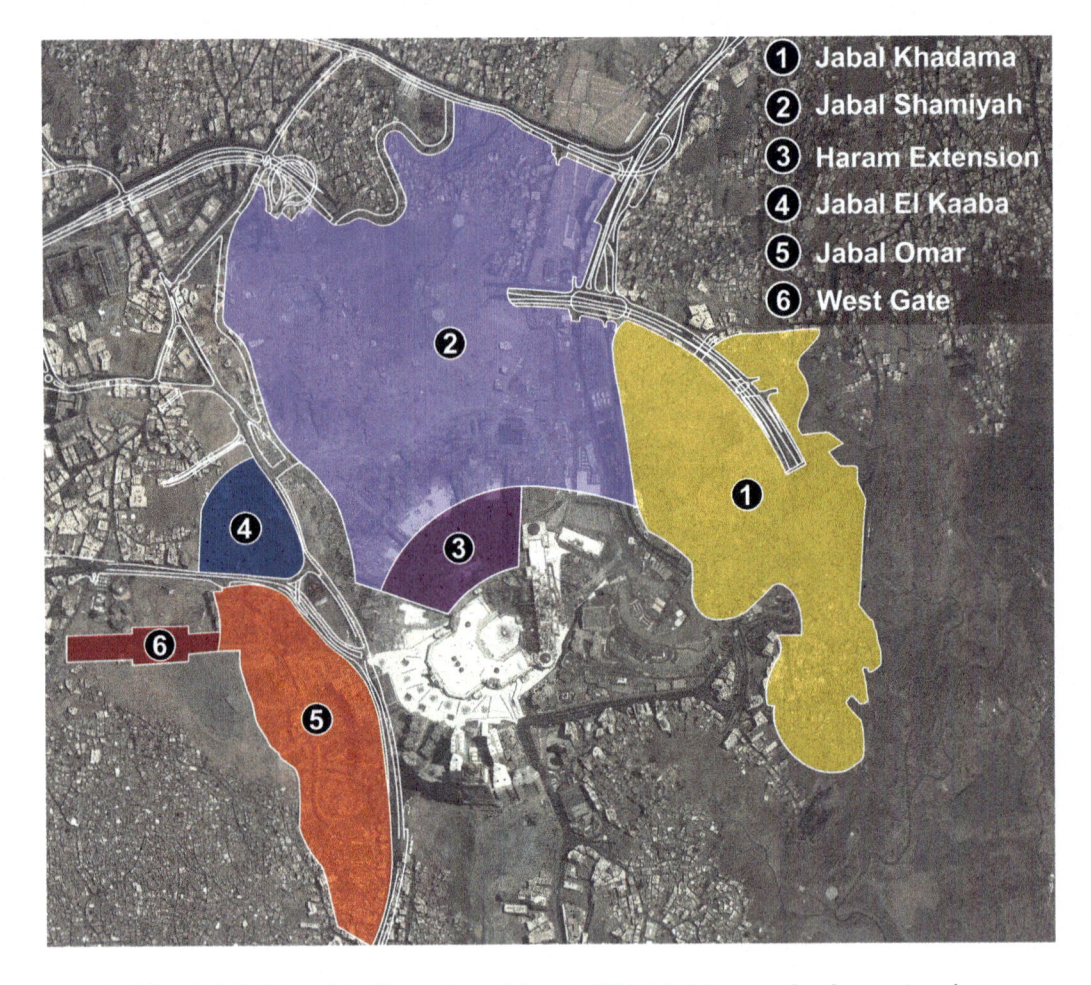

Figure 13.6 Subdivision of the Haram's periphery in Makkah into megadevelopment projects
Source: Author (based on Google Earth 2013).

Monofunctionality

In contrast to typical medinas in the Arab world, the urban cores of holy cities exhibit a mixture of commercial, handicraft and residential uses. Peters (1986: 76–7) described these as "*secondary service industries*, whose income derives directly from providing lodging, food and other nonsacral goods and services to the pilgrims." Compared to Cairo, Damascus or Istanbul, Makkah in the Middle Ages was a trading center focused on seasonal retail activity that excluded the more diverse activities of wholesale, import and manufacturing, and credit and banking (Peters 1986: 227, with reference to Wirth 1974/1975).

When holy cities lost their political functions to other capitals of the Islamic empire, they became mainly places of worship and scholarship. Commercial activities and social facilities clustered around the holy precinct, where education- and jurisdiction-related activities were associated with the mosque. At the same time, a tendency developed to emphasize *vertical sorting of uses* over horizontal segregation of functions. In particular, while the first two floors of buildings were kept for commerce (souqs), upper floors were used for temporary or permanent residence. According to Angawi (1988: 260), "The floor plans of many Mekkan houses were divisible into several independent sections (cuzlah, plural cuziat) which were separately rented to groups." Concurrently, buildings extended vertically, as opposed to clustering around courtyards. While "[i]n Cairo the street facade is minimal, and the real 'presentation' facade is in the internal courtyard[, in] Makkah the house is an extrovert presentation showing the most ornate aspect of the building" (Angawi 1988: 310). The prevalent typology in both Makkah and Madinah became the *tower house*, as opposed to the *courtyard house*, with an enclosed roof terrace being used as a protected open space (Bianca 2000: 223).

Another functional characteristic of medieval holy cities was a fine-grained distribution of functions that mirrored their intricate fabric of land ownership. In this regard, current trends toward land pooling, reparcelization and large-scale development have drastically altered a pre-existing organic morphology of mixed uses. Although local retail trade persists, as does the drive for speculation, the ever-increasing number of pilgrims has ushered in neoliberal economic practices that emphasize large-scale development and the dominance of global retail chains. In the absence of remedial, protective or preventive public policies, and with a new focus on private financing, the central districts of holy cities are turning into joint public/private commercial ventures.

When asked about the challenges of embarking on a $125 billion megaproject to expand the city's infrastructure and Holy Mosque, the mayor of Makkah observed:

> There are two difficulties—one of them is how you make the expansion of infrastructure to accommodate and work in parallel with the expansion of the holy mosque and the holy shrines. For that, you need more funds for projects and infrastructure that will draw the attention of the private sector to partner with the public sector in developing the infrastructure, the road, the mega-housing projects like Jabal Omar, like King Abdul Aziz road—these kinds of megaprojects in Mecca. (*Al Jazeera* 2009)

The outcome of this approach has been the subdivision of the Haram's periphery into megadevelopment parcels (Figure 13.6). These are conceived according to the principles of market-based urbanism, motivated by the high demand for space during the Hajj season. Such a strategy greatly discounts the issue of *seasonality*, that is, the lack of financial return during the remaining months of the year.

Seasonality

During the Hajj season, the ratio of pilgrims to the resident population is estimated to be around 3:1. This influx exerts considerable pressure on housing, transportation, public services, municipal utility systems and the network of roads and highways. When it comes to managing accessibility to the Haram area, Bianca (2000: 227–8) differentiated four periods of the year—a framework that may be taken as a general guide for other holy sites:

- Normal situation, applicable to usual workdays and involving mainly residents and business traffic.
- Holiday situation, relating to the increased influx of visitors from [Jeddah] and Taif during holidays, Fridays and Ramadan.
- Seasonal situation, resulting from an increase in the number of foreign visitors before and after the Hajj days, or from performing [Umrah] during certain favorable seasons.
- Hajj situation, concerning the peak days during the main pilgrimage season, when transportation from Arafat to Muna and to the haram has to occur during a fixed period of time.

The purpose of the suggested [public transport] system was to deal with the first three of the above cases. The fourth case involves such concentrations of people that no mechanical system can fully cope with the required turnover. There, pedestrian movement would have to prevail, but the public transport system could be useful for elderly or handicapped people, carrying them close to the Haram.

These problems of vehicular and pedestrian accessibility in and around holy cities are compounded by the need for prayer spaces within the Haram to accommodate the mass of pilgrims during the peak season. This issue has been addressed in successive urban design schemes by taking into consideration the fundamental concept in Islam that no special connection exists between "place and spirituality." As argued by Touba

(1997: 199), "Such a viewpoint provides a great deal of freedom to perform prayers at their proper times wherever a Muslim may be, on the principle that God is everywhere and the whole world is a temple of God."

As is the current practice from Istanbul to Cairo, any public space may be converted into sacred space for prayer (Figure 13.7). Such flexibility permits the use of streets and open spaces around the Haram as prayer spaces during the peak seasons of the Hajj, as illustrated by the 1985 plan for Makkah by Dar Al-Handasah:

> The building volumes of the new infill proposed between Sahah and Suheimi Streets were treated in such a way as to establish an architectural transition between the formal Haram structure and the northern part of the urban fabric. They were to have a flexible ground floor plan, allowing the available open space to be used for prayer whenever needed (particularly during the peak season), while during other periods it would be allocated to informal commercial use. This multi-functional approach would sustain the Haram's integration in the urban fabric, while preventing the central area from becoming a "dead place" during the low season.
>
> The total prayer surface within the boundaries of the new Haram extension amounts to approximately 160 000 square meters. By including the flexible ground floor space of the intermediate buildings and the surrounding pedestrian streets (available for temporary prayer use during peak seasons), this surface could be increased to about 240,000 square meters. The scheme could thus easily accommodate a maximum prayer capacity of at least 240,000 persons, which would meet the needs for the foreseeable future.

It is worth mentioning that this interchangeability between sacred and secular space is not tolerated in Western cities. In his presentation at "City Debates 2012," Yves Lion showed two projects for Islamic cultural centers in the Eighteenth Arrondissement of Paris, home to many North African immigrants (Figure 13.8). Due to a lack of mosque space, streets there were used on Fridays for prayer, "and each Friday the police car passed by to remind the believers that they are occupying public space." Since (according to a 1905 French law strictly separating state and religion) no religious buildings could be financed using public funds, the solution was to build Islamic *cultural centers* that would incorporate prayer spaces as part of a larger program of communal facilities and public services.

This fundamental difference in the conception and administration of public space in Western versus non-Western contexts highlights the issue of applying secular urban design principles to the holy cities of the Arab world and how the successive imports by foreign consultants of Western urban models have fared since the middle decades of the twentieth century. In addressing this issue, it is worth mentioning that differences in cultural values and practices go beyond conceptions about open space. They equally permeate such generic concerns of urban design as architectural conservation and urban identity and the interface between these public values and private development.

By examining successive plans for Makkah and Madinah and recent planning efforts in post-war mosaic and holy cities in Iraq, I will now attempt to derive a clearer understanding of the cumulative impact of imported design ideologies on the changing physical form of Muslim holy cities. I will work forward chronologically from the Modern and Postmodern periods until today.

Invariably, all such plans respond to two pressing needs. One is to clear space within the inner city to accommodate a growing influx of pilgrims. The other is to conserve the urban and architectural heritage of the religious–historic core. The following is an overview of how these dual constraints have been addressed by international and regional consultants since the 1970s and the extent to which their proposals have been implemented by local authorities. I will also explore current trends in rethinking the sacred core of holy cities in response to economic globalization and advances in transportation technology.

The two key reference on Makkah's architectural and urban heritage used here are by Sami Angawi and El Sayed Touba. Angawi (founder of the Hajj Research Center) has provided a detailed and comprehensive account of the development of Makkan domestic and sacred architecture and urban form that emphasizes the key role played by the Kaaba and Al-Masjid Al Haram. Touba has critically assessed the early master plans of Makkah by RMJM (1975) and Dar Al-Handasah (1985) and reflected on the issue of conservation from a comparative Western/regional perspective, as well as differing interpretations of heritage within the Islamic context itself.

Figure 13.7   Istanbul: The use of a street on Friday as prayer space
Source: Author.

Figure 13.8   Islamic cultural centers in the Eighteenth Arrondissement of Paris
Note: "Islamic Cultural Centre" Site Polonceau, Paris XVIIIᵉ (left); "Islamic Cultural Centre" Site Stephenson, Paris XVIIIᵉ (right).
Source: Atelier Lion associés.

Late Modernism: Integrating the Haram with its Periphery

In the early 1970s, during the age of late architectural modernism in the West and high architectural modernism in the Middle East, the firm of Robert Matthew Johnson-Marshall (RMJM) was commissioned by the Saudi Ministry of the Interior to develop the first master plan for Makkah. As explained by Touba (1997: 64–6), RMJM designated the Haram and its surroundings as a "Special Design Area" and envisioned the creation of a low-traffic zone around the Holy Mosque, an area then occupied by a decaying stock of buildings out of scale with their context. Furthermore, "[s]ince these development areas were the physical transition between the Haram and the general fabric of the Holy City, it was the intention of the special design proposals to integrate physically the Haram into the urban fabric as in the days of the Prophet."

Aware of the intense pressure for development and the need for policy controls, the plan recommended the relocation of institutional and office buildings as well as retail centers away from the Haram. However, it also acknowledged the existing mixed-use pattern and fine-textured distribution of activities in the area, and it proposed to retain this by avoiding "any enforcement of overall regulation on land use which would prohibit the flourishing of a variety of activities." As a way to prevent the harmful development of large-scale office and apartment buildings, "the regulations, for the Special Design Area, specified both a minimum and maximum plot size in order to retain the small scale activities."

Completed in 1975, the RMJM proposal showed a surprising sensitivity to the local and environment contexts, compared to the gargantuan gestures of today. However, the proposal went largely unimplemented, Touba noted, due to administrative restructuring and the unfulfilled need for additional technical guidance.

Early Postmodernism: Repairing the Haram's Periphery

Pressure on infrastructure and land speculation around holy precincts, which started in the 1970s, increased dramatically one decade later. Eventually, these forces led to the creation of artificial cuts through the old city structures of Makkah and Madinah and the destruction of the historic fabric around their central sanctuaries. At the beginning of the 1980s Stefano Bianca (1984: 21) described the dialectical attitude toward redeveloping versus repairing the historic fabric:

> Today, having passed the peak of the modern movement—or, if you prefer, standing on the brink of the postmodern age—we find ourselves in ambiguous situation. At one extreme are the often brutal, new large-scale developments promoted by the dynamics of today's economy and realized with the immense resources of modern technology. They introduce an alien scale and alien functional requirements into the historic city. At the other extreme—and as a reaction to the first—are the attempts at conservation that are often sterile because they do not consider the requirements of a living city.

In a pilot project for the area opposite to the King's Gate of Makkah's Holy Mosque, Bianca faced the challenge of integrating efficient public transportation solutions around the Haram with the repair of the destroyed urban form and natural landscape features. He has described his solution as follows (Bianca 2000: 231–2):

> The area at the northern exit of the tunnel, opposite the King's Gate of the Holy Mosque, posed a critical problem: a whole section of the former residential district on the hillside had been demolished, and the mountain slope was cut vertically at a height of approximately 20 metres, in order to build the recessed tunnel portals. This intervention caused a major townscape disruption in a sensitive location, opposite one of the main entries of the Haram and beneath the historic Turkish fort that sits above the tunnel. Accordingly, the pilot project for the train station opposite the King's Gate was conceived in such a way that it would reshape the disrupted slope by means of an integrated architectural intervention. The new infill structures were arranged as a series of gradually ascending buildings and terraces, crowned by the Jiyad Fort. The whole complex was planned to wrap the main station of the People Mover system into a larger complex with hotels, commercial and cultural facilities—complementary functions much needed in the vicinity of the Haram ... Thus the new building would not over-shadow the Holy Mosque, and the fort, an outstanding landmark of Mecca, would remain visible from the pedestrian plaza (the former Souq Al-Seghir).

Bianca's reconstitution of the hillside opposite the King's Gate thus emphasized the rugged topography surrounding the holy precinct. This constitutes a unique landscape feature shaped by four mountains: Jabal Khandama to the east, Jabal Abu Qubais to the west, Jabal Bakhsh to the south (with the Turkish fort on top), and Jabal Dhaf to the north.

The 1985 Dar Al-Handasah Master Directive Plan, the first comprehensive plan of Makkah, also emphasized this topography and the integrity of the landscape as an important identity-giver to the Haram and its surrounding urban region. It subdivided the city into six "cultural areas" (the Haram designated as the central zone), taking into consideration heritage buildings and their adjoining open spaces as well the pattern of activities and characteristic elements of the townscapes. It then presented three alternative plans for the central area, articulated around a common set of development guidelines: (a) raising buildings on colonnades to allow for the expansion of prayer and service zones during the Hajj season; (b) limiting the heights of buildings from seven to 15 floors outward from the Haram; (c) adopting a radiating street pattern centered around the Holy Kaaba; and (d) pedestrianizing, landscaping, and furnishing the plaza surrounding the Kaaba.

Despite its attempts at townscape preservation, Touba (1997: 109) has criticized this scheme both for providing an excessive level of infrastructure and for weakening the distinctive religious identity of the holy precinct:

> It is a well-known tenet in the basics of planning that, whenever you introduce a new road leading to one focal point, the problem of congestion is either exacerbated or at best temporarily delayed. To facilitate new roads leading to the Haram, Dar Al-Handasah recommended the demolition of homes and introduced piazzas around the Holy Mosque, with no isolation between the houses and the Mosque itself. The consultant considered no alternative plan except to create these surrounding piazzas which resulted in an alien pattern for an Islamic city ... An excessively bright lighting system designed by Dar Al-Handasah transformed the Holy Mosque into a daylight stadium. It is as if he did not appreciate the difference between the lighting of a soccer field and the soft lighting of a religious building. Moreover, the consultant incorporated bright, smooth marble and shiny brass with gold finish, giving the impression of an atrium in a five star hotel.

Although this critique may seem harsh considering the need to provide a well-lit environment for night mass prayer, it points to the emergence of a Postmodern speculative spirit that would become pervasive one decade later with the development of the periphery of the holy precinct. Regionally labeled "Gulf urbanism," this attitude toward design and development has now affected architecture and planning from Beirut to Dubai. Ultimately, it can be seen as a byproduct of increasing globalization and economic neoliberalization.

As noted by the Jones Lang LaSalle report (2010: 4), "the Muslim Holy Cities of Makkah and Madinah are unique real estate markets, benefitting from effectively unlimited visitor demand from the world's 1.8 billion Muslims." Today the proximity to the Holy Mosque has become the key factor in determining the price of land and revenue per hotel room, and the building of religious tourist accommodations adjoining the holy precinct is the driving force behind real estate investment in central Makkah. According to the *Guardian* report mentioned earlier, "a square foot around the Grand Mosque now sells for up to $18,000, mayor Osama Al-Bar said last year, dwarfing the Monaco average of $4,400" (Wainwright 2012).

Current Urban Design Trends

In Makkah, the first decade of the millennium witnessed the colonization of the hills surrounding the holy precinct with high-rise speculative structures. These capitalized on the radial topography that allowed strategic views toward the center. According to the Jones Lang LaSalle report (2010: 11), "[m]ore than 20 master plans have been submitted for individual large scale real estate developments in central Makkah in recent years. Several of these have now been approved with the projects progressing to the implementation phase."

As reported in the *Guardian*, a major manifestation of this movement is Abraj al-Bait, "which rises like Big Ben on steroids to tower 600m over the holy mosque of Makkah in the spiritual heart of the Islamic world. This thrusting pastiche palace houses an array of luxury hotels and apartments, perched above a five-storey slab of shopping malls." Furthermore:

> Along the Western flank of the city are the first towers of the Jabal Omar development, a sprawling complex that will eventually accommodate 100,000 people in 26 luxury hotels—sitting on another gargantuan plinth of 4,000 shops and 500 restaurants, along with its own six-story prayer hall. The line of blocks, which will climb to heights of up to 200 meters and terminate in a monumental gateway building, share the clock tower's Islamic-lite language: a clichéd dressing of pointed arches and filigree grillwork plastered over generic concrete shells. (Wainwright 2012)

I will now turn to a discussion of this and other recent urban design proposals for holy sites in the region that were presented and discussed at the "City Debates 2012" conference.

Modernism Revisited: Developing the Haram's Periphery

In 2006, the Jabal Omar project was the subject of an international competition promoted by the Jabal Omar Development Company (JODC), a Saudi joint-stock company established in 2006 to group together 5,000 owners of 1,200 real estate parcels covering an area of 232,000 square meters neighboring the Haram's western court. With a stipulated floor area ratio around 10, the project establishes legal grounds for tower structures of more than 30 stories. It will thus drastically reshape the townscape around the holy precinct.

At "City Debates 2012," Nezar AlSayyad, head of the Jabal Omar competition jury, commented that the winning entry by Yves Lion had been selected because it was seen as "the least offensive and the most sensitive" entry. Lion's proposal focused on key functional issues common to sites of worship—that is, centrality, fluidity of movement, and the interface between public and private spaces.

In presenting this work, Lion explained that a guiding principle behind the proposal was that "the primary understanding of the role of urban designers is to design public spaces not buildings—to configure and tie them to the place and to the topography, and not to fall into the trap of designing individual structures and malls." This understanding also conditioned the attitude toward the sanctity of the site: "We focused on a pragmatic approach in a place where spirituality does not need our contribution. The intention was to avoid monumentality because the real monument is the center. The spirituality translates into perspective views towards the Kaaba."

As a result of these views, the project emphasized "urban comfort," the "flow of people" and the "duality between the everyday situation and the exception of pilgrimage peak periods." The resulting design built on the integration of public platforms to the topography (Figure 13.9a), the fluidity of circulation leading to the prayer areas (Figure 13.9b), and the design of centrally directed visual corridors with sacred termination points (Figure 13.9c–13.9d). According to Lion: "Such an arrangement could be attained by envisioning the Central District as two entities: a public layer encompassing the ground and first floor, used for retail activities and public services; and an upper private layer including hotels and apartments bridging over streets and passages for environmental protection and a unique spatial experience."

Still, the primary consideration underlying the jury's decision was the optimization of views toward the Kaaba from the hotel accommodations, which determined the financial return on individual room units. This had been the central criterion advanced by the developer due to the speculative nature of the project. To this end, a mechanism with laser beams was programmed to measure, for the different submissions, the number of windows in each tower that would offer direct views of the Kaaba and the Haram.

What can be learned from Lion's proposal, however, is that excessive site exploitation does not necessarily preclude the accommodation of public amenities, nor sensitivity toward a sacred townscape. While pedestrian areas and other public spaces were carefully planned for protection from extreme weather conditions, the vertical residential structures above the communal podium were conceived as neutral visual elements shaped by a simple strategy of affording views to the Haram without an imposing presence on their own. In the 3D drawings submitted for the competition, these towers were kept diagrammatic in their expression. Indeed, Lion described these illustrations as "dessins théoriques," or conceptual drawings, to emphasize the intention to avoid competing visually with the sacred precinct.

In architectural terms, one might describe this project as a return to a Modernist design ideology that emphasizes functionalism and adaptation to physical and climatic context while deferring to the symbolic character of the site. As a response to the excessive economic neoliberalization at the start of the new millennium, one might call this "Modernism revisited." Instead of taking a radical and critical position toward the real estate speculation on the Haram's periphery, Lion rationalized his intervention through the notions of urban comfort, accessibility, visual permeability, and the layering of land uses. This allowed him to bring urban design back to its most common denominator: "serving the city."

Figure 13.9 Jabal Omar competition
Note: (a) integration within the topography of the area surrounding the Haram; (b) rendering of pedestrian corridors; (c) visual corridors leading to the prayer area; (d) radial spine leading to Haram.
Source: Atelier Lion associés.

Such an approach can be seen as a clear departure from the Postmodern flamboyance of the 1990s and 2000s, as expressed in the adjoining development of Abraj el Bait. There, in lieu of an urban design intervention, the hotel/commercial complex was envisioned first and foremost as large-scale architecture. The design focused on "building" and "image," with the result being the imposition of gargantuan scale and inappropriate symbolism—a clock tower in a timeless, transcendental location.

Centrality versus Centralities: Sites of Worship in Post-War Mosaic Cities

While sites of worship in holy cities command a central location and polarize the development of the totality of the urban context, sites of worship in mosaic cities are inscribed into a multifunctional and multicentered urban structure. This situation may be made further complex by spatial segregation and destruction, in post-war contexts like Beirut and Baghdad. Such a problematic context was clearly involved in the regional/international competition "to revive and develop the area of Adhamiyah" launched by Amanat (the Mayoralty of) Baghdad in 2010.

The historic Adhamiyah district is home to the shrine of Imam Abu Hanifa al-Numan, surrounded by five residential neighborhoods: Shuyoukh, Haibat Khatoon, Al-Hara, Safeena and Nassa. As defined in the competition brief, the project involved "the expansion of the structure of the shrine, and the construction of a guesthouse for visitors" (al-Mulhim 2012). According to Al-Mulhim, Khalid al-Essawi, a member of the National Investment Commission, explains:

> What makes Adhamiyah exceptional is the presence of a large number of shrines of many great scholars of Islam, which have become destinations for visitors coming from various Islamic countries, in addition to the presence of the royal cemetery in which members of the Iraqi monarchy family are buried ... There are also very old mosques that are hundreds of years old, in addition to its exceptional location on the shores of the Tigris River ... The project is one in a series that aims to develop the historic and heritage areas in Baghdad, which include renovating the Rasheed Street district, developing the area extending between this street and the Tigris River, and developing the area surrounding the Kadhimiya shrine.

In response to this challenge, an Italian group headed by Giuseppe Cinà, from the Politecnico of Torino, proposed a master plan, which was classified third in the competition. In presenting this work at the "City Debates 2012" conference, Cinà reported that his group started from the premise that "the rehabilitation of the shrine complex needs to be designed in close correlation with the overall rehabilitation of the surrounding neighborhoods." The work also needed to acknowledge "the strong operational limits of a city [like Baghdad] under reconstruction, [requiring] exceptional solutions" (Figure 13.10).

Another key premise identified by Cinà was that "cities are inherently inclusive," and that sites of worship constitute one identity among many, wavering between "competition and coexistence." Accordingly, the notion of heritage embraced in the work encompassed a diversity of districts and their urban fabrics, ranging from traditional centers where holy shrines are usually clustered to modern subcenters belonging to later stages of urban expansion. The project thus recognized five centralities (central places) instead of one, and attempted to reinforce the specific identity of each: (1) the Area of Abu Hanifa Mosque Square (religious identity); (2) the crossing of Nu'man and Il Iman al Adham Street (commercial identity); (3) the Antar Square (infrastructural identity); (4) Al-Bayt University (cultural/educational identity); and (5) the riverfront park of Al-Hara (civic identity).

Besides a *spatial and functional framework*, which focuses on "gates of conservation and innovation," the plan proposes a *regulatory framework* to govern the gradual and incremental change of "ordinary places." This dual strategy, combining innovation and conservation, synthesizes two urban design traditions. On the one hand, it reflects the grand tradition of spatial restructuring through the articulation of nodes and connections (as in Pope Sixtus's Rome or Haussmann's Paris). On the other, it embodies the morphological tradition of preserving the existing fabric through incremental change. The two traditions illustrate the notion of "inclusiveness" stressed by Cinà. Among the implications of this view is the need to accept ethnic/social diversity (the mosaic nature of cities) and a dual process of urban development. This means both a process for achieving joint public/private interventions at key cultural, commercial and infrastructural sites as well as incremental development on small sites controlled by building rules and regulations. Such an implementation process merges the grand gestures of eighteenth-century European urbanism with a Postmodern sensitivity toward diverse and symbolic urban conditions. Concurrently, it shares Lion's Modernist concern in Makkah for functionality and infrastructural fluidity. Overall, the proposed master plan may be interpreted as an attempt at merging Baghdad's religious and secular identities, in reaction to the increasing sectarian and political fragmentation of the city.

Political Fragmentation: Sites of Worship in Post-War Holy Cities

Although different in scope and program, the proposals by Lion and Cinà are both entries by foreign consultants responding to predetermined competition briefs. As outside observers, both designers possess a cultural and ideological distance that favors objectivity and innovation. However, such a disengaged viewpoint cannot provide pragmatic understanding of local administrative complexities or various stakeholder agendas, which inevitably stand in the way of effective plan implementation. In contrast, Iraqi consultants entrusted with local

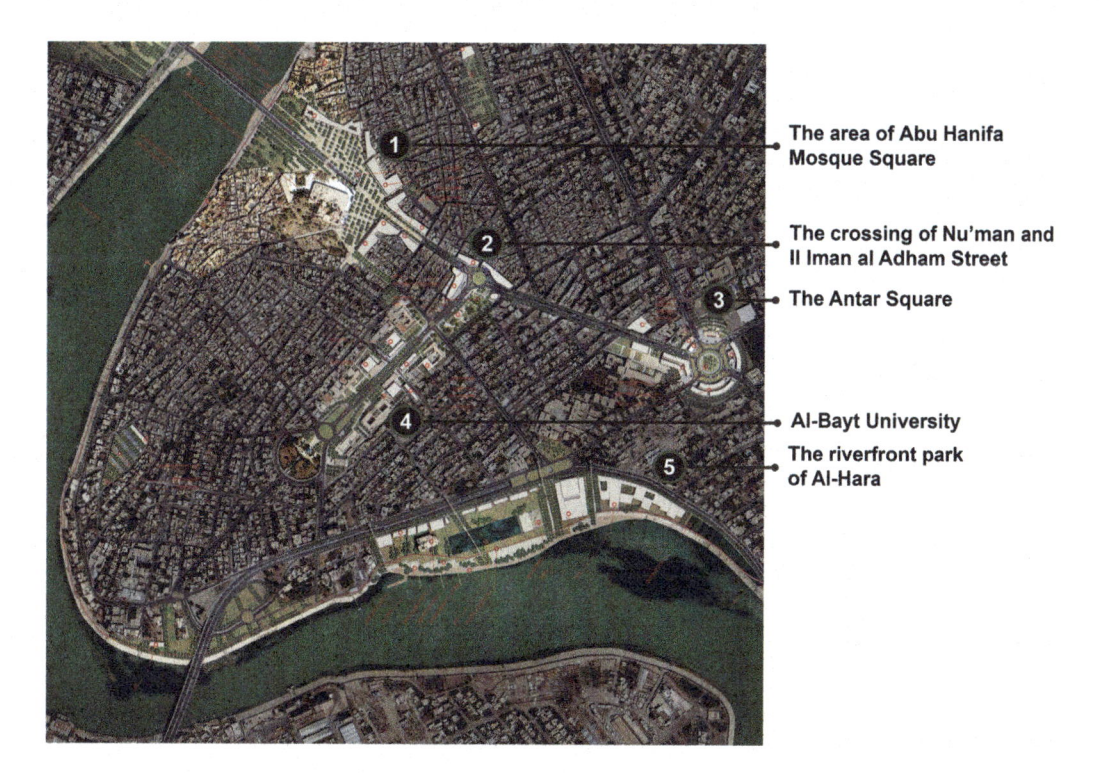

Figure 13.10 Urban requalification of the Abu Hanifa Mosque in the Adhamiyah neighborhood of Baghdad

Note: (1) the area of Abu Hanifa Mosque Square; (2) the crossing of Nu'man and Il Iman al Adham Street; (3) the Antar Square; (4) Al-Bayt University; and (5) the riverfront park of Al-Hara.
Source: Giuseppe Cinà.

master plans must operate on the ground to generate information about existing conditions. They also must interact with politicians, public officials and local residents, and so become entangled in a complex reality that makes the articulation of comprehensive and original visions more challenging.

Such a case is illustrated in the work of Dewan Architects & Engineers, an Iraqi consulting firm commissioned by the Ministry of Municipalities and Public Works to draft the master plans for Karbala and Najaf. As the chief holy cities for Shia Islam, Karbala and Najaf receive the highest number of pilgrims every year among Muslim holy cities after Makkah and Madinah. Karbala is the place of martyrdom of Imam Al Hussein and the commemorative site of the Day of Ashura. It is home to the shrines of Imam Al Hussein and his brother Abbas, and provides the ultimate burial location of pious Shia believers. Najaf is the renowned site of the largest cemetery in the Muslim world. It is also home to the Imam Ali Shrine, the second venerated figure after the Prophet, and an eminent center for learning and theology.

According to Emirates 24/7 (2010), in both cities, "[t]he scope of Dewan's contract include[d:] documenting and verifying the condition of the areas, and carrying out all required studies and surveys; analyzing and drawing conclusions based on the results; examining and presenting urban renewal alternatives; and preparing a comprehensive urban design report." Concurrently, "Dewan has to run several training workshops for the ministry as part of its 'knowledge sharing' programme."

In presenting Dewan's work at "City Debates 2012," Mohamed Al Assam, the firm's founder and managing director, alluded to "the challenges and obstacles [the consulting firm] faces every day." These include "problems inherited from Saddam Hussein and ... problems confronted now. The first [involved] the destruction of the old cities during the revolutions by the regime and the Iraqi army against the people. And then [came the] political problems/contradictions between the parties [currently] ruling Iraq." As Al Assam added, "before we had only one or five parties, now we have 100 ... We are all complaining and it is really affecting our work and progress."

Inhabited by a largely Shia population, both Karbala and Najaf were subject for 60 years to "negligence and destruction by the old regime." Moreover, in Karbala, "the area between the two shrines was demolished by the Saddam Hussein regime after the uprising in 1991 (since people used to hide there)." Yet the "the lack of awareness of the importance of buildings" and the "ignorance and limited knowledge and experience of officials" has now led to an ongoing pattern of destruction by the local authorities, themselves. According to Al Assam, they "start demolishing not according to [the consultant's] papers, but according to their needs."

For instance, "a very important area in Karbala, just outside the shrine of [Imam Al] Hussein," was cleared to create a link to another sacred site without referring to the urban design consultant. The same problem has arisen in Najaf, where Dewan is fighting to prevent the demolition of the old souq, in addition to "approximately 30 percent of the city, in an effort to offer a promenade from the main square to the shrine" and facilitate new development on either side. According to Al Assam, such measures are indicative of widespread "corruption," whereby the consultants' approval of building permits for construction and demolition is often undermined by side arrangements between the owners and the municipality.

Another key issue facing implementation is the entangled ownership status of private properties and "the absence of interest from original residents and landowners" in identifying themselves or improving their properties. Indeed, in many cases these owners may have migrated to suburban villas on the periphery or left the country altogether. Gradually, this has led to a condition where residential uses in old centers are being replaced by commercial ones to service the increasing influx of pilgrims.

As Al Assam concluded: "[T]he officials in Najaf and Karbala think we should design the city to take into consideration that the pilgrims are the priority. In Karbala, they are already asking us to clean around the two shrines an area that is enough for more than one million people at one single time. [This is] around three people per square meter, which is very high—the whole area is 330,000 square meters, which is one-third of the whole city of Karbala." He thus framed the "future of the holy cities" as a dialectic between "bricks and people," with no "magic solutions," and he refrained from advancing any firm proposals at this stage of the work.

What the Najaf and Karbala case studies reveal is a situation where urbanists are caught in the middle of a post-war transitional situation. In the case of such master planning efforts, any participative approach becomes problematic due to an increasingly fragmented political context. As Al Assam pointed out, in such conditions, "[the] ample opportunity for misinterpretation, disappointment, and insensitivity makes the prospect of intervention daunting from the outset." The problem is compounded by the duality of interests between design professionals and public officials, which arises out of corruption and administrative inefficiency.

Sites of Worship as Sites of Power: Governance, Conservation and Infrastructure

The cases of Najaf and Karbala, as well as of Makkah and Madinah, raise the tricky issue of "agency." On the local level, can urban designers be expected to mediate between the differing agendas of various stakeholders politically, economically and administratively? And from a wider perspective, it is also important to ask whether sites of worship belong to a global or a local community. Is their development a concern primarily of their host country, or of the Muslim world at large? Underlying these questions are the key issues of *governance* and *conservation*.

By way of a conclusion, I would like to reflect on this issue of governance by quoting the remarks of Sateh El-Arnaout from the "City Debates 2012" conference. These followed the presentations of Giuseppe Cinà and Mohamed Al Assam. I will also refer to El Sayed Touba's work again to discuss the differing attitudes toward conservation of Muslim scholars and urban design and planning professionals. And I would like to highlight recent visionary attempts at the future design interventions on sites of worship.

El-Arnaout began his comments by noting that sites of worship, normally discussed by urban designers from an operational perspective, also need to be envisioned in light of the socioeconomic realities of their populations, their governance structures, and their institutional setups. Such sites are not "isolated islands," they are also "sites of townships witnessing high population growth rates and rural to urban migration." These conditions are further compounded by seasonal dramatic variations created by the affluence of visitors and the influx of professional and migrant workers to serve the pilgrims. "Basically [holy cities] are economic hubs, and the challenge is how to make such cities work in a synchronized and harmonious way." In other words this involves bridging the gap between the spiritual, social and economic dimensions.

Concurrently, El-Arnaout noted, sites of worship are "places of power," as evidenced by "the governance dynamics between the worship sites, their host cities, and the host countries. You have the host city, and a worship site. Who takes the decisions regarding on-site/off-site developments? Is it the municipality, the Waqf, or the central government? There is always this dilemma of who retains the governance of these sites, and how to work with the political and, more and more, the religious leaderships." Increasingly, as in the case of Karbala and Najaf, "there is a need for consultation, consensus-building—mainly now when we have the clear expression of political parties. We need to reflect on the many conflicts the issue of religious governance is fostering in this part of the world."

El-Arnaout went on to list a number of examples of such conflicts: Jerusalem, with the problems of managing its religious sites; Egypt, "where building a church requires the prior approval of the president"; and Beirut, where the minarets of the Mohammad Al-Amin Mosque and the neighboring bell tower of the downtown Maronite cathedral compete for visual preeminence. In the Beirut case, between Solidere (the real estate company entrusted with rebuilding its central district), the municipality, and the religious Awqaf, "who is allowing that? Who is governing that?"

El-Arnaout further invoked the case of Makkah:

> Definitely we cannot talk about sites of worship without discussing Saudi Arabia and what is happening in Mecca which is again extremely controversial ... Is the developments of the holy sites (a clock tower that is 600 meters high just next to the Kaaba) and the real estate speculation around these sites in Mecca a local or a global responsibility? What authorities, states, and institutions represent the inhabitants and the pilgrims, and how do architects and urban designers steer their practice within these conflicts?

As I have attempted to show, the governance of sites of worship is a topic that has received relatively little investigation. Yet, despite sensitive issues that may emerge from discussing the intersection of political power and the custody of sacred sites, this is work that is needed. Such an investigation may reveal the limitations of urban design in enforcing change in complex administrative and political settings. And it may reveal the near impossibility of implementing master plans in the absence of clear consensus among different stakeholders.

Part of the problem may stem from the dialectic between development and conservation and the differing ideological stands toward sacred heritage between "religious scholars and conservationists." Thus, according to Touba (1997: 183, 184):

> [T]hose who stressed the need to save the past ... basically accept the idea of conserving the holiness of Makkah by conserving historic and religiously significant sites, but differ in the details of conservation, such as whether to save all old buildings or just selected ones, and whether to put some to commercial uses or as museums. The author is among those who believe that it is important to maintain a certain aura in Makkah to enhance the religious experience, rather than demolishing all buildings that stand in the way of development, thereby detracting from such a holy place. Makkah belongs to Muslims from all over the world. Pilgrims consider their visit as the most important journey in their entire life. To remove the soul of the city and wipe out the history associated with its physical monuments clearly denies all Muslims elements of their religious, historical and cultural past.

> One of the main arguments against conserving religious buildings ... was the belief that a true Muslim would not require any special place to pray and therefore did not need the ambience of historic and religious monuments to add to the event. There is a fear that maintaining historic and religious sites might lead to polytheism and the glorifying of graves. This was echoed by the Wahhabi doctrine and followers of that movement, including the Higher Committee of Religious Affairs in Saudi Arabia.

Touba (1997: 189) concluded that "[t]he gap must be narrowed between the two sides through dialogue and constructive thought." And he proposed a set of solutions mainly articulated around "limiting the number of pilgrims annually to match existing services."

Interestingly, Touba (1997: 189–202) also discussed different possibilities for "regaining the lost identity of Mecca." These included the conservation of remaining historic sites and buildings, their reconstruction, the recording of disappearing ones, and offer of incentives to owners to rehabilitate and conserve. Such recommendations have since been outstripped, however, by the neoliberal economic tide that has swept over the sites of worship and their vicinity for the past two decades.

Moreover, alternative ways of thinking are now emerging from design theorists and young academicians who are reframing holy cities with new visions of hybrid typologies and infrastructural townscapes. Sam Jacoby, in Chapter 8, refers to Deena Fakhro, one of his students at the Architectural Association, London, who produced a design thesis in 2008 on the theme of "The Holy City and Its Discontents." Fakhro's proposal aimed to reduce the redundancy of Hajj infrastructural services like the Jeddah airport, which is subject to an "annual 90% underuse." As explained by Jacoby:

> These infrastructures are consequently an economic burden, with Saudi Arabia spending each year billions of US dollars to construct and maintain them. These predicaments provoke the project to combine the economy of Makkah with regional ambitions to establish a globally competitive and Islamic knowledge economy—reducing dependence on a seasonal service industry. [Building on] a type study of circular airports and historical Islamic universities, a hybrid model part airport and university is proposed. During the peaks of pilgrimage, which coincide with academic holidays, it works as an airport, while at all other times it functions as a university. In response, three strategically located airport–universities in the valleys of Makkah are envisioned that re-establish three historically important gateways into the city from Jeddah, Madinah and Taif. This disperses incoming pilgrim flows and eases congestion, defines a limit to the urban sprawl and restores the ancient significance of the pilgrim's journey by heightening the experience of religious procession already on arrival to the Holy City.

Such experimental projects constitute a promising departure from the conventional thinking of the late Modernist and Postmodernist periods, which focuses on the dialectics of development and preservation. Instead, they explore broader concerns of regional restructuring and infrastructural reframing. However, they may also be interpreted as disillusionment with ever recuperating the lost identity of sites of worship.

References

Al Jazeera. 2009. Improving Mecca's Infrastructure. *Al Jazeera* [online]. Available at: http://www.aljazeera.com/focus/hajj/2009/11/200911250505146948.html [accessed: April 4, 2014].

al-Mulhim, M. 2012. Amanat Baghdad Launches Project to Develop Historic Adhamiyah District. *Mawtini* [online]. Available at: http://mawtani.al-shorfa.com/en_GB/articles/iii/features/iraqtoday/2012/04/20/feature-01 [accessed: February 17, 2014].

Angawi, S.M. 1988. *Makkan Architecture*. Doctoral dissertation, School of Oriental and African Studies, University of London.

Bianca, S. 1984. Designing Compatibility between New Projects and the Local Urban Tradition, in *Continuity and Change: Design Strategies for Large-Scale Urban Development*, edited by M. Bentley-Sevcenko. Cambridge: The Aga Khan Program for Islamic Architecture, 21–34.

Bianca, S. 2000. *Urban Form in the Arab World—Past and Present*. London: Thames & Hudson.

Emirates 24/7. 2010. Dewan in Deal for Urban Renewal of Iraqi Historic Cities. Available at: http://www.emirates247.com/lifestyle/living/dewan-in-deal-for-urban-renewal-of-iraqi-historic-cities-2010-11-03-1.312881 [accessed: April 4, 2014].

Jones Long LaSalle. 2010. Holy Cities: Saudi's Unique Real Estate Markets. Jones Lang LaSalle Middle East and North Africa [online], 1–16. Available at: http://www.joneslanglasalle.eu/ResearchLevel1/JLL%20MENA_Holy%20Cities_June%202010_EN.pdf [accessed: April 4, 2014].

Kister, M.J. 1972. Some Reports Concerning Mecca from Jahiliyya to Islam. *Journal of the Economic and Social History of the Orient*, 15, 61–93.

Peters, F.E. 1986. *Jerusalem and Mecca: The Typology of the Holy City in the Near East*. New York: New York University Press.

Touba, E.S.M. 1997. *Conservation in an Islamic Context: A Case Study of Makkah*. Master's Thesis [online], Durham University. Available at: http://etheses.dur.ac.uk/4981/ [accessed: April 4, 2014].

Wainwright, O. 2012. Mecca's Mega Architecture Casts Shadow over Hajj. *Guardian* [online]. Available at: http://www.theguardian.com/artanddesign/2012/oct/23/mecca-architecture-hajj1 [accessed: April 4, 2014].

Wirth, E. 1974/1975. Zum Problem des Bazars. *Der Islam*, 51, 203–60; and *Der Islam*, 52, 6–46.

Chapter 14
Sites of Conflict: Baghdad's Suspended Modernities versus a Fragmented Reality

Caecilia Pieri

Since the Tanzimat (Ottoman reforms), Baghdad has never ceased to suffer from aborted attempts at modernizing its urban form. Despite its leading role in the fields of modern arts and culture since the 1930s, imported models of urbanism have repeatedly proven inappropriate to the local context while being challenged by continuous political instability. A short historical overview shows that urbanism visions of Baghdad as the capital city of Iraq were mostly imposed from above, first by colonial powers and later by local governments with their own political and ideological agendas. This is instrumental in understanding Baghdad's urban context today (Figure 14.1), which is torn between two extremes: the center dating back to pre-modern and modern periods and being subject to neglect, physical degradation and slumification and projected large-scale peripheral neighborhoods conveying a global outlook.

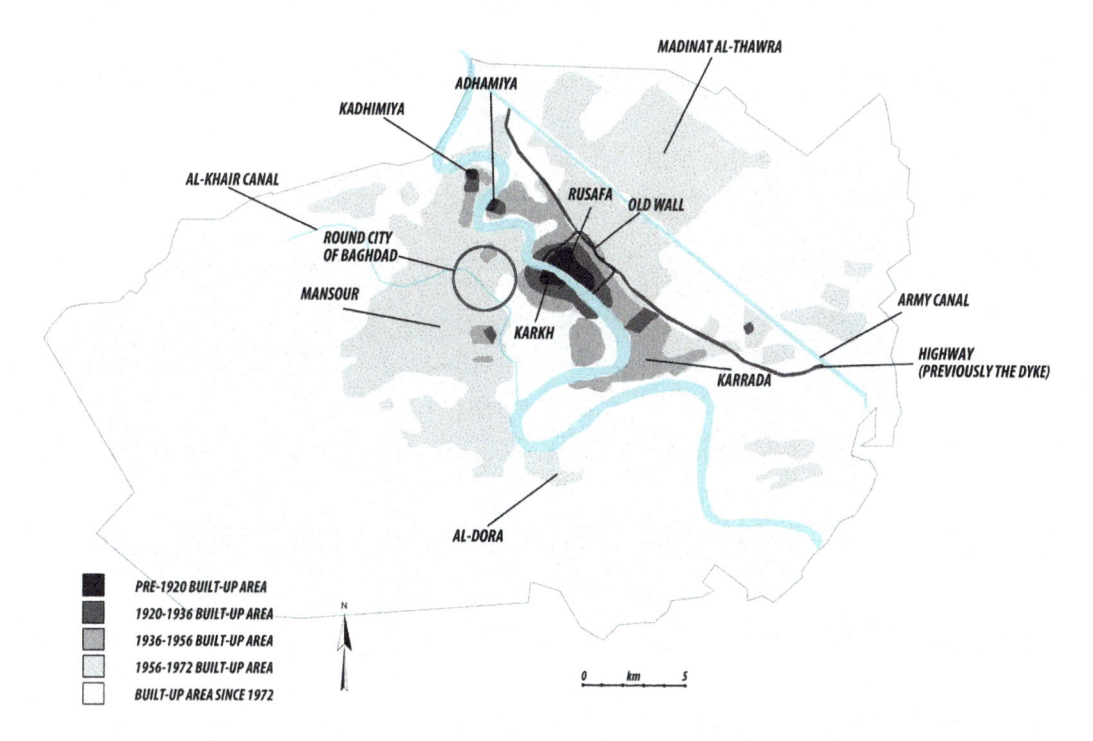

Figure 14.1 Physical growth of Baghdad from 1920 to present
Source: Author (infographics by Yaseen Raad).

As stated by Cooperson (1996), Baghdad remains a deceptive "literary trope," an "object of desire, cause of disappointment." The burden of Orientalism has left this city with an enduring image as the "Caliph's City"; this mythic past is masking the actual city being seen not for *what it is*, but for *what it was and is no longer* (Pieri 2008).Such lack of consideration for the urban reality may generate the repeated desire to create a "new Baghdad" through the radical gesture of *tabula rasa*.

1870s–1930s: Colonial Urbanism under the Late Ottoman Rule and the British Mandate

This approach began with the Tanzimat, which, in Baghdad, is generally associated with Midhat Pasha's rule (1869–71).[1] Under the French-educated Pasha, modernization entailed the destruction of the ancient walls—partially erected by the Seljukids in the eleventh century—and the Haussmannization of the periphery, emulating the Grand Boulevards of Paris and the Ring in Vienna (Figure 14.2). This attempt at importing and domesticating modernity, through the imposition of European urban models, was common in colonial territories—as witnessed in German Namibia, Dutch Indonesia, British India and French North Africa—and may be seen as a highly symbolic attempt to rewrite the history of Baghdad as the first political power to modify the city's medieval boundaries.

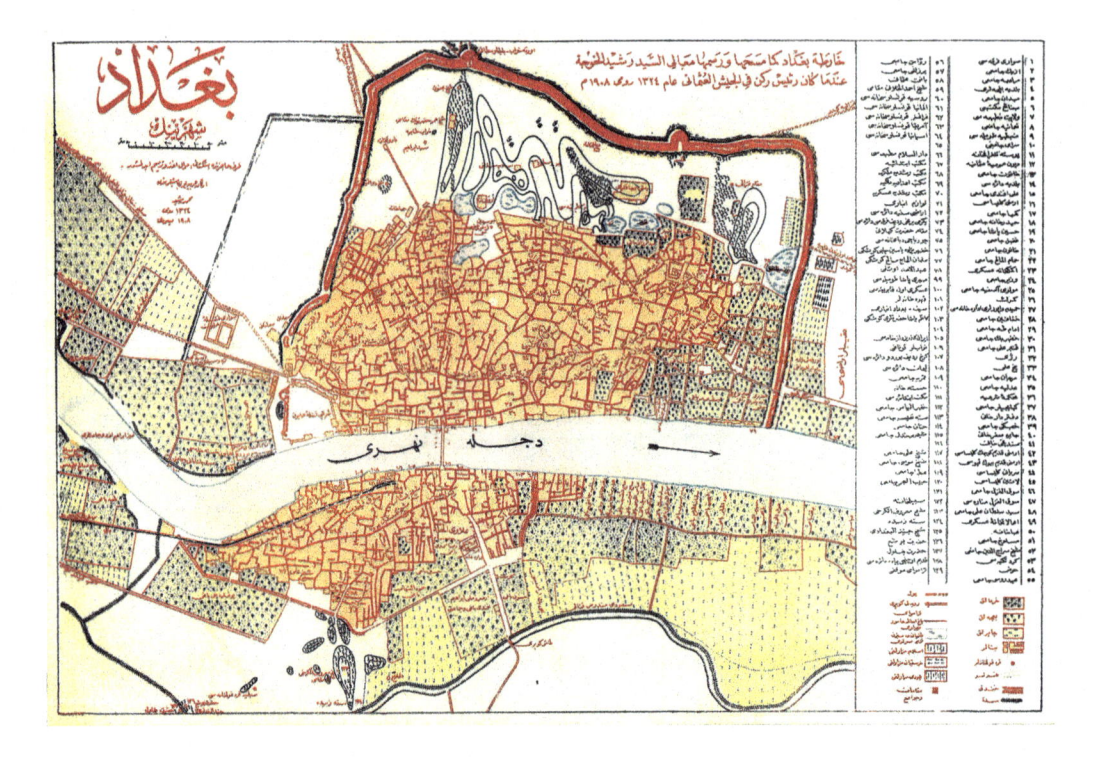

Figure 14.2   Baghdad's built up area in the late Ottoman era, 1908
Note: Author, Major Khoja.
Source: Susa 1957.

---

1   Important incentives for administrative reform have been previously launched in the 1830s by the Sultan Abdulmecid.

Near the end of the Ottoman rule, the first straight street in Rusafa—successively known as Khalil Pasha Street, New Street and finally Al Rasheed Street—was built by cutting across the traditional urban fabric, despite the resistance of the Sunni Awqaf (Figure 14.3). According to the British traveler Richard Coke, the work was carried out in only "one night-time by a gang of demolishers" and entailed the destruction of about 700 houses (Coke 1927). This opus was orchestrated by military engineers from Germany, allies of the Ottomans between 1915 and 1917. This illustrates another case of civic space subverted to a military agenda by facilitating the rapid crossing of the city from the southern gate towards the northern sectors, where various military and governmental facilities were situated.

In the aftermath of the 1917 British military victory and subsequent presence in Iraq, architecture and town planning were tailored to respond to a new agenda of foreign politics conveying Iraq's institutional and political status as a "sovereign country under assistance" (Nolde 1934) under the Mandate Treaty.[2] Again, urban design was derived from strategic military necessity, resulting in the implementation of infrastructural facilities related specifically to communications, security and logistics such as police stations, bridges, airports, post offices, tanks and clubs. In a more generic gesture, the first neighborhoods built along the existing axis to the south (known today as Saadoun Street) were a juxtaposed set of streets laid out according to a basic orthogonal grid. Such interventions dating from the 1920s and early 1930s can be interpreted as the "ground zero" of town planning. The *wide street* the British had previously used as a tool against riots in India (Home 1997) acted as a model for facilitating circulation for the newly introduced motor vehicles, as well for addressing sanitary needs and spatial regularization.

During this period, James Mollison Wilson—the first British Director of Iraqi Public Works Department (PWD) and a key figure in colonial town planning—explicitly spoke of an "Arab Renaissance" and of urban beautification (Sultani 1982), probably qualifying the new town he planned next to the military headquarters and airport (Phillips 1923) as well as the master plan of Adhamiyah neighborhood. The latter, typical of a Beaux-Arts radiating scheme, strangely recalls that of New Delhi. As Wilson had previously served as assistant to Sir Edwin Lutyens in India, he was instrumental in replicating this similar scheme in Iraq. Yet a budget shortage would soon put an end to these colonial attempts at modernizing Baghdad (Phillips 1923).

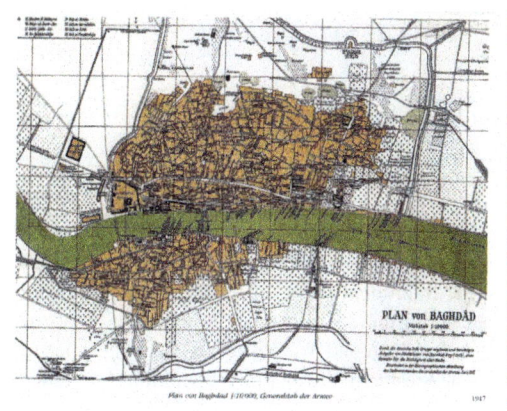

Figure 14.3   Rashid Street (called "New Street" until the late 1920s)
Note: Map of Baghdad in 1917 by the German Army showing Al Rasheed Street cutting through the traditional urban fabric (left); section of Al Rasheed Street building frontages (right).
Source: The German Army 1917, Wirth 2000 (left); author, December 2009 (right).

---

2   Official versions of the British mandate on Iraq can be found at the Public Record Offices, National Archives of London, under referenced files such as WO 106/6348 and PRO/ CO 730, among others.

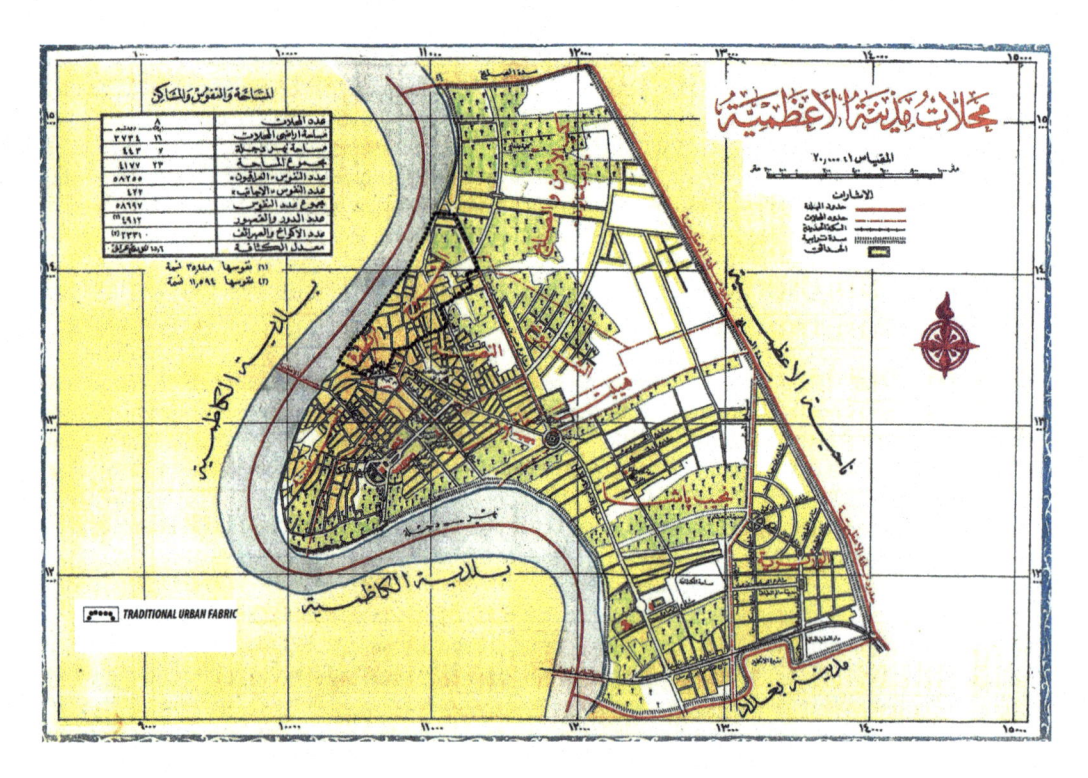

Figure 14.4 Map of Adhamiyah and Waziriya neighborhoods in the 1930s showing the juxtaposition of the traditional fabric sector (next to the river) and the new quarters with orthogonal grids and detached and semi-detached housing

Source: After Susa 1957 (infographics by Yaseen Raad).

1930s–1950s: "Regulation Urbanism" in an Independent Iraq

Following independence in 1932, Baghdad was faced with rapid urban growth due to rural-urban migration and the increase in work opportunities generated by oil revenues.[3] Although the first urban legislation[4] is sometimes associated with colonial Anglo-Indian urban schemes (Raouf 1985), it was more a recycled version of late Ottoman regulations[5] first implemented in other provinces such as Beirut as early as the 1890s (Ghorayeb 2000). As a consequence of these regulations, the traditional fabric of the old city was altered by the imposition of new street widths and alignments that led to the disappearance of the *zuqaq* [narrow passage]. In the new neighborhoods of Karrada, Saadoun, Adhamiyah and Waziriya,[6] six different types of plots were planned to accommodate detached and semi-detached residential structures resembling the garden city model (Figure 14.4). However such schemes were simply formal impositions not underlined by a social reform agenda.[7]

---

3 The first oil well was sunk in 1927 at Baba-Ghurghur, near Kirkuk.

4 The first set of urban regulations was decreed in Law #44 was first published in the *Iraqi Gazette* in October 1935.

5 The author provides a detailed comparison between the two texts in her thesis, chapter 3.2.1 and 3.2.2: 182–90 (forthcoming as a book, see bibliography at Pieri 2015).

6 Contrary to Gulick's statement (1976), Waziriya had not yet been built in the 1920s; archival research by the author revealed no evidence of it on a single map before 1936.

7 This is in contrast to earlier proposals for garden cities in the work of Ebenezer Howard, first defined in his 1902 book, *Garden Cities of To-Morrow* (1946).

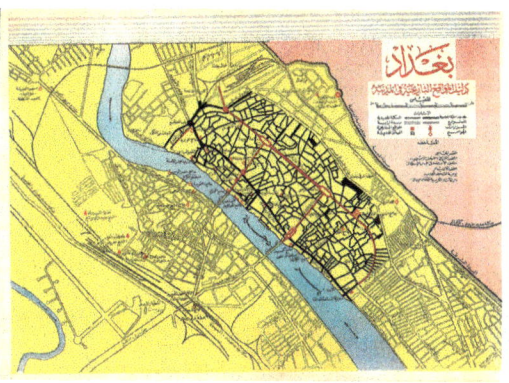

Figure 14.5 King Ghazi Street (today Kifah Street)
Note: In red, new urban cuts dating to 1938–40 (left); two-story mixed-use buildings on Wathba Street, January 2005 (right).
Source: After Susa 1957 (infographics by Yaseen Raad).(left); author (right).

Still in effect until the 1980s, these regulations marked a turning point in the history of the modern Iraqi city. They explicitly referred to the concept of *tanasuq* [harmony], possibly an Arabic adaptation of the notion of *embellissement* [beautification], a distinctive feature of European modernization since the eighteenth century in France (Harouel 1993). This may also be interpreted as a regional reiteration of the work of the Danger Frères, the French urbanists active in Algiers and Beirut as of 1931–2 (Ghorayeb 2000; Verdeil 2011). Urban extensions were planned to address the middle classes who migrated from their traditional houses in the old center towards the suburban villas of the periphery. Another major impact of modernization was the introduction of the notion of *public space*. Traditionally streets and open spaces had been controlled by the community and the residents themselves. Under the new legislation they fell under a centralized administration and were normalized by formal laws and regulations, marking a shift from *community* space to urban *public* space.

During this period, Ahmad Mukhtar Ibrahim was the first Iraqi to be appointed as government architect, having graduated from a foreign university, Liverpool University, in 1936. He planned and implemented King Ghazi Street with two major perpendiculars, cutting across the historic urban fabric and introducing a new urban typology of two-story, mixed-use buildings that is still visible today (Figure 14.5). Mukhtar was an architect, not an urbanist, but a similar phenomenon reportedly occurred in Iran and Egypt (Marefat 1988; Volait 2005) where local architects returning from Western universities were allocated high government positions not commensurate with their experience.

1950s: The Beginning of the World Bank's Influence

The 1950s marked a decisive step for Iraq, which witnessed the establishment of the Iraqi Development Board (IDB), a powerful government body in charge of an accelerated program of investment and modernization of infrastructure supported by the American-led International Bank for Reconstruction and Development (IBRD). This was marked by the report entitled *The Economic Development of Iraq*, published in 1952. Like the Marshall Plan for Europe, the IBRD report suggested the "*reconstruction*" of Iraq; but unlike post-war Europe, Iraq had not been destroyed through warfare.

The direction suggested by this report corresponded with the IDB's agenda and numerous promotional publications, official leaflets and brochures, declaring the country's enormous potential (Marefat 2007). The boom of oil revenues allowed for social reform, modernization and educational development, key conditions for the UK–US support in their effort to ensure Iraq's political allegiance (Baghdad Pact, 1955) against the

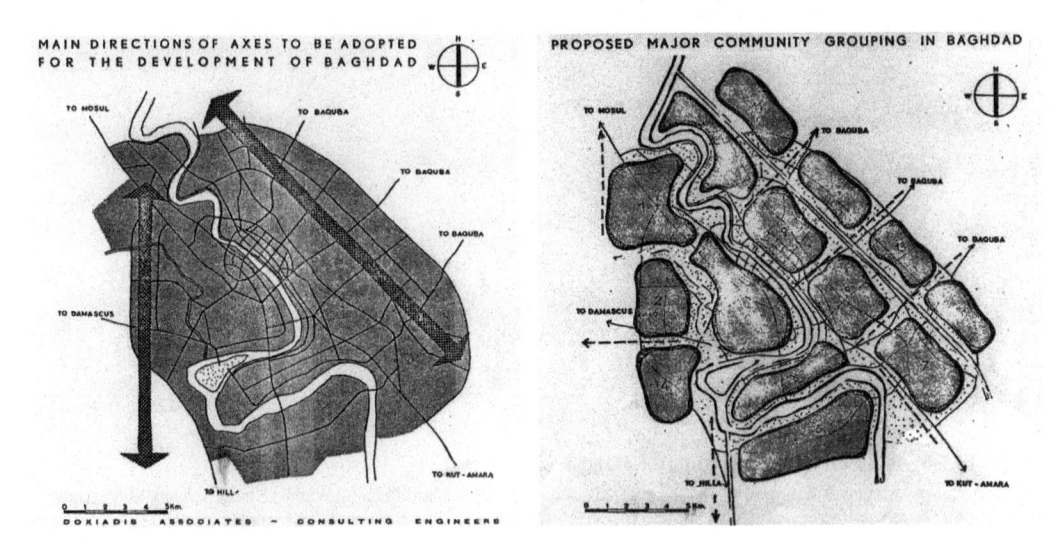

Figure 14.6 Doxiadis's master plan of 1958
Note: Showing proposed axes of development (left), and community grouping (right).
Source: Doxiadis original report; author's collection.

Cairo–Moscow axis. At the same time the national development agenda provided the impetus to call for international consultancy, again bringing Modernist ideologies in architecture and urbanism into Iraq. As such, International Modernism became a window of opportunity for Baghdad to secure international visibility as a model capital of a modern nation.

The influence of the World Bank triggered the process of Baghdad's metropolization, manifested both in long-term planning and the creation of schemes for peripheral extensions by foreign consultants such as Minoprio, Spencely and MacFarlane. This growth was also encouraged by the introduction of cooperative housing, which would eventually lead to localized homogenization based on occupation and income. The Greek urbanist Doxiadis, the acting representative of the World Bank in the Middle East, planned several *satellite cities* (Figure 14.6) that would put into practice his vision of the Dynapolis—what later became his theory of "Ekistics" (Doxiadis 1970). These were envisioned as rationalized extensions of community centers made up of low/middle income housing, organized according to the principles of the Athens Charter. As a solution for internal migration, Doxiadis also planned the first *resettlements* in Iraq, which were located into informal settlements known locally as the *sarifa* [built with corrugated tin] and the *kukh* [built with mud construction].

Since Modernist planning was easier to implement in non-developed areas, there was a noticeable disparity between the treatment of the urban periphery and the center of Baghdad. In 1957 the latter was to witness another gesture that would obliterate the existing urban fabric; Khulafa Street was superimposed on the existing street pattern to accommodate vehicular traffic. Concurrently the city suffered from an overall *laissez-faire* approach to planning with no attempts to promote the regeneration of the old core. Residential bourgeois neighborhoods grew under the continuation of the 1935 regulation and new suburban quarters sprung up among outlying palm groves, leading to the modernization of the empty outskirts. The spatial implementation of this global model reflected the lack of balance in the government's choices of urban policies, focusing on undeveloped areas where modernity could easily be implemented and publicized.

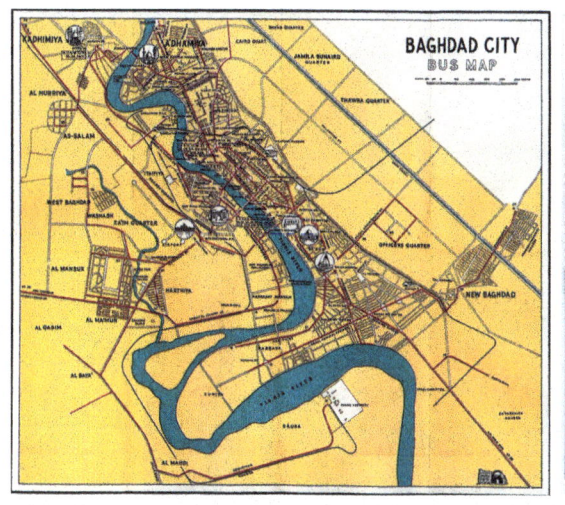

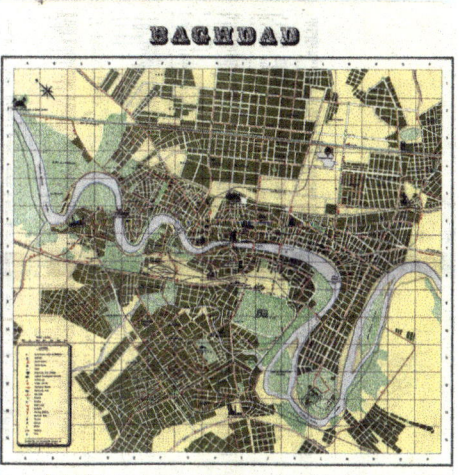

Figure 14.7 Peripheral growth during this period can be noted by comparing a bus route map from 1961 and a tourism map from 1971

Note: Left and right respectively.
Source: Author's collection.

After 1965: A Territory for Cold War Socialist Expansion

The 1958 national revolution marked the end of 30 years of British dominance backed by American support. The new rulers were anxious to break with the symbols of the former Western-oriented regime. Although Doxiadis was dismissed in 1959, Abdulkarim Qassem was pragmatic enough to implement several of his projects, including a new city, which was designed to house thousands of migrants relocated from the unhealthy living conditions of the *sara'if*. It was conceived as a local adaptation of the Dynapolis, with public amenities including hammams, mosques and communal squares. This is an exceptional case of a political leader taking concrete social needs into consideration; still Qassem is credited as having conceived himself of this city, which was called Madinat Al-Thawra.[8] Again during this time, the majority of public policies endeavored to find solutions for the peripheral extensions of the city while continuing to ignore the city center (Figure 14.7). However Qahtan Madfai, an Iraqi architect/urbanist trained in Cardiff, the UK and appointed to the PWD, focused on the problem of integrating the old with the new through a modern reinterpretation of the traditional urban morphology, an example of which can be seen in Bab-Sharqi (Figure 14.8).

Furthermore, the Iraqi National Revolution paved the way for new political alliances; starting in 1967, Eastern European experts were called in from Poland to launch an ambitious national master plan. The newly empowered Baath Party, which came to power in 1968, asked the PolService Company to come up with a comprehensive national plan. This gesture may have a dual interpretation concerning the import/export of urban models (Figure 14.9); on one hand Iraqi rulers were able for the first time to choose their own partners and consultants without foreign intervention; on the other, this cooperation may have been seen by Eastern Europeans as an opportunity to expand their own political ideologies by exporting their socialist urbanism model (Stanek 2012).

---

8   Madinat Al-Thawra was later renamed Saddam City, and is known today as Madinat Al Sadr.

206   *Urban Design in the Arab World*

Figure 14.8 Postcard of Bab-Sharqi showing typical buildings of the late 1950s as articulation between the old and the new city
Source: Author's collection; anonymous photographer.

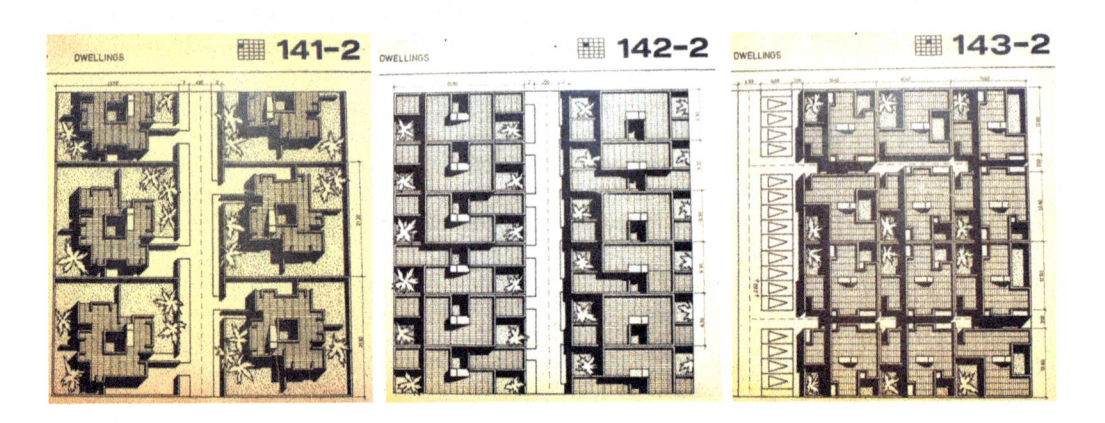

Figure 14.9 Schematics of dwelling types from the PolService of 1979
Note: Detached type (left); row type (middle); atrium type (right).
Source: PolService original report; author's collection.

1980s: Rewriting the National Identity Discourse in the Context of Iraqi Arab Leadership

Long-term plans for development were suspended by the rise to power of Saddam Hussein in 1979, leading to what is referred to as the Haussmannization of Baghdad (*Process* 1985) with the launch of major public works that transformed the capital into a construction site. Instead of the large-scale master plans of the previous decades, which aimed at responding to population growth, political will emphasized the reshaping of Baghdad's urban form to create the image of a grand capital matching Hussein's vision of Iraq as a major power. Foreign and Iraqi architects were given the mission of transforming this political agenda into a monumentalized Baghdad, emphasizing the direct relationship between politics and built form (Pieri 2008).

Saddam Hussein aimed at reviving the past grandeur of Iraq by projecting the glorious pasts of the Abbasids and Mesopotamians (Méténier 2006; Luizard 1994). The manipulation of historical Iraqi references became a key agenda of urban design, echoing the statement of Sethom:

> Many architects abuse heritage to justify the use of modern techniques in design, materials and construction within the framework of traditional Arab architecture ... Even when there is no clear basis for exploiting this heritage, this concept has been used many times by architects trying to gain acceptance of their designs. (Sethom 1985)

Accordingly, the Iraqi capital was divided into 14 sectors that were to be entirely reshaped and upgraded with new housing districts, public amenities and open spaces (*Process* 1985). Several neighborhoods were significantly transformed, either through the erasure of existing fabric or the privatization of public space. The enlarged Haifa Street was emulating a "*via triomphalis*" leading from the north to Karadat Maryam, the presidential and administrative neighborhood. The widening of the street erased part of the upper-class area adjacent to the former British Embassy as well as ancient neighborhoods inhabited by Hussein's political opponents; only some isolated elements remained in the middle of a totally reshaped area (Figure 14.10). New housing districts were built for public servants, punctuated with several key public buildings including the Rashid Theatre, the Saddam Art Center, the Ministry of Justice and the Baghdad Governorate. In Rusafa, the new Municipality was built by destroying the traditional fabric of the district. Facing the Presidential Palace, on the other bank of the river, the destruction of mansions dating back to the 1930s and 1940s allowed for the construction of the Abu Nuwas housing sectors, built for the presidential guard (Planar and Skarup & Jesperssen/ Abbad al-Radi, see Sultani and Pieri 2014). Lastly, the presidential neighborhood of Karadat Maryam itself was punctuated by new icons of military power; these included a new Monument to the Unknown Soldier in 1983 to replace the 1959 structure by Rifat Chadirji which was forcibly destroyed by the architect himself under presidential order, and the famed Arch of Victory, inaugurated in August 1989, whose style has been described as a hybrid "between Nuremberg and Las Vegas" (Makiya 2004).

In order for Baghdad to fully embody the new Arab leadership, Saddam Hussein needed a tool that would suit his nationalist agenda; the reshaped Iraqi capital had to become the monumental harbinger of this renewed collective identity. However, these changes responded more to symbolism, ideology and politics rather than to real urban needs. In parallel, the claim of an Iraqi identity also entailed the overall preliminary survey of urban heritage (Ottoman and twentieth-century housing), which was carried out under the aegis of a joint Western/local team (Bianca et al. 1983). The survey was limited to old Baghdad and the major part of the conservation plan was never implemented, partly because the war with Iran was soon to become the predominant presidential agenda.

Baghdad Today: Urbanism in a Post-War Context

Following the 14 years between the first Gulf War and the 2003 US-led invasion, the challenges facing the country today are immense. As was the case during the pre-Revolution decades, the current tools for urban management are again the product of foreign intervention—in this case the United Nations—as witnessed in two recent reports.

Figure 14.10 The enlarged Haifa Street
Note: Sketch map 1984 showing Haifa Street leading to the presidential quarter with some isolated buildings preserved in the middle of a totally reshaped area (left); Al-Dhahir houses preserved in Haifa Street (right).
Source: Baghdad Municipality 1984; author's collection.

The first, published through the Word Bank IBRD (2006), estimates Baghdad's housing deficit at 1.0–1.5 million units and identifies key constraints to the development of the housing construction industry. A rapid background study outlines clear recommendations promoting a shift from central-state governance to privatization, sector by sector, following a global neo-liberal agenda. They enable private foreign investment in housing and real estate and favor private sector access to financing at the expense of public contractor access to government subsidies (including equipment, materials and security services). The report also recommends a national investment law that would facilitate licensing, project development and sale, and the repatriation of profits.

The second report was published under the umbrella of the United Nations Human Settlements Program (UNHSP) and underlines principles of a good urban governance under four headings: the Well-Governed Iraqi City, the socially inclusive Iraqi City, the Productive Iraqi City and the economically sustainable Iraqi City (UN-Habitat 2007). These themes reflect current attempts at post-war reconstruction and are exemplified by recent urban competitions launched by the Baghdad Municipality. The competitions address short and mid-term operations in pericentral areas and follow a mainly market-based approach. The re-development of Kadhimiya, for instance, was awarded to an Emirati-Iraqi firm.[9] This project proposes to erase the dilapidated Ottoman structures surrounding the old core and to replace them with a new urban grid reminiscent of Haussmannian Paris. Yet, Kadhimiya could have offered a unique opportunity to foster a World Heritage project, comparable to the old city of Fez in Morocco. However the implementation of such a project could have been difficult given the time and financial limitations of the municipality and the growing logistical pressures of increasing pilgrimage to the area. In parallel, the Madinat Al Sadr project (on the former site of the Madinat Al-Thawra) was awarded to a British firm whose slogan is to promote "a global architecture, urbanism and design practice" (*Iraq-Business News* 2011). Al-Rashid Camp, another important project situated in the outskirts of southeastern Baghdad, foresees a mixture of Dubai-like towers and a green city with golf courses and lakes, raising questions of environmental sustainability.[10]

---

9 Images available at: http://www.dewan-architects.com/work_urban_planning_khadamiya.html [accessed: October 30, 2013].
10 Images available at: http://nplusn.pl/al-rashid-masterplan.html [accessed: October 30, 2013].

As for central Baghdad, the only current short-term project is the Al Rasheed Street Center, a Beirut-Solidere inspired scheme awarded to a Canadian-Iraqi firm that will be limited only to the left side of Al Rasheed Street leading up to the river Tigris.[11] On the other hand, the 2030 Baghdad master plan, a long-term development project, has been entrusted to a Lebanese firm which limited its heritage surveys to data gleaned from the PolService report of 1979 and the work of the Bianca-Fethi team (1983).[12]

Beyond Fragmentation: Functional and Sectarian Mixity as a Key to Social Peace

The current state of central Baghdad marks a stark contrast to the idealism of the above projects; the city center is characterized by physical degradation and functional slumification. Some of its inner sectors have been designated as slum areas by the UN report quoted above. Many living units are abandoned due to the successive waves of war-generated displacement between 2003 and 2008. Those still occupied are often inhabited by poor migrant families and temporary makeshift shops. The resulting social ruralization of the city center is manifested in residents congregating into small self-sustained networks replicating village community patterns, as discussed by Maath Alusi: "The city has been ruralized and the level of preparation for the new migrants has declined ... In Baghdad there is another reason: the lack of provision of urban-type services anywhere, and the ruralization of Iraq's centers of urbanization" (Alusi 2011).

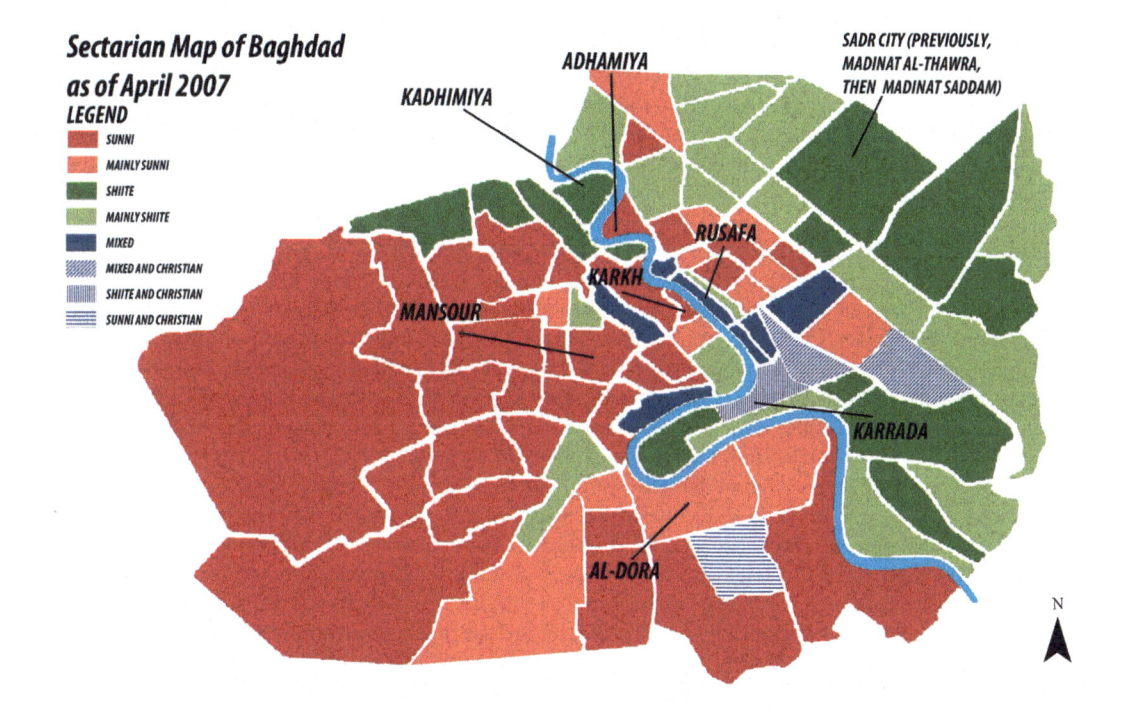

Figure 14.11   Sectarian map of Baghdad in April 2007
Source: Author, after AFP (infographics by Yaseen Raad).

---

11   G-Mimari Architectural. Information gathered by the author at Baghdad Municipality; data is not available to the public for the time being, especially considering that the ongoing project is currently on stand-by for legal problems.
12   Information gathered by the author from the offices of Khatib and Alami, Beirut, June 2012. The Baghdad Municipality also provided a PowerPoint presentation given by the author during a conference organized in Baghdad, March 2010.

Figure 14.12 Several levels of walling have become distinctive markers of Baghdad today, transforming neighborhoods into privatized areas as seen in Abu Nuwas, April 2013 and Jadriya, February 2011

Note: Left and right respectively.
Source: Author.

The situation is further complicated by a process of fragmentation, the first example of which was the creation of the Green (now International) Zone, with borders and sophisticated security devices that evoke the Iron Curtain in Eastern Europe or the militarized border between Southern and Northern Cyprus.[13] The sectarian reorganization of the state by the Coalition Provisional Authority (CPA) in 2003 has resulted in the spatial reproduction and codification of pre-existing sectarian differences (Figure 14.11), manifested and reinforced since 2007 by the implementation of a "walling strategy" (Damluji 2010). Concrete T-walls were used to isolate entire neighborhoods in order to protect them from increasing levels of insecurity as antagonistic Sunni insurgents and Shia militias fight for control throughout the city, which was described in the media as a "cropping up of mini-green zones" (Dagher 2007).

Beyond the need for security, the walls—still in place throughout the city today—have added to the overall phenomenon of segmentation and altered the perception and practice of public space. Besides the protection of institutions such as banks, museums, universities and schools, four distinct levels of walling can be seen throughout Baghdad (Figure 14.12). At the largest scale, walls encircle homogeneous neighborhoods—Sunni Adhamiyah or Shia Madinat Al Sadr—resulting in the clear segregation of communities and the reduction of shared public space. The second level is in the form of numerous checkpoints along main circulation axes; some of these have been reduced since the departure of the American troops in 2011, but they still exemplify the appropriation of public space for militaristic control. The third form is in blocking secondary axes—either by walls or by guards, or often both—effectively redefining the city's circulation patterns and access to living spaces. A final and more informal method is the privatization of public space created by the overlapping of private security apparatuses; this reinforces territorialized identities and forces a shift from collective spaces to communitarian spaces in a return to pre-modern urban practices. Neighborhoods are guarded by private militias, evidence that Baghdad is evolving according to the worst-case scenario of "self-enclosure," best illustrated in a recent article discussing young people that have reclaimed the creation of a gated city made especially for them.[14] This segmentation of the capital seems to have led to individual disinvestment in the public realm (Damluji 2010) and brings into question the possibility of any reconciliation, especially as long as governance and civil society lie in a suspended balance between recurrent reflexes of sectarian revenge and unsolved efforts to overcome them.

In spite of this fragmentation, examples of coexistence between various sects and social strata can still be found in the heart of Baghdad. Since 2011 the author has personally witnessed the return of affluent families from peripheral areas to poorer, centralized neighborhoods of a different confession, where they felt less

---

13   Personally witnessed by the author in July 1989 and January 2001 respectively.
14   http://www.niqash.org/articles/?id=3283 [accessed: May 5, 2014].

at risk from kidnapping. Is it possible to envision that the social, functional and sectarian mixity such as it existed in the twentieth-century city could once more turn out to be the key to modern social peace for the future of Baghdad?

References

Alusi, M. 2011. The Slums of al-Thawra Town, Saddam City, Sadr City. *Energy and Geopolitical Risk*, 2 (7 8), 27–35. Available at: http://www.mees.com/system/assets/000/001/201/original_Geopolitical_Risk_JULY-AUGUST_2011-3.pdf [accessed: March 4, 2014].
Bianca, S., Fethi, I., Lombardi, G. and Yamada, S. 1983. *Baghdad Historical Center Rehabilitation Project, vol. 1 Inventory of Monuments of Cultural Interest, vol. 2 Social Conditions, vol. 3 Macroframe Study*. Municipality of Baghdad. Unpublished.
Coke, R. 1927. *Baghdad, The City of Peace*. London: Butterworth.
Cooperson, M. 1996. Baghdad in Rhetoric and Narrative, in *An Annual on the Visual Culture of Islam*, vol. XIII, edited by G. Necipoglu. Leyden: E.J. Brill, 99–113.
Dagher, S. 2007. Baghdad Safer, but it's a Life behind the Walls. *The Christian Science Monitor* [online]. Available at: www.csmonitor.com/2007/1210/p01s-wome.html [accessed: December 10, 2007].
Damluji, M. 2010. Securing Democracy in Iraq: Sectarian Politics and Urban Segregation in Baghdad, 2003–2007. *TDSR*, 21(2), 71–87. Available at: http://iaste.berkeley.edu/pdfs/21.2g-Spr10Damluji.pdf [accessed: January 21, 2014].
Doxiadis, K. 1970. Ekistics, the Science of Human Settlements. *Science* [online], 170(3956), 393–404. Available at: http://www.ekistics.org/ekistic%20education%20modules/module%20c_ekistic%20frameworks/b.%20ekistic%20elements/ekistic%20elements_word.pdf [accessed: March 4, 2014].
Doxiadis & Associates. 1958. *Report of the Development of Baghdad: A Contribution to the Ideas for the Development of the Capital of Iraq*. Unpublished.
Economic Development of Iraq, The. 1952. Report of the Mission Organized by the International Bank for Reconstruction and Development (IBRD) at the request of the Government of Iraq. Baltimore: Johns Hopkins Press.
Ghorayeb, M. 2000. La transformation des structures urbaines de Beyrouth pendant le mandat français. Doctoral Thesis, Paris VIII—Institut Français d'Urbanisme, Paris.
Gulick, J. 1976. Baghdad: Portrait of a City in Physical and Cultural Change. *Journal of the American Institute of Planners*, 33(4), 246–255. Available at: http://www.tandfonline.com/doi/abs/10.1080/01944366708977925#.UxWwKKv8LIU [accessed: March 4, 2014].
Harouel, J.L. 1993. *L'embellissement des villes: l'urbanisme français au XVIIIe siècle*. Paris: Éditions Picard.
Home, R. 1997. *Of Planting and Planning: The Making of British Colonies*. London: Spon.
Howard, E. 1946 [1902]. *Garden Cities of To-Morrow*. 2nd Edition. London: Faber & Faber.
Iraq-Business News. 2011. Broadway Malyan Completes Masterplan for $10 Billion Sadr City [online]. Available at: http://www.iraq-businessnews.com/2011/08/03/broadway-malyan-completes-masterplan-for-10bn-sadr-city [accessed: October 30, 2013].
Luizard, P.J. 1994. Bagdad: une métropole moderne et tribale, siège de gouvernements assiégés. *Monde Arabe Maghreb-Machrek*, 143, 225–42.
Makiya, K. 2004. *The Monument, Art and Vulgarity in Saddam Hussein's Iraq*. 2nd Edition. London: Tauris.
Marefat, M. 1988. *Building to Power: Architecture of Tehran*. Doctoral Thesis, Harvard University, Cambridge, MA. Available at: http://18.7.29.232/handle/1721.1/14535 [accessed: March 4, 2014].
Marefat, M. 2007. 1950s Baghdad—Modern and International. *The American Academic Research Institute [TAARI] in Iraq Newsletter*, 2(2), 1–7.
Méténier, É. 2006. L'historiographie irakienne est-elle réductible à un simple discours idéologique? in *États et sociétés de l'Orient arabe en quête d'avenir 1945–2005, vol. 1: Fondements et sources*, edited by G. Khoury and N. Méouchy. Paris: Geuthner, 261–84.
Nolde, É. 1934. *L'Irak: origines historiques et situation internationale*. Paris: Librairie générale de droit et de jurisprudence.

Phillips, P. 1923. *Mesopotamia: The Inquiry of the London Daily Mail.* London: Associated Newspapers.
Pieri, C. 2008. Modernity and its Posts in Constructing an Arab Capital: Baghdad's Urban Space and Architecture. *Middle East Studies Association Bulletin* [online], 42(1/2), 32–9. Available at: http://www.jstor.org/stable/23063540 [accessed: March 4, 2014].
Pieri, C. 2015. *Bagdad. La Construction d'une Capitale Moderne, 1914–1960.* Beirut: Presses de l'Ifpo (forthcoming).
Pol-Service. 1979. *General Housing Program for Iraq*, 3. Pol-Service, Krakow/Baghdad: Dar al-'Imara.
Process. 1985. Special issue, *Medinat as-Salam: Baghdad 1979–1983*, 58.
Raouf, L. 1985. Tradition and Continuity in the Modern Iraqi House. *Ur, International Magazine of Arab Culture.* London: Iraqi Cultural Centre, 15–24.
Report on Iraq Housing Construction Sector Study—International Finance Corporation. 2006. World Bank International Bank for Reconstruction and Development, Planning and Development Collaborative International [PADCO].
Sethom, H. 1985. Urban Renaissance in Baghdad. *Albenna*, 4(21–22), Dar al Funun al Saudiyya, 76–9.
Stanek, L. 2012. Miastoprojekt Goes Abroad: The Transfer of Architectural Labour from Socialist Poland to Iraq (1958–1989). *The Journal of Architecture* [online], 17(3), 361–86. Available at: http://dx.doi.org/10.1080/13602365.2012.692603 [accessed: March 4, 2014].
Sultani, K. 1982. Architecture in Iraq between the Two World Wars, 1920–1940. *Ur, International Magazine of Arab Culture.* London: Iraqi Cultural Center, 93–105.
Sultani, K. and Pieri, C. Architecture in Iraq from 1914 to 2014: From pre-modernity to uncertain challenges. *Architecture from the Arab World 1914–2014*, George Arbid ed., exhibition catalogue, Pavilion of the Kingdom of Bahrain, 14th International Architecture Exhibition, Venice: Musumeci, 133–4.
Susa, A. 1957. *Atlas Baghdad.* Baghdad: Taba'a al-wataniya al-'iraqiya; in Arabic.
UN-Habitat—Global Urban Research Unit. 2007. *The State of Iraq Cities Report 2006/2007.* Newcastle: Newcastle University.
Verdeil, E. 2011. *Beyrouth et ses urbanistes: une ville en plans (1946–1975).* Beirut: Presses de l'IFPO.
Volait, M. 200. *Architectes et architectures dans l'Égypte moderne, 1830–1950. Genèse et essor d'une expertise locale.* Paris: Maisonneuve et Larose.
Wirth, E. 2000. *Die Orientalische Stadt im Islamischen Vorderasien und Nordafrika.* Mainz: Philip von Zabern Verlag.

Chapter 15
Sites of Contestation:
Tahrir Square; From Appropriation to Design

Robert Saliba, Hussam Hussein Salama and Nathan Cherry

Editorial: Robert Saliba

As mentioned in the introductory chapter on "crossing the boundaries between the utopian and the real," urban design has often played the role of a mediator between *idealized pasts* and *idealizing futures*, and a channel for importing and domesticating modernity. The making of boulevards and squares in the eighteenth- and nineteenth-century European context was a celebration of the strongly emerging bourgeois city in its entrepreneurial spirit, its belief in modern transport technology, and the creation of a stage set for the display of bourgeois status and wealth. Underlying this society of spectacle was the military agenda of controlling public space as a potential setting for demonstrations and political contestations. Transferred to the colonial context, either through the superimposition by mandatory powers or self-imposed modernization by local rulers, formal squares retained their agenda of military control (mainly of the indigenous population), however they redefined the conventional understanding and practice of open space in the European provincial territories extending from North Africa to the Levant. The notion of *public space* in the traditional Arab-Islamic cities existed only as *institutional space*. The political and the religious were integrated, and the mosque was the setting within which the social and political discourse took place. With the mounting dialectical interface between the religious and the secular, and the authoritarian and the democratic, public space in the region has evolved from an aesthetic and functional infrastructural entity toward fulfilling its vital potential as a center for democratic exchange, political contestation and military confrontation. This transformation occurred in stages for the past 100 years as a reflection of the changing political regimes and the maturation of people's radical consciousness. Tahrir Square, as the embodiment of the Arab Spring in the collective imagery, is the archetype of public space that illustrates the formation and dynamic transformation of political and civic spatial practices in the region. Tahrir Square has already been imprinted/designed through people's own appropriations, heroic actions and dreams. Shall urban designers be entrusted with the *shaping of a strategic node* that in turn, is shaping a nation's future? Do designers have the political and professional legitimacy to propose/impose their own interpretations and visions on such an iconic public space? Do they have the professional and disciplinary tools to regulate and constrain its occupation by contesters and demonstrators?

Two professionals/scholars each contribute their own views toward answering these questions, that is: the *historical*, the *pragmatic* and the *conceptual* in an attempt to bridge the gap between the visionary and the real, and between the perceived, the conceived and the lived.

Hussam Hussein Salama in his "Formation and Transformation of Tahrir Square" provides a sweeping historical overview of how Tahrir Square shaped and has been shaped by the political life of Egypt on the backdrop of government secularization and Cairo's evolving modernization. Nathan Cherry in his "Design for Revolution: Accommodating the Multiple Vocations of Tahrir Square," sheds a designer's professional view on a square that will become in the future "the vessel of everyday life of a working Democracy"; the backdrop is Times Square, Trafalgar Square and the National Mall in Washington, DC.

Formation and Transformation of Tahrir Square:[1] Hussam Hussein Salama

The modernization of Cairo featured the emergence of the square as a new typology of public spaces. Several *Sahas* (public plazas) were transformed into squares during the late nineteenth century. Many of these squares were converted later to roundabouts to accommodate motorized vehicles (Figure 15.1). The role of new public spaces and more specifically public squares in shaping political life in Egypt began to flourish by the beginning of the twentieth century. In 1919, the place that is known today as Tahrir Square [*Midan Al Tahrir*] hosted one of the most important revolutions in Egyptian history, led by Saad Zaghlul against the British Occupation. Since then, the square, called Ismailiya Square at the time (referencing Khedive Ismail), unofficially earned the name *Tahrir* [*liberation*]. This *Midan* [square] was originally a greenfield that was supposed to be designed to emulate the Charles de Gaulle Square in Paris. This vision was never implemented and the square was gradually shaped over time, especially after the construction of the Egyptian Museum in 1902 (see AlSayyad 2011), and the surrounding series of palaces as part of the new Al Ismailiya district. Since the 1919 revolution, Tahrir Square became the main arena of public protest in Egypt; however, it could be argued that this place did not host significant forms of social discourse compared to other public spaces in the city such as Al Azbakiya and Al Orman Gardens.

The modernization of Cairo, a movement by the elite who benefited economically and politically, featured a gradual process of secularization of government—the state contribution to urban development gradually diminished in favor of both local and foreign enterprises. Western influences were obvious in Cairenes' way of life at the time, and more than ever, the city became open to the Western culture. As noted by Tignor (1984), during the periods before World War I, and between World War I and World War II, local industrial and commercial bourgeoisie, composed of both foreigners and Egyptian business elites, played an important role in the Egyptian economy. Three groups dominated development in Egypt: the British political and military establishment; the European individuals and enterprises through metropolitan capital; and landed oligarchy (Tignor 1984: 8). New residential projects such as Al-Maadi, Garden City and Heliopolis began to emerge by the beginning of the twentieth century. The Garden City district was developed by Frantz Sofio, Charles Bacos and George Maksud, the owners of the Nile Land & Agricultural Company. The development of the Heliopolis district, by the Belgian industrialist Baron Empain, began in 1905. These projects created new forms of class spatial segregation that did not exist in Old Cairo (Tignor 1984: 5).

After the 1952 revolution against King Farouk, Egypt experienced a dramatic shift toward socialism, redefining the meaning of public space and its boundaries with the private realm. This introduced the concept of *melk el hokoma* [property of the government] that occupied Egyptians' conception of public space for the following six decades, a victory against the Feudal System that controlled the country for decades. After being developed and operated by local and foreign enterprises for decades during the early twentieth century, lands, real estate projects, major retail chains, theaters, gardens and most public parks were fully or partially acquired by the Egyptian government under the Nationalization Program, a process that portrayed a reversal of the widely discussed concept of *privatizing public space* (see Sennett 1977; Banerjee 2001). In order to gain people's support, the government made many of these properties and public spaces, previously limited to social elites, accessible to the public regardless of their social or economic class.

In 1960, Tahrir Square earned its name officially and became the icon of freedom and liberation in Egypt. However, at that time, the tendency of the ruling regime to hinder all forms of opposition has limited the role of public space in political life/discourse; although these places were made accessible to all Egyptians, they were continuously monitored by the secret police. It was not until President Nasser announced his resignation after the defeat in the 1967 war that people returned back to public space, protesting his decision. For the first time since the 1952 revolution, massive crowds spent the night in the streets and squares of Egypt demanding Nasser to stay in office.

---

1   An extended version of this section of the chapter was published in 2013 by Archnet-IJAR: *International Journal of Architectural Research* [online], 7(1), 128–38. Available at: http://archnet.org/gws/IJAR/11042/files_10681/7.1.10-hussam%20h.%20salama-pp128-138.pdf [accessed: March 20, 2014].

Figure 15.1 The transformation of the *Saha* of Sultan Hassan Mosque to a modern square during the late nineteenth-century modernization project

Note: Many of the public open spaces in Cairo were landscaped in order to inject the European round-shaped public squares into the indigenous urban fabric of the city. These new landscapes were later transformed into roundabouts to allow vehicular access.

Source: Author on archival photos.

When President Sadat came to power in 1970, he began to gradually abort the rigid socialist ideals that ruled the country for nearly two decades. He embraced the open door policy [*infitah*] and shifted the economy toward capitalism. These economic changes in the market dynamics benefited many local small investors and entrepreneurs who took advantage of the new business opportunities, in general, and the demand for imported goods, in particular. A new class of nouveau riche began to emerge mainly in Cairo, reshaping the urban development trends in the city—social segregation and inequality started to emerge, triggering societal conflicts and tensions. This was translated into two forms of public resistance to many social and economic policies: one by socialists; and the other by Islamists. For socialists, public space provided a place to protest against capitalism—in 1977, they led a massive riot that is referred to as the *Bread Riots* against subsidization cuts. Protests began in Tahrir Square and then moved to many other parts of the city. This reintroduced the role of the square in shaping political life in Egypt. For Islamists, it was the mosque that hosted their secret meetings and political discourses. By the end of the 1970s and after Sadat signed the peace treaty with Israel, Islamists intensified their opposition to the regime. Mosques, and more specifically those in poor neighborhoods and squatter settlements, became the hubs of political Islamic discourse. These were the places where the Muslim Brotherhood and other Islamic movements recruited their members. These forms of resistance to secular government reached their peak during the early 1990s when some areas in Cairo such as Imbaba were nearly governed by Sheikhs and were labeled: "The Islamic Republic of Imbaba."

When Mubarak came to power in 1981 after the assassination of Sadat, his regime activated the emergency laws, hindering most of the political opposition activities, and prohibiting any form of public gatherings in mosques except during the times of prayer. The Mubarak administration followed the same economic policies of Sadat and started the Privatization Program through which many of the public enterprises were sold to local and foreign investors. This has triggered a new wave of anger and opposition that never materialized into a public discourse until the late 1990s. At the time, the introduction of the Internet, cell phones and satellite television opened venues for Egyptians to start constructing a new form of public sphere that had the capacity to host political discourse away from the police's watch. The digital world became the main public sphere for Egyptians—the percentage of people using the Internet escalated from 0.7 percent in 2000 to 32.6 percent in 2011. These new technologies contributed to the emergence of what Howard Rheingold (2002) calls *the smart mobs* or groups of people who manage to use communications technology to activate and organize social actions and events in the real world (Rheingold 2002). These groups tend to initiate events, call for protests and political activities in the cyber world and then take it to the physical public space. In that sense, public places become hubs for flows of information and ideas generated locally and globally. Political blogs, tweets, emails and Facebook posts created linkages between digital and physical realms, gradually pushing political discourse back to public spaces. These communication tools facilitated the formation of several movements that played a significant role in reshaping the socio-political environment in Egypt, as noted by Herrera (2011):

> Social movements belong to people and not to communication tools and technologies. Facebook, like cell phones, the Internet, and twitter, do not have agency, a moral universe, and are not predisposed to any particular ideological or political orientation. They are what people make of them.

Many opposition movements in Egypt—conservatives such as the Muslim Brotherhood, or liberals such as Kefaya—managed to make use of these new technologies and cyber spaces to spread their ideals and beliefs. Bloggers and political activists focused on recruiting members online and were continuously calling for protests. Blogs, Facebook, YouTube and many other Internet forums become the new political arenas where people expressed their political opinions and criticized the performance of the government.

It took a few years for this digital public discourse to materialize into physical action. On April 6, 2008 an activist posted a call for a nationwide one-day civil disobedience. The call was widely spread via emails and SMSs. It was surprisingly successful especially in the industrial city of Mahala where thousands of workers protested against the regime and its privatization policies, tearing down a poster of Mubarak and calling for change. The historic act paved the way for more protests later on, and marked the beginning of a new era of political discourse in public space. Protests became common in major cities in Egypt—places such as the stairs in front of the Syndicate of Journalists building, the sidewalks around the Parliament and Prime

Minister Office became places of political discourse. However, participation was always limited to political activists, and in few cases, workers and governmental employees; the majority of Egyptians refrained from these activities fearing prosecution.

When the revolution in Tunisia succeeded in overthrowing President Zine El Abidine Ben Ali after 24 years in power, Egyptians realized that political change was possible. A call for a nationwide protest on January 25, 2011 was posted on Khalid Said's Facebook page. After a few days, the call was spread across the country and political activists began to campaign online. Protests were strategically planned with urban public spaces in mind. Based on previous experiences, activists were aware that security forces tend to attack demonstrations in their early stages before gaining crowds. Accordingly, the plan was to avoid formal public spaces and start marching in multiple urban squatter settlements and irregular narrow streets until a large mass of people is formed. This strategy managed to confuse secret police and security forces that were suddenly confronted with huge masses emerging from multiple zones across the city. With no plan for what to do next, protest leaders did not expect that the demonstrations would survive for long. Interestingly, after a couple of hours of marching through main streets, massive protests across Cairo were all moving toward Tahrir Square, which became the main magnet for contestation at city scale (Figure 15.2).

Figure 15.2   Freedom of expression in Tahrir Square
Note: During the 2011 Egyptian revolution, expressive banners, caricatures and wall newspapers became the only communication tools that reflected local culture and interests, replacing the digital social media that was blocked by the government (above); after the end of violent confrontations that took place in the first week of the revolution, gathering nodes of discussions and entertainment emerged as ceremonial places that were regularly visited by families who took pictures and became part of the historic event (middle); since the resignation of Mubarak, the walls of the square carry strata of visual representations that document the dynamics of political discourse in Egypt during the last two years (below)
Source: Photograph by Mohamed El Wakeel (above–middle); author (below).

The occupation of Tahrir Square and many other public spaces across the country was a statement of rejection of state domination—a reclamation of people's right to the public realm. Tahrir Square became the "discursive space," using Habermas's definition of public space, "in which individuals and groups congregate to discuss matters of mutual interest and, when possible, reach a common judgment" (Hauser 1998). The square was gradually transformed into a city-within-the-city. In three days, camping areas, media rooms, medical facilities, gateways, stages, restrooms, food and beverages carts, newspaper booths and art exhibits were established in the square—a process of space adaptation and divergence which featured astonishing forms of social organization and administration. For protestors Tahrir Square became an urban utopia—a place of community engagement, collective projects and social discourse, and most importantly, freedom of speech and expression.

Design for Revolution: Accommodating the Multiple Vocations of Tahrir Square:[2] **Nathan Cherry**

Tahrir Square, once a neglected crossroads in downtown Cairo, has now become part of the global consciousness. Egypt's recent 18-day revolt centered in the square, and it was there that citizens of all ages and classes succeeded in ousting President Mubarak in February 2011. The square erupted in a night-long celebration after his announced resignation, with shouts of "Everyone who loves Egypt, come and rebuild Egypt." This space is the vessel in which a revolution is occurring. Going forward, it is likely that the square will become even more important in the everyday life of a working democracy. What can comparable spaces contribute to that process, and what urban design tools could help to optimize the square's function as the cradle of a new democratic Egypt?

Location, Location

Tahrir Square adjoins the 6 October Bridge, which crosses the Nile River and is one of the city's most heavily trafficked east–west arterials. Cairo's street layout generally follows a radial plan, which led to its nineteenth-century reputation as the *Paris of the Nile*. The location of the square is important because it is at the first downtown traffic exit after the bridge. However, to get traffic beyond this point, the city has built an extremely disjointed network of arterial streets culminating in a clumsy traffic circle at the heart of the space. In short, Tahrir is an auto-dominated environment that pedestrians can control only with massive numbers.

The uses around the square are also somewhat disjointed. On the northeast side is a plaza with statues and the Omar Makram Mosque. The square sits on the northern terminus of the historic Qasr al-Ayn Street and the western end of Talaat Harb Street. Qasr el-Nil Street, which crosses the plaza's southern side, gives the plaza direct access to the Qasr al-Nil Bridge.

The area also includes the Egyptian Museum, the National Democratic Party (NDP) headquarters building, the Mogamma government building, the headquarters of the Arab League building, the Nile Hilton Hotel, and the original downtown campus of the American University of Cairo. Because of the isolated and institutional nature of these uses, the square tends to be more active during the day and around building entrances; it has only has limited pedestrian activity after dark on most days.

Even before this year's events, Tahrir Square was more closely associated with violent protest than as a "place to be." Unsurprisingly, the street environment includes a series of over-scaled and barren sidewalks with little street life or pedestrian amenity. Bringing in more mixed uses and choreographing the sidewalks for better day-to-day public interaction—generally creating more reasons for people to congregate there, not just for protest—will be essential. Ultimately, Tahrir Square must change into a place of day-to-day public life, celebration and self-expression, not just protest.

---

2   A previous version of this section was published in 2011 by the *American Planning Association* [online], 77(4), 22–4. Available at: https://www.planning.org/planning/2011/apr/designforrevolution.htm [accessed: March 30, 2014].

Sizing up the Space

Tahrir Square is most easily seen and understood by car, not only because of access but also because of the physical size of the space. The overall dimensions are roughly 400 by 1,200 feet, or about 11 acres, excluding some adjoining undeveloped building parcels to the west. If the undeveloped parcels are added, the entire space balloons to more than 22 acres, most of which is either open land or grassy areas between traffic rights-of-way. The result is an amorphous and unstructured public realm.

Crossing the space from end to end takes as long as five minutes on foot, which implies that it might be better organized as a series of smaller interconnected spaces of more individual character. Block size is an issue, with oversized parcels of roughly 600 by 800 feet adjoining the square, making the district somewhat difficult for pedestrians to traverse. Underground passages pull pedestrians from street level and farther isolate the space from human activity.

When comparing Tahrir Square (Figure 15.3a) to other spaces with a similar role in Western cultures, three examples immediately come to mind: Times Square in New York City (Figure 15.3b); Trafalgar Square in London (Figure 15.3c); and the National Mall in Washington, DC (Figure 15.3d). Public protest and assembly have a long history in all three places. Among them were protests against the Vietnam War in the 1960s, demonstrations supporting women's and gay rights in the 1970s and 1980s, and antiwar protests within the past decade. All of these spaces are considered the heart of their respective cities: the place to go for public speech on a grand scale, where the largest gathering space is coupled with the greatest urban activity, mix of people and cultures.

These sites are relatively small. Times Square is four acres in size (140 feet by 1,200 feet); Trafalgar Square is five acres (roughly 450 by 500 feet); and the Mall, although much larger (about 70 acres in size, roughly 4,800 by 650 feet), is broken into smaller "parterres" of roughly 650 by 600 feet.

During the recent protests in Egypt, similar demonstrations occurred in Times and Trafalgar squares. The tightness of those spaces seemed to contribute to the gravity of the moment. What is also different is that each space has a variety of buildings around the perimeter and ground-floor uses that engage the sidewalk. In short, these are spaces of assembly, but they are also essential places to be in the daily life of the city. Without a greater sense of enclosure, variety, street life and quality, Cairo residents might eventually find that Tahrir Square will become less prominent in the life of the city.

Even the National Mall, where more than a million people have congregated (most recently during President Obama's swearing-in ceremony in 2009), has the advantage of its shape: a long, thin configuration linking the Capitol to the Washington Memorial. At a width of 650 feet, the Mall can accommodate many people without obliging officials to shut down adjacent streets.

However, when an event of such scale is not occurring, the Mall retains a certain intimacy by being broken into three sub-areas: a central open green with flanking areas of dense tree canopy. Retail kiosks recently have been added within the flanks, and that promotes pedestrian activity—at least during the daytime. Integrating activities and uses within the public right-of-way might similarly be of benefit to Tahrir Square.

Moving the People

In order to appropriately demonstrate the magnitude of their dissatisfaction with the Egyptian government, the protesters needed a place that could accommodate large numbers of people in a relatively short time span. With Cairo's notorious traffic problems, many had to get there by transit or foot. Tahrir Square fit the bill because of its location adjacent to the Sadat Station, which sits at the junction of the Metro system's two main lines, thereby linking to Giza, Maadi, Helwan and other districts and suburbs of Greater Cairo. The underground passages were a blessing in this case because they allowed pedestrians to reach and cross the square without having to brave the broad, busy roads.

International business and tourism will continue to be an important part of the Egyptian economy, and it is safe to say that Tahrir will rise in prominence as a destination and regional gathering place.

Learning from examples such as Chicago's Millennium Park, the people of Cairo might consider adding features such as bike rentals, information kiosks, way-finding, and nearby parking facilities. Those additions

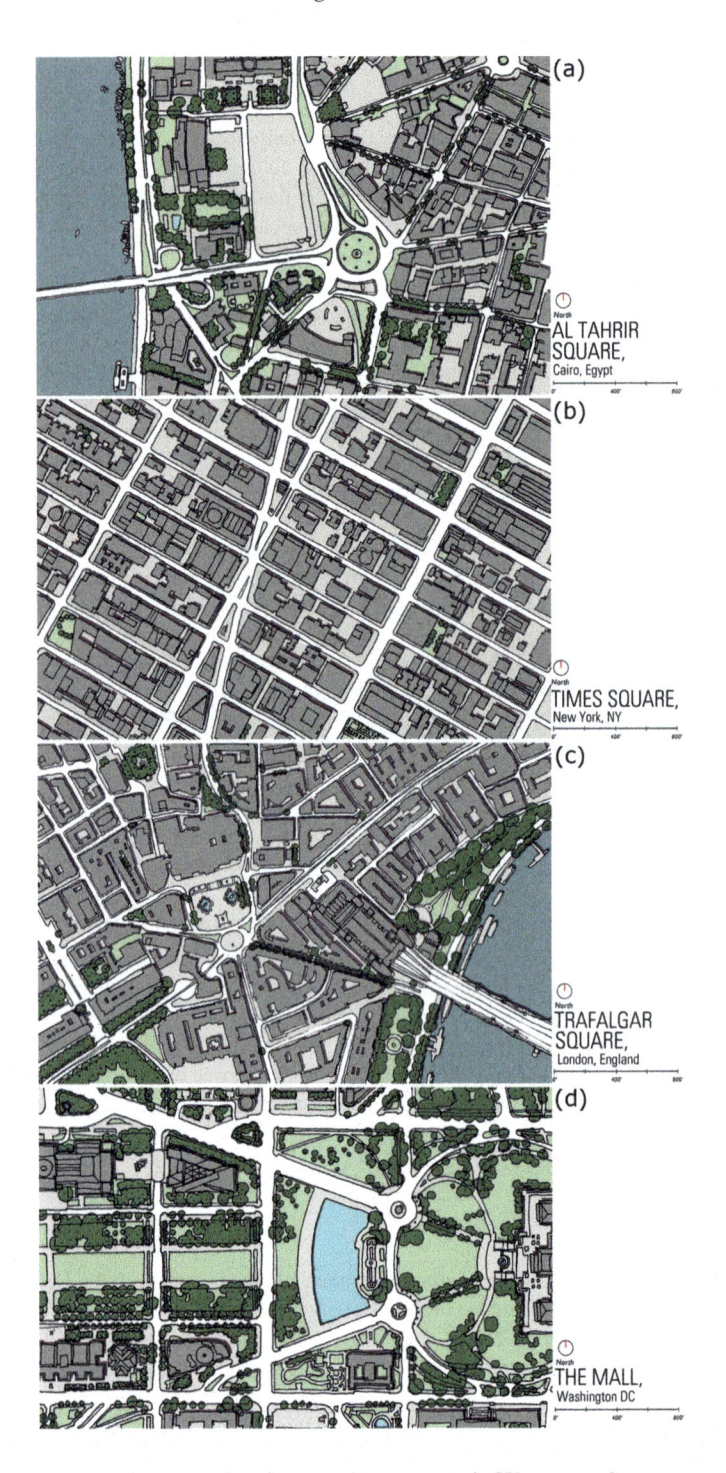

Figure 15.3 Comparison between Tahrir and other squares in Western cultures
Note: (a) Tahrir Square, Cairo; (b) Times Square, New York City; (c) Trafalgar Square, London; (d) The National Mall, Washington, DC.
Source: RTKL Associates Inc. 2014. All rights reserved.

could make the square an important point of departure by allowing visitors to park at the perimeter of downtown, orient themselves, and move into the rest of the city. This strategy would help to improve the significant traffic and pollution challenges the city confronts as it continues to grow.

Special Events

When an event as momentous as the downfall of a regime and the creation of a new democracy happens, the space becomes part of the public domain, a unique part of the culture. Think of the significance of the Place de la Concorde in the life of Paris or Faneuil Hall in Boston, taking this into account will mean that the square should be organized to accommodate major annual celebrations while also handling the basic daily needs of the city.

One of the advantages of having a compact urban grid such as in New York City is the ease with which a district can be closed to traffic within minutes, leaving other options for movement just a block or two away. Traffic was recently eliminated between 42nd and 47th streets along Broadway in order to attract more pedestrians to Times Square. Likewise, Trafalgar Square has been changed from a four-sided traffic island configuration to a three-sided peninsula, with the National Gallery and steps spilling out into the space to encourage better pedestrian flow—a change that has greatly benefited the pedestrian and bike linkages to the surrounding communities.

Layering and modulating the space into a series of smaller interconnected spaces that can accommodate a variety of events would help to animate the space and break down its scale when no major event is occurring. Programming weekly, monthly and special events within the space would help to keep it lively throughout the year.

A successful February 2011 celebration will be essential to the future life of the square, so thinking ahead about what will be needed to accommodate these events (infrastructure, facilities, logistics, among others) will be essential to future planning efforts of the city and region.

More Options: Other Ideas for Tahrir Square

Street Configuration and Traffic Flow

From a pedestrian perspective, it would be good to reduce automobile access to the square, either by simplifying the street network, bringing the bulk of the traffic from the bridge one block to the east or west, or eliminating the traffic circle within the square altogether. Reducing traffic flow would allow a more balanced interaction of pedestrians and cars within the space and increase the ability to close down the square for special events. Strengthening the pedestrian connection between the National Museum and the main event space is another improvement that would further augment and choreograph pedestrian flow.

Improved Entries and Exits

The narrow passage between the 6 October Bridge and the square now has historical significance, in that it was the street where protestors fought valiantly against pro-Mubarak forces. Can this site be made into a pedestrian street, with amenities and historical markers more appropriate to the gravity of the event and the place?

Broadcasting Facilities

Because of government interference during the revolt, one of the protestors' biggest challenges was their inability to communicate with each other and the outside world. A new administration will want to assure that freedom of speech is a right upheld by the new constitution, which should be expressed within Tahrir Square in some meaningful way. As Times Square represents the heart of communication in New York, perhaps a new broadcasting facility would be an appropriate symbol of a new transparency and free flow of information in the new Egypt.

Amphitheater Seating

At the far end of the square, the Egyptian museum's front steps can be used as stadium seating with views of the event space beyond. Coupled with an information kiosk, Internet cafe and newsstand, this area could become an information hub for all current activities and events happening in Cairo.

Animated Signage

Although a variety of signage already surrounds Tahrir Square, much of it is the traditional billboard variety. The introduction of modem LED displays and sound towers could provide animation to the space and access to news, commercial messages and current events.

Light and Sound

Towers that incorporate light-and-sound technology would definitely help the flexibility of the space and speed the set-up time for major performances and other events by providing a built-in capability to amplify and light the space when needed.

Mixed Uses

Additional density would bring more interest to the district. A number of open lots around the square could be redeveloped as mixed-use blocks. Residential, office, retail and hotel uses with terraced views of the square would help to build a constituency and populate and energize the space.

Water

Fountains help to break the space into several sub-areas, mitigate the ambient temperature, and provide white noise, reducing traffic noise. During major events, the fountains could be turned off for safety.

As Churchill famously said: "We shape our buildings; thereafter they shape us." Egypt has the opportunity to create a new foundation upon which to build a future with a sense of newfound equity, inspiration and purpose. The reshaping of Tahrir Square could be an important early accomplishment of a new democratic Egypt.

References

AlSayyad, N. 2011. A History of Tahrir Square. *Harvard University Press Blog* [online]. Available at: http://harvardpress.typepad.com/hup_publicity/2011/04/a-history-of-tahrir-square.html [accessed: January 17, 2013].

Banerjee, T. 2001. The Future of Public Space: Beyond Invented Streets and Reinvented Places. *Journal of American Planning Association* [online], 67(1), 9–24. Available at: http://dx.doi.org/10.1080/01944360108976352 [accessed: February 4, 2014].

Hauser, G. 1998. Vernacular Dialogue and the Rhetoricality of Public Opinion. *Communication Monographs* [online], 65(2), 83–107. Available at: http://dx.doi.org/10.1080/03637759809376439 [accessed: February 4, 2014].

Herrera, L. 2011. Egypt's Revolution 2.0: The Facebook Factor. *Jadaliyya* [online]. Available at: http://www.jadaliyya.com/pages/index/612/egypts-revolution-2.0_the-facebook-factor [accessed: February 12, 2011].

Rheingold, H. 2002. *Smart Mobs: The Next Social Revolution*. Cambridge, MA: Perseus Publishing.

Sennett, R. 1977. *The Fall of the Public Man.* New York: Knopf.
Tignor, R. 1984. *State, Private Enterprise, and Economic Change in Egypt, 1918–1952.* Princeton: Princeton University Press.

PART V
Prospects: Future Urban Design Agendas

Chapter 16
Estidama as a Model for Sustainable Urbanism in the Arab World: The Case Study of Abu Dhabi[1]

John Madden

Estidama: A Program that Embeds Sustainability as a Way of Life

While urban areas cover approximately 2 percent of the earth's surface, over 50 percent of the world's population is now living in cities, projected to increase by the year 2050 to an estimated 70 percent (United Nations 2013). This migration is having considerable environmental impacts associated with human activities, contributing to more than 80 percent toward global economic output, 60 to 80 percent of global energy consumption, and 70 percent of CO^2 emissions (UN-Habitat 2011). These global trends are evident in Abu Dhabi's transformation from a series of small remote nomadic tribal settlements to a burgeoning metropolis with a population approaching one million. Remarkably, this transformation occurred over the course of less than one generation. Settlement patterns of the past (based on familial and tribal relationships) were rapidly transplanted with the rational orthogonal grid layout of arterial streets responding to the modernist car-centric era of the 1960s and mega blocks punctuated with glass towers that have become the urban structure of Abu Dhabi today.

By 2007, a pivotal decision by the governing leadership to change the course of Abu Dhabi's future physical growth through the *Abu Dhabi Urban Structure Framework Plan: 2030* (Plan Capital 2030) set forward a fundamentally new vision outlining a number of key directions with a focus on environment, identity and livability. Based on directions laid out in Plan Capital 2030, the Abu Dhabi Urban Planning Council (UPC) created Estidama [Arabic for sustainability] in 2008 to guide future development to address the ecological/climatic, traditional and cultural, and economic development needs of the region. The Estidama initiative also set a clear mandate to improve the long-term health of cities and communities within the emirate of Abu Dhabi founded on the balance between the four pillars of sustainability (the environmental, economic, social and cultural aspirations) (Figure 16.1). "Estidama touches on all aspects of life in Abu Dhabi—the way we build, the way we resource, the way we live out daily lives, the choices we make as employers—all in an effort to attain a sustainable way of living" (Abu Dhabi Urban Planning Vision 2010: 77). Accordingly, Estidama is not just a policy or program, but a fundamental new "sustainable philosophy or mindset" behind planning, designing, constructing and operating all types of developments in a manner that enables future generations to sustain themselves and transform Abu Dhabi into a model of sustainable urbanization.

Ultimately, adopting the *Estidama philosophy* will depend on actively integrating it across governance bodies and authorities, which will guide Abu Dhabi's future through a coordinated policy framework. Through the course of its formulation and implementation, the UPC helped to ensure that the Estidama philosophy and approach have been integrated into every aspect of urban planning and development. The Estidama approach placed greater emphasis on contextual, place-based design over short-term economic gains. An essential tool created by the UPC is the Pearl Rating System (PRS),[2] a green building credit-based system meant to incentivize and guide all new physical development to become more environmentally sensitive and climatically responsive in its design, construction and ongoing operations. The PRS has incorporated some of the basic principles of other third party rating systems that have been developed around the world, such as

---

1 This chapter is a modified version of an original online publication: Madden, J.P. 2010. Sustainable Urbanism in Abu Dhabi. *ISOCARP* [online]. Available at: http://www.isocarp.org/fileadmin/user_upload/publications/Review_06_Specimen_Chapter_.pdf [accessed: June 3, 2014].

2 For additional information refer to the Estidama website: http://www.estidama.org/ [accessed: June 5, 2014].

Figure 16.1   The four pillars of Estidama (sustainability)
Source: Abu Dhabi Urban Planning Council.

LEED and BREEAM; the key difference was that this rating system has a monitoring and enforcement aspect both developed and directly administered by the UPC. Another advantage of the PRS is that the system is fully adapted and integrated into the regulatory frameworks developed by the UPC, including new building codes and development regulations, enabling the alignment of multiple regulatory tools to address sustainability from buildings to large-scale master-planned communities. The PRS is also context sensitive and focuses on how the built environment responds to the extreme heat and humidity of a coastal desert; a core mandate of the PRS requires that passive design strategies be undertaken throughout the planning and design stages of the application process. Accordingly, it places greater emphasis on the credit weighting toward water and energy efficiency. The PRS for communities encourages large master-planned proposals to incorporate traditional neighborhood patterns such as the *fareej* [housing cluster] centered around a *Midan* [square] that supports community uses and connected by pedestrian *sitkkas* [narrow pedestrian routes]. Key strategies include the orientation of the street grid and building plots to allow penetration of prevailing northwest coastal winds through the building site. The built form can also contribute positively to the local microenvironment by orienting the buildings to provide shade on the public realm and providing variations in height to help direct winds downward to the pedestrian realm without creating a wind tunnel effect. Appropriately implemented, these factors will help realize immense benefits in the livability and comfort within the built environment. Credits also encourage the use of *grey water* or treated sewage effluent (TSE) for irrigation and district cooling systems. Abu Dhabi has commissioned the construction of a treated sewage effluent (TSE) plant which will have a capacity of converting 430,000 cubic metres of sewage per day and will use processes such as ultra-filtration treatment and ultraviolet light disinfection (Todorova 2010).

The Estidama Pearl Rating System for Communities, Buildings and Villas

The UPC invited developers to pilot the new rating systems with a variety of selected project applications prior to officially implementing the program. This allowed a number of improvements to be made to clarify credit intents and to better explain calculation methodologies and performance requirements for each of the rating systems. The findings from the pilot phase, compiled with best practices research as well as life-cycle cost–benefit analysis for achieving graduated levels (from one to five pearls) of rating systems helped to assess the impacts associated with each of the rating systems. The above empirical research and analysis concluded that the following results, associated with the four pillars of the Estidama program, would be achieved:

- energy and water savings;
- increased return on investments;
- healthier places to live, work, study and play;
- improved productivity, retail sales and student performance;
- greater tenant retention;
- enhanced reputation and marketability;
- recognition from the leadership of Abu Dhabi.

It was estimated that significant operational savings of approximately 11,000 GWh in the residential sector alone could be realized which equates to a financial savings to the society in the order of AED 2.6 billion per annum at current cost (2010) of production of electricity (Figure 16.2a). Similar outcomes would

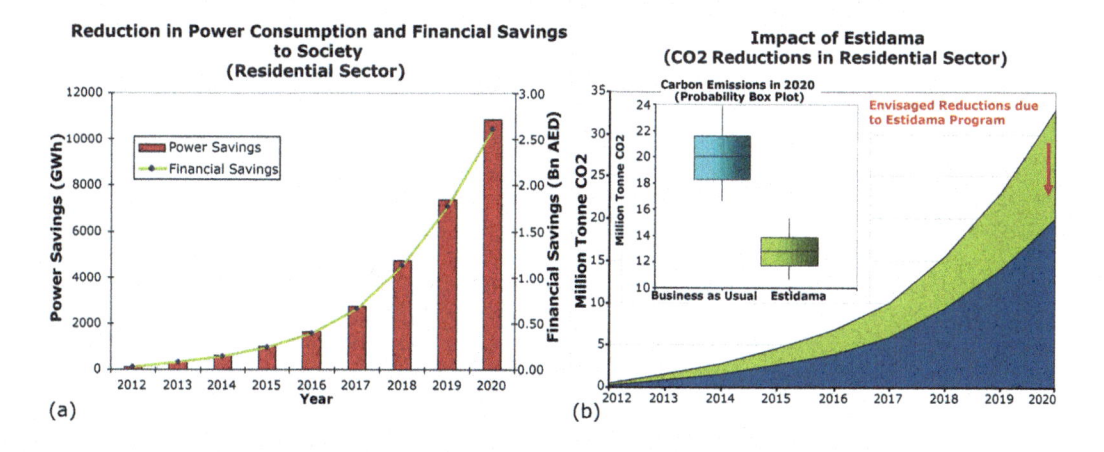

Figure 16.2 Impact of Estidama

Note: (a) reduction in power consumption and financial savings to society; (b) CO_2 emissions reduction in residential sector
Source: Development Review and Corporate Research, Abu Dhabi Urban Planning Council.

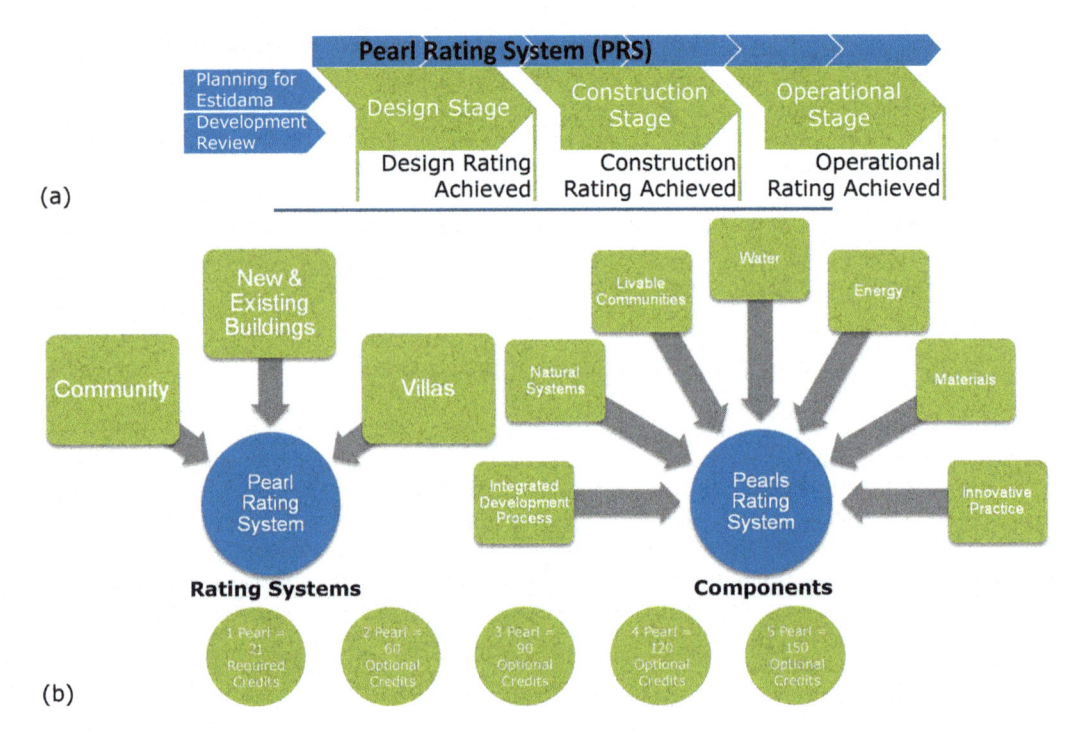

Figure 16.3 The Estidama Pearl Rating System (PRS)
Note: (a) Estidama stages; (b) performance and design matrix, Estidama.
Source: Estidama Program, Abu Dhabi Urban Planning Council.

be anticipated for the commercial, retail, hotel and public sector buildings as well. The PRS will also result in significant reduction in carbon emissions. With the potential energy savings that are achieved through the government mandated requirements toward energy efficiency, it is estimated that the PRS has the potential to reduce carbon emissions by over 35 percent over a "business as usual" approach to new development over the next 10 years (Figure 16.2b). The Pearl Rating System takes an integrated approach by addressing sustainable design at all stages in the life of buildings and communities—planning, design, construction and operation (Figure 16.3a).

The PRS was organized into seven categories that address performance and design metrics (Figure 16.3b), intended to help the design team conserve resources and increase efficiency across the three archetypes of new developments: community master plans, multi-story buildings and single-family villas (Abu Dhabi Urban Planning Council 2010a, 2010b, 2010d). The credits within each of the PRS were organized into the following seven credit categories:

- Integrated Development Process: ensuring that sustainability goals are identified at the beginning of the process and each design discipline is working together to identify innovative design approaches that potentially increase the project's quality and long-term value while reducing risk.
- Natural Systems: conserving, preserving and restoring the region's critical natural environments and habitats.
- Livable Communities: improving the quality and connectivity of outdoor and indoor spaces.
- Precious Water: reducing water demand and encouraging efficient distribution and alternative water sources.
- Resourceful Energy: targeting energy conservation through passive design measures, reduced demand, energy efficiency and renewable sources.

- Stewarding Materials: ensuring consideration of the "whole-of-life" cycle (from extraction and manufacturing to transportation, useful life and disposal) when selecting and specifying materials.
- Innovative Practice: additional credits can be achieved if the design approach demonstrates innovation in its application or innovation through the design process that led to an overall improvement, which is not represented in the other credit categories.

Initially, the PRS was envisioned as a voluntary market transformation too. However, in May 2010, the Urban Planning Council directed that the fledgling PRS be officially launched in November of 2010 and mandated that every new private development was to achieve a minimum of one-pearl certification. To demonstrate its commitment to sustainability, leadership mandated that all government-funded development projects achieve a minimum of two pearls. The Estidama team worked with the Abu Dhabi Education Council to achieve three-pearl certification on over 50 schools slated to be built over the next 10 years. Since its launch in the fall of 2010, the program has certified over 565 buildings of which 350 have achieved the mandatory two-pearl certification. During the same period there have been over 10,700 villas certified, demonstrating the impact of the program in a relatively short period of time (Figure 16.4). The mandatory credit requirements were mapped into the statutory development review process with a supporting step-by-step guide entitled "Planning for Estidama." The objective was to create a seamless application process to ensure that the objectives were being implemented. Additionally, as a further step, the UPC created a dedicated team that had the responsibility to develop a series of focused Estidama training programs ranging from introductory to advanced courses tailored for a variety of stakeholder needs. Training was developed for different government agencies offered in both Arabic and English. Accordingly, it had the responsibility of building technical capacity, addressing the varying and specific needs of stakeholders involved in development and construction—regulators, developers, businesses, applicants and investors. The Estidama training program has trained hundreds of municipal regulatory review staff and management how to administer the program, verify complete applications, how to undertake technical review and provide technical assistance. A separate certification program was developed to ensure that participants understood and comprehended the intent, methodology and application of the program requirements. Participants that successfully passed the certification exam were given the designation of a Pearl Qualified Professional (PQP). To ensure compliance with the PRS, every applicant team was

Buildings Numbers by Rating

	1 Pearl	2 Pearl	3 Pearl	4 Pearl	5 Pearl
Buildings	155	349	54	6	1

Villa Numbers by Rating

	1 Pearl	2 Pearl	3 Pearl	4 Pearl	5 Pearl
Villas	1679	8444	595	0	0

Figure 16.4 Numbers of building and villas that have been rated
Source: Estidama Project Log, Abu Dhabi Urban Planning Council.

required to engage a PQP to prepare the PRS application submissions to the UPC and municipal regulators. To date, the Estidama program already has certified over 1125 PQPs and over 7,000 participants have taken Estidama courses. Additionally, the Estidama training program also focused on creating awareness for future occupants and owners who would benefit from the program, since ultimately their actions will influence how successful the program is in terms of reducing ecological footprint associated all three PRSs (Communities, Buildings and Villas). The training program also developed a sustainable materials database identifying core supply chains and procurement professionals, and listing specifications, performance metrics and which credits they addressed. The purpose was to support design teams in promoting the selection of sustainable materials and technical specifications compliant with the PRS credit requirements as common practice.

As mentioned before, the impetus for the Estidama program was based on the urban design and sustainability policy directions laid out in Plan 2030 (Figure 16.5). The advisors of His Highness Sheikh Mohamed Bin Zayed Al Nahyan, Crown Prince of Abu Dhabi and Chairman of the Abu Dhabi Executive Council identified global experts in the field of sustainability, along with urban designers, planners and transportation engineers to undertake the ambitious job of establishing an urban design framework to guide the growth of the emirate. A series of maps and diagrams were produced identifying environmentally sensitive areas, natural habitats, mangroves, cultural landscapes and historic buildings, transportation networks, land use patterns, built form (height) and figure ground diagrams, open space and park systems. These maps were used to provide a diagnostic on the existing conditions and to understand where future growth could

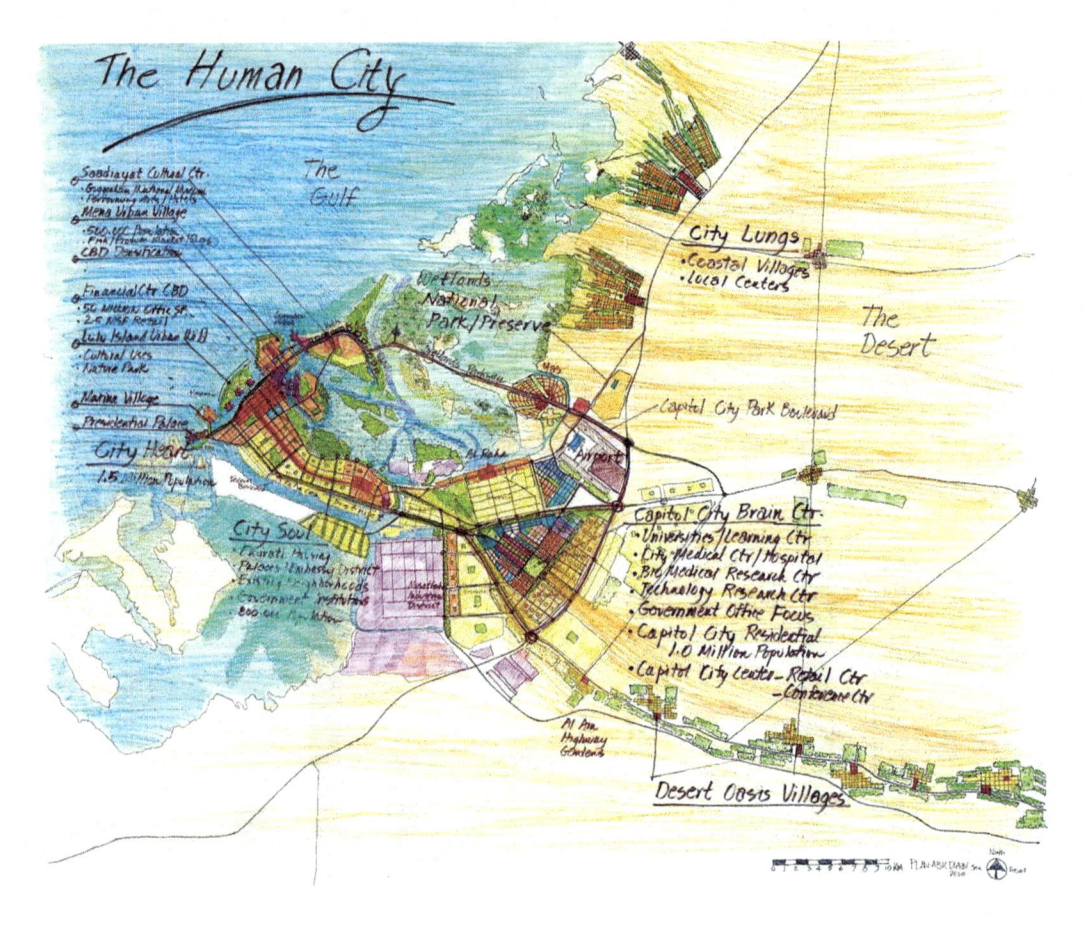

Figure 16.5   Plan 2030 concept sketch titled: *The Human City*
Source: Abu Dhabi Urban Planning Council.

be accommodated without threatening the natural ecology, cultural and historic assets. Economic forecasts were undertaken based on Economic Vision 2030 and equated these growth forecasts for each sector of the economy (leisure and tourism, retail, office-commercial, administration and management, manufacturing, light and heavy industry, and so on), and derived a gross floor area projection to accommodate growth in each of those economic sectors to a planning horizon of 2030. The next step was to allocate a spatial and built form dimension to those gross floor areas and to map out a series of frameworks and basic structure plans for land use, transportation, environment, open space, parks, built form and density. The result was a visionary new document called Abu Dhabi Plan 2030 (Plan 2030), articulating the guiding principles that support moving toward a more sustainable region, and providing clear policy directions to pursue green building standards and sustainable infrastructure as well as ensuring that new development protects the environment and reflects the unique cultural traditions of the region. Conceptual plans and schemes were formulated for key areas including the proposed expansion of the central business district, Masdar City, Capital District, Grand Mosque District and Lulu Island. A series of more detailed studies were sketched illustrating potential designs for emirate neighborhoods, revitalization of downtown blocks and new eco-villages in selected desert and coastal areas.

Case Study: The Capital District

The Capital District (Figure 16.6a) forms the gateway to Abu Dhabi and is one of the major strategic initiatives of Plan Capital 2030. The Capital District master plan provides a long-term vision toward 2030 for the development of a global twenty-first-century capital based on sound planning principles, sustainable criteria toward environmental quality and energy consumption, and a desire to provide the highest quality of life possible for all its citizens (Abu Dhabi Urban Planning Council 2009).

The plan for this 45 square kilometer site provides for a projected population of 370,000 residents. The Capital District is one of the most ambitious urban development projects being planned in the United Arab Emirates. In creating this new city, the master plan has capitalized on the site's physical assets—its centrality within the region and accessibility to both Abu Dhabi Island and to emerging developments on the mainland, its proximity to a well-connected street network, coastal climate and breezes, and its adjacencies to existing residential neighborhoods.

The site's triangular shape provided strong cues for organizing development around proposed high capacity transit lines through the site and in creating a series of symbolic and visual axes that link important civic spaces and landmarks, terminating at a central civic space that will represent the nation.

The Capital District is planned as a sustainable, compact, mixed-use city, comprised of high-density transit-oriented communities, employment, major universities, hospitals and knowledge-based employment sectors, as well as a lower density Emirati neighborhood. A central driver behind the master plan vision is the symbiotic relationship between land use and transportation in the creation of high quality, attractive district and neighborhood centers, vibrant streets and public spaces, and well-planned cultural and community facilities, all served by a world-class public transportation system.

The Capital District will be the new seat of national government and house a diplomatic and embassy neighborhood. It will also serve as the city of Abu Dhabi's second business district, providing over 100,000 jobs in a dynamic mixed-use urban core. In addition to a dense network of open spaces and community uses to support the local population, the Capital District will host an Olympic caliber 65,000 seat National Stadium as well as various sports venues and conference facilities. New universities and research facilities will position the city as a hub for education and research. The new city will also be a leader in environmental sustainability, with requirements for the use of highly energy efficient building structures, district cooling systems, water sensitive landscaping and irrigation and an overall urban design plan that promotes connectivity and pedestrian comfort.

Again, Abu Dhabi's desert and coast climate will pose significant challenges to maintaining human comfort in outside urban environments. The plan seeks to mitigate the negative impacts of thermal heat gain through comprehensive systems of shade and ventilation throughout the urban environment.

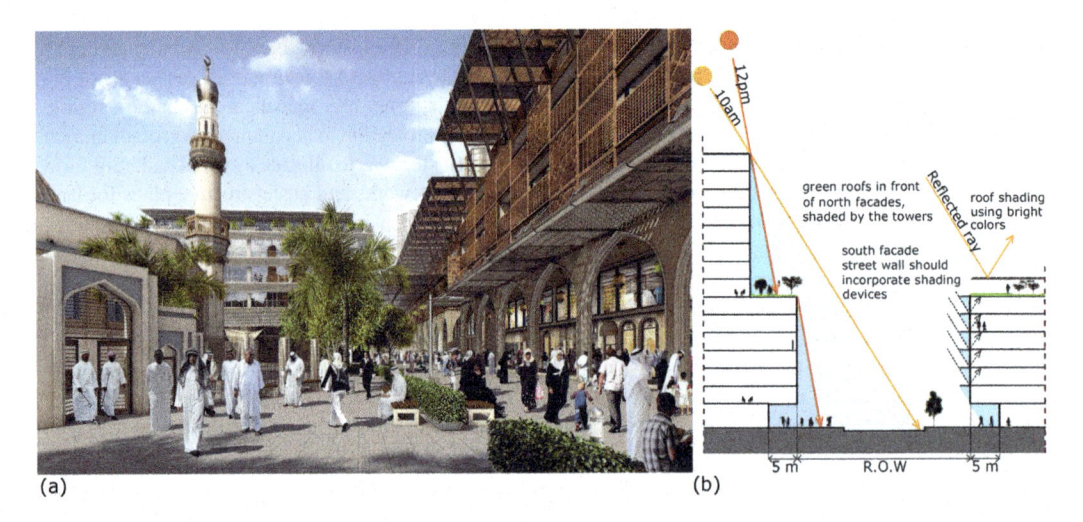

Figure 16.6 The Capital District
Note: (a) integration of built form into the public realm; (b) solar shading from street-wall setbacks.
Source: Abu Dhabi Urban Planning Council.

The fundamental principles guiding the geometry of the plan seek to naturally ventilate the city by having roadways, block orientation, landscape and building form oriented to capture the prevailing winds as a cooling source (Figure 16.6b). Throughout the planning process, modeled design scenarios were tested in order to understand the implications from a wind and cooling standpoint.

Based on results from these studies and additional scientific research, strategies were developed to guide decision-making with regard to the orientation of streets and the positioning and dimensioning of buildings in order to best take advantage of the wind. Also, shading devices such as arcades, trellis and landscaped canopies are planned as a complex network of places that allow pedestrian movement, solar protection and refuge from the harsh climatic conditions of Abu Dhabi. Sustainable practices toward conservation of energy and water are key priorities of the Capital District plan. The plan optimizes building energy use and water consumption through the application of *green building* practices as defined by the government's Estidama program. The design of the public realm and open space systems will incorporate xeriscaping strategies that use drought-resistant plantings and materials that significantly reduce the consumption of potable water. Recycling centers will be located within the ground floor of public parking facilities and encourage individuals and households to recycle. In addition to enhancing urban fabric and community infrastructure that will enable the values, social arrangements and culture of the Emirati communities to be preserved, Capital District clearly aims to manifest Abu Dhabi's role and stature as a capital city.

Case Study: Masdar

Masdar (Figure 16.7) is planned to be a mixed-use development strategically located on the metropolitan mainland of Abu Dhabi between the international airport, Capital District and approximately 17 km from the existing central business district at the north end of Abu Dhabi Island. The plan aspires to create a carbon-neutral and zero-waste city, which will become a model for demonstrating traditional and high-tech approaches to sustainability in the region. The 640 hectare site of Masdar will accommodate 40,000 residents and approximately 50,000 employees when fully built (Masdar City 2014).

Figure 16.7 Oblique view of Masdar development proposal
Source: Abu Dhabi Urban Planning Council.

The focus of the development is centered on the Masdar Institute of Science and Technology (MIST) and the headquarters of the International Renewable Energy Agency (IRENA). The first phase of the development will have an academic and research focus on sustainable technologies and alternative energies. In addition to the educational facilities, the mix of land uses include commercial, community and residential uses which help to create a job–housing balance which in turn reduces the potential number of commuter trips. The planned mix of land uses will also help create a more vital community and sense of place.

The master plan for Masdar incorporates traditional Islamic–Arabic design with advanced sustainability techniques into a contemporary architectural expression (Figure 16.8). The spatial footprint of the development (Figure 16.9) is very compact but is relatively low in scale with predominate building heights ranging from four to seven stories. Studies have shown that the optimal densities to support a basic provision of commercial services and public transport is about 5,000 people within a catchment area of 300 metres walking radius. This equates to a design population density of 200 people per hectare. To induce greater pedestrian trips, the Masdar plan proposes densities of 245 people per hectare, which reduces the effective pedestrian catchment areas to nearly 150 metres (Figure 16.10).

The transportation strategy is premised entirely on alternative modes to the private automobile. All trips within the Masdar development will be either by transit, walking or cycling (Figure 16.11). To achieve this, the plan proposes a hierarchy of transit systems including a personal rapid transit system (PRT) and a network of bicycle and pedestrian routes that are seamlessly interconnected. A compact development footprint, a comprehensive alternative transportation network and strategically clustered public facilities and amenities induce a greater number of pedestrian trips. The transportation strategy alone will reduce carbon dioxide emissions by 7 percent (Masdar City 2010).

The planned orientation and layout of the development responds to climate and its geographic location (Figure 16.12). Through solar analysis and thermal dynamic modeling, the design strategy of Masdar evolved to minimize solar radiation and thermal heat gain. The entire city's street orientation and urban structure were rotated by 45 degrees to the northwest to minimize solar gain within the public realm and along building facades thereby reducing the potential cooling load of buildings and improving overall microclimate and outdoor thermal comfort. Building height to street width ratios help to maximize solar shading.

The combined passive solar strategies with the improvement in building energy efficiencies (high efficiency building envelopes, ventilation and air conditioning systems, improved shading devices, and so on) is estimated to help to reduce CO_2 emissions by up to 56 percent (Masdar City 2010).

Masdar plans that all of the energy to be used within Masdar City will be generated through renewable sources including:

- 8 percent waste to energy;
- 16 percent evacuated tube collectors;
- 36 percent concentrated solar power (CSP);
- 42 percent photovoltaic.

The utilization of renewable energy is estimated to reduce carbon emissions by approximately 24 percent compared to *business as usual*. The development of Shams 1, a 100MW concentrated solar plant (CSP) in the Western Region of Abu Dhabi, will contribute significantly to the renewable energy supporting the operations of the development. Apart from the CSP plant, the alternative energy generation, waste management, wind farms, bio-remediation fields, and grey water recycling are almost entirely integrated within the site. Solar PVs panels have also been integrated onto the roofs providing 1,800MWh of electricity each year in addition to thermal solar hot water collectors that satisfy almost 75 percent of the hot water demand (Gonchar and Nambiar 2011).

The Masdar project has also targeted the development to be zero waste. In the initial stages it has already implemented this strategy by diverting construction waste generated on site as well as using residual concrete and wood waste from surrounding construction sites to be incorporated into the initial phase of development. Scrap wood waste is converted into wood chips to place over landscaped areas and footpaths. This material helps to reduce evaporation of irrigation water in landscaped areas as well as replacing asphalt or concrete for footpaths which helps reduce embodied carbon and heat island effect. Masdar has targeted 50 percent of the materials that are used on site to be either reused or recycled with 33 percent of non-recycled waste being converted to energy. Plans include systems for 17 percent of all organic materials to be composted or converted into bio-fuels (Figure 16.13) (Masdar City 2010).

Education and awareness will be a critical component to shifting behavior to meet sustainability targets. To help assess the success of the Masdar sustainability initiative, an intelligent metering and building control system has been planned to monitor water, energy and waste. These systems are intended to help inform and educate occupants as to how they rank against the established targets. Ongoing monitoring to assess progress will play an important role in ensuring compliance with such targets.

The Masdar plan will be integrated with regional transportation infrastructure with an emphasis on accommodating the planned metro and tram network. Further, its immediate proximity to the international airport will create an easy and efficient public transit link between Masdar and the International Airport, Capital City, Raha and the existing central business district on the northern edge of Abu Dhabi Island.

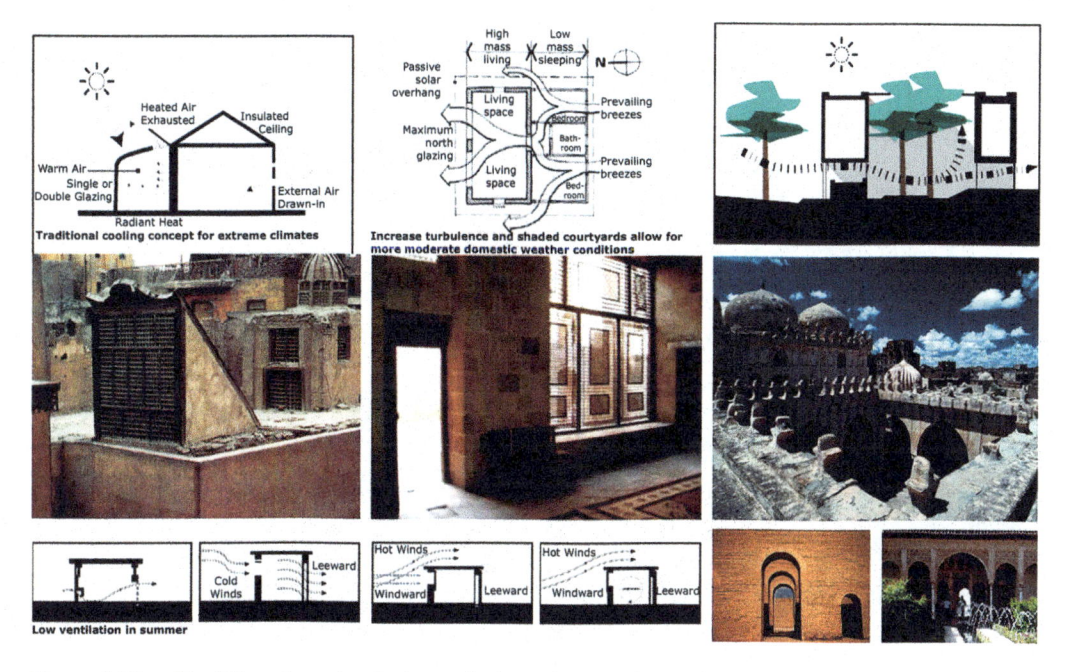

Estidama as a Model for Sustainable Urbanism in the Arab World 237

Figure 16.8 Traditional passive design techniques in Islamic architecture
Source: Abu Dhabi Urban Planning Council.

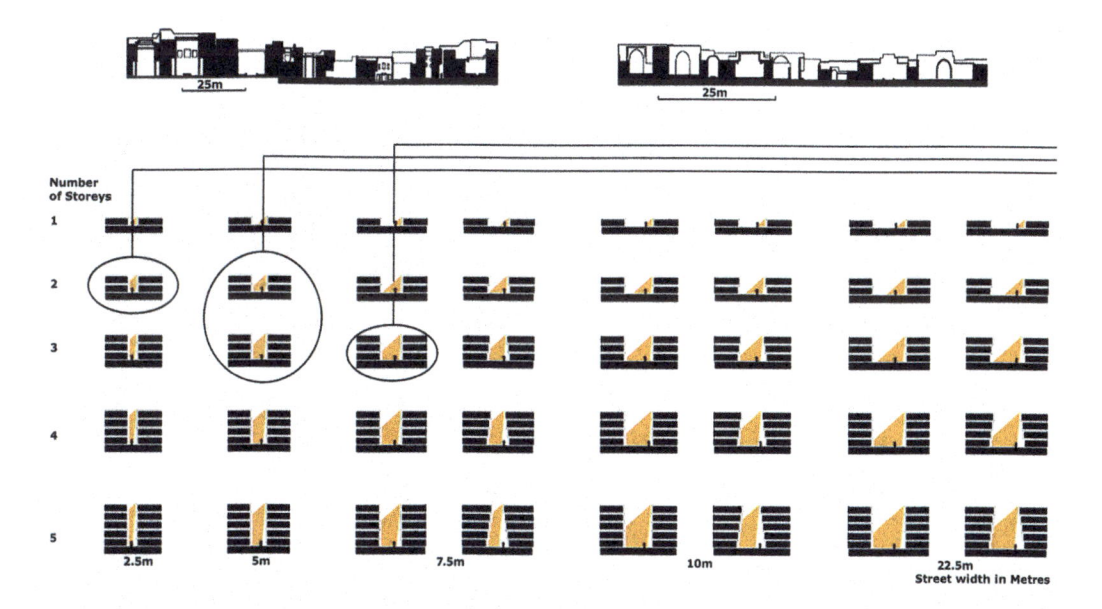

Figure 16.9 Solar shading analysis
Note: Street widths to building height ratios.
Source: Abu Dhabi Urban Planning Council.

238   *Urban Design in the Arab World*

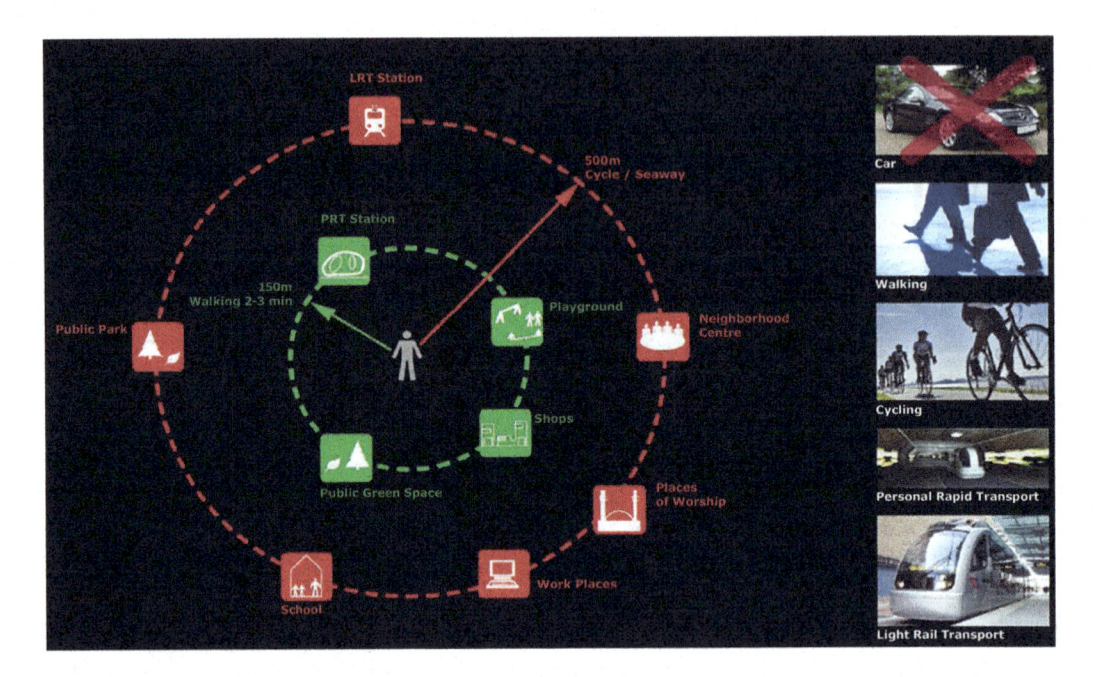

Figure 16.10   Transportation strategy, Masdar
Source: Abu Dhabi Urban Planning Council.

Figure 16.11   Pedestrian routes with passive and active solar shading
Source: Abu Dhabi Urban Planning Council.

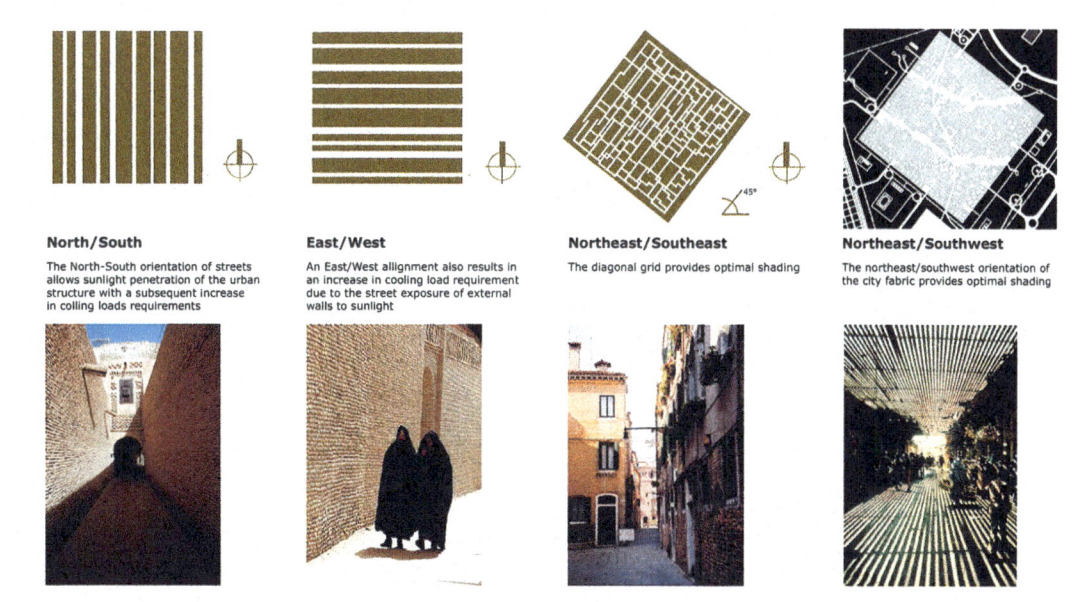

Estidama as a Model for Sustainable Urbanism in the Arab World 239

North/South
The North-South orientation of streets allows sunlight penetration of the urban structure with a subsequent increase in colling loads requirements

East/West
An East/West allignment also results in an increase in cooling load requirement due to the street exposure of external walls to sunlight

Northeast/Southeast
The diagonal grid provides optimal shading

Northeast/Southwest
The northeast/southwest orientation of the city fabric provides optimal shading

Figure 16.12 Grid orientation and built form, Masdar
Source: Abu Dhabi Urban Planning Council.

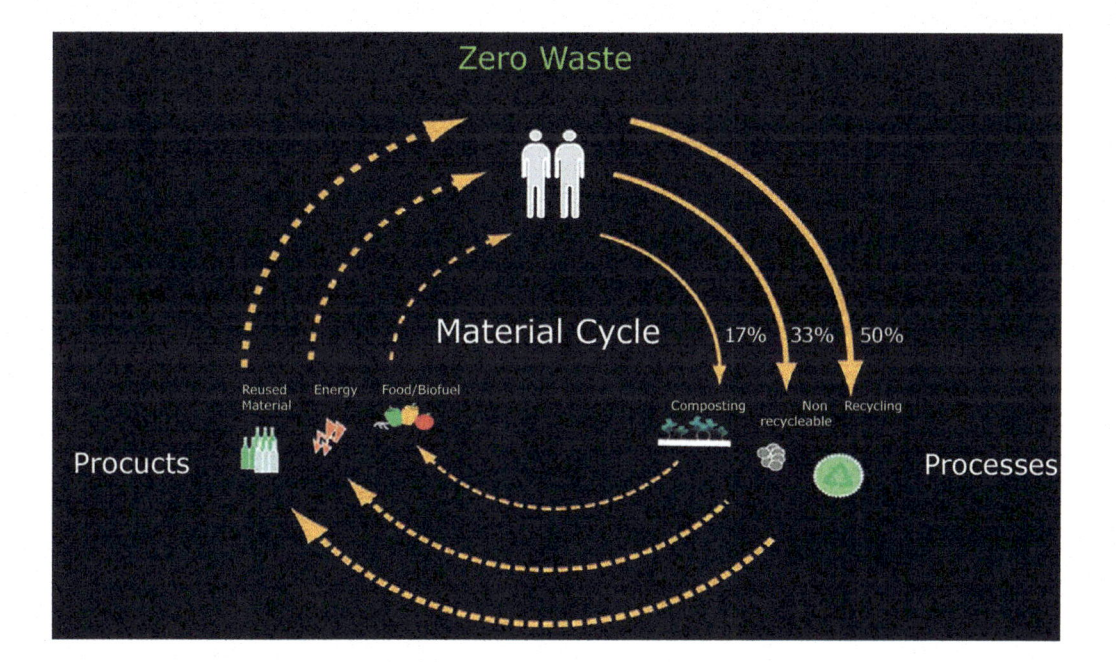

Figure 16.13 Zero waste and material reuse strategy
Source: Abu Dhabi Urban Planning Council.

Conclusions

With the PRS Estidama program, Abu Dhabi Vision 2030 presents a new trajectory for growth that prioritizes the protection of the environmental assets and restoration of the natural systems that give the emirate its unique identity. As examples, both the Capital District and Masdar case studies highlighted innovations in urban design, planned according to context-sensitive design and sustainability principles. The PRS systems also help to mitigate and effectively respond to the rapid physical growth and the resulting impact on the sensitive desert and coastal environments. Ultimately, the continued success in the implementation of Estidama depends on two factors: the capacity of the PRS to promote an *empirical awareness* as the guiding principles behind a more sustainable urban design practice; and *the replicability of elements of the PRS pilot program* in other Arab Gulf regions with similar climatic conditions tested through future plans to export Estidama to all seven emirates.

Empirical Awareness

The long-term value of Estidama is that it underscores the importance of *empirical evidence-based methods* in dispelling the myths associated with inflationary costs and increased construction delays. These two threats underpinned the importance of building capacity and knowledge among affected stakeholders to address knowledge gaps and demonstrate how the objectives could be met with practical visual explanatory guides and a database of materials (with costs) to help address the credit requirements. Costing studies and analysis were undertaken on actual projects that applied the Estidama Pearl Rating System and concluded that the project budgets and schedules were not significantly impacted. A comprehensive Estidama training program was designed to target a wide range of groups from students to executives that would collectively become *agents of change* in the built environment. On one hand, children and families are taught how individual lifestyle choices can reduce the percentage of their ecological footprint. On the other hand, contractors, suppliers and urban design professionals were provided with a detailed costing analysis of the mandatory PRS credits; the purpose is to disprove the notion that the system creates inflationary costs associated with consultants charging additional premiums and *contingencies*. Over 75 percent of ownership expenses occur after design and construction, and yet 75 percent of decisions driving costs are taken before detailed design is even completed. This underscores the importance of getting the facts right from the beginning. As such, the Abu Dhabi Planning Council commissioned a cost consultant to review the budget associated with achieving 1–5-pearl certification. The report concluded that attaining 1–2 pearls would add a 2–4 percent cost premium but result in a 25–30 percent reduction in water and nearly 35–40 percent savings in energy.

Replicability

The Estidama PRS was formulated and launched in Abu Dhabi not as a static policy or regulation that can simply be adopted in other cities. Rather, it is a system that has evolved from a need to respect and incorporate unique Arab cultural influences in the built environment and to encourage contemporary expressions of Arab urbanism at large that responds to the historic urban design traditions and architecture from master planning to the building scale that have both aesthetic and functional performance value. Credits require projects to demonstrate passive cooling design principles through: optimizing building and street orientation; reducing window to wall ratios; requiring highly insulated building envelopes; incorporating light shelves to redirect and diffuse direct sunlight; and water-efficient landscaping. All of these credits and design principles are applicable to other regions within the Arab Gulf and North Africa in different ways. It is important to note that the UPC's priority was to ensure that the implementation processes were refined through a quality improvement cycle[3] before being effectively *exported* to other countries in the MENA region. The results determined that a successful implementation requires a sweeping change of the planning/design of projects across a range of design disciplines that were involved in preparing development applications. It embodied a whole new

---

3   Quality Improvement Cycle is a planned sequence of systematic and documented activities and actions that are targeted toward improving a process.

approach to the design and regulatory review process. The Estidama and development regulations explicitly required proof that from the outset, an integrated design process was being used that incorporated key design disciplines to achieve synergistic improvements over *business-as-usual* designs. On the regulatory review side, various disciplines including urban designers, transportation and development planners, ecologists and civil engineers would collaborate to provide integrated solutions and design directions to the applicant team. This was a conscious effort to move away from departmental silos of design to a collaborative and integrated design process. Therefore, any planning system in the Arab Gulf that adopts the PRS is encouraged to provide a systematic roadmap and guides for applicants to address the integrated development requirements, important to assessing applications from various departmental criteria. This process requires a *champion* who can strategically advise on how to integrate the system within existing and emerging regulatory reviews. A facilitator, with specialized technical training, should also be assigned to provide guidance to the applicant, address conflicting comments, and reduce bureaucratic delays and excessive *transactions*. Accordingly, to ensure that the content, skills and abilities was being properly comprehended in the Arab Gulf, the Pearl Qualified Professional certification process targeted consulting firms from the entire Middle East; the training program encompassed web-casts administered online to increase regional accessibility. Furthermore, a testing and PQP certification process is provided through Prometric[4] which administers the testing and certification exams. Ultimately the adaption of the Estidama program requires leadership and support to shift the decision-making paradigm that identifies clear sustainability objectives with a supporting plan, implementation and monitoring strategy. More importantly, training and capacity building that incorporates evidence-based approaches will help shift attitudes and behaviors, which, in turn, help strengthen the support from those that are impacted.

References

Abu Dhabi Urban Planning Council. 2009. *Capital District Master Plan Summary*. Abu Dhabi: UPC.
Abu Dhabi Urban Planning Council. 2010a. *Building Rating System: Design & Construction (Version 1.0)* [online: The Pearl Rating System for Estidama]. Available at: http://estidama.org/template/estidama/docs/PBRS%20Version%201.0.pdf [accessed: August 26, 2013].
Abu Dhabi Urban Planning Council. 2010b. *Community Rating System: Design & Construction (Version 1.0)* [online: The Pearl Rating System for Estidama]. Available at: http://estidama.org/template/estidama/docs/PCRS%20Version%201.0.pdf [accessed: August 26, 2013].
Abu Dhabi Urban Planning Council. 2010c. *Introduction to Abu Dhabi Urban Planning Council (UPC)* [online: Abu Dhabi Urban Planning Council]. Available at: http://www.upc.gov.ae/template/upc/docs/UPC_Media%20Kit_English.doc [accessed: August 26, 2013].
Abu Dhabi Urban Planning Council. 2010d. *Villa Rating System: Design & Construction (Version 1.0)* [online: The Pearl Rating System for Estidama]. Available at: http://estidama.org/template/estidama/docs/PVRS%20Version%201.0.pdf [accessed: August 26, 2013].
Abu Dhabi Urban Planning Vision. 2010. *Abu Dhabi Economic Vision 2030*. Available at: http://www.upc.gov.ae/template/upc/pdf/abu-dhabi-vision-2030-revised-en.pdf [accessed: August 26, 2013]
Gonchar, J. and Nambiar, S. 2011. *Masdar Institute and Estidama Pearl Rating System, Abu Dhabi*. Architectural Record [online]. Available at: http://archrecord.construction.com/projects/portfolio/2011/05/masdar_institute.asp [accessed: August 26, 2013].
Masdar City. 2010. *The Global Centre of Future Energy*. Available at: http://www.masdarcity.ae/en/ [accessed: August 26, 2013].
Masdar City. 2014. *Masdar City at a Glance*. Available at: http://www.masdar.ae/assets/downloads/content/270/masdar_city.pdf [accessed: March 9, 2015].

---

4 Prometric is a third-party independent test development and delivery agency that the UPC contracted to administer the testing and certification of Pearl Qualified Professions (PQP) for each rating system. A PQP designated professional is required on all applicant teams to help prepare the required submittals and ensure quality assurance on submitted materials.

Todorova, V. 2010. Treated Sewage Will Reduce Gulf Water Use. *The National* [online]. Available at: http://www.thenational.ae/news/uae-news/environment/treated-sewage-will-reduce-gulf-water-use [accessed: August 26, 2013].

UN-Habitat. 2011. *Global Report on Human Settlements 2011: Cities and Climate Change* [online: United Nations Human Settlements Programme]. Available at: http://www.unhabitat.org/downloads/docs/GRHS2011_Full.pdf [accessed: August 26, 2013].

United Nations. 2013. *World Economic and Social Survey 2013: Sustainable Development Challenges* [online: Department of Economic and Social Affairs]. Available at: http://www.un.org/en/development/desa/policy/wess/wess_current/wess2013/WESS2013.pdf [accessed: August 26, 2013].

Chapter 17
Re-Engineering the Twenty-First-Century City: Future Directions for Urban Design in the Arab World

Anne Vernez Moudon

Urban design has a rich history as a theory-driven field guiding practice. The theory is normative, defining ideal urban forms. Today, theories abound, especially with the recent rise in popularity of different "urbanisms." Dozens of types of urbanisms have been reported including the "new," "post," "everyday," "digital," "noir," "messy," and so on, urbanism (Barnett 2011), further energizing a field already full of good ideas. Yet rarely are the actual applications of urban design theories evaluated to establish a reliable knowledge base for practice. This is unfortunate because, as Jane Jacobs noted, "designing a dream city is easy, rebuilding a living one takes imagination" (Jacobs 2004).

Many disciplines, which are complementary to urban design, provide substantive knowledge on how city form functions and affects society and economy (Moudon 1992). This chapter illustrates how research in other disciplines offers evidence for the direction of future urban design interventions. The focus is on one issue that is being flagged by different streams of research: the over-reliance on motorized transport for inner-city mobility, which is common to all post-industrial and most post-colonial cities. Specifically, the proliferation of private cars, trucks and buses against a weak background of transit and human-powered travel (walking, buggies, bicycles and so on) has severe impacts on the use of urban land, as well as on the health of humans and their environment. The recent resurgence of "sustainability," a buzzword to encapsulate the future redemption of cities, in part recognizes the problem associated with urban motorized transport. However, the sustainability "movement" remains fractured within the hands of the different professions, none of which seems to embrace a comprehensive understanding of the negative impacts of motorized transport. Hence for example, "green" buildings made of healthy recyclable materials are commonly set within large parking lots or on top of large garages, which encourage their users to drive to and from them, and often provide no other travel alternative than the private automobile. As well, many newer buildings in places ranging from Switzerland to Korea use triple glazing or protective balconies to shield users from the noise and pollutants of an adjacent motorway, thus in effect turning their back to the ills of the ambient urban environment. Environmental pollution and nuisances, many of which, as we will see, come from motorized transport, are the *tiger in our midst*. Unfortunately, only one option seems to be used to fight this tiger: that of putting his potential victims in a cage. It does not require much thinking to realize that while this approach may work for safaris, it is not appropriate for cities, from which the tiger must be removed.

Motorization is a common theme for cities in the developed and developing world. Cities in the Arab world are no exception: motorization dominates in all of its cities, large and small, rich and less rich; it chokes the historic cores of the many ancient settlements and entirely shapes the new emerging cities in the desert. Fleshing out what is known about the impacts of extreme urban motorization helps rethink how cities should be designed and built. Already, and somewhat unexpectedly, some cities are re-engineering themselves, showing the way for future urban design in the Arab world.

Evidence from Research

Research tells us that the over-reliance on inner-city motorized transport impacts society, economy and environment in several domains: that of urban form and infrastructure; of human behavior and productivity; of the quality of the environment; and of human health.

Urban Form and Infrastructure

Motorization requires substantial investments at both the individual (vehicle purchase, insurance, gas, maintenance, repair and related taxation) and the collective (infrastructure in the form of roads and streets, as well as ancillary services such as gas stations, repair shops and, of course, parking) levels. Until about two decades ago, high levels of motorization were confined to Western and developed nations and their cities, which had responded to rapidly increasing rates of individual car ownership with investments in supporting infrastructure. Over the years, however, Western experience has shown that investments in motorized infrastructure in turn spur higher utilization rates by the traveling public, and encourage motorized freight at the expense of cheaper and less polluting rail or water-based freight systems.

Motorization is linked to wealth. Measuring wealth by national Gross Domestic Product (GDP), high and medium GDP countries in the Arab world have a disproportionally high level of motorization, measured by motor-vehicles per capita. Lebanon, a medium GDP country, has 0.43 vehicles per capita, compared to Bahrain (0.51), a high GPD country (World Bank 2008; International Monetary Fund 2011). Jordan has a high 0.15 vehicles per capita, compared to other lower GDP countries such as Turkey and Egypt, both at 0.04 vehicles per capita (Figure 17.1). Outside of the Arab world, high GPD countries also have a range of motorization rates. The United States is leading with 0.81, while South Korea remains low at 0.35.

Curiously, however, if motorization is an inevitable byproduct of economic development and its associated demand for individual mobility, the relationship between wealth and motorization is not linear, suggesting that levels of motorization are policy- and not market-driven, the result of deliberate taxation policies affecting vehicle purchase, gas prices, insurance and so on. Reinforcing the weak market effect on motorization rates is the large variation in the share of public investment in motorized transport infrastructure among wealthy urbanized regions. The US has the most extensive motorway infrastructure in the world. It is particularly prominent in cities that experienced major growth since the 1980s. Yet importantly, even in these highly motorized cities, levels of infrastructure vary substantially: Phoenix has 1.46 lane-miles of roads per 1,000 population, compared to 1.2 in Atlanta and Dallas (Poole 2006). In terms of motorway and arterial lanes per area served, Atlanta has 2 lane-miles per square mile, Dallas 2.5, and Phoenix a whopping 4 lane-miles per square mile (The Public Purpose 2002). Furthermore, comparing US with European city-regions, the

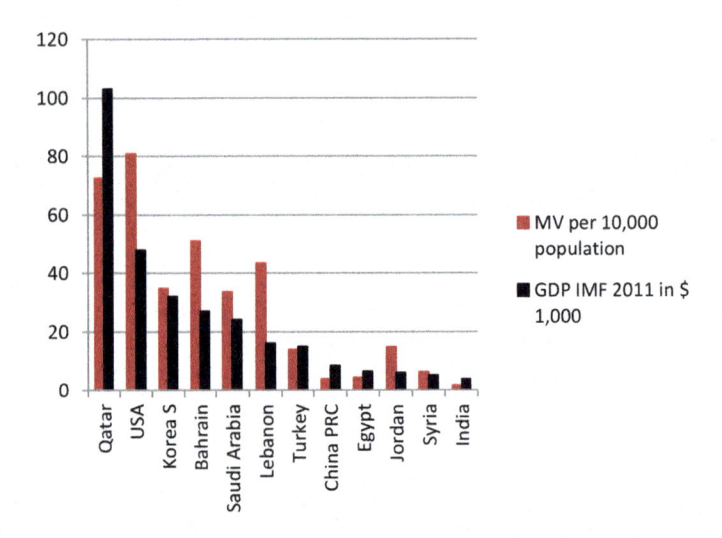

Figure 17.1   Gross Domestic Product (GDP) per capita and motorization
Note: Motor vehicles include automobiles, SUVs, vans and commercial vehicles; and exclude motorcycles and other motorized two-wheelers, 2007–8.
Source: Author (after World Bank 2008; International Monetary Fund 2011).

latter have on average about *one-fourth* of the motorways per km² (Bialas-Motyl 2008). Of note, the relation between road density and GDP is also non-linear in EU countries. To simplify the comparison, on average, major Western European cities, with about half the rate of motor-vehicles per capita than the US, have *half of the motorway infrastructure* that is present in US cities. With regard to motorized infrastructure, cities of the Arab world appear to follow the US model of unabashed institutional support for individual car transport in the newer cities of the Gulf, and the European model in the historic and older cities in other parts of the Middle East and North Africa. European and Arab statistics show that neither rates of motorization nor investments in motorized infrastructure are linearly associated with the wealth and welfare of a country or with its population's standard of living. Taxation and public investment policies are what determine travel-mode-based mobility and accessibility patterns.

In cities, the cost of urban motorways includes more than that of buying vehicles and building the corresponding infrastructure. Motorways consume extremely valuable urban land, the productivity of which (in the form of return on investment and taxation) is not included in municipal finance tallies. For example, motorway "intersections," now called "highway interchanges," easily cover 2 km² (500 acres), taking as much space as do the historic core of ancient cities or entire neighborhoods of the early twentieth century. These large areas are often combined with environmental mitigation measures, where more than half of the space is taken not by traffic but by water catchment basins. Many also contain planted or green areas for "beautification" purposes. The value of these areas as open space for recreation is rarely questioned in spite of their known high levels of pollution, and often deafening ambient noise levels. And the land costs and loss in tax base associated with highway interchanges is never taken into consideration, because these are public works, exempt from tax and opportunity cost assessment.

Urban motorways are mainly dedicated to provide mobility to that single user, the motorist. For accessibility, motorists must rely on city streets, which themselves cover a minimum of 25 percent of urban land. Since today most of this street space is dedicated to automobiles, the land it occupies should be tallied as motorized infrastructure. Adding parking to space taken by vehicles further exacerbates the imbalance and adds to the cost of intra-city travel. At minimum, a car needs two parking spots to function, which amount to 56 m² (28 m² per stall to allow for maneuvering) (Kay 1997). At this rate, each car takes almost twice as much standing space in a city than individual residents of Shanghai used in 2001 (33 m²); and about one-third of the space that a residents of London used (160 m²) (Bertaud 2001).

While parking vehicles adds significantly to the demand for urban land, the real costs of parking are typically kept separate from transportation costs, and instead are included in the land use or land improvement category. Whether in the form of parking at-grade or parking garages, parking is attached to the cost of public and private land development, and as such is shared by everyone, including the non-motorized traveling public (the young, the old and the poor) and transit riders (Shoupe 2005). In the US, there are an estimated three *nonresidential* parking spaces (that is, excluding parking at places of residence) for every car, adding up to almost 800 million nonresidential parking spaces for a total of 22,400 km² (800 million spaces at 28 m² per stall, the total amounts to more than twice the size of Lebanon and one-eighth of that of Syria) (Ben-Joseph 2012). In comparison, the number of cars in Beirut is estimated to be about 800,000 (two million people x 0.4 cars per capita in Lebanon). At three stalls per car, this translates into an equivalent of 67.2 km² being occupied by parking. Further assuming that about one-third of this parking takes place in the basement of buildings, and another third is on-street, parking at-grade would still take some 22.4 km² of Metropolitan Beirut's 200 km² (Perry 2000). Finally, adding parking at-grade to street space, cautiously estimated at 25 percent of the city surface, more than 36 percent of the land of Beirut is likely to be used exclusively for cars (Figure 17.2).

Few if any jurisdictions tally up the staggering total amount of urban space dedicated to motor vehicles. If they did, they would be able to monetize the true costs of policies that favor individual motorized transport. And public awareness of these true costs would surely dampen the common support for such means of inner-city travel.

Figure 17.2   Expanses of roads and parking in Istanbul, Dubai, Aleppo and Beirut
Note: Clockwise from top left: highway interchange in Istanbul; highway interchange in Dubai; roads and parking in Aleppo; roads and parking in Beirut.
Source: Clockwise from top left: Google Earth 2010, GeoEye; Google Earth 2011, Europa Technologies; Google Earth 2011, GeoEye, Basarsoft, ORION-ME; Google Earth 2014.

Behavior

Cars are overused, especially in small or dense cities where distances between activities are short and could easily be accommodated by other means of transport. In the US again, where distances between activities are longer than in the rest of the world, 27 percent of auto trips are shorter than 1.6 km (about a 20-minute walk), and 40 percent are shorter than 3.2 km (U.S. Department of Transportation 1990; U.S. Department of Transportation 2000). In central cities, it is estimated that 30 percent of car traffic is generated by people looking for a parking spot (Shoupe 2005). A final statistic that should convince the skeptic: a car is parked 95 percent of its life (Ben-Joseph 2012).

For almost 50 years, transportation planners have focused on the economic benefits of driving for individuals, and have downplayed its personal and social costs. Yet the emphasis on automobile travel and especially the Single Occupant Vehicle (SOV) mode also has long-term effects on behavior and the perception of travel. Daily travel budgets in Western economies are estimated at 90 minutes per day; of that budget, Los Angelinos spend an average of 100 percent (Fruin et al. 2007) and Europeans 50 percent, in a car (Aliaga 2005). That period of time accounts for 33–45 percent of total exposure to diesel and ultrafine particles. Research in Germany indicates that work absenteeism would be reduced by 16 percent if workers had a negligible commute (van Ommeren and Gutiérrez-i-Puigarnau 2009).

Research also shows, not surprisingly, that habitual behaviors and attitudes toward and perceptions of travel options within cities can be thwarted by a lack of travel options. Children who have been driven all their life are not likely to walk or bike for transport in adulthood, nor will they be inclined to consider taking public transit (Baslington 2008). For many teenagers, driving a car is seen as a rite of passage into adulthood, and for the old, driving is proof of status in today's society. Statistics do not seem to matter: astoundingly, fatality rates per licensed drivers aged 16 to 19 are on average 25 percent greater than for the general population (Imai and Mansfield 2008); for those 75 years and older, the rates are twice as high as for the population aged 24–65 (Loftipour ct al. 2013). In Saudi Arabia, the right to drive is sex-based and appears to be a more contentious issue today than dress code restrictions.

Environment

Motorized transportation systems are a major source of the three primary air pollutants, CO_2, NOx and VOC, which have long been linked to greenhouse gas emissions as well as to increasing rates of asthma and cancers. One study found a six-fold increase in childhood cancers in households living adjacent to high traffic roads (with more than 20,000 vehicles per day) (Pearson et al. 2000).

Legislative efforts to curb environmental pollution in Western nations lag behind the growing rates of motor-vehicle use. Already three decades old in the US, most of these efforts have aimed at main point sources of pollution (Figure 17.3a, shown in green as "off-highway" sources). Mitigation rather than reduction seems to be the approach taken to curb the environmental impacts of motorized transportation. Electric or biofuel-powered vehicles are touted as solutions, while highway construction continues unabated in many developing economies. Importantly, air and water quality are typically monitored at a coarse scale: in many urbanized regions, they are measured at less than a handful of points, which provide general levels of exposure but fail to identify the many "hotspots" present in areas where populations are concentrated. Yet such hotspots invariably correspond to lower-income areas, thus implicitly confirming the ill-effects of motorized transport.

Monetizing the environmental costs of vehicles by type shows that improvements could be achieved (Litman 2012). Local emissions for compact cars are 10 percent lower than those of an average car, and 20 percent lower in global warming costs. Vans and light trucks are estimated to produce 80 percent more local air pollution than an average car. For motorcycles, the local air pollution is twice that of an average car, but half the greenhouse gas emission. Electric vehicles only provide some relief, as they still produce brake, tire and road dust particulates comparable to gasoline-powered vehicles.

Beyond air pollution, roads, highways, bridges and car parks also contribute significantly to water pollution, with contaminants from vehicles and activities associated with transportation infrastructure being washed off vehicular areas. Another known environmental byproduct of motorization is outdoor ambient noise, which is steadily rising in populated areas. Numerous psycho-physiologic outcomes of sustained exposure to ambient noise are being documented to include annoyance, reduced performance, aggressive behavior and increased risk of myocardial infraction. In response, the World Health Organization produced guidelines on occupational and community noise. The EU followed by mandating noise surveillance and abatement programs in cities (Moudon 2009).

Health

The human health impacts of the over-reliance on inner-city motorized transport fall into two categories: motorized transport as an agent of death, injury and trauma; and of a rise in chronic diseases ranging from respiratory ailments to sedentary behaviors, which lead to mental stress, obesity, type 2 diabetes and cardio-vascular diseases (CVD) (World Health Organization 2013).

Motor-vehicle collisions are third in causes of disability-adjusted life year loss (DALYs) (Mathers et al. 2005): they are projected to be more than 10 times higher than those from malaria and tuberculosis, and twice those of HIV/AIDS in 2030. Fatalities and severe injury rates related to motor-vehicle collisions are higher than those of any war since World War II (World Health Organization 2004). Lebanon, Jordan and Saudi Arabia lead in both motor-vehicle-related DALYs and fatalities per capita, ahead of China, India, Egypt and

248   *Urban Design in the Arab World*

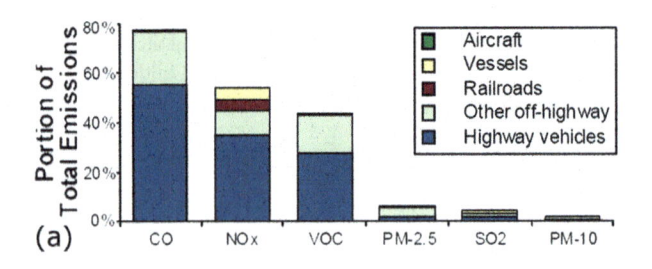

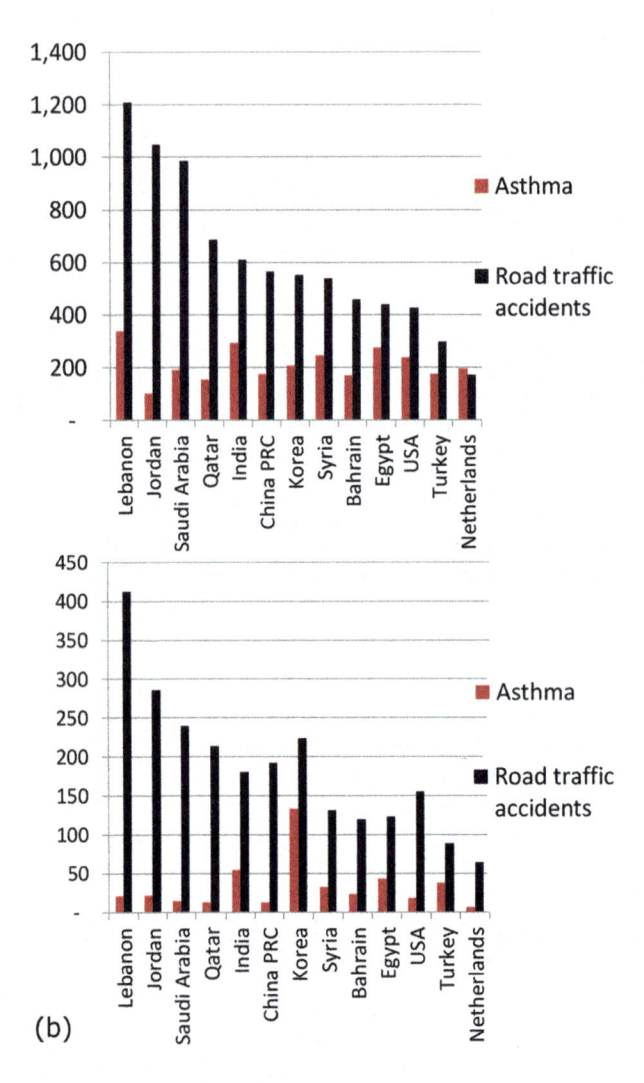

Figure 17.3   Evidence from environmental research
Note: (a) transportation as a major contributor of many air pollutants (2002); (b) health impacts of motorization. (1) estimated disability-adjusted life years (DALYs) per 100,000 population (2002): rates for road traffic accidents and asthma causes; (2) estimated deaths per 10,000 population (2002): rates for road traffic accidents and asthma causes.
Source: (a) Litman 2012, original source: ORNL (2005), Transportation Energy Data Book, US DOE, Table 12.1; (b) author (after World Health Organization 2004).

the US. Turkey and the Netherlands have the lowest rates of the group. Korea has similar fatality rates to Saudi Arabia's. DALYs and death rates go hand-in-hand with rates of asthma, a disease that is related to air quality (Figure 17.3b).

Chronic diseases have replaced infectious diseases as the number one public health concern worldwide. The use of automobiles, together with increased motorization and robotization at all levels of life (from Cuisinarts to escalators, and ubiquitous TVs to computers), has propelled the majority of urban residents to adhere to sedentary lifestyles. The prevalence of physical inactivity is at the root of many ailments, from CVD to obesity. In the US, 65 percent of US adults and adolescents are not sufficiently physically active to support good health and about 26 percent are not active at all. Research shows that the most popular form of physical activity across various population strata is walking (Lee and Moudon 2004). Yet, and not so ironically, walking is rarely considered as a mode of travel by most departments of transportation in developed economies.

Obesity rates have doubled in the 20 years between 1980 and 2000. Today 65 percent of the world's population lives in countries where overweight and obesity status kills more people than underweight status (World Health Organization 2013). Thus T.R. Malthus's early nineteenth-century predictions of the dangers of population growth that would preclude progress and strain "earth to produce subsistence for man," are meeting an unexpected challenge: mass processing of food products has facilitated the control of food costs to meet the demand of the sky-rocketing population growth over the last 50 years; yet processed foods are cheap only because they are low in nutrients and high in fat and sugar. In consequence, their consumption, which is acute in lower-income populations, parallels the increasing rates of overweight and obesity.

Today 69 percent of US adults are overweight and 36 percent are obese (National Institute of Diabetes and Digestive and Kidney Diseases (NIDDK) 2013). Overweight is defined as Body Mass Index (BMI) greater than 25 kg/m^2, corresponding to a 167 cm person weighing more than 70 kg. Being obese corresponds to a BMI greater than 30 kg/m^2 (167 cm and 84 kg). Overweight and obesity rates seem to be especially high in English-speaking countries (for example, the US, the UK, Ireland and Australia). In comparison, the Netherlands has about 48 percent overweight and 16 percent obese; and Greece has 55 percent overweight and 18 percent obese. The lowest rates are in China and Japan. However, while rates in Japan seem stable, widespread economic growth in China could lead to significant increases in these rates. One study found that between 1989 and 1997, Chinese men who acquired a vehicle experienced a 1.8 kg greater weight gain and had a 2 to 1 odds of becoming obese, compared with those whose vehicle ownership did not change (Bell et al. 2002).

Statistics available for the Arab world are hard to believe. A recent Canadian study noted that obesity rates in Saudi Arabia, Egypt and the United Arab Emirates are rising due to the adoption of Western-style eating habits. It estimated that approximately one-third of the population aged over 15 years in each of these countries is obese (Agriculture and Agri-Food Canada 2011). Several studies note that the rates differ substantially between men and women:

- In Saudi Arabia, among middle-aged people, 34 percent of men and 45 percent of women were obese (Baxter 2010).
- In Lebanon, for adult men and women (more than 20 years of age), the prevalence of overweight was 57.7 percent and 49.4 percent, respectively. In contrast, obesity was higher overall among women (18.8 percent) than men (14.3 percent) (Sibai et al. 2003).
- In northern Jordan, age-standardized prevalence of obesity was 28.1 percent for men and 53.1 percent for women (Khader et al. 2008).

How Motorways Came to Colonize Cities

With little doubt, the emphasis on motorized transport *in cities* over the past three or more decades has brought not the individual mobility that it first promised, but economic, social and environmental costs that cannot be sustained, especially in the light of projected growth in urban populations worldwide. How did we get where we are now? Why is motorization a global phenomenon?

The Allure of the Car

Motorways have their origins in the parkways of the eastern part of the US in the 1900s (Gandy 2003). Parkways were romantic encapsulations of the new motorcar age, which embodied man's elusive idea of leisure and freedom of movement through an erstwhile work-intensive countryside. A century later, this idea is still very much alive and indeed it is the leading theme of most of ads and commercials selling cars today. Tellingly, the length of motorcades and the number of Sports Utility Vehicles (SUVs), four-wheel drive (4WD), limos (and double limos), Suburbans, and so on, correlate perfectly with the rank and popularity of the traveling official. Even the most farsighted and ecologically minded politicians eschew the blinding hypocrisy of relying on such vehicles for local travel. Notable exceptions have been Mayor Mike Bloomberg of New York City, who rides the subway to work, and Boris Johnson, the cycling Mayor of London.

The automobile landscape has changed radically since the early twentieth century, when cars were relatively scarce and cities relatively small. Parkways morphed into autobahns and expressways during and after World War II. Also, while parkways were regional facilities, autobahns and motorways jumped in scale to that of national and international transport networks. First built in Germany and the US, the networks were originally envisioned as national rather than urban systems, and deemed essential for defense and industrial development (the US 1956 National Interstate and Defense Highways Act was an evident sign of the emergence of the military-industrial complex). So-called freeways only became *urban* systems after World War II, first in such outlier places as Detroit, the automobile capital, and Los Angeles, which was then less of a city than a city-region. Both the interstate network and the regional experiments were seen as "advanced" and "modern" ways to deal with the emergence of city-regions.

Opposition to the disruptive effects of massive engineering schemes on local neighborhoods quickly erupted in the 1970s, and the subsequent struggles in cities like New York, Boston (with the first grassroots opposition to an urban expressway), Toronto, Seattle and so on, have been documented (Gillham 2002). Yet, national and local governments continued to finance motorways in and around cities, thus facilitating a suburbanization that was welcome by landowners at the then-fringes of cities; and by both romantics and conservatives who had long seen the city as a place of business which was inappropriate for family life (Fishman 1987). Early on, a nascent car industry had of course been an integral part of the political machine, which in the US and Europe fostered the construction of motorways, and eventually exaggerated the delights of suburban life. In the US, the car industry successfully led efforts to eradicate all existing urban rail systems (Detroit and Los Angeles only being iconic examples) across the country. Today, the demise of rail systems and the savage history of urban and national "colonization" by motorways seem to be repeating themselves in places like Poland under the aegis of the EU. And motorways are the primary transport in the Arab world where, with the exception of Egypt, most of the French- and British-built rail systems have been abandoned or dismantled.

Most regrettably, the age of the motorway came along when the world population exploded. In retrospect, few could foresee the combined impact of population and economic growth on the demand for urban transport in the aftermath of World War II. Unfortunately, then and now, few take seriously Lewis Mumford's prediction that the building of a highway "has about the same result upon vegetation and human structures as the passage of a tornado or the blast of an atom bomb" (Mumford 1963).

Transportation Planners Take Over City Planning

Where were urban designers and planners at the crucial time when cities began to grow exponentially? Briefly, they were struggling with housing issues and debating early century neighborhood-level dogmas, which were pitching Modernism against Garden Cities (Hall 1988). To date, the cogent transportation dimension of Garden Cities (with a local and regional rail system linking small and large towns) continues to escape debate. Failed urban renewal programs saw US planners turn to regulate suburban development with a vague anti-urban model (decentralization, low densities and separation of land uses) (Walker 1982; Jacobs 2004). Post-World War II European planners launched into the development of satellite new towns with, again, untested models borrowing simplistically from either Modernist or Garden City theories. The Soviets took to mass-housing production pretty much in lieu of city planning. These models were and continue to be opportunistically or mindlessly exported to or adopted by the old colonies.

Meanwhile, the growing demand for national transportation systems consolidated the political base of the transportation engineering and planning professions. Their technical approach to "new mobility standards" further legitimized ongoing national defense strategies that included the development of motorways. While demonstrating the functional and economic utility of new motorway networks, they used their influence to develop a research base that came in handy to justify a growing, and eventually tentacular, body of standards and regulations touting greater mobility and safety. Their eventual grip on infrastructure development and research was built from the top down, using the original influence on national-level systems and trickling it down to state and local levels. These engineering-based empires are present to date in the US and Europe, and they are being exported to or emulated in many developing economies. Resistance to increased motorization exists in some cities, but it typically lacks a unified political platform and the resources to fight a rigid system of established standards. Demands for changing the post-World War II motorway networks in the inner-city and for adapting it to the reality and the needs of contemporary cities remain largely unmet.

Worldwide today, most cities of more than 500,000 that are not crisscrossed by major throughways linking them to a national road network are those in regions with low political and economic power. As a result, in many developing economies, motorways have come to embody wealth and prosperity. As shown, this is an unfortunate confusion of cause and effect. Motorization does not make cities rich and powerful. Now, the opposite seems to be true. At first glance, only a handful of such wealthy, "self-conscious" cities as Paris, Amsterdam and perhaps San Francisco, seem busy "de-motorizing" and removing cars from their midst. A more detailed review actually points to a reversal of pro-car policies in several surprising cases, some of which are discussed below.

New Practices

The evidence points to the obvious need to re-engineer the city. At the core of this re-engineering is revisiting and perhaps reversing policies that have favored the private automobile as a means of urban travel. By concentrating travelers in efficient and comfortable transit systems, facilitating the safe use of small motor-vehicles such as smart cars, motorbikes, mopeds, encouraging bicycling and walking for short trips, urban space can be regained, the quality of air and water can be improved, and people can lead more active lives. Such re-engineering approaches seem to be simple enough and do not require major public investment. Indeed they are being taken in a few major cities, which are de-emphasizing the automobile in the urban environment: Seoul, New York City and some large cities in China are such cases.

Seoul

Seoul used to be routinely referred to as a "concrete jungle" in the Asian press. With a population of 10.4 million, Seoul is one of the densest cities in the world. It is a city of superblocks with "avenues" as wide as 100 m crisscrossing its tight 353 km^2 geographic extent. These avenues contain at least six, but more commonly 16 or more, vehicular lanes. The Seoul superblock has its origins in the Westernization of Asian cities, under various waves of Japanese colonization, itself inspired by Baron Haussmann's Paris work in the mid-nineteenth century (Sohn 2003). As seen earlier, Korea has one of the highest traffic collision rates in the world. Since the mid-2000s, great efforts have been made to re-conquer Seoul from the car. Under Lee Myung-Bak, then Mayor of Seoul, and president of the country from 2008 to 2013, three projects have reclaimed street space for public use. They are anchored along 1.2 km of Sejongno Avenue (named after King Sejong, the creator of Hangeul, the Korean alphabet), downtown Seoul's principal north–south spine. At the northern end lies Gwanghwamun Gate, and at the southern end is Seoul's City Hall. Midway between City Hall and Gwanghwamun Gate is Cheonggye Square, where the Cheonggyecheon stream restoration project starts.

The first project, Gwanghwamun Square was inserted in the middle of Sejongno Avenue: 33 m wide and 600 m long (20,000 m²), the square now connects Gwanghwamun Gate and Cheonggye Square (Figure 17.4). Opened in August 2009, it includes many different activities divided into several sections.

The second project, Seoul Plaza, lies 600 m south of Gwanghwamun Square along Sejongno Avenue. Located in front of City Hall, it was the subject of a design competition in 2004 to replace a four-way intersection of four diagonal streets, which served as a shortcut to adjacent streets, and two small plazas, that had been squeezed within the intersecting diagonal streets (Figure 17.5). About 15,000 m², the new plaza was built in one-and-a-half months (March–April 2004), and transformed the number one institutional center of the metropolis into a people-oriented place.

The third intervention runs east–west, along a restored Cheonggyecheon Stream, which was the heart of Seoul for 600 years. Records of the Joseon period (1392–1897) indicate that 86 bridges had been built over the stream (Shin and Lee 2006; Park n.d.). During the Japanese colonial period (1910–45), those displaced from their farmlands migrated to Seoul and flocked along the banks of Cheonggyecheon. They built shanties and the Cheonggyecheon was used as an open sewage system. In the 1940s, a section of the river was covered for the first time, leading the way for a post-World War II complete canalization of the river to accommodate both sewage and vehicular traffic. In 1976, the Cheonggye Elevated Highway was constructed above the existing street as a 50–80 m wide and approximately 6.3 km long structure. It carried 102,747 out of the 168,556 vehicles using the corridor. The project to demolish the elevated highway and to replace it with a stream and linear park was announced in 2003, promoting three themes for urban rejuvenation: history, culture and nature

Figure 17.4   Seoul: Sejongno Avenue before and after Gwanghwamun Plaza
Note: Clockwise from top left: Sejongno Avenue 2005; Sejongno Avenue 2010; Sejongno Avenue 1995; Gwanghwamun Plaza 2010.
Source: 2010 Seoul: Seoul 2009/2010 urban form and landscape. Seoul: Seoul Metropolitan Government, 2010.

Re-Engineering the Twenty-First-Century City 253

Figure 17.5 Seoul Plaza in front of City Hall before and after
Note: Clockwise from top left: Seoul Plaza 2003; 2006; before 1995; ca. 2005; ca. 2000; 2006; 1990; 2010.
Source: Photographs dated 1990, 1995 and 2005 (2010 Seoul: Seoul 2009/2010 urban form and landscape. Seoul: Seoul Metropolitan Government, 2010); photographs dated 2000, 2003 and 2006 (courtesy of Young Ook Kim); photograph dated 2010 (*Yonhap News*, 27 May 2009).

Figure 17.6   Seoul, Cheonggyecheon
Note: Elevated highway and road ca. 2000 (left); restoration ca. 2005 (right).
Source: 2010 Seoul: Seoul 2009/2010 urban form and landscape. Seoul: Seoul Metropolitan Government, 2010.

(Figure 17.6). Two-lane streets remained on either side of the stream/park, which was sunk about 5 m from the street level. The restored stream runs the entire 6 km and is accessible at 17 locations. Accomplished in less than three years, this major project opened to the public in September 2005.

The district along the Cheonggyecheon stream was home to more than 200,000 merchants and 60,000 shops, many of which are being relocated to the outskirts of Seoul. Some gentrification is taking place, though more slowly than expected due to the downturn in the world's economy. Seoul planners claim that creating the environment with clean water and natural habitats was the most significant achievement of the project. The recovered stream helps to cool down the temperature in the nearby areas by an average of 3.6°C. After the demolition of the elevated highway, the number of vehicles entering downtown Seoul decreased by 2.3 percent; bus users increased by 1.4 percent; and subways users by 4.3 percent, for a daily average of 430,000 people (Park n.d.).

The case of Seoul is telling for a society with high motorization levels, comparable to those of Saudi Arabia, but lower than Lebanon's. While the scope of the changes made in very little time may be hard to completely emulate in places where public works proceed at a much slower pace, Seoul is a prime example of how vehicular traffic can be radically curbed within the heart of large and vibrant cities without major repercussions on their economy or on the mobility within them.

New York

Similarly to Seoul, the case of New York City shows that a mayor can make a difference. In the late 1990s, Mayor Rudolph Giuliani had put barriers on sidewalks along Fifth Avenue in Midtown Manhattan to prohibit pedestrians from crossing the street and to facilitate car traffic at some intersections. Although virulent protests forced a reversal of this policy, the fact that even the idea of restricting the heavy pedestrian traffic on one of the city's premier avenues had percolated up to the mayor's office was stupefying. Less than a decade later, however, under Mayor Bloomberg, not only have the city's traffic and transportation policies changed radically, but actual changes have being implemented that profoundly modify the city's streetscape. Bloomberg launched a Sustainability Agenda in 2007, embodied in the PlaNYC, which included congestion pricing. While the bid to levy a fee of $8.00 on all cars entering Manhattan during peak hours and on weekdays failed, the plan remained with its twin goal of attracting an additional one million people while reducing the city's carbon footprint by 30 percent by 2030. Janette Sadik-Khan was appointed as Commissioner of the Department of Transportation (NYDOT) in 2007, and in 2009, NYDOT's strategic plan laid out the accelerated goal of doubling bicycle commuting between 2007 and 2012 and tripling it by 2017. By 2011, the city, where bicycling was previously embraced by a tiny minority of "green" citizens and fearless messengers

Figure 17.7 New York City: Broadway and First Avenue
Note: (a) clockwise from top left: Times Square 2009; 2010; 2000; 2010; (b) First Avenue.
Source: (a) photographs dated 2000 and 2009 (courtesy Gordon Price); photographs dated 2010 (author); (b) author 2010.

competing with FedEx and DHL, had already reached its first goal. Remarkably, the rising volume of cyclists was accompanied by a decline in the numbers of cyclist injuries and fatalities (Pucher et al. 2010).

New York's cycling infrastructure was expanded to include cycle tracks, buffered bike lanes, special bike signals, bike boxes at intersections, and green-lane markings. In 2009, the 561-mile bicycle network had 134 miles of physically separate facilities; 282 miles of on-street bike lanes; and 146 miles of suggested bike routes without any special provision. The city's street space was being radically re-engineered. On Broadway, this most iconic street in Manhattan, more than one-third of the roadway was taken away from motorized traffic and given to cyclists, pedestrians and plaza areas complete with plants, tables and chairs. Unthinkable just a few years ago, Times Square is now closed to through-traffic (Figure 17.7a). The NYDOT won the battle waged by automobilists and especially taxi companies, who argued that the closing of the street would "kill" business, by first piloting the project and monitoring traffic during a trial period. The pilot demonstrated that indeed, as Jane Jacobs had noted two decades prior, existing traffic managed to flow elsewhere as this erstwhile main thoroughfare was closed to motor vehicles, without any new bottlenecks being created.

New York City also has an extensive Plaza Program with the aim of having all New Yorkers live within a 10-minute walk of quality open space. NYDOT works with not-for-profit organizations to create plazas throughout the city and to transform underused streets into vibrant social spaces.

The Bicycle

New York City is only one of the world cities developing its bicycle infrastructure. The two-wheeler is quickly becoming a fashionable choice for in-town travel (Figure 17.7b). By the end of World War II, bicycling was down-rated as the poor-person's means of travel, the victim of motorization. Only a few wealthy societies, notably in the Netherlands and Denmark, carried on nurturing their bicycle culture. In Japanese cities, bicycles continued to serve as a mid-range mode of travel between slow walking within residential neighborhoods and riding efficient transit systems. The advantages of bicycles or two-wheelers are obvious: they are inexpensive; the per-person space they take up is small, leading to great efficiencies in road use and parking flexibility (parking can easily take place at building entries, or even within dwellings and office spaces); travel speed for short inner-city distances are optimal (there is no waiting for the bus). If that wasn't enough, cycling is recognized today as non-polluting, quiet, and directly benefiting the health of its rider. The mode's undeniable qualities are now becoming obvious to many city leaders. Ironically, however, technological advances, not common sense, have elevated urban cycling to high status in wealthy cities. Indeed, bike-share programs had emerged in a few European cities in the 1980s, but the concept did not take off until about 2007, when the Paris Vélib program was launched, using credit-card-activated kiosks to collect fees and sensing technology to track the location of the "vehicles." With about 20,000 bicycles and more than 1,400 stations where people can pick up or drop off the bicycles, Vélib also benefits from major changes in the street network to accommodate cycle priority lanes and bike tracks.

Stylish Vélib (it is regularly tagged and vandalized by youth objecting to what they perceive as a bourgeois toy) helped to inspire many other bicycle-sharing programs, including those in Sao Paulo, Brazil; Montreal, Canada; Washington, DC; Mexico City, Mexico; Brisbane, Australia; and many other cities, all places where very few people ever bicycled in recent memory (Schroeder et al. 2009). This is a case where marrying cool technology and the aura of the "City of Light" trumped prior attempts at sustainable transportation policy. Indeed, only after Vélib became popular was attention paid to China, which had started to reverse its motorization policies earlier. In 2005 Beijing already had a 10,000-bicycle and 1,000-station bike-share program, an admittedly small program relative to the size of the city. With the world's largest number of bicycles and bicyclists, China had experienced a drastic decline in average bicycle ownership, from 197 bicycles per 100 households to 113 between 1993 and 2007 (Shaheen et al. 2011). Still, being a low GDP country, China's share of trips by bicycle had remained high, compared to that of Western countries (Tang et al. 2011).

In view of China's unprecedented growth in urban population, it became clear that continuing to focus on motorization within cities would lead to congestion and unbearably low levels of air quality. As a result, transit expansion plans were eventually given priority over roads, and several cities embarked on developing bike-share programs. Standing out from other bike-share programs that promote autonomous short-distance travel in the densest parts of cities, many Chinese bike-share programs are designed to complement transit expansion plans (Figure 17.8). The approach is therefore similar to that of Japan, where the bicycle is meant as an access mode to transit. It brings additional efficiencies to transit, allowing stations to be spaced farther apart than if riders were expected to walk to transit. Fewer stations mean fewer stops, which in turn mean faster transit service.

Within less than four years of the Beijing bike-share program, Hangzhou and Wuhan each had programs with 20,000 bicycles and about 1,000 stations, and Shanghai had about 7,000 bicycles and 2,500 stations. Chizhou, Jiangyin, Tongliang, Zhoushan now also have such programs (Tang et al. 2011). As of March 2011, Hangzhou Public Bicycle operated 60,600 bicycles with 2,416 fixed stations in eight of the city's core districts (Shaheen et al. 2011). The Hangzhou bike-share smart card is integrated with the public transit system. Research showed that users most frequently used a bike-sharing station closest to either home (40 percent) or work (40 percent) (Shaheen et al. 2011). Interestingly, bike-share card-holders had a higher rate of auto ownership than nonmembers, likely because those who did not have a car had their own bicycle.

Bicycles are becoming a viable means of urban travel in large cities. The potential of electric bike technology is particularly promising. In the next few years, China is expected to purchase 20 electric bicycles per 1,000 population (that is 24 million bicycles), compared to 30 in Germany and three in the US.

Future Directions

Evidence from research raises serious questions about the wisdom of furthering urban motorization. Cities need to be re-engineered to guarantee their effectiveness as centers of commerce and culture, as well as to insure their environmental soundness and the health of their population. If these goals fit the currency of sustainability, then sustainability must acknowledge that re-engineering the city starts with de-motorizing it. Seoul, New York, Hangzhou and many other cities focusing on de-motorization provide innovative directions and make strategies to re-capture urban space for humans real and reliable. These cities serve as models for future generations of urban design plans and interventions.

Figure 17.8 Shanghai public bicycles
Note: Clockwise from top left: street with bicycle ca. 2004; 2011; public bikes end of metro line 10, 2011; 2011.
Source: Author.

Old and New Cities

The Arab world is host to most of the ancient cities remaining on the globe. Respecting these cities' legacies while making them livable will generate immense benefits, locally and globally. Yet many of these cities are now littered with cars and parking lots. In the twenty-first century, their design and land use trails behind that of the European precedents that aimed at preserving their heritage and, in so doing, are now some of the most prized cities worldwide. The cases of Seoul and New York were introduced to show that returning urban space to people-supportive activities is no longer the privy of quaint European cultural ideology. Heralding history and culture through urban form has recently evolved to apply to newer urban places as well. Welcome by both indigenous populations and visitors, de-motorization is also an environmentally and economically sound investment. Using this approach to re-engineer the ancient cities of the Arab world is long overdue given the cities' high cultural status. A number of these cities were restructured with superblocks to accommodate the car in the second half of the twentieth century. It will take little more than political leadership to tame traffic within the superblocks, as has been done in Japan and Korea. Regarding the use of "smart" bicycles for short-distance inner-neighborhood travel, cultural differences, and specifically clothing customs, need not be a hindrance: long-robed women rode bikes in 1920s urban Europe, and today, women in similar attire exercise at outdoor gyms in Turkey's cities. The current proliferation of bike-share programs in places with no prior familiarity with this mode of travel indicates that the two-wheeler is as much a matter of fashion as it is a commonsensical approach to urban mobility. Perhaps bicycles will come last to the beautiful cities of the Levant and North Africa, but in the meantime a portion of the cars must be removed to make room for livability and grandeur. More walking and low-impact transit (for example, streetcars) are the way to get started, as shown in many cities and neighborhoods, rich and less rich, that have invested in the technology. Urban advocates faced with pedestrianization often raise the specter of gentrification (the process by which a new population of higher means displaces existing residents of lesser means) (Lees et al. 2010). Yet pedestrianization itself is not ever the cause of gentrification: it may be contemporaneous with gentrification only insofar as it is implemented in areas or neighborhoods where the land uses, together with land development regulations, favor the rich. By extension, any improvement to an area or neighborhood (for example, tree planting, street cleaning, emergence of "nice" new buildings, and so on) runs the risk of triggering gentrification, not because improvements necessarily displace the less rich, but because land development or redevelopment is by nature predatory. Measures to prevent or at least contain gentrification can be and have been taken if the political will to do so exists. Witness Rotterdam, Grenoble, Manchester, Raleigh, San Diego, Geneva and Istanbul, all cities of varying history, character and economy, which are vibrant in their own ways in their post-car reincarnation.

The Middle East also has some of the most "modern" cities in the world. The form and structure of these cities show that the forces of modernization are undeniably stronger than those of culture. Indeed the new cities of the desert have more in common with Las Vegas than with their ancient precedents: their forms look similar to those of "Sin City"; malls and cars dominate; and they both deny their desert environment. Yet large modern cities need not be entirely car-dependent. Again, the examples of Seoul, New York and Hangzhou serve as potent models of approaches to re-engineering.

Learning from Research

Seriously considering the results of many different strands of research suggests that the age of urban motorization needs to come to an end. Motor vehicles have their place in long-distance travel and as shared urban transit, but they can no longer invade cities, which should be reserved for their original beneficiaries, people. Research makes it evident that continuing to rely solely on cars for inner-city transportation carries enormous societal costs to the environment and human health. Furthermore, blindly investing in vehicular infrastructure does not improve urban mobility, and only stifles the productive use of valuable urban land. Motorization rates in the Arab world are already high relative to other countries and they plague both oil- and non-oil-producing countries. As in the US, they are disproportionate to GDP in Saudi Arabia, Lebanon and Jordan. In Syria and Turkey, they are proportionately much higher to GDP than in China. Without change, the future may be even bleaker. Arab countries won't be protected from the daunting prospects for motorization in the developing world, where car imports are projected to be 21 million per year, growing at 45 per cent per year, against 36.2 million cars per year in industrialized countries. Also, cars sold to developing countries will be produced primarily in China, at standards that are expected to be lower than those of cars produced in the US, Europe and Japan. If this is true, this means that cars coming to the developing world will pollute, kill, injure, harm at higher rates than projected today. Arab countries already have some of the highest rates of DALYs and fatalities from motor-vehicle collisions. Also associated with high levels of motorization and adding to the health burden are the startling obesity rates at a time when economic development has yet to match that of such obesogenic countries as the US, the UK, Australia and South Africa. Leaders need to figure out what is going on and seek to reverse the trends.

Reasons for optimism can be found in the number of elevated roadways which have been torn down and the several such roadways which were planned but never built (CNU 2011). Metro lines and Bus Rapid Transit (BRT) systems are beginning to appear in many large cities (Deng and Nelson 2011). Dubai has built about 100 km of rail since 2009 and has 100 km in planning. Shanghai has 400 km and a plan for 877 km by 2020. Riyadh, Saudi Arabia, with a population of more than one million and no organized public transportation system, advertises plans for a 1,200 km bus network within three years, including 120 km devoted to BRT, with 70 km of bus lanes, 900 bus stops and five park-and-ride sites (Lippert 2011). BRT joins the streetcar, an old technology, which, modernized, has been re-integrated into many medium-sized cities since the late twentieth century.

Leadership and Changing Professional Models

If re-engineering the city is de-motorizing it, perhaps the most important and effective approach is to rein in mainstream transportation experts. The cases of Seoul and New York, not to mention Paris and London, show that a mayor (Delanoé in Paris and Johnson in London) can have a decisive impact on a city's transportation system. Politicians and their staff also need to be closely watched for their typically cozy relationships with large-scale corporate road builders.

Urban designers have a chance to play an effective role because they have by tradition been the go-betweens in urban planning and development. Together with urban planners, urban designers must proactively integrate transportation into their portfolios and cease to leave the transportation sector to transportation specialists. The latter must be re-trained to abandon their focus on vehicles and turn to serving human not vehicular mobility and accessibility. Urban designers' versatility, relative lack of dogmatic principles (specifically relative to transportation and urban planning) and comprehensive approach to cities make them well-positioned to become facilitators of not only a rapprochement between transportation and urban planning, but also of a return to considering people (the person and the collective) as the center of urban life. Finally, to consolidate their impact on city planning, urban designers must make research from many fields an integral part of their professional portfolios. Doing so will give them the evidence base for implementing necessary and immediate change in cities.

References

Agriculture and Agri-Food Canada. 2011. *Saudi Arabia, Egypt and the United Arab Emirates Consumers, Markets, and Demand for Grain-Based Products.* International Markets Bureau Market Analysis Report [online]. Available at: http://www.gov.mb.ca/agriculture/statistics/agri-food/middle_east_grain_products_en.pdf [accessed: September 3, 2012].

Aliaga, C. 2005. *Populations and Social Conditions* [online]. Available at: http://epp.eurostat.ec.europa.eu/cache/ITY_OFFPUB/KS-NK-06-004/EN/KS-NK-06-004-EN.PDF [accessed: January 25, 2013].

Barnett, J. 2011. A Short Guide to 60 of the Newest Urbanisms. *Planning* [online], 77(4), 19–21. Available at: http://www.uc.edu/cdc/urban_database/urban_imaging/60_Newest_Urbanisms.pdf [accessed: October 11, 2014].

Baslington, H. 2008. Travel Socialization: A Social Theory of Travel Mode Behavior. *International Journal of Sustainable Transportation* [online], 2(2), 91–114. Available at: www.tandfonline.com/doi/abs/10.1080/15568310601187193 [accessed: October 14, 2014].

Baxter, E. 2010. Obesity Rate Among Saudi Men and Women Hits 70%. *Arabian Business.com* [online]. Available at: http://www.arabianbusiness.com/obesity-rate-among-saudi-men-women-hits-70--343513.html [accessed: September 3, 2012].

Bell, C., Ge, K. and Popkin, B.M. 2002. The Road to Obesity or the Path to Prevention: Motorized Transportation and Obesity in China. *Obesity Research* [online], 10(4), 277–83. Available at: http://onlinelibrary.wiley.com/doi/10.1038/oby.2002.38/full [accessed: October 11, 2014].

Ben-Joseph, E. 2012. *Rethinking a Lot: The Design and Culture of Parking.* Cambridge, MA: MIT Press.

Bertaud, A. 2001. *Metropolis: A Measure of the Spatial Organization of 7 Large Cities* [online]. Available at: http://alainbertaud.com/wp-content/uploads/2013/06/AB_Metropolis_Spatial_Organization.pdf [accessed: July 22, 2013].

Bialas-Motyl, A. 2008. Regional Road and Rail Networks. *Statistics in Focus- Transport* [online]. Available at: http://www.thepep.org/ClearingHouse/docfiles/Regional.Road.Rail.Transport.Networks.pdf [accessed: July 24, 2013].

Congress for New Urbanism (CNU). 2011. *Freeways Without Futures.* Available at: http://www.cnu.org/highways/freewayswithoutfutures [accessed: July 15, 2013].

Deng, T. and Nelson, J. 2011. Recent Developments in Bus Rapid Transit: A Review of the Literature. *Transport Reviews* [online], 31, 69–96. Available at: http://www.tandfonline.com/doi/abs/10.1080/01441647.2010.492455#.VDlErucVfbk [accessed: October 11, 2014].

Fishman, R. 1987. *Bourgeois Utopias: The Rise and Fall of Suburbia*. New York: Basic Books.
Fruin, S., Westerdahl, D., Sax, T., et al. 2007. Measurements and Predictors of On-road Ultrafine Particle Concentrations and Associated Pollutants in Los Angeles. *Atmospheric Environment* [online], 42(2), 207–219. Available at doi: 10.1016/jatmosenv.2007.09.057 [accessed: October 11, 2014].
Gandy, M. 2003. *Concrete and Clay, Reworking Nature in New York City*. Cambridge, MA: MIT Press.
Gillham, O. 2002. *The Limitless City, a Primer on the Urban Sprawl Debate*. Washington, DC: Island Press.
Hall, P.G. 1988. *Cities of Tomorrow, an Intellectual History of Urban Planning and Design and in the Twentieth Century*. Oxford: Blackwell Publishing.
Imai, S. and Mansfield, C. 2008. Disparities in Motor Vehicle Crash Fatalities of Young Drivers in North Carolina. *North Carolina Medical Journal* [online], 69(3), 182–7. Available at: http://intranet.ecu.edu/cs-dhs/chsrd/Pubs/upload/Dispariities-in-young-driver-mortality.pdf [accessed: October 11, 2014].
International Monetary Fund. 2011. *Gross Domestic Product (GDP) Per Capita 2009–2011*. World Economic Outlook Database. Available at: http://en.wikipedia.org/wiki/List_of_countries_by_GDP_%28PPP%29_per_capita [accessed: January 20, 2013].
Jacobs, J. 2004. *Dark Ages Ahead*. New York: Random House.
Kay, J.H. 1997. *Asphalt Nation: How the Automobile Took Over America, and How We Can Take It Back*. New York: Crown Publishers.
Khader, Y., Batieha, A., Ajlouni, H., et al. 2008. Obesity in Jordan: Prevalence, Associated Factors, Comorbidities, and Change in Prevalence Over Ten Years. *Metabolic Syndrome and Related Disorders* [online], 6(2), 113–12. Available at: http://online.liebertpub.com/doi/abs/10.1089/met.2007.0030 [accessed: October 11, 2014].
Lee, C. and Moudon, A.V. 2004. Physical Activity and Environmental Research in the Health Field: Implications for Urban and Transportation Planning Research and Practice. *Journal of Planning Literature* [online], 19(2), 147–81. Available at: http://jpl.sagepub.com/content/19/2/147.short [accessed: October 11, 2014].
Lees, L., Slater, T. and Wyly, E. (eds) 2010. *The Gentrification Reader*. London: Routledge.
Lippert, W. 2011. Big Public Transport Plans for Riyadh, Saudi Arabia. *Public Transport International* [online], 59(6), 24–5. Available at: http://trid.trb.org/view.aspx?id=1097820 [accessed: October 11, 2014].
Litman, T. 2012. *Transportation Cost and Benefit Analysis II—Air Pollution Costs*. Victoria Transport Policy Institute. Available at: http://www.vtpi.org/tca/tca0510.pdf [accessed: August 3, 2013].
Loftipour, S., Sayegh, R., Chakravarty, B., et al. 2013. Fatality and Injury Severity of Older Adult Motor Vehicle Collisions in Orange County, California 1998–2007. *Western Journal of Emergency Medicine* [online], 14(1), 63–68. Available at: http://www.ncbi.nlm.nih.gov/pmc/articles/PMC3583287/ [accessed: October 11, 2014].
Mathers, C., Ma Fat, D., Inoue, M., et al. 2005. Counting the Dead and What they Died From: An Assessment of the Global Status of Cause of Death Data. *Bulletin of the World Health Organization* [online], 83(3), 171–7. Available at: http://www.scielosp.org/scielo.php?pid=S0042-96862005000300009&script=sci_arttext&tlng=enen [accessed: October 11, 2014].
Moudon, A.V. 1992. A Catholic Approach to Organizing What Urban Designers Should Know. *Journal of Planning Literature* [online], 6(4), 331–49. Available at: http://jpl.sagepub.com/content/6/4/331 [accessed: October 11, 2014].
Moudon, A.V. 2009. Real Noise From the Urban Environment: How Ambient Community Noise Affects Health and What Can be Done About It. *Am J Prev Med* [online], 37(2), 167–71. Available at: http://www.sciencedirect.com/science/article/pii/S0749379709002955 [accessed: October 11, 2014].
Mumford, L. 1963. *The Highway and the City: Essays*. New York: Hartcourt: Brace & World.
National Institute of Diabetes and Digestive and Kidney Diseases (NIDDK). 2013. *Weight Control Information Network, National Health and Nutrition Examination Survey (NHANES 2009–2010)*. Available at: http://www.win.niddk.nih.gov/statistics/#b [accessed: January 20, 2013].
Park, K.-D. n.d. Cheonggyecheon Restoration Project. Seoul, Seoul Metropolitan Government, Korea. *JFES-WFEO Joint International Symposium on River Restoration*. Hiroshima University.
Pearson, R., Wachtel, H. and Ebi, K. 2000. Distance-weighted Traffic Density in Proximity to a Home is a Risk Factor for Leukemia and Other Childhood Cancers. *Journal of the Air & Waste Management*

Association [online], 50(2), 175–80. Available at: www.tandfonline.com/doi/abs/10.1080/10473289. 2000.10463998 [accessed: October 11, 2014].

Perry, M. 2000. Car Dependency and Culture in Beirut: Effects of an American Transport Paradigm. *Third World Planning Review (University of Liverpool)*, 22(4), 395–409.

Poole, R.W., Jr. 2006. *Reducing Congestion in Atlanta: A Bold New Approach to Increasing Mobility (No. Policy Study 351)*. Reason Foundation. Available at: http://reason.org/files/d1553a97e45b89fd4de254a121184c4b.pdf [accessed: August 3, 2013].

Public Purpose, The. 2002. *Lane Miles Per Capita 1999: US Urbanized Areas Over 1,000,000 (1999 Texas Transportation Institute Data)*. Available at: http://www.publicpurpose.com/hwy-tti99ratio.htm [accessed: January 20, 2013].

Pucher, J., Thorwaldson, L., Buehler, R. and Klein, N. 2010. Cycling in New York: Innovative Policies at the Urban Frontier. *World Transport Policy and Practice* [online], 16, 7–50. Available at: http://ejb.rutgers.edu/faculty/pucher/CyclingNY.pdf [accessed: October 11, 2014].

Schroeder, B., Hagen, J., Leve, Z. and Peñalosa, A. 2009. Bike-sharing Goes Viral. *Sustainable Transport*, Winter(21), 24–9. Available at: http://trid.trb.org/view.aspx?id=912617 [accessed: October 11, 2014].

Shaheen, S.A., Zhang, H., Martin, E. and Guzman, S. 2011. China's Hangzhou Public Bicycle: Understanding Early Adoption and Behavioral Response to Bikesharing. *Transportation Research Record* [online], 2247, 33–41. Available at: http://trb.metapress.com/content/14w44476227gt101/ [accessed: October 11, 2014].

Shin, J. and Lee, I. 2006. *Cheon Gye Cheon Restoration in Seoul, Korea*. Proceedings of the ICE—Civil Engineering [online], 159(4), 162–70. Available at: http://www.icevirtuallibrary.com/content/article/10.1680/cien.2006.159.4.162 [accessed: October 11, 2014].

Shoupe, D. 2005. *The High Cost of Free Parking*. Chicago: American Planning Association.

Sibai, A.M., Hwalla, N., Adra, N. and Rahal, B. 2003. Prevalence and Covariates of Obesity in Lebanon: Findings from the First Epidemiological Study. *Obesity Research* [online], 11, 1353–61. Available at: onlinelibrary.wiley.com/doi/10.1038/oby.2003.183/full [accessed: October 11, 2014].

Sohn, J.-M. 2003. Colonial City Planning and its Legacy, in *Seoul Twentieth Century: Growth & Change of the Last 100 Years*, edited by K.-J. Kim. Seoul: Seoul Development Institute, 433–60.

Tang, Y., Pan, H. and Shen, Q. 2011. *Bike-Renting Systems in Beijing, Shanghai and Hangzhou and Their Impact on Travel Behavior*. Transportation Research Board Annual Meeting. Washington, DC: Transportation Research Board.

U.S. Department of Transportation. 1990. *Nationwide Personal Transportation Survey*. Federal Highway Administration. Available at: http://nhts.ornl.gov [accessed: August 3, 2013].

U.S. Department of Transportation. 2000. *National Household Travel Survey*. Federal Highway Administration. Available at: http://nhts.ornl.gov [accessed: August 3, 2013].

van Ommeren, J. and Gutiérrez-i-Puigarnau, E. 2009. *Are Workers With a Long Commute Less Productive? An Empirical Analysis of Absenteeism*. Available at: http://www.tinbergen.nl/discussionpapers/09014.pdf [accessed: September 4, 2012].

Walker, D. 1982. *The Architecture and Planning of Milton Keynes*. London: The Architectural Press.

World Bank. 2008. *Number of Motor Vehicles Per 1,000 People*. International Road Federation, World Road Statistics and Data Files. Available at: http://en.wikipedia.org/wiki/List_of_countries_by_vehicles_per_capita [accessed: January 20, 2013].

World Health Organization. 2004. *Death and DALY Estimates by Cause and WHO Member State 2002*. Available at: www.who.int/entity/healthinfo/statistics/bodgbddeathdalyestimates.xls [accessed: January 20, 2012].

World Health Organization. 2013. *Obesity and Overweight*. Fact Sheet No 311. Available at: http://www.who.int/mediacentre/factsheets/fs311/en/ [accessed: January 20, 2013].

Index

Events

1954, earthquake, Saida, Lebanon 73
1990s, Resistance, Islamic Republic of Imbaba, Egypt 216
9/11 (September 11, 2001) 1, 17, 23

Aga Khan Award for Architecture 2, 6, 21, 29, 32, 33, 35
    Aga Khan Award for Architecture, 11th cycle 32, 33, 35
    Aga Khan Award for Architecture, 12th cycle 33
Arab Renaissance 201
Arab Spring 1, 9, 23, 32, 65, 213
Ashura 193
Assassinations
    1981, Sadat 216
    2005, Rafic Hariri 107, 135

Earth Summit 1992, Rio de Janeiro 117

Hajj 100, 102, 185
    days 185
    infrastructures 100, 196
    season 185, 186, 189
Haret Hreik charette, Department of Architecture and Design, AUB 41, 43

International competition(s), urban design 58, 60, 89
    2000, Garden of Forgiveness 60
    2004, Seoul Plaza 252
    2004, the Grand Axis, Martyrs' Square 60
    2006, King Abdullah Financial District (KAFD) 168
    2007, Haret Hreik 41
    Holy cities 177, 178
    International landscape design competition, City Park, Solidere 63
    Jabal Omar 177, 179, 190, 191
    UIA international open event, Souqs of Beirut, Solidere, 1994 58
    UIA open design competition, Beirut's House of Arts and Culture, Ministry of Culture, Solidere 60
International conferences 2, 21, 177
    2010 International Conference, Preservation and Rehabilitation of Iraqi City Centers, Mayoralty of Baghdad 177
    City Debates 2011, Department of Architecture and Design, AUB 5
    City Debates 2012, Department of Architecture and Design, AUB 2, 7, 177, 179, 186, 190, 192, 193, 194

Invasions, occupations
    1982, Israeli Invasion, Saida, Lebanon 73
    2003 US-led invasion, Baghdad, Iraq 76, 207
    2006–8, Martyrs' Square, Pro-Syrian occupation, Beirut 107
    American occupation, Iraq 80
    British Occupation, Egypt 214
    French invasion, Algeria 18
    Napoleon, short-lived urban-based occupation of Egypt 18
    Tahrir Square, occupation 213, 218

Nahr el Bared Relief Campaign 131, 144

Protests
    Anti-Syrian protest, 2005, Beirut 107
    Antiwar protests, Vietnam War, 1960s 219
    Bread Riots, protest against capitalism, 1977, Egypt 216
    Nationwide protest, Egyptians, January 25, 2011 217, 218, 219, 221
    Policy, restricting the heavy pedestrian traffic, 1990s, New York, Fifth Avenue 254
    Public protest, Egypt 214, 219

Revolutions
    1919 revolution, Egypt 214
    1952 revolution, Egypt 214
    1958 Iraqi National Revolution 205
    2011 Egyptian revolution 9, 213, 214, 217, 218
    2011 Tunisian revolution 217
    Arab Revolution 1
    Tunisian Revolution 217

Uprising, Iraq, 1991 194

Wars
    1960s, Vietnam War 219
    1967 war, Egypt 214
    1975–90 civil war, Lebanon 40, 51, 58, 63, 87, 104, 106, 107, 135, 144
    2006 war between Israel and Hezbollah 7, 39, 40, 41, 131
    Arab-Israeli war 39
    Civil war, Syria, ongoing 115, 129
    Cold War 205
    Gulf War 76, 207
    Iran–Iraq War 207
    World War I 214
    World War II 147, 214, 247, 250, 251, 252, 255

Institutions, Organizations, and Political Parties

Abu Dhabi Education Council 231
Abu Dhabi Urban Planning Council (UPC) 70, 227, 228, 229, 230, 231, 232, 233, 234, 235, 237, 238, 239, 240, 241
Adrian Dalsey, Larry Hillblom, Robert Lynn (DHL) 255
Aga Khan Trust for Culture 35
   Regionalism in Architecture, Modern Approaches to Regionalism and Symbolism in Its Regional and Contemporary Context 32
Agence France Presse (AFP) 209
Agorastidou + Noukakis 60
Al-Azhar University, madrasa, Cairo 100
Al-Bayt University, Baghdad 192, 193
Al-Manar Television, Lebanon 47
Al Rasheed Street Center, Baghdad 209
Allies & Morrison 57
Amal, political party, Lebanon 135, 142
American Planning Association 218
American University of Beirut (AUB) 2, 7, 8, 35, 39, 40, 41, 43, 44, 47, 104, 131, 132, 134, 138, 139, 177
   Center for Civic Engagement and Community Service (CCECS) 47, 131, 132, 134
   Community Projects and Development Unit (CPDU) 8, 47
   Department of Architecture and Design 40, 43, 131
   Department of Civil and Environmental Engineering (CEE) 134
   Department of Landscape Design and Ecological Management (LDEM) 44, 47, 134
   Office of Institutional Research and Assessment (OIRA) 132
   Reconstruction Unit (RU) 39, 40, 41, 43, 44, 49, 131
American University of Cairo 218
Architectural Association (AA), London 90, 97, 98, 99, 101, 102, 103, 105, 107, 109, 148, 196
   Diploma Unit 101, 102, 103, 105
   Projective Cities 97, 98, 99, 107, 109
Archnet-IJAR 214
Ashkal al Alwan Homeworks, Beirut 85
Associations de la Sauveguard de la Ville de Tunis, Nabeul 36
Atelier Lion associés, Paris 183, 187, 191

Baath, political party, Iraq 205
Baghdad Municipality, Mayoralty 76, 177, 191, 208, 209
Beirut Arab University 135
Beirut Art Center 85
Beirut Municipality 80, 143
Beit bil-Jnoub [*House in the South*] 47, 48, 49
Biomedical R&D, Riyadh 9, 168
Birdlife International 46, 47

Capital Market Authority, Saudi Arabia 168
Central Fund for the Displaced, Lebanon 47
Cities Alliance (2006), Brussels 115

Coalition Provisional Authority (CPA), Iraq 210
Congress of New Urbanism (CNU), United States of America 258
Council for Development and Reconstruction (CDR), Lebanon 39, 139, 150, 154
Council of the South, Lebanon 47, 48
Cruz y Ortiz 60

Dar Al-Handasah 182, 186, 188, 189
Department of Energy (DOE), United States of America 248
Dewan Architects & Engineers 11, 177, 182, 193, 194
Dirab Development Company, Riyadh 168

Emirates 24/7, Dubai 193
European Neighborhood Partnership (ENP) 75
European Neighborhood Policy Instrument and Cross Border Cooperation (ENPI-CBC) 75
European Union (EU) 75, 245, 247, 250

Facebook 216, 217
Fatah el Islam 131
FedEx 255
Fields Operation 148
Free Patriotic Movement 142
Future Party, Lebanon 135, 138, 142

G-Mimari Architectural 209
Gallery Sfeir-Semler, Beirut 85
German Technical Cooperation (GTZ), Gesellschaft für Internationale Zusammenarbeit (GIZ) 8, 115, 116, 117, 118, 119, 121, 122, 124, 125
Ghobeiri Municipality 131, 135, 136, 138, 142
Greater Riyadh Authority 36
Gulf Cooperation Council (GCC) 4
Gustafson Porter 59

Hajj Research Center 186
Haret Hreik Municipality 42
   Haret Hreik Municipal Council 42
Hariri Foundation for Sustainable Human Development (HFSHD), Lebanon 131, 134, 139, 143
Harvard Graduate School of Design 97
Harvard University 21
Henning Larsen Architects 9, 10, 167, 168, 169, 170, 171, 172, 173
Herzog & de Meuron 59
Hezbollah, political party, Lebanon 23, 39, 40, 41, 42, 43, 47, 131, 142
Higher Committee of Religious Affairs, Saudi Arabia
Higher Council of Relief, Beirut 47
House of Arts and Culture, Beirut 60

International Bank for Reconstruction and Development (IBRD) 203, 208
International Renewable Energy Agency (IRENA) 235
International Union for the Convention of Nature (IUCN) 72

Iraqi Development Board (IDB) 203
Iraqi Gazette 202
Iraqi Public Works Department (PWD) 201, 205

Jabal Omar Development Company (JODC), Riyadh 190
Jihad al-Bina, Lebanon 40
Jones Lang LaSalle 189

Kefaya, opposition movement, Egypt 216
Khatib and Alami 67, 72, 75, 76, 209
King Abdullah University of Science and Technology 100
Krupp Company, Germany 117

Lebanese Army Forces 131
Lebanese Council of Ministers 47
Lebanese Environment and Development Observatory (LEDO) 150, 154
Lebanese Order of Engineers and Architects (OEA) 42
Lebanese University 104
Liverpool University 203

March 8th, political party, Lebanon 135
March 14th, political party, Lebanon 135
Masdar Institute of Science and Technology (MIST) 235
Massachusetts Institute of Technology 21
MedCities 75
Ministry of Environment, Lebanon 150, 154
Ministry of Justice, Iraq 207
Municipal Council, al-Qleileh 47
Muslim Brotherhood 216

National Democratic Party (NDP), political party, Egypt 218
National Institute of Diabetes and Digestive and Kidney Diseases (NIDDK) 249
New York Department of Transportation (NYDOT) 254, 255
Nile Land & Agricultural Company, Egypt 214

Oak Ridge National Laboratory (ORNL), United States of America 248
Office for Metropolitan Architecture (OMA) 148

Politecnico of Torino 192
PolService Company, Poland 205, 206, 209
Port Authority, Beirut Central District 62
PROAP 60
Professors World Peace Academy 21
Public Pension Agency, Saudi Arabia 168
Public Record office, Iraq, National Archives of London 201

Rashid Theatre, Baghdad 207
Robert Matthew Johnson-Marshall (RMJM) 186, 187, 188
RTKL Associates Inc. 220
Rusafa, Municipality, Baghdad 207

Sabra Market Street Committee, Beirut Metropolitan Region 134
Saddam Art Center, Baghdad 207

Saida municipality 72, 75, 79
Saudi Joint Stock Company 190
Saudi Ministry of the Interior 187
Skidmore Owings & Merrill (SOM) 62
Society for the Protection of Nature in Lebanon (SPNL) 46, 47
Solidere, Beirut 7, 51, 53, 54, 55, 56, 57, 58, 59, 60, 61, 62, 63, 64, 106, 107, 108, 195, 209
Stoss LU 148
Sukleen 138, 143
Syndicate of Journalists, Egypt 216
Syrian Refugees' Collective Shelters, 2013 132

The Guardian 189

U.S. Department of Transportation 246
Uberbau 115, 116, 117, 119, 121, 122, 124, 125, 128
UNESCO Protocol 52
UN-HABITAT 48, 65, 208, 227
Union of International Architects (UIA) 58, 60
Union of Municipalities of Sour, Bint Jbeil and Jabal 'Amil, Lebanon 48
United Nations (UN) 39, 117, 207, 227
United Nations Development Programme (UNDP) 40, 134
United Nations Educational, Scientific and Cultural Organization (UNESCO) 52
United Nations Human Settlements Program (UNHSP) 208
United Nations Interim Force in Lebanon (UNIFIL) 46, 47
Urban Agriculture Training Center, Saida 132, 133
Urban Task Force, United Kingdom 70

Valode et Pistre 60

Wa'd, Lebanon 41, 43, 44
Waqf, Awqaf 22, 46, 195
West 8 148
World Bank 177, 203, 204, 244
World Health Organization (WHO) 70, 247, 248, 249

Youth Mobilization and Development in Beirut and its Suburbs 134
YouTube 216

People

Abdul Nasser, Gamal, President, Egypt 1, 17
Abu-Lughod, Janet 22
Al-Asad, Mohammad 1, 4, 9
Al Assam, Mohamed 193, 194
Al-Bar, Osama, Mayor, Makkah 189
al-Essawi, Khalid 192
Al-Farabi 18
Al-Harithy, Howayda 3, 4, 6, 7, 39, 49, 131
Al-Hathloul, Saleh 22
Al-Mulhim, Mahmoud 192

Al Nahyan, Mohamed Bin Zayed, Sheikh Crown Prince of Abu Dhabi, Chairman of the Abu Dhabi Executive Council 232
Akbar, Jamel 22
Allen, Stan 148
AlSayyad, Nezar 1, 2, 3, 4, 17, 18, 19, 20, 21, 22, 23, 49, 177, 190, 214
Alusi, Maath 209
Angawi, Sami 177, 181, 184, 185, 186
Ardlan, Nader 22

Bacos, Charles 214
Bakhtiar, Laila 22
Batatu, Hanna 32
Baudelaire, Charles 87
Bayat, Asef 23
Becker, Louis 170, 171, 172, 174
Ben Ali, Zine El Abidine, President, Tunisia 217
Benjamin, Walter 87, 88
Berri, Nabih, Speaker of the House 135
Bianca, Stefano 5, 177, 180, 181, 185, 188, 207, 209
Bloomberg, Michael, Mayor, New York 250, 254
Bollens, Scott 132
Brunschvig, Robert 19

Carr-Ellison, Drew 170, 171, 172
Chadirji, Rifat 207
Cherry, Nathan 9, 213, 218
Churchill, Winston 222
Cinà, Giuseppe 177, 192, 193, 194
Coke, Richard 201
Cooperson, Mike 200
Corner, James 86, 88, 89, 148
Cuthbert, Alexander 1

Dash, Kevin 57, 60
De Planhol, Xavier 19
Debord, Guy 88
Delanoé, Bertrand, Mayor, Paris 259
Doxiadis, D.A. 76, 204, 205
Durand, Jean-Nicolas-Louis 97, 110

Ecochard, Michel 135, 145
Ehlers, Eckart 22
Eisenmann, Peter 90, 94
El-Arnaout, Sateh 177, 194, 195
El Chami, Yasmina 104, 107, 109, 110
Elsheshtawy, Yasser 1, 2, 4, 5
Empain, Baron 214

Fakhro, Deena 100, 101, 102, 103, 196
Farouk, King, Egypt 214
Fawaz, Mona 4, 6, 41, 42, 43, 44, 67
Foster, Norman 58

Ganczarski, Marcin 97, 98, 99

Gilloch, Graeme 88
Giuliani, Rudolph, Mayor, New York 254
Guattari, Félix 90, 94
Gulick, John 202
Gustafson, Katherine 60

Habermas, Jürgen 218
Hadid, Zaha 58, 60
Hakim, Besim 22
Hamadeh, Shirine 2, 5
Hamieh, Christine Sylva 40
Harb, Mona 4, 6, 23, 41, 42, 43, 44, 67
Hariri, Rafic 63, 107, 135
Hariri, Saad 135
Haussmann, Baron 52, 149, 180, 192, 200, 207, 208, 251
Heidegger, Martin 29
Hejduk, John 87, 88
Hempel, Anoushka 60
Herrera, Linda 216
Hourani, Albert Habib 20
Howard, Ebenezer 202
Hussein, Saddam 193, 194, 207

Ibn Khaldun 18
Imam al Hussein 193, 194
Ismail, Adel 20
Ismail Pasha, Khedive 214

Jabr, Abdelhalim 177
Jacobs, Jane 52, 243, 250, 255
Jacoby, Sam 8, 97, 180, 196
Jairazbhoy, Rafique Ali 20
Jeshi, Hassan 43
Johnson, Boris, Mayor of London 250, 259

Koolhaas, Rem 89, 96

Lapidus, Ira 20, 21
Le Corbusier 104
Le Roy, Julien-David 110
Le Tourneau, Roger 19
Lee, Christopher 110
Lion, Yves 177, 179, 186, 190, 192
Lu, Duanfang 3
Lutyens, Edwin, Sir 201
Lynch, Kevin 89

Mac Ginty, Roger 40
Mackay, Benton 67
Madfai, Qahtan 205
Mahmood, Saba 23
Makhzoumi, Jala 4, 6, 7, 44, 45, 46, 47, 65, 67, 68, 72, 73, 75, 80, 91
Maki, Fumihiko 58, 60
Maksud, George 214
Malthus, Thomas Robert 249

Mansour, Fadi 104, 105
Marçais, Georges 19, 20
Marçais, William 19, 20
Marino, Peter 60
Massignon, Louis 19
McCann, Eugene J. 80
McHarg, Ian 89
Midhat Pasha 200
Mitchell, Tim 22
Moneo, Rafael 58, 60
Monier, Ahmed 20
Mossop, Elisabeth 150
Mostafavi, Mohsen 72, 90, 148
Mubarak, Hosni, President, Egypt 216, 217, 218, 221
Mugerauer, Robert 29
Mukhtar Ibrahim, Ahmad 203
Mumford, Lewis 67, 250
Myung-Bak, Lee, Mayor of Seoul, president of the country from 2008 to 2013 251

Najle, Ciro 72, 90, 94, 148
Napoleon, Bonaparte 18
Nasr, Joe 2, 3, 5, 6
Nasrallah, Hassan 40
Nouvel, Jean 58

Obama, Barack, President, United States of America 219
Olmsted, Frederick Law 149

Pamuk, Orhan 3
Peters, Francis E. 178, 183, 184
Piano, Renzo 58
Poole, Kathy 148, 149
Pope Sixtus V 99, 180, 192
Prophet, the, Muhammad 17, 180, 187, 183, 193
Pungetti, Gloria 44, 72, 91

Qassem, Abdulkarim 205
Quatremère de Quincy, Antoine-Chrysostome 97, 110

Rheingold, Howard 216
Rogers, Richard 58, 60
Roy, Ananya 3

Sadat, Anwar, President, Egypt 216
Sadik-Khan, Janette 254
Saggaf, Abdul Aziz 21
Said, Edward 3, 21, 22
Said, Khalid 217
Salama, Hussam Hussein 9, 213, 214
Sauvaget, Jean 19, 20
Schwartz, Martha 60
Schwarzer, Mitchell 6, 7
Sejong, King 251
Serageldin, Ismail 21
Shibli, Rabih 8, 45, 47, 48, 49, 131
Sofio, Frantz 214

Spivak, Gaytri 22
Spoerry, Francois 57
Stern, Samuel Miklos 20
Stokman, Antje 148, 149
Sultan Abdulmecid 200

Tange, Kenzo 66
Tignor, Robert 214
Touba, El Sayed 177, 180, 182, 185, 186, 187, 188, 189, 194, 195, 196
Tschumi, Bernard 89
Turner, Tom 89

Vidal, Olivier 60
Vidler, Anthony 88
Volait, Mercedes 2, 3, 203
von Grunebaum, Gustave 19, 20, 21

Waldheim, Charles 89, 90, 148
Wang, Yuwei 97
Weber, Max 18, 20
Wilson, James Mollison 201
Woods, Lebbeus 86, 87, 88, 94

Zaghlul, Saad 214
Zenlund, Darrow 32

Places

Airport(s)
    Abu Dhabi, international airport 234, 236
    Charles de Gaulle's Terminal 1, Paris 101
    Jedda airport 100, 196
    King Abdulaziz International Airport 100
    Tegel Airport, Berlin 100
Al Dahiya 41, 42, 67
Ancient Tell, Beirut Central District 52, 61, 108
Andalusian Spain 34
Arab region(s) 22, 29, 32, 131
Aurelian Wall, Rome 98
Avenue(s)
    Avenue Habib Bourquibah, Tunis 35, 36
    Avenues, New York 254
    Avenues, Seoul 251
    Emile Lahoud Avenue, Beirut 90
    Fifth Avenue, New York 254
    First Avenue, New York 255
    Sejongno Avenue, Seoul 251, 252
Boulevard(s)
    Abu Nuwas river boulevard, Baghdad 76
    Grand Boulevards, Paris 200
    Maritime boulevard, Saida 73, 75
    Park Avenue, New York 52
Bridge(s)
    6 October Bridge, Cairo 218, 221
    Qasr al-Nil Bridge, Cairo 218

Building(s)
  Citadel
    Citadel, Aleppo 116, 118, 127
    City Hall, Seoul 251, 252, 253
    Çoban Mustafa Pasa Complex, Istanbul 100, 101
    Egyptian museum, national, Cairo 214, 218, 221, 222
    Faneuil Hall, Boston 221
    Grand Theatre, Beirut Central District 55, 60
    Hotel Palestine, Baghdad 12
    Lazaria Center, Beirut Central District 56
    Madinat al-Zahra Museum, Cordoba 34
  Grand Serail, Beirut Central District 52
  Maqam
    Maqam Nabi 'Umran, al-Qleileh 45, 46
  Mosque(s)
    Abu Hanifa Mosque, Baghdad 177, 193
    Al-Azhar Mosque, Cairo 101
    Al-Masjid al Haram, Makkah 186
    El Dana mosque, Beirut 138
    Grand Mosque, Makkah 189
    Holy Mosque, Makkah 179, 182, 185, 187, 188, 189
    Mohammad Al-Amin Mosque, Beirut Central District 195
    Omar Makram Mosque, Cairo 218
    Prophet's Mosque, Madinah 180, 183
    Sultan Hassan Mosque, Cairo 215
    Umayyad Mosque, Aleppo 129
  National Gallery, London 221
  Nile Hilton Hotel, Cairo 218
  Sokollu Mehmet Pasa Complex, Istanbul 100, 101
  Starco Center, Beirut Central District 56

City(ies)
  Aleppo 4, 8, 19, 20, 30, 32, 115, 116, 117, 118, 119, 120, 121, 122, 123, 124, 126, 127, 128
  Amman 67, 69
  Baghdad 7, 9, 12, 65, 66, 67, 71, 72, 75, 76, 77, 78, 79, 80, 177, 178, 191, 192, 193, 199, 200, 201, 202, 203, 204, 207, 208, 209, 210, 211
  Beijing 70, 256
  Beirut 2, 3, 4, 6, 7, 8, 9, 23, 35, 39, 40, 41, 42, 44, 51, 52, 53, 54, 55, 56, 58, 60, 61, 62, 63, 64, 65, 67, 71, 72, 80, 85, 86, 87, 89, 90, 91, 94, 96, 104, 106, 107, 108, 110, 120, 131, 132, 134, 135, 136, 138, 142, 143, 147, 148, 151, 152, 153, 154, 155, 158, 159, 161, 162, 177, 178, 189, 191, 195, 202, 203, 209, 245, 246
  Boston 149, 221, 250
  Cairo 3, 4, 13, 20, 22, 23, 65, 75, 100, 101, 184, 185, 186, 204, 213, 214, 215, 216, 217, 218, 219, 220, 222
    Paris of the Nile 218
  Copenhagen 167, 170
  Cyprus 210
  Dallas 58, 244
  Damascus 3, 4, 19, 20, 22, 65, 66, 67, 68, 69, 71, 80, 119, 167, 168, 184
  Doha 35, 63
  Erbil 69, 80
  Fez 19, 208
  Frankfurt 71
  Geneva 258
  Giza 219
  Grenoble 258
  Hangzhou 256, 258
  Heliopolis 214
  Helwan 219
  Istanbul 71, 100, 170, 184, 186, 187, 246, 258
  Jeddah 8, 100, 185, 196
  Jerusalem 4, 178, 195
  Karbala 9, 11, 177, 178, 180, 182, 199, 194, 195
  Liverpool 172, 203
  London 85, 167, 171, 196, 201, 219, 220, 245, 250, 259
  Los Angeles 250
  Madinah 18, 100, 177, 178, 180, 181, 183, 185, 186, 188, 189, 193, 194, 196
  Makkah [Mecca] 9, 100, 101, 102, 103, 110, 177, 178, 179, 180, 181, 182, 183, 184, 185, 186, 187, 188, 189, 193, 194, 195, 196
  Manchester 258
  Manhattan 254, 255
  Masdar 14, 233, 234, 235, 236, 238, 239, 240
  Memphis 17
  Najaf 117, 180, 182, 193, 194, 195, 149, 186, 187, 192, 200, 208, 214, 218, 221, 251, 256, 259
  New Delhi 201
  New York 14, 85, 172, 219, 220, 221, 250, 251, 254, 255, 256, 257, 258, 259
  Paris 85, 87, 88, 101
  Raleigh 258
  Rome 97, 98, 99, 100, 110, 180, 192
  Rotterdam 258
  Rourkela, Indian New Town 117
  Saida 7, 67, 69, 72, 73, 74, 75, 77, 79, 80, 132
  San Diego 258
  Sanaa 21
  Seoul 14, 251, 252, 253, 254, 256, 257, 258
  Shanghai 245, 256, 257, 258
  Sour 48
  Taif 100, 185, 196
  Tehran 23
  Tripoli, Lebanon 72
  Wuhan 256
  Yathrib 17, 18
Conservation Area, Beirut Central District 52, 61, 108
Corniche
  Abu Nuwas River Corniche green corridor, Baghdad 76
  Beirut Corniche 62
  Corniche El Nahr, Beirut 87, 90, 91, 94

Pierre Gemayel Corniche, Beirut 90
Country(ies)
   Afghanistan 1, 17
   China 18, 247, 249, 251, 256, 257, 258
   Egypt 1, 9, 13, 17, 18, 20, 22, 65, 195, 203, 213, 214, 216, 217, 218, 219, 222, 244, 247, 249, 250
   India 18, 20, 117, 200, 201, 202, 247
      Mughal 20
   Indonesia 23, 200
   Iran 1, 17, 22, 40, 203, 207
   Iraq 9, 11, 12, 22, 65, 75, 76, 79, 80, 177, 178, 180, 182, 186, 192, 193, 194, 199, 201, 202, 203, 204, 205, 207, 208, 209
   Israel 7, 39, 40, 41, 73, 131, 132, 216
   Italy 58, 97
   Japan 249, 251, 252, 255, 256, 257, 258
   Korea 243, 249, 251, 257
   Kuwait 21, 40
   Lebanon
      North Lebanon 131
      Northern suburbs, Lebanon 90
      Southern Lebanon 39, 44
      Southern suburbs, Lebanon 7, 23, 40, 41, 42, 131
   Namibia 200
   Pakistan 1, 17
   Palestine, Occupied Palestinian Territories 65, 73, 132, 135
   Qatar 35, 40, 54, 63
   Saudi Arabia 9, 10, 21, 36, 40, 54, 100, 167, 168, 171, 172, 173, 187, 190, 195, 196, 247, 249, 254, 258
   South Korea 244
   Switzerland 243
   Syria 17, 19, 22, 30, 32, 65, 68, 107, 115, 118, 119, 120, 128, 129, 132, 135, 144, 245, 258
   Tunis 23, 36, 217
   Turkey 1, 17, 23, 101, 118, 119, 188, 244, 249, 257, 258
   United States 6, 67, 244
   Vietnam 219

District(s)
   Al Ismailiya district, Cairo 214
   Al Medina, Aleppo 127
   Al Rihab, Beirut Metropolitan Region 131, 135
   Beirut Central District (BCD) 4, 7, 51, 52, 53, 54, 55, 56, 58, 60, 61, 62, 63, 64, 106, 108
   Canary Wharf, London 171
   Capital District, Abu Dhabi 14, 233, 234, 240
   Dirab, Riyadh 168, 170, 171, 172, 173, 174, 175
   Garden City, Cairo 214
   Gemmayzeh, Beirut 108
   Ghobeiri, Beirut Metropolitan Region 131, 135, 136, 138, 142
   Grand Mosque District, Makkah 233
   Haram district(s) 177, 183
   Haret Hreik, Beirut Metropolitan Region 7, 39, 41, 42, 43, 44
   Hotel District, Beirut 58, 61
   Jdeideh, Aleppo 127
   Jeddah Central District 63
   Kadhimiya, Al Anbar, Iraq 177, 192, 208
   King Abdullah Financial District (KAFD), Riyadh 9, 10, 168, 170
   Knightsbridge, London 172
   Knowledge Economic City, Madinah 100
   Maadi, Cairo 214, 219
   Madinat Al Sadr, Baghdad 67, 205, 208, 210
   Madinat Al-Thawra, Baghdad 205, 208
   Montmartre, Paris 85
   Nahr district, Beirut Metropolitan Region 151
   Rasheed Street district 192
   Rusafa, Baghdad 75, 201, 207
   Saifi Village, Beirut Central District 56, 57, 58, 60
   Sin el Fil, Beirut 90
   Soho, London 85
   Um Al-Qura Economic City, Makkah 100
   Wadi Abou Jamil, Beirut Central District 52, 58

Emirate(s) 233, 240, 233, 240, 249
   Abu Dhabi 14, 70, 227, 228, 229, 230, 231, 232, 233, 234, 235, 236, 237, 238, 239, 240
   Abu Dhabi Island 233, 234, 236
   Dubai 4, 58, 80, 189, 208, 246, 258
   Riyadh 9, 36, 167, 168, 170, 171, 172, 258

Garden(s) and Park(s)
   Al Azbakiya, Cairo 214
   Al-Hara, Riverfront park 192, 193
   Al Jalaa Park, Damascus, Syria 68
   Al Orman Gardens, Cairo 214
   Basateen, Saida 75
   City Park, Beirut City Center 61, 63
   Community garden, Frankfurt 70, 71
   Downsview, Toronto 85, 89
   Emerald Necklace, Boston 149
   Freshkills, New York 85
   Garden of Forgiveness, Beirut Central District 59, 60, 61, 108
   Hadiqat al Jala'a, Baghdad 66
   Hadiqat al Umma, Baghdad 66
   Hadiqat Teshreen, Baghdad 66
   Millennium Park, Chicago 219
   Parc de la Villette, Paris 85, 89
   Park al Sa'doun, Baghdad 66
   Quweik Park, Aleppo 126
   Waterfront Park, Beirut Central District 60

Garrison Town(s)
   Basra 18
   Fustat 18
   Kufa 18

Gate(s)
   Gwanghwamun Gate, Seoul 251, 252
   King's Gate, Makkah 188

Ghouta agricultural enclave, landscape, Damascus 67, 69

Gulf 58, 63
   Arab Gulf 167, 174, 240, 241
   Gulf cities, states 4, 31, 245

Highway(s)
   Beirut-Jounieh highway 90
   Cheonggye Elevated Highway, Seoul 252, 254
   Coastal highway, Lebanon 90
   Highway interchange, Dubai 246
   Highway interchange, Istanbul 246
Haram 180, 181, 183, 185, 186, 187, 188, 189, 190, 191

Indian subcontinent 20
Informal settlement
   Muhajireen, Damascus 67
Island
   Lulu Island, coast of Abu Dhabi 233

Jabal
   Arafat, Makkah 185
   Jabal Abu Qubais, Makkah 188
   Jabal 'Amil, Southern Lebanon 48
   Jabal Bakhsh, Makkah 188
   Jabal Dhaf, Makkah 188
   Jabal Hafeet, Abu Dhabi 70
   Jabal Khandama, Makkah 188
   Jabal Omar, Makkah 177, 179, 185, 189, 190, 191
   Mount Qassioun, Damascus 67
   Mount Sannine, Mount Lebanon range 52, 58

Kaaba, Makkah 102, 179, 183, 186, 189, 190, 195
   [Sacred House] 179
Karantina slaughterhouse, Beirut Metropolitan Region 135
Karkh, Baghdad 75
King's Cross railyards, London 85

Levant 7, 19, 22, 213, 257

Maghrib 18
Mashreq 7, 65, 66, 67, 68, 69, 71, 72, 73, 77, 79, 80, 81
MENA region 117, 240
Middle East 1, 17, 18, 20, 54, 129, 167, 187, 204, 241, 245, 258
   Arab Middle East 1, 20
   Greater Middle East 1, 17
Monument(s)
   Monument to the Unknown Soldier, 1983, Baghdad 207
   Washington Memorial, Washington, DC 219

Neighborhood(s)
   Abdoun, Amman 67
   Abu Nawas, Baghdad 210
   Adhamiyah, Baghdad 177, 191, 192, 193, 201, 202, 210
   Al-Hara, Baghdad 192, 193
   Bab-Sharqi, Baghdad 205, 206
   DUMBO, New York 85
   Eastern docklands, Amsterdam 85
   Fheis, Amman 67
   Greenwich Village, New York 85
   Haibat Khatoon, Baghdad 192
   Hey el Gharbi, Beirut 135
   Imbaba, Cairo 216
   Jadriya, Baghdad 210
   Jamila, Baghdad 67
   Karadat Maryam, Baghdad 207
   Karem el Zaytoun, Beirut 132, 134
   Karrada, Baghdad 202
   Mezza, Damascus 67
   Nassa, Baghdad 192
   Saadoun, Baghdad 202
   Safeena, Baghdad 192
   Shmeisani, Amman 67
   Shu'la, Baghdad 67
   Shuyoukh, Baghdad 192
   Tariq el Jdideh, Beirut 131, 135
   Waziriya, Baghdad 202
North Africa 19, 186, 200, 213, 240, 245, 258

Peninsula(s)
   Greenwich peninsula 85
   Iberian Peninsula 34
Plaza(s)
   Al Haram plaza, Makkah 182
   Bank Audi Plaza, Beirut Central District 57
   Gwanghwamun Plaza, Seoul 252
   Seoul Plaza 252, 253

Qanaya, Saida 75, 79

Raha, Abu Dhabi 236
Refugee Camp(s)
   Ain Al Helwa Palestinian camp, Saida 73, 132, 133
   Nahr el Bared Camp, North Lebanon 131
   Shatila, Beirut Metropolitan Region 135
   Sabra, Beirut Metropolitan Region 131, 134, 135, 136, 138, 139, 140, 142, 144
Ring Road(s)
   Old City ring, Aleppo 126, 127
   Ring road, Beirut Central District 53, 54, 55, 61
   Ring, Vienna 200
River(s), Nahr
   Awali River, Southern Lebanon 72, 75, 77
   Barada River, Damascus 67
   Charles River, Massachusetts 149
   Cheonggyecheon Stream, Seoul 251, 252, 254
   Diyala River, Iran, Iraq 75
   Euphrates River, Iraq, Syria, Turkey 118
   Nahr Abou Ali, North Lebanon 147
   Nahr Antelias, Mount Lebanon 147
   Nahr Beirut, Beirut River, Beirut Metropolitan Region 8, 9, 67, 85, 87, 90, 135, 147, 148, 151, 152, 153, 154, 158, 159, 161, 162
   Nahr El Mot, Beirut 147

Nile River, Egypt 218
Qanat al Jaish, Baghdad 75
Quweik, riverbed, Aleppo 118, 126
Sainiq River, Southern Lebanon 72
Tigris River, Iraq, Syria, Turkey 75, 76, 77, 79, 192, 209

Sadat Station, Cairo 219
Saha(s)
   Saha of Sultan Hassan Mosque 215
   Saha, Sabra, Beirut Metropolitan Region 135
Shrine(s) 182, 185, 192
   Holy shrine, Al Anbar, Iraq 177, 192
   Holy Shrine, Makkah 177
   Imam Ali Shrine, Najaf 180, 182, 193
   Shrine of Imam Abu Hanifa al-Numan, Baghdad 192
   Shrine of Imam Al Houssein, brother Abbas, Karbala 193, 194
   Twin shrines, Karbala 180, 182
      Holy Shrine, Karbala 177
Souq(s)
   Beirut Souqs, Beirut Central District 58, 60, 64
   Souq Al-Seghir, Makkah 188
   Souq Sabra, Beirut Metropolitan Region 131, 134, 135, 136, 139, 140, 142, 144
   Souq Waqif, Doha 35
Sports City, Beirut 135
Square(s)
   Abu Hanifa Mosque Square, Baghdad 192, 193
   Antar Square, Baghdad 192, 193
   Charles de Gaulle Square, Paris 214
   Cheonggye Square, Seoul 251, 252
   Khan Antoun Bey Square, Beirut Central District 60
   Martyrs' Square, Beirut Central District 52, 55, 60, 61, 106, 107, 108, 193
   Najaf's main square 182
   National Mall, Washington, DC 213, 219, 220
   Place de la Concorde, Paris 221
   Tahrir Square, Cairo 9, 13, 213, 214, 216, 217, 218, 219, 220, 221, 222
   The Etoile, Beirut 64, 108
   Times Square, New York 213, 219, 220, 221, 255
   Trafalgar Square, London 213, 219, 220, 221
Street(s)
   Al Rasheed Street (called "New Street" until the late 1920s), Baghdad 192, 201, 209
   Allenby Street, Beirut Central District 52, 55
   Broadway, street, New York 221, 255
   Foch Street, Beirut Central District 52, 55
   Haifa Street, Baghdad 207, 208
   Khalil Pasha Street, Baghdad 201
   Khulafa Street, Baghdad 204
   King Ghazi Street (today Kifah Street), Baghdad 203
   Maarad Street, Beirut Central District 52, 55
   Nu'man and Il Iman al Adham Street, Baghdad 192, 193
   Qasr al-Ayn Street, Cairo 218
   Qasr el-Nil Street, Cairo 218
   Rue Weygand, Beirut Central District 55
   Saadoun Street, Baghdad 201
   Sabra Market Street, Beirut Metropolitan Region 134
   Sahah Street, Makkah 186
   Suheimi Street, Makkah 186
   Talaat Harb Street, Cairo 218
   Wathba Street, Baghdad 203

Tower(s)
   Abraj al Bait Towers, Makkah 189
   Big Ben, London 189
   Clock tower, Makkah 179, 183, 189, 191, 195
   Petronas Towers, Kuala Lumpur 35

Village(s)
   Al-Hajarayn, Yemen 31
   Al-Qleileh, Lebanon 7, 39, 44, 45, 46, 47, 48
   Bint Jbeil, Lebanon 48
   Siddiqine, Lebanon 48
   Zibqine, Lebanon 48, 49

Wadi Hanifa 36, 168
Waterfront(s)
   Beirut Marina 58, 62
   Bourj Hammoud, waterfront, Beirut Metropolitan Region 90, 150, 151, 154, 160
   Lebanese coast 90, 147, 148, 150, 151
   New Waterfront, reclaimed land, Beirut City Center 51, 52, 55, 58, 60, 61, 62, 63, 64
   Port First Basin, Beirut Central District 61, 62
   Quai de la Seine 85
   Saida, waterfront 75, 77, 79
   St George's Bay, Beirut City Center 52

Terms and Concepts

Advocacy 33
Aerotropolis 8, 102, 104
Agri-tourism 79
Alam Al-Fikr (1982) 21
Aleppo 2025 City Development Strategy (CDS) 115, 116, 118, 120, 128, 129
Amenity 70, 79, 218
   corridor(s) 76, 77
   gardens 76
   green spaces 75, 149, 151
   landscapes 70
Arab Chronicles 20
Archeology 3, 51, 73, 79
Architectural awards 33, 34
Asthma 14, 247, 248, 249

Baghdad Comprehensive City Development Plan (CCDP) 7, 72, 75, 76, 77, 78, 79, 80
Beautification 79, 97, 201, 203, 245
Beaux-Arts 201
Bike-share program 256, 257

Biodiversity 46, 70, 77, 126
Body Mass Index (BMI) 249
Boulevard(s) 52, 73, 75, 76, 99, 126, 149, 150, 180, 182, 200, 213
Brownfield, redevelopment, reuse 63, 70, 85
Build-to-line frontage development 56
Building Research Establishment Environmental Assessment Methodology (BREEAM) 14, 228
Built-up Area (BUA) 168, 52, 55, 56

Cancers 14, 247
Capitalism 18, 22, 216
Car ownership, rate 54, 244
Cardio-vascular diseases (CVD) 14, 247, 249
Catalyst(s) 4, 6, 8, 60, 63, 86, 88, 96, 133, 148
Cemeteries 66, 67, 79, 192, 193
Centrality(ies) 21, 22, 178, 179, 180, 182, 190, 191, 233, 191
City
    Annex 168
    Cosmopolitan 7, 58
    Holy 4, 100, 102, 177, 178, 179, 180, 183, 184, 185, 186, 187, 189, 191, 192, 193, 194, 195, 196
    Mixed-use 233
    Mosaic 178, 179, 186, 191, 192
    Multi-confessional 7
    Post-colonial 29
    Provincial 2, 100, 202, 213
    Satellite 76, 168, 171, 204, 250
Civic space 1, 5, 106, 201, 233
Civil society 23, 33, 36, 41, 79, 80, 210
    Stakeholder(s) 2, 8, 29, 32, 41, 43, 48, 64, 72, 80, 104, 110, 115, 116, 117, 118, 131, 132, 133, 134, 139, 143, 170, 177, 192, 194, 195, 231, 140
Civitas 17
Coastal agriculture 69
Colonialism 1, 2, 3, 5, 9, 18, 20, 22, 29, 30, 32, 36, 66, 199, 200, 201, 202, 213, 252
    Neo-colonialization 175
    Post-colonial(ism) 2, 3, 5, 22, 29, 31, 32, 243
Communal 2, 8, 154, 160, 190
    Agriculture 154
    Church 98
    City space 173
    Facilities 186
    Landscape 46
    Squares 205
Community Based Learning (CBL) 131, 138, 143
Community Based Projects 131, 133, 134, 135, 143
Concentrated solar power (CSP) 236
Concrete T-walls 12, 210
Cultural tourism 127

Date palm orchards 69, 76, 79
Demarcation lines 5
Desert 233, 243, 258
    Climate 172, 233
    Coastal 228

Ecology 70
Environment 258, 240
Fingers 70
Sand belt 70
Seasons 168
Steppe 118
Developing world 70, 71, 85, 86, 243, 258
Disability-adjusted life year loss (DALYs) 247, 248, 249, 258
Discourse(s) 3, 7, 44, 148, 216
    Academic 1
    Architectural 2
    City-region 7, 80
    Corporate 7, 51, 64
    Cultural 6, 29
    Design 29
    Ecological 6
    Globalization 2
    Greening 6, 7, 65, 66, 68, 70, 71, 72, 75, 76, 77, 79, 80
    Historical 3
    Islamic 216
    National identity 207
    Normative 33, 97
    Participative 7, 39
    Political 213, 216, 217
    Post-colonial 1, 2, 3, 22
    Public rights 80
    Reconstruction 44
    Social discourse 214, 218
Disneyfication 127
Displacement 39, 40, 47, 65, 76, 86, 209, 252, 258
Dubaization 4

Ecocorridor 79
Ecology 4, 5, 6, 7, 8, 9, 36, 44, 45, 65, 67, 68, 70, 72, 73, 75, 77, 89, 117, 118, 126, 147, 148, 149, 150, 154, 161, 162, 163, 227, 233
    Ecological corridor 77, 148
    Ecological degradation 147
    Ecological footprint 67, 232, 240
    Ecological impact 7, 68
    Ecological integrity 77
    Ecological Landscape Associations (ELAs) 44, 45
    Ecological Landscape Design 7, 44, 65, 72, 77, 80
    Ecological networks 149
    Ecological restoration 149
    Ecological sciences 72
    Ecological systems 67, 79, 154
    Ecological treatments 154
    Ecological water management 149
    Ecologically efficient cities 168
    Ecologically minded politicians 250
    Ecologists 241
Economic Vision 2030 233
Ecosystem(s) 67, 68, 148, 150, 151
    Agro-ecosystem 75
    Living ecosystem 76, 77
    Riparian ecosystems 77

Ecotone management 79
Editorial Urban Design 162
Envelope controls 55
Environment 17, 39, 44, 46, 51, 61, 62, 66, 68, 70, 72, 75, 77, 79, 85, 90, 148, 154, 162, 168, 188, 227, 228, 230, 233, 240, 243, 247, 248, 245
    Auto-dominated 218
    Environmental benefits 148
    Environmental challenges 7, 65
    Environmental costs of vehicles 247, 249
    Environmental disaster zone of landfills 36
    Environmental health 79, 258
    Environmental impact(s) 7, 68, 227, 247
    Environmental mitigation measures 245
    Environmental policy 80
    Environmental pollution 243, 247
    Environmental potentials 115, 116
    Environmental protection 190
    Environmental quality 76, 233
    Environmental restoration 240
    Environmental soundness 256, 257
    Environmental strategies 77
    Environmental sustainability 70, 77, 208, 233
    Environmental toxicity 14
    Environmentally sensitive design 227, 232
    Environmentally sustainable urban greening 65, 68
    Microenvironment 229
Estidama 14, 227, 228, 229, 230, 231, 232, 234, 240, 242
European Landscape Convention (ELC) 72
Exploitation, ratio(s), coefficient 52, 55, 56, 58, 190

Fareej [housing cluster] 228
Flâneur 87, 88
Functionality 150, 192
    Monofunctionality 120, 178, 184
Fundamentalism 3, 23
    Fundamentalist city 23

Garrison towns 18, 22
Gated neighborhoods 67
Gentrification 80, 85, 254, 258
Globalization 1, 2, 3, 9, 10, 167, 171, 175, 186, 189
Grassroots Approach to Reconstruction 47, 132
Green Line 104
Green–blue network 78, 79
Greenhouse Gas (GHG) 154, 247
Gross Domestic Product (GDP) 244, 245, 256, 258
Gross National Product (GNP) per capita 54
Gulfication 4

Hadarah, civilization 17
Haussmannization 200, 207
Health Promotion and Community Health (HPCH) 134
Heritage, conservation, preservation 2, 3, 4, 5, 7, 23, 35, 36, 46, 47, 51, 52, 55, 60, 61, 62, 67, 68, 70, 72, 73, 75, 77, 79, 106, 108, 118, 120, 127, 167, 177, 186, 188, 189, 192, 194, 195, 196, 207, 208, 209, 230, 234, 257
High traffic roads 247
Highway(s) 5, 53, 54, 55, 61, 90, 102, 108, 117, 120, 123, 126, 127, 151, 180, 185, 200, 245, 246, 247, 250, 252, 254, 246, 252, 254
Historic cores 5, 55, 60, 61, 64, 67, 75, 180, 186, 243, 245
Housing 106, 108, 117, 123, 127, 185, 202, 204, 207, 208, 228, 235, 250
Human Immunodeficiency Virus/Acquired Immune Deficiency Syndrome (HIV/AIDS) 247

Identity(ies) 2, 3, 4, 5, 17, 21, 23, 29, 31, 32, 34, 35, 52, 53, 68, 80, 88, 92, 94, 95, 106, 108, 118, 123, 126, 127, 148, 167, 171, 172, 173, 175, 178, 186, 188, 192, 196, 207, 227, 240
    Arab 17, 31
    Civic 192
    Collective 32
    Conflicting 34
    Ethno-religious 29, 31
    Imagined 31
    in cities in the Arab world 23
    Infrastructural 192
    Iraqi 207
    Islamic 2, 31, 34
    National 1, 2, 108, 207
    Political 106
    Religious 189, 192
    Sectarian 32
    Secular 192
    Subaltern 32
    Territorialized 210
    Townscape 178, 179, 183
Ideological construct(s) 2, 7, 31, 32
Ideological frameworks 5, 131
    Community-based 4, 5, 131, 132, 133, 168
    Empirical-based 4, 5
    Formal/conceptual-based 4, 5
    Market-based 4, 5, 51, 185, 208
Ideology(ies) 2, 6, 31, 32, 33, 41, 106, 148, 167, 186, 190, 192, 195, 199, 204, 205, 207, 216
    European cultural 157
    Imported design 186
    Modernist 204
        Modernist design ideology 190
    Political 205
    Populist 31
Important Bird Area (IBA) 47
Industrial zone(s), transitional 5, 90, 123
Inequality 80, 148, 216
Infill development 55, 56
Informality 1, 4, 5, 65, 67, 115, 118, 119, 120, 127, 129, 131, 133, 135, 138, 142, 186, 204, 210
Infrastructure 4, 5, 8, 9, 14, 39, 40, 51, 60, 61, 62, 63, 70, 73, 75, 76, 85, 88, 89, 90, 92, 94, 100, 104, 118,

123, 126, 127, 129, 135, 139, 147, 148, 149, 150, 151, 153, 154, 160, 162, 163, 168, 177, 178, 179, 180, 185, 188, 189, 192, 194, 196, 201, 203, 213, 221, 236, 243, 244, 245, 247, 251, 258
   Civic, community 127, 160, 234
   Cultural 8, 85, 86, 92, 94, 96, 148
   Cycling, bicycle 255
   Hybrid 162
   Infrastructural breaks 5, 180
   Infrastructural landscape 70, 71, 147, 158, 149, 150, 154, 155, 160
   Infrastructural sites 5, 192
   Social 63, 123, 178
   Sustainable 233
   Water 147, 149, 150, 154, 160
Inner-city central districts 5, 251, 256
Inner-city neighborhoods 5
Interdisciplinary 4, 8, 21, 23, 75, 79
Islamic Architecture and Urbanism (German 1983) 21

Laissez-faire 41, 204
Landscape(s)
   Agricultural 79, 123
   Cultural 44, 45, 46, 67, 70, 75, 77, 79, 232
   heritage 68, 70, 75, 77, 79
   Infrastructural 70, 71, 147, 148, 149, 150, 154, 155, 160
   Multifunctional 46, 70, 77
   Natural 45, 67, 70, 188
   Pastoral 68, 69
Landscape urbanism 7, 8, 72, 85, 86, 88, 89, 90, 92, 94, 96
   Network and territory, articulations 92, 93
   Synthetic ecologies 94, 95, 96
Leadership in Energy and Environmental Design (LEED) 14, 228
Legibility 102, 178, 179
Levantine villas 52
Light Emitting Diode (LED) 222
Livability 7, 41, 42, 43, 80, 227, 229, 258
Local Agenda 21 (LA21) 117, 118, 120, 123, 124, 126, 127

Madaniyah 17
Man-made islands 4
Marxian principles 32
Master planning 4, 8, 9, 51, 52, 53, 55, 56, 58, 60, 61, 62, 63, 64, 67, 76, 79, 80, 86, 178, 182, 186, 187, 189, 192, 193, 194, 195, 201, 204, 205, 207, 209, 228, 230, 233, 235, 240
   City Center master plan 52, 64
   Landscape master plan 78
   Market-Responsive Master Plan 52
   Metro Master Plan 63
   Sector plan 62
Medina(s) 1, 17, 18, 20, 22, 23, 36, 184
Megaprojects 183, 185
Metro line 257, 258
Midan [square] 214, 228

Microclimate 65, 79, 236
Mixed-use 14, 53, 60, 63, 188, 203, 222, 233, 234
Mobility 4, 87, 116, 120, 124, 126, 147, 154, 159, 161, 162, 243, 244, 245, 249, 251, 254, 257, 258, 259
Modernity, Western 2, 3, 9, 29, 88, 200, 213
   Postmodernity 3
Mosque(s) 19, 21, 23, 31, 100, 101, 102, 138, 180, 182, 184, 186, 189, 192, 205, 213, 216
Motorization rates 244, 258
Multidisciplinary 43, 138, 147, 148, 149, 162
   design 162
Museumification 2, 127

Nationalism 1, 2, 3, 17
Nationalization Program 214
Neoliberal, politics, trends, models, economy 65, 67, 80, 185, 196
Neoliberalization 189, 190
Non aedificandi 61, 162
Non-governmental Organization (NGO) 39, 40, 46, 47, 48, 49, 79, 80, 129, 132, 143

Obesity 14, 247, 249, 258
Oil rich cities, countries 4
Open door policy [*infitah*] 216
Orientalism 2, 3, 7, 18, 19, 21, 20, 21, 22, 200

Pan Arabism 1, 17
Parochialism 3
Pearl Qualified Professional (PQP) 231, 232, 241
Pearl Rating System (PRS) 14, 227, 228, 229, 230, 231, 232, 240, 241
Pedagogy 9, 44, 131
Pedestrianization 46, 52, 55, 60, 61, 77, 90, 92, 108, 126, 132, 138, 147, 151, 154, 159, 160, 167, 168, 172, 180, 185, 186, 188, 189, 190, 191, 218, 219, 221, 228, 233, 234, 235, 236, 238, 254, 255, 258
Peripheral districts 5
Pilgrim 100, 102, 177, 179, 180, 182, 183, 184, 185, 186, 193, 194, 195, 196
Pilgrimage 9, 100, 102, 177, 178, 180, 183, 185, 190, 196, 208
Plan 2030 14, 227, 232, 233
Plan Abu Dhabi 2030 70
Plan Al Ain 2030 70
Plaza Program 255
Post-war, reconstruction, destruction 3, 4, 5, 6, 7, 9, 39, 40, 41, 42, 43, 44, 45, 46, 47, 48, 49, 51, 63, 72, 86, 87, 106, 115, 129, 131, 139, 186, 191, 192, 193, 194, 196, 203, 207, 208
Poverty 1, 3, 75
Private development 4, 5, 149, 151, 178, 182, 186, 231
Privatization 106, 170, 207, 208, 210, 216
Prophet hajjis 183
Public health 14, 65, 70, 149, 249
Public Private Partnership (PPP) 51, 63
Public Space 4, 7, 23, 29, 30, 36, 43, 51, 52, 55, 60, 61,

67, 80, 89, 98, 100, 101, 104, 106, 108, 116, 117, 127, 148, 149, 153, 154, 159, 160, 161, 162, 163, 170, 172, 178, 182, 186, 190, 203, 207, 210, 213, 214, 216, 217, 218, 233

Quality living 65, 79
Quran 17

Ramadan 185
Rapid transit 180
 Bus Rapid Transit (BRT) 55, 123, 126, 258
 Personal rapid transit system (PRT) 235
Real Estate, speculation, bubble 6, 7, 9, 60, 63, 70, 75, 106, 123, 128, 127, 170, 177, 179, 180, 182, 183, 185, 188, 189, 190, 195, 208, 214
Refugee studies 4
Refugee, camp 4, 5, 51, 65, 76, 129, 131, 132, 135, 144
Regeneration 51, 167, 204
Regionalism 2, 3, 29, 32, 33, 36
Religiosity 23
Renewal 9, 51, 58, 63, 64, 85, 177, 193, 250
Research and Development (R&D) 132
River valleys 5, 70, 90
Road traffic accidents 248
Ruralization 209
Rural-urban migration 65, 195, 202

Saha(s) 131, 135, 214
Saida Urban Sustainable Development Strategy (USDS) 7, 72, 74, 75, 77, 78, 79, 80
Scholar(s) 2, 3, 9, 17, 18, 19, 20, 21, 22, 23, 192, 194, 195, 213
Scholarship 17, 20, 21, 23, 32, 184
 Arab 18
 European 19
 Middle East 20
 Nationalist tradition, 1980s 2
 Orientalist tradition, pre-1960s 2, 18, 20, 22
 Revisionist tradition, late 1960s and 1970s 2
Seasonality 178, 185
Sectarian 32, 39, 106, 107, 138, 178, 192, 209, 210, 211
Sites
 of conflict 1, 9, 12, 199
 of contestation 1, 9, 13, 213
 of globalization 1, 9, 10, 167
 of power 194
 of worship 1, 9, 11, 177, 178, 190, 191, 192, 194, 195, 196
Situationists 88
Special design area 187, 188
Star Architects 58
Streetwall, control, building 55, 56, 57
Suburb, garden 135
Suburban 1, 87, 175, 194, 203, 204, 250
 Development 250
 Informal settlements 4
 Neighborhood rebuilding 4

Suburbanization 250
Sustainability 4, 8, 14, 61, 62, 70, 77, 115, 119, 123, 173, 208, 227, 228, 230, 231, 232, 233, 234, 235, 236, 240, 241, 243, 254, 256
 Management 79

Terrorist bombing 5
Theory(ies) 1, 90, 97, 142, 143, 243
 Architectural 97
 Culturist 19
 Ekistics 204
 Garden City 202, 250
 Modernist 250
 Normative 243
 Social 8
 Urban design 8, 243
Think tank 116
Town planner 48
Townscape(s) 3, 52, 58, 177, 178, 179, 183, 188, 189, 190, 196
 Cultural 178
 Disruption 188
 Identity 178, 179, 183
 Infrastructural 196
 Legibility 178, 179
 of holy cities 179, 190
 of the margins 3
 Political 178
 Preservation 189
 Sacred 179, 190
 Value 52, 58
Transdisciplinarity 79
Transdisciplinary planning 79
Transitional districts 5
Transportation 14, 64, 70, 76, 79, 92, 116, 118, 123, 126, 127, 129, 147, 149, 151, 154, 163, 168, 172, 179, 180, 185, 186, 188, 213, 231, 232, 233, 235, 236, 241, 245, 246, 247, 248, 249, 250, 252, 254, 256, 258, 259
 Car-based transport strategies 53
 Motorized transport 14, 243, 244, 245, 247, 249
 Public transport 54, 55, 63, 92, 126, 154, 168, 172, 180, 185, 188, 233, 235, 258
 Transport infrastructure planning 123
Treated sewage effluent (TSE) 229
Type 2 diabetes 14, 247
Type(s) 8, 97, 100, 101, 108, 110
 Church 97, 100
 Fundamental 97, 100, 102
 Generic 22
 Landscape 90, 92
 Lebanese central hall 106, 107, 108
 of settlements 5
 of urban narratives 4
 Study 98, 100, 102, 196
 University 104
Typological Transformation 101

Typology(ies) 97, 100, 108, 110, 127, 183, 185
   Detached-house 76
   Modernist 55
   of public spaces 214
   Urban 203

Umrah 100, 185
univerCity 8, 104
University campuses 34, 35, 66
Urban agriculture 66, 70, 77, 79, 132, 133
Urban design 1, 3, 4, 5, 6, 7, 8, 14, 29, 41, 51, 64, 89, 97, 148, 162, 167, 170, 174, 176, 177, 178, 179, 190, 191, 193, 194, 195, 201, 207, 213, 232, 233, 240, 243, 256
   3D urban design plan 55
   Agenda(s) 14, 225
   as a catalyst for change 6
   as a profession-oriented discipline 8
   as architectural conservation 186
   as ideology and as praxis 6
   Consultant 194
   Contemporary 1, 8, 51, 64
   Controls 55
   Discipline in flux 1
   Editorial 162
   Emerging discipline 1
   Focus 1
   Framework 178, 232
   Good practice in 6
   Ideas competition 41, 60, 177, 178
   in the Arab World 1, 14, 29, 177, 243
   in the Muslim world 29
   in the region 6, 8
   Interventions 4, 191, 243
   Issues 6, 9, 178
   Matrix 4, 5
   on the margins 1, 8
   Participative urban design process 138
   Perspective 177
   Practice 1, 5, 8, 167, 240
   Principles 186
   Projects 177
   Regional geography of 4
   Research 8
   Role of 5
   Schemes 185
   Skills 64
   Strategies 148
   Street-based 55
   Studies 6
   Studio projects 86
   Theory(ies) 8, 243
   Third world 3
   Tools 9, 218

Traditions 192, 240
Trends 189
Urban design thinking 1, 6, 8
   the *discursive* 6, 27
   the *hybrid* 6, 7, 83
   the *operational* 6, 8, 113, 134
   the *visionary* 6, 9, 165, 213
Urban designers 1, 14, 58, 97, 148, 170, 190, 194, 195, 213, 232, 241, 250, 259
Urban geography 17
Urban heat island effect (UHI) 147, 151
Urban renewal 9, 63, 85, 177, 193, 250
Urban wildlife habitats 70
Urbanity 5, 34, 35, 88, 97, 98, 99
Urbanist 86, 135, 194, 203, 204, 205
Urbanization 7, 9, 17, 18, 32, 65, 67, 80, 97, 147, 148, 170, 174, 209, 227
Urbanism 2, 3, 5, 6, 17, 18, 20, 21, 22, 23, 32, 148, 199, 204, 243
   Arab 1, 2, 5, 14, 17, 240
   Architectural 8, 97, 100, 110
   Colonial 200
   Concentric 182
   Contemporary 9, 148, 162
   Digital 243
   Discursive 6
   Eighteenth-century European 192
   Everyday 243
   Global 208
   Gulf 189
   Imported, exported 2, 199
   Islamic 17, 18, 20, 21
   Landscape 7, 8, 72, 85, 86, 88, 89, 92, 94, 96
   Market-based 185
   Messy 243
   Middle Eastern 21
   Muslim 19, 21
   New 243, 258
   Noir 243
   Post 243
   Post-war 9, 207
   Regulation 202
   Research-based strategic 115
   Socialist 205
   Sustainable 14, 227
   Toast-rack, 182
   Typological 97
'urf [local customs] 133

Vernacular architecture 57
Volatile Organic Compound (VOC) 247

Watercourses 72, 73, 75, 77, 79, 147, 149